Measurement Issues in Criminology

Kimberly L. Kempf
Editor

Measurement Issues in Criminology

Foreword by Joseph G. Weis

Springer-Verlag
New York Berlin Heidelberg
London Paris Tokyo Hong Kong

Kimberly L. Kempf
Department of Administration of Justice
College of Arts & Sciences
University of Missouri-St. Louis
St. Louis, MO 63121-4499

Library of Congress Cataloging-in-Publication Data

Measurement issues in criminology/Kimberly L. Kempf, editor.
     p.   cm.
     Includes bibliographical references.
     ISBN 0-387-97260-9 (alk. paper)
     1. Criminology—Research—Methodology.   2. Criminal statistics.
     I. Kempf. Kimberly L.
     HV6024.5.M43   1990
     364'.072—dc20   90-9517

Printed on acid-free paper

Typeset by Asco Trade Typesetting Ltd., Hong Kong
Printed and bound by Edwards Brothers, Ann Arbor, MI
Printed in the United States of America.

9 8 7 6 5 4 3 2 1

ISBN 0-387-97260-9 Springer-Verlag New York Berlin Heidelberg
ISBN 3-540-97260-9 Springer Verlag Berlin Heidelberg New York

Avoid the fallacy fallacy. When a theorist or methodologist tells you you cannot do something, do it anyway. Breaking the rules can be fun!

Travis Hirschi
Procedural Rules in the Study of Deviant Behavior,
21 (2) Social Problems, pp. 171–172.

Foreword

To my knowledge, *Measurement Issues in Criminology* is the only anthology in the field of criminology that, from a variety of disciplinary perspectives, addresses a broad range of topics and issues in the measurement of crime. This is not surprising, given the relative neglect of methodological issues by criminologists. Unfortunately, the legacy of a multidisciplinary "scientific study of crime" includes what may be a misplaced emphasis on the products rather than the procedures of research. Historically, criminologists have focused on the causes and control of crime, leaving the methods and problems of doing research to the methodologists in their respective parent disciplines of sociology, psychology, economics, or political science. Consequently, criminology has not developed its own methodology and, therefore, has lagged behind the traditional disciplines in both the creation and application of methodological refinements, often compromising the quality of criminological research.

There is a growing awareness of this void in criminology, to which *Measurement Issues in Criminology* is a response that addresses both generic measurement issues, as well as those that are unique in studying crime. Its publication is timely—criminology has been in a period of theoretical groping for the past two decades, attributable in part to unresolved measurement problems. Before our understanding of crime can move forward, our ability to observe accurately and consistently the phenomena to be explained must be improved. Otherwise put, valid and reliable measurement is essential in both theory construction and testing. That theme will be evident throughout the book to the intended audience of graduate students of criminological research methods and professional criminologists.

Measurement Issues in Criminology is a welcome addition to the small but growing literature on the methodology of criminological research. With its broad range of high quality papers on many of the most critical issues on measurement in criminology, it will be a standard reference on measuring crime.

Joseph G. Weis
University of Washington
Seattle

Preface

In *Measurement Issues in Criminology*, several of the principal issues in measurement confronting criminologists today are explained by experts who are well acquainted with the benefits and problems associated with each topic. In addition to conveying the techniques and procedures necessary for successful measurement, the authors share advice gleaned from their own research experiences. Topics suited to certain research designs, data sources, and analytic techniques are identified, as are other topics for which such measurement is inappropriate. Besides providing illustrations of typical applications, the authors discuss specific obstacles encountered in their work and the courses pursued to overcome them. Current research covering a variety of substantive areas, as well as some findings never before published, also are reported. The intended audiences of this book are students of research methods, particularly students at the master's degree level, and scholars in criminology to whose own work the experiences and findings reported by the authors will be relevant.

In preparing this book, the authors endeavored to provide a resource in criminology for teaching graduate students, or advanced undergraduates, the important elements in research. Research methods for criminology typically have been taught with textbooks from another science, often not directly relevant to criminology, or with a collection of published articles. In the latter situation, knowledge of measurement issues is often implied, because the articles are written for other criminologists, and usually students suffer as a result. In the case of textbooks, sometimes considered cookbooks for research, in which the rules, or recipes, for measurement are outlined, students are ill prepared to cope with the atypical challenges faced in an actual study. The aim of *Measurement Issues in Criminology* is to serve as an instructional tool to fill this void. In one sense, this is a cookbook, because conventional formulas and instruments used in criminology are explained. However, the additional resources available in this book are more valuable, such as what to do when not all the ideal scientific ingredients are present or protocol is somehow unavailable. Authors do not assume existing knowledge of methodological issues; chapters are written with entry-level graduate students in mind. The humility and wisdom of hindsight that come with research experience, but usually do not get journal articles published, is valuable information. Perhaps most important, this book exposes readers to controversy. As the chapters reveal, consensus on the best measurement procedures does not always exist in criminology.

One reason for controversy is that criminology itself is somewhat contentious. While humanities, especially philosophy and art, have aided criminology, contributions from the social and natural sciences provided the foundation from which the science of criminology evolved. Actually, whether criminology is a science is an issue of debate. Most criminologists, however, adhere to the scientific method. And although many definitions of criminology are offered, the one I prefer is the following: *Criminology is the scientific study of crime, criminals, and society's reaction to both.* Contributions to this book reflect this view.

This book also illustrates that a multidisciplinary science carries with it both a blessing and a curse. Criminology can reap the benefits of scientific advances made elsewhere, but it must cope as well with the difficulties encountered there. The contributors to this book are all too familiar with this situation. In addition to being criminologists, the authors represent the fields of sociology, psychology, social psychology, political science, engineering, social work, and criminal justice. As a result, their writings provide general guidance, as well as stimulate thought with their unique perspectives and biases.

Obviously, not every field of expertise or every important measurement issue in criminology can be included in one book. Criminologists with skills from biology, economics, anthropology, history, and communication are not represented here. There are no chapters devoted specifically to cross-cultural comparative designs or historical research. Issues in sampling, variable construction, questionnaire format, and objectivity are referred to within the context of other topics. Other valuable issues are no doubt absent as well. And, this book is not a statistical manual, although many techniques of analyses are discussed. The assortment of sophisticated multivariate modeling techniques available, as well as the variety of accessible computer applications developing to execute them, render that information less important here.

Measurement Issues in Criminology provides detailed information about 10 major methodological issues for a wide range of substantive topics. In the first chapter, Drs. Bernard and Ritti identify what constitutes a theory and clarify the important role of theory in science. Criminologists must distinguish between theory and the folk wisdom of well-meaning citizens in order to contribute knowledge and assist in the development of effective criminal justice policy. For these and other reasons, the scientific method cannot function and the wheel of science cannot evolve without theory.

The authors offer several examples of research missing the guidance of theory and explain how this absence worked to the detriment of those studies. Guidelines for constructing and testing theory are presented. These instructions are important because, as Drs. Bernard and Ritti argue, criminology has not grown as a science should due to poorly specified theories and the neglect of even the best theory by research.

While it is true that theoretical development in criminology has been meager in recent years, there are many reasons to expect greater attention to theory during the 1990s. Technical advances in research will be used to test existing theories. New ideas will appear, too. Debates over integration of existing theories likely will grow louder, and even the delineation between positivism and classicism may achieve renewed controversy. Students of criminology must be equipped to participate in these debates. Valuable exercises may be developed from the resources provided in the chapter on theory in this book. For example, Drs. Bernard and Ritti present criteria needed to falsify a theory. As a classroom exercise, try applying these criteria to the theory of crime you consider to have the most intuitive appeal. How does it hold up under scrutiny? Or evaluate the role of theory in selections within a single journal issue. Are hypotheses tested, and if so, how well? Remember, descriptive research is not scientific, according to Drs. Bernard and Ritti.

Patrick Jackson describes the major sources of information about crime, criminals, public perceptions, and criminal justice processing, as well as some less recognized locations of data. Each source developed independently and in response to designated purpose. It is important to realize these purposes and understand the procedures used in collecting these data, their limitations, and the unique advantages they offer. Media accounts of the crime rate, for example, are based on sources such as the Uniform Crime Reports or the National Crime Survey. If public perception of the fear of crime escalates in response to media reports, criminologists must explain whether such fear is justifiable based on the original source of data. Dr. Jackson explains the different potential uses of these data sources, how they complement each other, and how they differ. Findings are presented to convey the issues of comparability among data sources, as well as evaluate their ability to answer the important questions in criminology. As illustrated, even relatively new innovations within these sources are not without their limitations.

Prevalence, incidence, rates, and other descriptive measures are explained by Paul Tracy, and the formulas for their calculation are presented. It is important that these concepts be understood, because they constitute one of the necessary first steps in almost all studies, applicable to quantitative as well as qualitative methods. Some of these measures may serve as actual variables in analyses. All are fundamental to more advanced statistical applications. These concepts can be quite confusing, easily substituted for one another in error. Using a series of tables and figures and data for 27,160 subjects, Dr. Tracy conveys the substantive meaning of these terms and clearly shows how they differ.

In chapter 4, Sandra Wexler explains the ethical obligations of scientists to those they are studying. This knowledge is important particularly to criminology, because special concerns exist when sensitive topics and behaviors, such as criminality, are being observed. The requirements of ethical science are considered by many to be at odds with high methodological standards. Dr. Wexler refutes this claim, arguing instead that criminologists should delight in knowing that ethical and methodological requirements are compatible. This is valuable information for a measurement issue that criminologists too often ignore.

Experiments are generally considered the most valuable tools in science, but ethical, legal, and practical constraints often prevent their use in criminology. Jeffrey Fagan offers advice by which these difficulties can be overcome. He argues the merits of the natural experiment as a vehicle to test theory and evaluate policy. Elements needed to design natural experiments are identified and their capabilities explained. Sources of error are identified and potiential solutions suggested. Study designs of three natural experiments on very different substantive topics are examined. Findings and conclusions from these studies are evaluated according to their value as natural experiments.

In "Exploring the Offender's Perspective: Observing and Interviewing Criminals," Drs. Wright and Bennett demonstrate the many virtues of ethnographic study. Many topics in criminology are ideally suited to field investigation, and for some it is the only method available to acquire the desired information. Criminologists, however, have been reluctant to pursue these methods of observation, instead remaining within the comfortable arena of the ivory academic tower. Evidence exists that indicates the offender's perspective is gaining vogue. As Drs. Wright and Bennett discuss, many of the worries associated with participant-observation research are without foundation. Moreover, the benefits to be obtained are considerable. Interesting examples from their own work, as well as from others', illustrate the techniques and helpful hints for overcoming problems. Students are well advised to take their scientific questions to the field.

Longitudinal research designs are discussed in the next chapter, by Elizabeth Piper Deschenes. Four major types of longitudinal designs are presented, as well as the unique advantages and limitations accompanying their use. The relative merits of longitudinal and cross-sectional designs for establishing causation are debated. Design issues, such as choices between samples and populations, data sources, prospective or retrospective investigation, and identified and evaluated using examples from current research in criminology. Longitudinal designs have been very popular in criminology during the last two decades. Their use has provoked recent controversy. Although clearly an advocate of longitudinal research, Dr. Deschenes outlines the basis to this controversy. The arguments presented by each side can make for lively classroom debates.

Criminologists offer society a valuable service through evaluations of policy changes following legislation, court decision, or administrative decree. In "Issues in Legal-Impact Research," Drs. Horney and Spohn highlight the contributions provided by policy research as well as the difficulties that may be experienced during these types of evaluations. Using their own assessment of rape reform legislation and work by others on the impact of deterrence on drunk driving laws, court-ordered prison reforms, and mandatory gun laws, Drs. Horney and Spohn illustrate the principal measurement issues associated with legal-impact research. As these examples portray, unique situations occur in every investigation therefore general guidelines serve as helpful reference. Conceptualization of the intended goals and procedures by which they are expected to be attained are especially important. Informed choice of data sources best capable of providing unbiased information also is crucial to successful evaluation. These and other design issues are explained in convincing manner in this chapter. Policy changes affecting crime, criminals, and the criminal justice systems occur almost daily. Students might try developing a plan to assess the impact of one of these changes in their local area.

In "Time Series, Panel Design, and Criminal Justice: A Multi-State, Multi-Wave Design," Drs. Kohfeld and Decker convey their belief in the advantages of time-series studies over other procedures for important questions about processes and change in criminology. Considerations of sequencing, timing, and causal order are discussed. Methods for conducting good time-series analyses are explained using examples of unemployment and crime as well as a detailed account of their own research on the deterrent effects of capital punishment. There are many modes of time-series research, some of which can involve sophisticated statistical models; so this chapter is challenging.

The final chapter of this book explains the strengths and weaknesses of studies using secondary data sources. Criminologists have tended to avoid projects based on data collected and coded by others. Criminology has accumulated data, at the very least, and this reinvention of the wheel is no longer always necessary. As Drs. Laub, Sampson, and Kiger argue, secondary data sources offer unlimited potential for new knowledge. Their work locating, recoding, and reanalyzing data from the mammoth study by Sheldon and Eleanor Glueck serves to illustrate the varied and creative uses for archival data. Perhaps best of all, the advice provided in this chapter can be put to immediate use, because a variety of data sources available for secondary analysis are identified in chapter 2 and actual data are presented in the previous chapter.

Measurement Issues in Criminology identifies procedures and topics about which special considerations exist in the science of criminology.

Students must be taught these concerns. They must be provided the conventional wisdom used to execute these techniques, as well as caveats available in order to overcome difficulties they may encounter. An increase in student enrollments and the addition of new degree programs in criminology and criminal justice provide clear indication that graduate training in criminology is a growing need. Criminology also must grow as a science. Better links between theory and research must be established. Greater awareness of data sources and research designs and of procedures for utilizing them must be more widely known. Greater opportunities for triangulation, using multiple approaches, must be explored in criminology. The research of students and scholars, alike, should benefit from the information provided in this book.

I thank all of the authors for their contributions and their advise on the overall design of this book. I would like to thank the staff at Springer-Verlag for their encouragement and supervision of this project.

Kimberly L. Kempf
St. Louis, Missouri

Contents

Epigraph v
Foreword vii
Preface ix
Contributors xvii

1   The Role of Theory in Scientific Research
    Thomas J. Bernard and R. Richard Ritti   1

2   Sources of Data
    Patrick G. Jackson   21

3   Prevalence, Incidence, Rates, and Other Descriptive Measures
    Paul E. Tracy Jr.   51

4   Ethical Obligations and Social Research
    Sandra Wexler   78

5   Natural Experiments in Criminal Justice
    Jeffrey A. Fagan 108

6   Exploring the Offender's Perspective: Observing and
    Interviewing Criminals
    Richard Wright and Trevor Bennett 138

7   Longitudinal Research Designs
    Elizabeth Piper Deschenes 152

8   Issues in Legal-Impact Research
    Julie Horney and Cassia Spohn 167

9   Time Series, Panel Design, and Criminal Justice: A Multi-State, Multi-Wave Design
    Carol W. Kohfeld and Scott H. Decker 198

10 Assessing the Potential of Secondary Data Analysis: A New Look at the Glueck's *Unraveling Juvenile Delinquency* Data
    John H. Laub, Robert J. Sampson and Kenna Kiger 241

Biographies 258
Author Index 263
Subject Index 269

Contributors

Trevor Bennett, Ph.D., Institute of Criminology, University of Cambridge, Cambridge, Cambrideshire, CB3 9DT, England

Thomas J. Bernard, Ph.D., Administration of Justice, Pennsylvania State University, University Park, Pennsylvania 16802, USA

Scott H. Decker, Ph.D., Administration of Justice, Center for Metropolitan Studies, University of Missouri-St. Louis, St. Louis, Missouri 63121, USA

Elizabeth Piper Deschenes, Ph.D., UCLA Drug Abuse Research Group, University of California, Los Angeles, Los Angeles, California 90024-3511, USA

Jeffrey A. Fagan, Ph.D., School of Criminal Justice, Rutgers, the State University of New Jersey, Newark, New Jersey 07102, USA

Julie Horney, Ph.D. Criminal Justice, University of Nebraska at Omaha, Omaha, Nebraska 68182, USA

Patrick G. Jackson, Ph.D., Criminal Justice Administration, Sonoma State University, Rohnert Park, California 94928, USA

Kenna Kiger, M.A., Department of Sociology, University of Illinois at Urbana-Champaign, Urbana, Illinois 61801, USA

Carol W. Kohfeld, Ph.D., Political Science, Center for Metropolitan Studies, University of Missouri-St. Louis, St. Louis, Missouri 63121, USA

John H. Laub, M.A., Ph.D., College of Criminal Justice, Northeastern University, Boston, Massachusetts 02115, USA

R. Richard Ritti, Ph.D., Administration of Justice and Sociology, Pennsylvania State University, University Park, Pennsylvania 16802, USA

Robert J. Sampson, M.A., Ph.D., Department of Sociology and the Institute of Government and Public Affairs, University of Illinois at Urbana-Champaign, Urbana, Illinois 61801, USA

Cassia Spohn, Ph.D., Criminal Justice, University of Nebraska at Omaha, Omaha, Nebraska 68182, USA

Paul E. Tracy, Jr., Ph.D., College of Criminal Justice, Northeastern University, Boston, Massachusetts 02115, USA

Sandra Wexler, Ph.D., University of California, Berkeley, Berkeley, CA 94720, USA

Richard Wright, Ph.D., Administration of Justice and Fellow, Center for Metropolitan Studies, University of Missouri-St. Louis, St. Louis, Missouri 63121, USA

1
The Role of Theory in Scientific Research

THOMAS J. BERNARD and R. RICHARD RITTI

Most researchers in criminology or criminal justice would describe what they are doing as behavioral or social science. The term *science* would likely connote for them having to do with fact rather than opinion, with description of social relations rather than beliefs about how people ought to behave. Numbers would come to mind as well for a large group of us, expressing results in quantities rather than qualities. Explanation and prediction from theory are yet other mental images conjured up by the word "science."

Our contention in this chapter is that of all these things, theory alone is the distinguishing feature of the scientific enterprise. True, some of the others are necessary or desirable, but regardless of measurement precision, quantification, or power of analytical tools, the activity is not science unless it involves an explicit theory. We argue, then, that there is no such thing as a purely descriptive piece of scientific research.

This is not to say that useful and interesting things cannot be done without the involvement of an explicit theory. For example, we might gather statistics on the numbers of citations for driving under the influence (DUI), organize these by police jurisdictions, and analyze these data against traffic fatalities. This might produce some eye-opening results, so who cares whether or not there's a theory involved.

Why we ought to care is the concern of this chapter. We ought to care because we in fact are operating on some implicit, unstated theory that relates DUI to traffic fatalities—how else could we have chosen to examine those variables among the hundreds available to us? We ought to care because that very implicitness of our theory can lead to sloppy investigation, to misleading or meaningless conclusions, and to the failure to include a crucial variable. Finally, we ought to care because our understanding of the DUI problem will never go beyond low-level empirical description unless we develop an adequate conceptual framework.

An explicitly stated theory, even though it may be rudimentary, is necessary to (a) define a question as a scientific question, (b) give a question meaning under the canons of scientific inquiry, (c) provide a means for selecting variables and measures, and (d) make possible the interpretation of results. This is not an argument for a rigid, formula-like approach to doing research. Science, after all, is in some measure art and intuition and not merely the careful statement of all hypotheses in the approved *NULL* form. But the existence of an explicitly stated theory that spawns those hypotheses is always necessary for the reasons that we now explore.

Science and "What Everyone Knows"

"You've all had the weekend to prepare your problem statements, so let's see what you've come up with. Lesley?" With that, Professor Faust's Research Methods I class has been called to order, and Lesley is now outlining the research problem she has chosen for her class project.

"Um, I know that this may not seem like much, but it really took me a long time. Well, I think I want to do something on the relationship between body image and female criminality." Lesley glanced hopefully at Faust as she continued.

"We know that males commit most of the violent crime, and then I was reading this article on body image, and how people describe themselves on this scale of body image, and how this predicts other kinds of things like occupational choice. Then I thought that maybe we could use this as a predictor of the type of crime that females commit. So I'm going to administer this scale to a sample of our residents and see the extent to which the 'male' and 'androgynous' types tend to commit different kinds of offenses from the 'female' types."

"I see," nodded Faust, "but just what would lead you to expect such differences?"

"Well it's what I just said, we know that males are more likely to. . . ."

"Yes, I know that is what you just said, Lesley, but that's not the point I am trying make," Faust interrupted. "I want to know—to see in writing— exactly why, exactly what line of reasoning leads you to posit this relationship."

Following additional clarification and discussion, it's Stanley's turn. And Stanley does have it all laid out for the professor. In fact, he's pretty much convinced that he's ready to go.

"I'm going to do a comparative study of two medium security prisons, one with a low incidence of complaints about excessive use of force by custodial personnel, and the other with a high incidence." (Stanley works for the state Board of Corrections.)

"My theory is that differences in the socialization process of the two inmate groups will account for the differences in behavior. I plan to use participant observation combined with available data from personnel records." Stanley went on to detail his data collection procedures, as well as how the socialization process shaped behavior through group pressure to conform to norms.

"Finally, I'll be using minority status, sex, age, educational attainment, and family SES as control variables."

"How so?" was Faust's rather unhelpful comment.

"Um, I don't think I get your drift, Professor. Do you mean, why just those variables and not some others? I think the answer to that is, is . . . well, you've got to draw the line somewhere!"

"Certainly. No, perhaps I should rephrase my question. Of all the possible variables, what instructed you to choose those? As I listened to your reasoning, nowhere were any of them explicitly mentioned. Education, for example, what has that to do with socialization?"

"Why sure it does, Dr. Faust. See, the more education a person has. . . ." Stanley went on to detail his reasoning.

Folk Theory Versus Scientific Theory

These brief scenarios reflect some typical approaches that beginning students take to the unaccustomed business of designing a research project. That is,

- Commonly, they settle first on a methodology and a set of variables, rather than a theoretical framework.
- The motivation for both the method and variable selection is largely implicit, half formed, derived by analogy from an existing piece of research.
- The supporting rationale, when asked for, is often couched in terms of "What everyone knows," or in our language, in terms of "folk theory" as opposed to scientific theory.

The main characteristic of a folk theory, as opposed to a scientific theory, is that it is not explicitly stated. There are several good reasons why researchers should take time to explicitly state the theories underlying their research. First, at least some commonly held folk theories simply are wrong. For example, one common folk theory is that poverty causes crime, but the evidence against this is fairly strong (cf. Vold & Bernard, 1986). Second, many folk theories are not necessarily wrong, but when specified and tested as a scientific theory, they prove to be so complex that their truth or falsity is unclear. Numerous examples can be mentioned—the idea that if we punished criminals more severely, then crime would decrease throughout the society (cf. Blumstein, Cohen, & Nagin, 1978); the belief that poor people commit more crime than other people (cf. Tittle, Villemez, & Smith, 1978); and the belief that there are a relatively small number of "career criminals" who account for a large majority of serious crimes (cf. Hirschi & Gottfredson, 1988).

Finally, at least some folk theories contain inherently unscientific concepts in the sense that they are empirically unavailable. For example, at the beginning of this century, many people believed that crime was caused by biological inferiority (cf. Vold & Bernard, 1986). Researchers attempted to specify and test this folk theory, but they were unable to define the concept of biological inferiority in a scientific way. In practice, what they did was to measure the physical and biological characteristics of criminals and then define those characteristics as evidence of biological inferiority (Gould, 1981). There was no independent way to specify the concept of biological inferiority so that the relationship between it and criminality could be examined.

Folk theories have great intuitive appeal since they are based on "what everyone knows." Unless explicitly stated, their pitfalls never become apparent, and research that is based on them can be wasted effort. Thus, research undertaken without an explicit statement of the theory is subject to all of the above possible problems. We therefore argue that scientific research *begins* with the explicit statement of the theory on which it is based. Other elements, such as the methodology and the selection of the variables, come only after the explicit statement of the theory.

Theories in Science

Fact Versus Concept

For the purposes of our discussion we refer to a *fact* as a direct observable. For example, possession of a firearm is a fact; red hair is a fact. A *concept* is an abstraction based on several direct observables. Socioeconomic status, deviance, culture are concepts. Indeed, a concept such as culture is a higher order concept, itself being defined by a group of lower order concepts. Concepts cannot be directly observed. For example, direct observation can reveal that a person possesses a gun, that the person points it at another person, that the gun discharges, that the other person falls to the floor, and that the person is now dead. Two people, each observing this sequence of actions, may reach different conclusions about whether a crime has occurred. Direct observation itself cannot determine this—rather, some judgmental calculus involving various criteria must be employed before a person can make that decision. Deviance and crime are concepts, not facts, and as such, they cannot be observed directly. There is always a gap between observations and concepts, but that gap may be greater or smaller.

Empirically oriented researchers sometimes formulate concepts that are quite close to observable data—i.e., the gap is very small. Theories based on such concepts are highly testable, but they have little appeal because, in a sense, they just summarize existing data (e.g., Hindelang, Gottfredson, & Garafalo, 1978). At the other end of the spectrum, theorists sometimes propose concepts that are highly intuitive and appealing but that are distant from observable data (e.g., Sutherland & Cressey, 1978). The appeal of such theories arises because they reflect widely-held folk theories about crime and criminals. These theories may be fruitful in that they may be the source of an enormous range of insights and predictions (e.g., see DeFleur & Quinney, 1966). The problem for researchers is to specify the concepts sufficiently so that the theory can be tested.

Whether the gap is large or small, the point is that the gap between concepts and observations necessarily exists in all theories. This gap means that some form of judgmental calculus must be employed in translating observations into concepts.

Scientific Theories

What then is a scientific theory? There are many definitions, but we prefer the following: A theory is a set of concepts bound together by explicit relationships and causal priorities. For example, "crime is generated by social structural strain," "crime emerges when social control is weakened or absent," and "crime results from normal social learning" are all theoretical statements that link various concepts in specific relationships. None of these concepts (social structural strain, social control, social learning, crime) are directly observable. These familiar examples illustrate some of the following characteristics of theory.

First, theories are necessarily incomplete. There are undoubtedly circumstances under which the generalization does not hold. More can be added and qualifications appended. Therein lies the utility of the phrase made famous by economists—*ceteris paribus*—other things being equal. As working models, as simplifications of reality, theories must be incomplete to be useful. If predictions from theory are so crude as to be useless, then some elaboration is necessary.

Second, theories are necessarily incorrect, at least in some detail. Even some of the best established laws of physics, theory whose truth is so well established that it can serve as the basis for technology, are approximations that in some minor (though theoretically important) circumstances do not square with observation.

Third, theories themselves are never tested, only the observable consequences of the theory. This is because a proper theory is phrased in terms of concepts and, therefore, is at least one level removed from observables. Consequently, it is the predictions made by a theory about empirical observables—facts—that alone can be tested.

What Constitutes a Scientific Issue?

In our discussion thus far, we have simply assumed that a suitable issue for scientific investigation has been chosen. But once again as we inquire into the role of theory in scientific research, we find the question to be a bit more complicated than it might at first seem.

"Any question becomes a scientific question if I deem it so!" might be your reply. And we must admit that to some extent your position would be correct. But any question? Out of the endless possible combinations of facts, concepts, and causal assertions, how is it that we (1) settle on a very few questions as worthy of scientific investigation and (2) decide that a particular question is framed appropriately to be deemed a scientific issue? It is true that one can use various methods of pure empiricism, such as ransacking the data in search of relationships. But even if one finds such relationships, the larger issue concerns the point at which a question becomes a scientific question, as opposed to a simple empirical inquiry.

The answer to that, we argue, lies in the construction of a theoretical/ conceptual framework that both explains and predicts the observations at hand. To illustrate our argument, let's look at an issue that has received a considerable amount of empirical attention—but somewhat less theoretical specification: the question of race and crime.

The Question of Race and Crime

There seem to be some fairly strong empirical associations between race and crime in the United States and elsewhere (e.g., Nettler, 1984, pp. 136–138). Certainly sufficient folk theory exists that would support an argument about race as a causal factor in some sense: "Everybody knows" that when racial minorities (read Black, Hispanic, or Native American, depending on where you are) move into a neighborhood, the crime rate goes up. Do we then have a scientific question? And if we do, just what is it?

We have a scientific question about the relationship between race and crime only if we have an explicitly stated scientific theory that links those two concepts. That is, we must posit some form of inductive generalization that both predicts and explains the connection between race and crime; and we cannot merely rely on empirically establishing that such a connection exists. Unless such a theory exists, then there is no proper scientific issue, despite the abundance of relevant empirical data.

Some of the theories that attempt to explain these data use race as a surrogate, as an indicator for another concept such as culture (e.g., Wolfgang & Ferracuti, 1972) or intelligence (e.g., Gordon, 1976). If race is only a surrogate, then the scientific question is not one of the relationship between race and crime, but something very different. Other theories focus on problems with the concept of crime (e.g., there is not an association between minority status and insider trading) or with the impact that race has on enforcement (e.g., Wolfgang, Figlio & Sellin, 1972, p. 252 found that race was the most significant factor determining a police officer's decision to arrest).

If the question is defined specifically as race and criminality, then the theory must explicitly define the concept of race in some defensible way and state explicitly and plausibly, in an empirically testable way, just what the linkages and causalities are. Such a theory would almost certainly have to focus on biological and genetic heritage if race is to be involved as something other than a surrogate. Short of such a theory, however, no amount of correlational, multicorrelational, or particorrelational evidence will establish a scientific issue.

With these ideas in mind, let us turn to the method of science: the construction and testing of theoretical propositions.

Constructing and Testing Theories

Induction and Deduction

Induction involves working from empirical observables to the construction of generalizations. The converse process is deduction: working from generalizations to observables. The process of theory *construction* is inductive: it involves building generalizations from observables. The process of theory *testing* is deductive: empirical observables are deduced from the theory and compared with observed facts.

The formal name given to these empirical consequences deduced from theory is *hypothesis*. So the process of hypothesis formation is simply the formal statement of the implications that the theory holds for what may be observed *if* the theory is correct. Even relatively simply theoretical statements may spawn numbers of hypotheses formally stating relationships or differences in magnitude implied as consequences of the state of the world as modeled by the theory.

Consider this syllogism:

1A. If all horses have tails, then Mr. Ed (a horse) will have a tail.
1B. All horses have tails.
1C. Therefore Mr. Ed has a tail.

This is a deduction: if A and B are ture, then C logically is also true. But what if B and C reversed to read as follows?

2A. If all horses have tails, Mr. Ed will have a tail.
2B. Mr. Ed has a tail.
2C. Therefore all horses have tails.

Logically, this syllogism is incorrect—Mr. Ed's tail entitles us to say nothing about the class of all horses. But that does not mean that 2C is false—in fact, it may be true that all horses have tails. What we have done here is create an inductive generalization: We have moved from observations of Mr. Ed (and presumably numerous of his comrades) to a generalization about horses. The result is a "theory" that can be verified or falsified only by empirical investigations, not by logical analysis. Induction, then, is the method of creating scientific theories. The single hypothesis generated in this case would be: "A horse will have a tail." Strictly speaking, hypotheses are to be framed in *null* terms, that is, "A horse has no tail." Each instance of rejecting the null hypothesis then provides further support for the validity of the theory.

Several points can be made about scientific theories from this simple example. Note that the truth of 2C can never be established short of producing observations of all horses part, present, and future. Further observation of tails on horses can only make the theory more plausible but can never confirm its truth. This is true of all scientific theories.

What happens if we find a horse without a tail? We could reject 2C as simply false: For the purist, just one counterexample is sufficient to falsify any inductive generalization. But we may take other paths. For example, we may revise our theory in some way so as to incorporate the existence of a few deviant horses, or we may redefine what we mean by a horse to exclude the offending animal. In practice, then, it is possible to hold on to the proposition that all horses have tails in the face of fairly extensive evidence to the contrary.

We have just described some important consequences of the scientific method; so they are worth repeating.

1. No amount of continued verification of the empirical consequences (i.e., rejecting null hypotheses) can ever finally establish the truth of a scientific theory. However, it may become increasingly plausible to the extent that we consider it proven.
2. A single counterexample is sufficient to invalidate a scientific theory as it stands. We may throw the whole thing out as a result, or we may modify the theory in some way so as to incorporate the discrepant finding.
3. The possible modifications include
   - revision—i.e., changing what is postulated about the relationships or causal sequences;
   - redefinition—i.e., altering the concepts in some fashion;
   - elaboration—i.e., adding new concepts and/or relationships.
4. Because modifications are almost always possible, there often is no clear point at which there is unanimous agreement that a scientific theory has been falsified.

This final point can become a problem when people have nonscientific reasons for adhering to a scientific theory. For example, scientists who work for years developing a particular theory will generally find that their personal reputation and prestige are tied up with that theory. Such scientists may continue to modify their theory in the face of intractable counterinstances, long after others have abandoned it.

The problem is more severe in the social sciences, where theories often have implications for political and social values. Scientists may be initially attracted to one theory rather than others because that theory supports their deeply held values. Those same scientists then have a motive to modify rather than reject the theory when confronted with a counterinstance. For example, at the present time, at least some criminologists continue to modify and reformulate virtually every theory of crime that has been put forth in the last 200 years (Vold & Bernard, 1986). As a result, the falsification of social science theories sometimes seems like an impossible task.

The Verifiability Theory of Meaning

Despite these problems falsifying theories, falsification itself is central to what it means to be scientific. Specifically, any assertion qualifying as a scientific assertion must, at least in principle, be able to specify the conditions under which it will be falsified.

Scientific discourse is not the only kind of discourse. Ethical values and religious beliefs are extremely important areas of human discourse, perhaps much more important than the types of issues discussed in the social sciences. But no matter how important they are, assertions about human values and religious beliefs cannot be falsified. Therefore, such assertions lie outside the scientific arena.

This criterion of falsifiability appears to be straightforward and noncontroversial, but it is an important question that can be asked about many theories. For example, Hirschi and Gottfredson (1980) argued that Sutherland (1947) constructed his theory is such a way that it could not be falsified. The same issue has been raised about behavioral psychology (e.g., Burgess & Akers, 1968). Akers (1985), whose social learning theory combines those two, has responded by arguing that indeed it is possible to falsify his theory, yet he does not state specifically what observations *would* falsify the theory. To the extent that crucial observations remain unspecified, there will still be disagreement about whether such theories are scientific.

The same question can be asked about other theories. For example, *in principle* what observations would falsify the "rational choice" theories (e.g., Cornish & Clarke, 1986), as well as the earlier economic and classical theories that make similar arguments (see Vold & Bernard, 1986)? What human behaviors could we observe that would reveal these theories to be incorrect? What if, for example, we observe that, given the possibility of enormous gain and little cost, a potential crime remains uncommitted? If these theorists then suggest that the agent's benefit/cost calculus is such that the benefits did not outweight the costs after all, then have we not gotten into a nonfalsifiable position? It then would seem that there is not conceivable observation that would falsify the theory. If such is the case, as *science* these theories are meaningless.

The issue of falsifiability becomes particularly crucial when a theory confronts a counterinstance—i.e., when some observable pattern contradicts the predictions of the theory. One of the possible responses to that situation is to revise the theory to incorporate the discrepant empirical finding.

Because it addresses a counterinstance, there is some temptation to revise the theory in such a way as to rule out all possible future counter-instances—i.e., to make the theory nonfalsifiable.

Consider the following discussion of the deterrent effect of police, as presented by McPheters and Stronge (1976, pp. 376–396). These theorists take an economic position that predicts that increased police expenditures should be associated with decreased crime rates. The counterinstance they faced was that numerous studies have found the opposite—that increased police expenditures are associated with increased crime rates.

McPheters and Stronge therefore revised their theory to incorporate this discrepant empirical finding. They hypothesized that the increased police expenditures indeed deter a portion of the crime, so that crime rates would have been even higher without those expenditures. They conclude that, despite the consistent positive relation between expenditures and crime, "increased police expenditures do have a definite deterrent impact upon criminal activity."

The question raised here is: What will falsify such an argument? As McPheters and Stronge have phrased it, if crime rates go down, it supports the deterrence hypothesis, and if crime rates go up, it also supports the deterrence hypothesis. If there is no observation that can falsify this hypothesis, then this is not meaningful as a scientific statement.

Falsification and the Content of the Theory

To ask the question, In principle, what will falsify this theory? is to ask for a clear and precise statement of what the theory asserts. Often, what a theory asserts is not terribly clear. To ask what will falsify a theory is to ask for the nonnegotiable bottom line: What is it that this theory asserts that is so fundamental to the theory that, if it is contradicted by observations, the theory itself should be dumped? Thus, establishing exactly what will falsify a theory also establishes exactly what the theory asserts.

One of the present authors (Bernard, 1987a) has analyzed strain theories in an effort to state their propositions in falsifiable form. Merton's (1968) theory, for example, can be summarized in the following falsifiable propositions:

1. There is cross-cultural variation in the value placed on monetary success—i.e., in the link between monetary success and social status or prestige.
2. Cross-cultural variation in the value placed on monetary success is positively related to rates of utilitarian, profit-oriented criminal activity.
3. Within a given society, rates of utilitarian criminal behavior in different groups is inversely related to the access those groups have to legal means of acquiring wealth.
4. Within a given society, access to the legal means of acquiring wealth

varies according to social structural location. Specifically, in American society, there is a positive relation between access to legal means of acquiring wealth and social class position, with the lowest social class having the least access and the highest social class having the most access.

Similar sets of falsifiable propositions were presented for Cohen's (1955) and Cloward and Ohlin's (1960) theories.

Agnew (1987) responded that Bernard had misinterpreted these theories, which instead make falsificable predictions about individual frustrations. The major point here is that, apparently, it is not clear what these theories assert. To ask, "In principle, what will falsify Merton's strain theory?" is to ask for a precise and exact statement of what the theory asserts. If that question generates contradictory and conflicting answers, then the content of Merton's theory is not well understood. A similar point can be made in reference to an article Bernard (1987c) wrote about Hirschi's (1969) control theory.

Variables and Measures

Earlier we defined a theory as "a set of concepts bound together by explicit relationships and causal priorities." Concepts, we noted, are abstractions derived from observables, and they are used to compose the theory.

Variables represent the state of observables. The particular observables that will be important for testing a given theory are those that are related to, represent, or reflect the concepts in that theory. Thus, variables represent concepts directly or in combination with other variables.

Concepts and variables are not the same thing, since more than one variable may be taken to represent a concept. For example, the concept of "deviance" may be represented by several variables, including engaging certain actions or adhering to particular attitudes or values. Those actions and attitudes can be directly observed, whereas the concept of deviance cannot. It is apparent that there are a variety of variables that are related to, or might be taken to represent or reflect, the concept of deviance.

It might seem tautological to say this, but variables must exhibit variation. That is, under different conditions, there must be differences in what is observed, so that we can link those differences to the predictions of the theory. Those differences then must be "measured" in some way.

Measures are ways of determining the level of a variable within the framework of a particular investigation. That is, measures are ways of recording the variation that a variable exhibits. Measures are not the same thing as variables, since more than one measure may be seen as a valid indicator of the variable.

Because these ideas were developed first within the physical sciences, we will illustrate them first using Newton's law (a very well established theory)

Force = Mass × Acceleration. Note first that force, mass, and acceleration all have common-sense meanings but that none are direct observables. Take acceleration: That's how fast your automobile gets from 0 to 60. Literally, it is the rate of change in velocity (in speed, to civilians) per unit time. In terms of direct observables: length per unit time per unit time.

In terms of measures, we could measure length by reading the auto's odometer, or we could use a tape measure. For time we undoubtedly would use a stopwatch. From these we calculate acceleration. We can then calculate mass (weight divided by the acceleration of gravity) and, in turn, the force required to bring about the observed state of affairs. We could also determined the power required, the amount of work done, and so on, all by using the measures of mass, length, and time (the so-called MLT system of physics).

These useful physical concepts are hardly arbitrary inventions. They are members of a family of concepts closely related within a coherent conceptual system. In the social sciences, the situation is not as tidy. A variable may be reflected in many measures that demonstrate only a limited degress of agreement with one another (if that!). The observable result is that the concepts mirrored in the different measured variables do not agree. The resulting problem is one of *validity*: i.e., the extent to which different measures really represent the underlying concept.

Validity

Validity historically has been a problem for both the physical and the social sciences. Social sciences have used several methods to address the problem of validity. One has been *construct validity*: the extent to which the observed behavior of measures accords with the prediction from theory. Yet quite obviously, this is a bootstrap procedure, one dependent on the preexistence of the theory that the measures are designed to verify!

An alternative approach, that espoused first by the physical sciences and imported to social science is that of the *operational definition* of concepts. "Every scientific concept must be connected to experience by means of precisely given operations, which tell us how to apply the concept. . . . For example, if a biologist is to use the term 'Mammal,' he must be able to tell us exactly how we determine whether a given animal is a mammal" (Kemeny, 1959, p. 127). Unfortunately, what we social scientists don't learn from this is how a scientific consensus develops in support of this set of operations. Yet another problem is that even in the physical sciences actual work seldom conforms to the letter of the prescription. Yet, operationalism is a solution to the validity problem in that it enables scientists to circumvent the definitional problems that may render tests of competing theories incommensurable.

Is this the solution for the social sciences? Experimental psychology (perhaps not a social science), especially learning theorists, quite self-consciously adopted the notion. For example, one does not refer to a "hungry" rat (and a genetically standard rat, at that). Rather, we have 12- or 24-hour "deprived rats," trials to criterion, and so on. All in all, allowing for some problems in the cognitive area, the approach seems to work.

But what of the investigator interested in alienation, or deviance, and the like? No parallel solution is apparent. What set of operations defines alienation, for instance? The answer frequently offered is that of a composite scale of N items, each reflecting some aspect of the universe of content.

Says who? The immediate difficulty is that an infinite number of such operational definitions is possible, and many of these will not show a substantial degree of agreement with others. The difficulty appears to be that we are not really defining operations here, but variables, and there is no discernible framework within which agreement is likely.

Admittedly to oversimplify, there is no analogy to the physical MLT structure that constrains, and to some extent defines, the types of operations possible. What we have then is what Torgerson has termed *measurement by fiat*, in fact just the problem that operationalism is presumed to avoid (Torgerson, 1958, p. 22). Then why the problem? Optimistically, we might invoke the differential levels of development in the social and physical sciences. Further refinement of theory and concept will correct all. But we wonder. There do appear to be some fundamental differences in the two vocations, differences in the nature of concepts, measures, and theories. At this point, all we are prepared to say is that universally accepted sets of measures that define concepts appear to be crucial to theory development, and without theory there can be no science of criminology.

Variables and Measures in Criminology

One of the authors (Bernard) has argued that many tests of the various types of criminology theories have used variables and measures that do not validly represent the concepts in those theories and that the results of those tests therefore do not apply to the theories. These arguments are related to the argument described above about what will actually falsify a theory. Research testing strain theories has typically measured strain with individual-level variables. For example, Merton's theory is frequently tested with measures of frustration resulting from perceptions of blocked legitimate opportunity. But Bernard (1987a, 1987b) argues that Merton's theory predicts at best a weak relation between individual frustration and criminality, and it also predicts that people in a situation of social structural strain would resort to illegal opportunities even if they are not frustrated. Frustration plays no causal role in Merton's theory, so that measures of frustration cannot be used to test the theory.

The problem is that Merton's theory makes social structural, not social psychological, assertions. His concepts describe properties of social aggregates (structures and cultures) and not properties of individuals. Those concepts are causally linked to rates and distributions of crime, not to individual criminal behavior. Research that measures the properties of individuals and links them to the likelihood that the individual will engage in crime simply cannot be used to test Merton's theory.

Using the four falsifiable propositions that Bernard attributes to Merton's theory (pp. 10–11 above), we can construct measures for each of these propositions, but none would focus on an individual's feelings of frustration. An appropriate measure of proposition 1, for example, would be an attitude survey measuring linkage between monetary success and social prestige, administered to two or more cultural groups. The variation we would be looking for would be *among cultures*, not among individuals within in a culture. If no variation appears among cultures, then this element of Merton's theory can be considered falsified.

Comparable arguments were made for the other elements in Merton's theory and for Cohen's (1955) and Cloward and Ohlin's (1960) strain theories. The conclusion of the article was that virtually all research purporting to test these theories did not actually do so. The point is that variables and measures must be carefully chosen to represent the concepts in the theory, or the research simply will not apply. The failure to choose variables and measures carefully is one reason why so little falsification has been achieved in criminology.

Bernard also raised questions about the adequacy of self-reported data as a measure for testing the concepts in control theory (see Bernard, 1984; Vold & Bernard, 1986, pp. 245–247). Self-report surveys almost always are done with normal (i.e., nondelinquent) groups, such as high school or college students. Such a sample has a very small portion of seriously delinquent youths to begin with and tends to lose most of the data on those youths for a variety of reasons. In order to generate variation, a weak measure of delinquency is created that concentrates on trivial offeness.

Bernard argues that the results of such surveys are best viewed as explaining the variation between overconformity and underconformity (i.e., square kids vs. wild kids) in a basically nondelinquent population. These results can be extended to serious delinquents only if the same causal processes are at work there as in normal populations, something that is asserted (e.g., Hirschi, 1969, p. 41) but not demonstrated. In fact, more recent research (Cernkovich, Giordano, & Pugh, 1985) suggests this is not the case. All of these problems with self-reported measures go back to the very first self-report survey (Nye, 1958) and were pointed out by Toby (1959).

Many of the problems with testing strain theories originated with control theorists (Bernard, 1984). Control theory is a social psychological theory, and control theorists have a tendency to see other types of criminology theories also as social psychological theories (e.g., Hirschi, 1969). Thus, strain theories were interpreted in social psychological terms, as asserting that there are variations in the "driving forces" to crime. This made them

directly comparable to control theories, which assert that there are variations in the "restraining forces." While such an interpretation was convenient for setting up comparative research, it was fundamentally inaccurate.

The point is that when researchers select variables and measures in testing a theory, close attention must be paid validly representing the concepts
in that theory. As fundamental a point as that seems, it has been consistently and egregiously violated in criminological research. The result is an
overall lack of progress within criminology.

Theory and Methodology

The masthead of *Psychometrika* proudly proclaims that this prestigious
journal is one devoted to the development of psychology as a "rational,
quantitative science." By default, it also would imply that only true science
can meet that description, a view more than likely held by many of our
colleagues. Carried a bit further, there also are many of us who have been
trained to believe that only the methodology of the true experiment is fully
scientific, in that only in this way can extraneous effects be controlled and
causality established. But whether you accept this or not, you are more
than likely saying, yes, but what does research design per se have to do
with theory? Haven't you just argued that empirical data (facts) and theory
are quite different things? Well, yes, we have. Yet it is also true that data
are collected under a theory of how the facts arrange themselves in the
observable world. An example will help illustrate the point.

Some years ago, one of the present authors (Ritti) was involved as a
consultant to several colleagues who were interested in the relationship
between aging and "quality of life." Conditioning variables were income
and gender (or some such). Because they had been trained in the tradition
of the experiment, their first impulse was to lay out a matrix of "treatment"
cells of 10-year increments in age by high and low income. Cells were to
contain equal numbers, of course, so that the data could be analyzed within
an experimental design. Immediately apparent was the problem of finding
sufficient numbers of high-income 80+ year old males. Life doesn't seem to
work that way. But for the researchers, this is far more than a practical
problem. Their method of data collection and subsequent analysis doesn't
support a theory of society in which there are many fewer 80- than 50-year-
olds, and fewer still of high income, and even fewer males to boot. What
can possibly be learned from sorting out main and interaction effects
reflecting the quality of life in a society that doesn't, and more than likely
couldn't, exist?

The point is that an experimental design is implemented properly only
with reference to a theory that supports those procedures. Perhaps more
obvious are examples based on other members of the general linear model
family, stepwise regression and path analysis. Forward stepwise regression
is popular because it affords a "best" model in the sense of accounting for

the most variance in the dependent variable with the fewest independent variables. Unfortunately, given the generally low reliabilities and relatively high levels of interdependence among social science variables, stepwise regression is also a suspect tool for analysis (as opposed to prediction). Though the details are beyond the scope of this chapter, the difficulty stems from the fact that clusters of related independent variables account for essentially the same piece of the dependent variable. Once a single variable is included, very likely on some additional chance variation, the remaining variables in the cluster are effectively excluded from further analysis. Models derived in this fashion can appear to be very different from those posited on theoretical grounds. In fact, however, were the model to be specified before analysis in accordance with theory, it might easily be nearly as good as the "best" model, differing only in its lack of capitalization on chance variation. And with models such as those using path analytic, or LISREL techniques, a theoretical framework is not only desirable, it is absolutely necessary.

Quantitative Versus Qualitative Methods

Before we conclude this section, it seems necessary to comment on the perennial issue of the relative merits of quantitative as opposed to qualitative research methods. As noted at the top of this section, there is the tendency to equate measurement quantification with science, at least as a necessary condition for true scientific inquiry. But science is a method, not a measurement technology. Many of the earth and life sciences are latecomers to quantification, having had long and useful histories as qualitative or taxonomic sciences. As we have argued, there is a distinction between the purely empirical and the theoretical, with the latter being the *sine qua non* of science, A regression equation may be empirical and predictive, but it is not of itself an example of science. Furthermore, becoming more precise is not equivalent to becoming more scientific.

True, there may be reasons to mistrust qualitative work in the social sciences. Unlike fossil bones or plants, the phenomena under investigation may be ephemeral, not available for inspection by other interested researchers. But then, are questionnaire data inherently less suspect? Are the circumstances antecedent to the generation of the responses any more publicly available? Ultimately, the issues are the same for both types of data and are questions concerning the adequacy of methodology rather than adherence to the science model.

The Crucial Role of Theory in Policy Research

While the term *policy research* could signify a range of policy-relevant inquiries, what we mean here is the following: a project designed specifically to answer questions about the desirability of different policy alternatives by testing them in a field situation. The reason for this narrower focus is that it is in this situation that theoretical considerations are most likely to be neglected. What we want to know, after all, is which of our alternatives is best. Theory may seem to be beside the point. Furthermore, if much of what we know is based on past experience with operational programs, there may not even be a body of theory available to describe what we are doing.

A recent example comes to mind. One of us was involved in a project to test the effectiveness of a home heating subsidy program for low-income families. It involved a true experimental design, with a sample of the eligible population assigned randomly to treatments and controls. The treatment involved a complicated formula for allocating available program funds to substantially reduce the customer's monthly payments due, together with an arrangement for systematically reducing the backlog of the customer's past due bills (which might be in the thousands of dollars). The goal was to get a higher overall percentage payment by bringing the payments due down to a level that the customer could handle.

Question: Why would such a program work? The social services people and the utility people—who, after all, aren't paid to spin theory—had a hunch that if bills were affordable, people would get used to paying them and subsequently the habit would "stick." Additionally, for every 3 months of satisfactory participation, customers would be granted an additional reduction in their accrued past debt, and this would be further incentive to stay current. So they basically had only a folk theory to support a methodologically sophisticated experiment.

Okay, so what? If it works, who cares? And if it doesn't, we can try another variant. Besides, we plan to collect a lot of data on all kinds of economic, social, and demographic variables, then interview participants at the end of the experiment. What more can you ask?

Well, the first thing might be, What theory of human social behavior supports such an intervention? How do people in the inner city cope with the financial burdens of everyday life on incomes that average $5,000 a year? And what kind of educational and cultural background is assumed by an elaborate payment incentive arrangement that requires months of deferred gratification? Trying to frame these questions properly amounts to more than idle academic theorizing—it represents the only way to assess the outcome of the experiment adequately.

Suppose we get lucky and it works, which most often will not be the case. What have we learned? Just this: that in this particular population, in this particular place, and under these particular circumstances, something worked. There is no guarantee that the particular procedure is exportable, nor do we have any defense against political critics who assail the program as demonstrating something very different from our interpretation. No, only if we have an adequate theoretical/conceptual framework and a body of data collected explicitly to test that framework will we have a solid basis for interpreting the outcome.

And if it doesn't work? At least we now have a basis for assessing our failure and revising the program. Our theory posits certain intermediate linkages and causalities that give rise to the end result. Inspecting the data collected explicitly to assess these linkages may help us to understand where the hypothesized process failed. But, you might ask, what of the data you were going to collect anyway, and what of those interviews? Well, if that information is going to be of use to us, first we need to be lucky in guessing correctly which variables will be crucial; and second, we will have to construct after the fact the theory we should have had in the first place in order to test those crucial linkages.

It should be apparent that what we are going to have to do in any event to utilize even partially the results of our experiment is just what we should have, and could have done at the outset. So why not do it right in the first place? The theory doesn't have to be all encompassing; it doesn't have to be complete—theories never are. And it doesn't even have to be correct! All it needs to be is explict rather than implicit, a framework to guide and motivate data collection and analysis.

Conclusion

If criminological research is to be scientific, then theory is absolutely necessary, although not sufficient. This is because the product of the scientific endeavor is *theory*, not fact or policy. Our conception of science as involving incremental growth and development depends on the existence of theory.

Scientific understanding grows through the elaboration and specification of a body of theory—of concepts and the causal linkages among those concepts. From this model of the social world, researchers deduce observable consequences that then can be checked against empirically observed facts. This empirical checking is also a necessary, although not sufficient, condition for science, and it is the concern of methodology. The alternation between theory and research is an interactive process that results in the falsification of some theories and the accumulation of knowledge within the context of other theories—i.e., in progress within the discipline.

In physics, the research enterprise is formally split between theorists and experimentalists. The job of the theorist is to formalize, abstract, and extend the findings of the experimentalist, while the job of the experimentalist is to devise methods for testing the implications of theory against physical reality. The talents required of each are sufficiently different and sufficiently well elaborated to require such a split.

While there is a balance between theory and methodology in physics, it seems to us that the theoretical aspect of the scientific enterprise is sometimes given insufficient attention by researchers in criminology. In the last 20 years, the field of criminology has become increasingly quantified, and an enormous amount of research has been published. As we point out above, all research tests theory of some type, regardless of whether the theory is stated well or badly. Thus, one would have to say that there has been an enormous amount of theory testing in criminology over the last 20 years.

Despite this fact, no theories in criminology have been falsified in the last 20 years. Whether there has been an accumulation of knowledge within the context of other theories is not at all clear, and any assertion on this issue would elicit wide disagreement among criminologists. Thus, despite enormous amount of research, criminology does not appear to have progressed as a scientific discipline in the last 20 years (Bernard, forthcoming).

The failure of criminology to progress as a discipline, it seems to us, comes from the failure to take theory seriously in designing and implementing research. Too much emphasis is placed on the sophistication of methodological and analytical techniques, and too little attention is paid to the careful specification of the theoretical issue that is being addressed. No matter how sophisticated the research techniques, progress in criminology as a science cannot occur unless that research is based on explicit and intelligent theory.

References

Agnew, R. (1987). On "Testing structural strain theories." *Journal of Research in Crime and Delinquency*, *24*(4), 281–286.

Akers, R.L. (1985). *Deviant behavior*. Belmont, CA: Wadsworth.

Bernard, T.J. (1984). Control criticisms of strain theories. *Journal of Research in Crime and Delinquency*, *21*(4), 353–372.

Bernard, T.J. (1987a). Testing structural strain theories. *Journal of Research in Crime and Delinquency*, *24*(4), 262–280.

Bernard, T.J. (1987b). Reply to Agnew. *Journal of Research in Crime and Delinquency*, *24*(4), 287–290.

Bernard, T.J. (1987c). Structure and control. *Justice Quarterly*, *4*(3), 409–424.

Bernard, T.J. (Forthcoming). Twenty years of testing theories: what have we learned and why? *Journal of Research in Crime and Delinquency*.

Blumstein, A., Cohen, J., & Nagin, D. (Eds.). (1978). *Deterrence and incapacitation*. Washington, D.C.: National Academy of Sciences.

Burgess, R.L., & Akers, R.L., (1968). A differential association-reinforcement theory of criminal behavior. *Social Problems*, *14*, 128–147.

Cernkovich, S.A., Giordano, P.G., & Pugh, M.D. (1985). Chronic offenders. *Journal of Criminal Law & Criminology*, *76*(3), 705–732.

Cloward, R.A., & Ohlin, L.E. (1960). *Delinquency and opportunity*. New York: Free Press.

Cohen, A.A. (1955). *Delinquent boys*. New York: Free Press.

Cornish, D.B., & Clarke, R.V. (1986). *The reasoning criminal*. New York: Springer-Verlag.

DeFleur, M.L., & Quinney, R. (1966). A reformulation of Sutherland's differential association theory and a strategy of empirical verification. *Journal of Research in Crime and Delinquency*, *3*(1), 1–22.

Gordon, R. (1976). Prevalence. In M.W. Klein (Ed.), *The juvenile justice system* (pp. 201–284). Beverly Hills, CA: Sage.

Gould, S.J. (1981). *The mismeasure of man.* New York: Norton.

Hindelang, M., Gottfredson, M., & Garafalo, J. (1978). *Victims of personal crime.* Cambridge, MA: Ballinger.

Hirschi, T. (1969). *Causes of delinquency.* Berkeley, CA: University of California Press.

Hirschi, T., & Gottfredson, M. (1980). Introduction: The Sutherland tradition in criminology. In T. Hirschi and M. Gottfredson (Eds.), *Understanding crime.* Beverly Hills, CA: Sage.

Hirschi, T., & Gottfredson, M. (1988). Science, public policy, and the career paradigm. *Criminology, 26*(1), 37–56.

Kemeny, J.G. (1959). *A philosopher looks at science.* Princeton: Van Nostrand.

McPheters, L.R., & Stronge, W.B. (1976). Law enforcement expenditures and urban crime. In L.R. McPheters & W.B. Stronge (Eds.), *The economics of crime and law enforcement.* Springfield, Ill: Thomas.

Merton, R.K. (1968). *Social theory and social structure.* New York: Free Press.

Nettler, G. (1984). *Explaining crime.* New York: McGraw-Hill.

Nye, F.I. (1958). *Family relationships and delinquent behavior.* New York: Wiley.

Sutherland, E.H. (1947). *Criminology.* Philadelphia: Lippincott.

Sutherland, E.H., & Cressey, D.R. (1978). *Criminology.* Philadelphia: Lippincott.

Tittle, C.R., Villemez, W.J., & Smith, D.A. (1978). The myth of social class and criminality. *American Sociological Review, 43*(5), 643–656.

Toby, J. (1959). Review of family relationships and delinquent behavior. *American Sociological Review, 24*, 282–283.

Torgerson, W.S. (1958). *Theory and methods of scaling.* New York: Wiley.

Vold. G.B., & Bernard, T.J. (1986). *Theoretical criminology.* New York: Oxford.

Wolfgang, M.E. & Ferracuti, F. (1972). *The subculture of violence.* Beverly Hills, CA: Sage.

Wolfgang, M.E., Figlio, R.M. & Sellin T. (1972). *Delinquency in a birth cohort.* Chicago: University of Chicago Press.

2
Sources of Data

PATRICK G. JACKSON

. . . no people, ever, have been more diligent in counting themselves, their opinions, conditions, and behaviors. The largest behavioral science studies in terms of numbers of subjects, numbers of tests, and money expended have been American, and no other land tries to tally such a grand range of activities—from tax filings to bedroom pleasures. (G. Nettler, 1989, p. 36)

Introduction

The search for answers to questions about crime and attempts to control it eventually leads most researchers to data about its nature and distribution. Investigators who study crime or social problems have long sought out data necessary to frame or revise research questions, test hypotheses, or interpret findings.[1] Today, data sources are used to unravel the reasons for crime or deviance, determine the impact of crime prevention or rehabilitation programs, assess changes in crime or crime rates, model the careers of offenders, estimate the risk of victimization, determine defendant dispositions after arrest, and address numerous other questions.

Resolution of theoretical questions in the field is critically tied to the reliability and validity of data sources. Over the past two decades, there has been a growing recognition of the problem of measuring crime and the development of new and refinement of older data collection systems. The advent, routine administration and (in varying degrees) enhancement of nationally representative victim surveys (Bureau of Justice Statistics, 1989), nationally representative self-report survey data on youth crime, and impending changes in the country's oldest and widely used data source—the Federal Bureau of Investigation's (FBI's) Uniform Crime Reports (UCR) (Federal Bureau of Investigation, 1988b)—are perhaps the most visible manifestations of this concern.

The purpose of this chapter is to examine and evaluate the major sources of data about crime. It is useful to conceive of data sources, and the procedures that underlie them, as products of quite varied forms of complex social organization, each of which has distinctive implications for the test-ing or generation of theories about crime. Existing data collection systems have been developed to respond to specific and/or more general problems or concerns.[2] Accordingly, a fundamental point is that *no data source is useful for addressing all questions that arise in the study of crime*. For exam-ple, some sources are more suitable for addressing epidemiological or etiological questions where others are useful for examining the amount or nature of change in rates of victimization and the characteristics of victims. The development of new sources or forms of data, such as longitudinal information about individual offenders, is sometimes undertaken to address new questions about the patterning of criminal careers (see, e.g., Blumstein, Cohen, Roth, & Vishor, 1988).

The preferences of researchers for particular sources of data have changed over the decades. Some of the earliest criminological studies re-lied upon statistics gathered and recorded by governmental agencies, parti-cularly at the level of indictment or court processing. For many years, this source of data was deemed most valid, since it was assumed that the accuracy of data was greater as criminal cases penetrated further into the system. Biderman and Reiss (1967) refer to this viewpoint as the "institu-tionalist." However, an alternative view—the "realist"—has gradually gained ascendancy. It sees as most useful or valid those criminal statistics that are collected as close to the criminal event as possible (Sellin, 1951). The main reason for this is that statistics collected at a point closer to the crime event are presumably not as affected by administrative rules.

It seems self-evident, however, that the accuracy, validity, or reliability of, for example, police-based data are also conditioned by a variety of factors including administrative rules, such as crime classification proce-dures, victim willingness to report crimes that they are aware of, police professionalization, the nature of the offense, and many other factors. Thus, the currently prevailing realist position is not immune from criticism. Moreover, the weakness of the institutionalist position is not entirely a function of technical problems of measurement. For example, even though data sources linking offenders to case dispositions are improving, they, like other official statistics, have problems. In any event, whether the institu-tionalist position will attain the legitimacy presently accorded the realist position in mainstream criminology remains to be seen. This seems unlike-ly so long as researchers cling to the enduring positivistic quest for the individual causes of criminal behavior rather than to the factors that condi-tion the patterning and consequences of the societal reaction to crime.

Information Sources

The major sources of data that are examined here include the FBI's UCR, the National Crime Survey (NCS), and the National Youth Survey (NYS). In addition, we briefly consider offender-based data systems for tracking

the disposition of defendants after arrest and mention other sources dealing with the characteristics of prisoners, jails, and jail inmates as well as
public opinion data about crime.

The nature and meaning of information about crime cannot be divorced
from the social context within which it is generated. Most commonly,
information about crime events[3] is derived from one or more of the following social sources: actual, alleged, or potential offender(s); actual or
potential victim(s) or witnesses; and/or some official agency such as the
police and/or some third party. Only some crime events lead to arrest.
Different measurement procedures—self-report, victim surveys, and
police reports—generate distinctive kinds of information about such
events because they tap offenders, victims, and police reactions to them,
respectively, and for various reasons each only defines certain kinds of
information as relevant. Although we have only scratched the surface, it
seems clear that the information about crime gained from each may not
correspond exactly.

As shown in Figure 2.1, examples of offender- or potential-offender-
based information about delinquency and crime can be found in self-report
surveys. Victim-based information, whether by individual, household, or
business, is found in national surveys of potential victims. Information
from officials is found in such varied sources as UCR data or court-based
statistics such as Offender-Based Transaction Statistics (OBTS). Public
opinion about crime can also be found in a variety of nationally representative surveys.

Data about crime ordinarily are taken from one of these sources,
although researchers frequently compare the results of crime estimates
generated from one source of data to another and seek to explain any
differences. However, like the fabled blind people and the elephant, a sole
reliance upon a single information source may give rise to a limited perspective about crime. Obviously, the nature of the research question dictates which information source(s) can or should be used. Ideally, investigators use a data source that is best suited to the theoretical concepts, level of
analysis, and/or questions under examination. An analysis of the differing
sources of data will aid in deciding on the utility of various sources for the
researcher's purposes as well as the limitations and advantages of each data
source. This may in turn be helpful in determining the necessity of original
data collection.

Asking the Police: The Uniform Crime Reports

The first source of data considered in detail is the FBI's UCR. Prior to a
critical discussion of the UCR, Savitz (1982, p. 4) notes that it is "without
question the most important and valuable source of official criminal statistics" in the United States. More recently, Gove, Hughes, and Geerken
(1985, p. 491) have concluded that UCR data "have much more validity"
than the NCS for certain crimes (rape and aggravated assault) and that, for

FIGURE 2.1. Social contexts of information about crime.

Victims and offenders		
Name of data & source	Source of data	Data gathered
Uniform Crime Reports (UCR) Federal Bureau of Investigation	Offenses reported to police; records of police arrest	Offense(s), age, sex, race, city size, region, offenses cleared, law enforcement characteristics

Offenses measured include Index offenses: attempted or completed homicide, rape, robbery (personal and commercial), aggravated assault, burglary (commercial and household), larceny (commercial and household), motor vehicle theft, arson; and a lengthier list of non-Index offenses.

National Crime Survey (NCS) Bureau of Justice Statistics; collected by U.S. Bureau of the Census	Potential victims: individuals and businesses; national probability sample of households and businesses	Number/type of victimizations for rape, robbery, assault, burglary, theft; reasons for not reporting to police, age, sex, race of offender; characteristics of victim

Offenses measured: attempted or completed rape, robbery (personal), aggravated and simple assault, household burglary, larceny (personal and household), motor vehicle theft.

National Youth Survey (NYS) Boulder, Colorado	Potential youth offenders; national probability sample of youth ages 11–17 in 1976; youth panel is followed each year	Self-reported crime and delinquency; personal and prior record characteristics

Offenses measured: all UCR Index offenses except homicide and arson (at least in early surveys); 75% of non-Index offenses; and a wide range of "all other" offenses; for 1979–1980 and 1984–1985, police records of arrest are included.

Adjudication of defendants		
Information source	Social context	Data gathered
Prosecutor Management Information Systems (*PROMIS*) Selected county or state courts (e.g., New York)	All persons charged with one or more felony offenses	Personal and prior record of defendant; type disposition and sentence; evidential factors
Offender-Based Transaction Statistics (*OBTS*) (e.g., California)	All persons charged with one or more felony offenses	Personal and prior record of defendant; type disposition and sentence

Corrections and punishment		
Annual Survey of Jails (*ASJ*) Bureau of Justice Statistics	Local jail facilities; response to mailed questionnaire to jail personnel	Characteristics of inmates & jails; average daily population pretrial & sentenced population
Survey of inmates of state correctional facilities Bureau of Justice Statistics (collected by Dept. of the Census)	Inmates in prison; stratified probability sample of inmates; in-person interviews	Social and demographic; prior record, job & income; drug use
Uniform Parole & National Probation reports (UPR, NPR) Bureau of Justice Statistics	Probation and parole officials	Number of offenders on probation/parole by region; jurisdiction & method of release

those Index crimes that wind up in UCR (except arson), UCR data "are at least as valid [as] and probably more valid than the data from victimization surveys." This view is probably not shared by all, but it does point to some academic support for UCR data.

In evaluating the UCR data, one finds it instructive to note briefly its historical roots. Although data collection under this system began in 1929, the FBI did not assume the responsibility until 1930. In its early years, there was discussion over whether responsibility for collection of these data should be given to the FBI, since the information could be used as a basis for appropriations requests or expansion of powers and equipment. In fact, the prestigious Wickersham Commission concluded that the compilation and publication of such statistics should not be delegated to an agency involved in the administration of criminal law (National Commission on Law Observance and Enforcement, 1931, p. 5). However, for a variety of reasons the program was placed under FBI jurisdiction (see Maltz, 1977). Other data collection systems have not been placed under the jurisdiction of an agency with such a potential interest in the results and have not appeared to experience the sustained level of skepticism met by the UCR.

The UCR is based upon police records of reported crime (for Index offenses only, discussed below) and arrests for crime. It is published yearly and based upon monthly information reported by police and other agencies. In its formative years, the UCR largely relied upon the voluntary cooperation of local police departments to collect information, but increasingly, reporting has become mandatory.

As a data source, UCR data are grounded in a lengthy filtering process involving victims, witnesses, and police. The process is usually instigated by a citizen's decision to report an offense, which is then acted upon by police, who eventually forward relevant information to the UCR. This brief description of the process by which decisions are made is more applicable to index offenses (excluding arson) than non-Index offenses. A number of decisions are involved in this process. Citizens must perceive that an offense has occurred and define it as worthy of police intervention; police in turn must decide whether a crime has occurred and eventually to forward the information to appropriate authorities for inclusion in the UCR. None of these decisions is a foregone conclusion.

Some Findings

The UCR pays great attention to "Crimes Known to the Police," those coming to the attention to the police and that are "founded" or accepted. It is especially concerned with so-called "Index crimes" because these are defined as more important due to their seriousness and/or frequency. At least until 1979, when arson data were first included in publications along with the other Index offenses, the Index offenses have largely fallen within exclusive police jurisdiction.

Over the years, the number of law enforcement agencies reporting data to the UCR has grown. In 1988, approximately 98% of law enforcement agencies in the United States reported information to the UCR program; participation is greater in Metropolitan Statistical Areas (MSAs) (99%) than rural ones (90%). The FBI *estimates* crime levels for nonreporting areas in some tables as well as for agencies that do not submit an entire year's worth of data. These estimates are based upon the "known crime experiences of similar areas within a state [and] are computed by assigning the same proportional crime volumes to nonreporting agencies" (Federal Bureau of Investigation, 1989, p. 3). A recent criticism of this practice as it applies to juveniles is available in Schwartz (1988). The problem is that it is unclear whether reporting and nonreporting agencies have similar crime volumes (Savitz, 1982). The assumption is not valid for the offense of arson (see Jackson, 1988; and below).

As mentioned, until recently there were only seven Index crimes, including attempted or completed murder and nonnegligent manslaughter, forcible rape, robbery, aggravated assault, burglary, larceny-theft, and motor vehicle theft. After approximately two decades of these Index-crime categories, however, in 1979 the FBI provisionally added arson to the list in response to congressional mandate. It was then permanently added in 1982 by the Anti-Arson Act of 1982. For a variety of reasons, both the International Association of Chiefs of Police and other experts, including the head of the UCR section of the FBI, suggested that arson not be treated as an Index offense (U.S. Senate Subcommittee, 1978).

Some examples of UCR Index-offense and arrest data are reported in

Tables 2.1 and 2.2. Table 2.1 displays the Index of Crime for the United
States from 1979 to 1988, including the total number of Index offenses and
number of each Index offense for each year (excluding arson), percentage
changes in number of offenses, the rate of the Index offenses (i.e., number
of reported offenses per 100,000 population) for each year, as well as the
percentage change in the rate of each Index offense between differing time
periods. In 1988, for example, there were 13,923,100 Index offenses, of
which 1,566,220 were violent crimes (defined as murder, rape, robbery,
and aggravated assault) and 12,356,900 property crimes (defined as burglary, larceny-theft, and motor vehicle theft). The rate of Index offenses was
5,664.2 in 1988, which was an overall 1.8% increase over 1979; the violent
crime rate rose 16.1% and the property crime rate 0.2%. These increases
in rates, particularly violent crime, differ substantially from the NCS,
which are discussed below.

Most reported offenses included in the Index do not result in arrest, the
primary means by which offenses are "cleared" by the police. Clearances
through "exceptional means" also occur when police are unable to place
formal charges against an alleged offender, such as when the individual is
dead, a victim refuses to cooperate, or extradition is denied. Only 21% of
1988 Index offenses were cleared in 1987, including 46% of the violent
offenses and 18% of the property offenses. This is important information
since the age, race, gender, and related characteristics of individuals reported in the UCR only refer to persons arrested (Federal Bureau of Investigation, 1989a, p. 157). It is unclear whether the characteristics of arrested
individuals are the same as those who are not.

Table 2.2 displays the number and rate of individuals arrested for Index
and non-Index offenses by population group and includes arson. For example, the rate of Index property crime per 100,000 population is greatest in
cities with a population of 250,000 and over (1,259.5) and lowest among
those with less than 10,000 population (744.3). Similar statistics for Index
crimes are also presented by region and for individual states. Other tables
in the UCR break down the number and rates of crime by race/ethnic
origin, sex, and age.

Limitations of Police Statistics

The extent to which offenses are reported to police and the question of
what explains the difference between police and victim reports of crime—
the latter of which are much higher than police reports—has been examined through victim surveys, some results of which are discussed separately below. Researchers have found that a victim's failure to report a
potentially criminal event is due to a variety of factors, including whether a
weapon, injury, or financial loss was involved in the crime event (Gottfredson & Gottfredson, 1988). In addition to these, the use of force (including
a weapon), whether the assailant was a stranger, the invasion of a home, or

TABLE 2.1. Index of crime, United States, 1979–1988

Population[1]	Crime Index total[2]	Violent crime[3]	Property crime[3]	Murder and non-negligent man-slaughter	Forcible rape	Robbery	Aggravated assault	Burglary	Larceny-theft	Motor vehicle theft
Number of offenses:										
1979-220,099,000	12,249,500	1,208,030	11,041,500	21,460	76,390	480,700	629,480	3,327,700	6,601,000	1,112,800
1980-225,349,264	13,408,300	1,344,520	12,063,700	23,040	82,990	565,840	672,650	3,795,200	7,136,900	1,131,700
1981-229,146,000	13,423,800	1,361,820	12,061,900	22,520	82,500	592,910	663,900	3,779,700	7,194,400	1,087,800
1982-231,534,000	12,974,400	1,322,390	11,652,000	21,010	78,770	553,130	669,480	3,447,100	7,142,500	1,062,400
1983-233,981,000	12,108,600	1,258,090	10,850,500	19,310	78,920	506,570	653,290	3,129,900	6,712,800	1,007,900
1984-236,158,000	11,881,800	1,273,280	10,608,500	18,690	84,230	485,010	685,350	2,984,400	6,591,900	1,032,200
1985-238,740,000	12,431,400	1,328,800	11,102,600	18,980	88,670	497,870	723,250	3,073,300	6,926,400	1,102,900
1986-241,077,000	13,211,900	1,489,170	11,722,700	20,610	91,460	542,780	834,320	3,241,400	7,257,200	1,224,100
1987-243,400,000	13,508,700	1,484,000	12,024,700	20,100	91,110	517,700	855,090	3,236,200	7,499,900	1,288,700
1988-245,807,000	13,923,100	1,566,220	12,356,900	20,680	92,490	542,970	910,090	3,218,100	7,705,900	1,432,900
Percent change: number of offenses:										
1988/1987	+3.1	+5.5	+2.8	+2.9	+1.5	+4.9	+6.4	-.6	+2.7	+11.2
1988/1984	+17.2	+23.0	+16.5	+10.6	+9.8	+12.0	+32.8	+7.8	+16.9	+38.8
1988/1979	+13.7	+29.7	+11.9	-3.6	+21.1	+13.0	+44.6	-3.3	+16.7	+28.8
Rate per 100,000 inhabitants:										
1979	5,565.5	548.9	5,016.6	9.7	34.7	218.4	286.0	1,511.9	2,999.1	505.6
1980	5,950.0	596.6	5,353.3	10.2	36.8	251.1	298.5	1,684.1	3,167.0	502.2
1981	5,858.2	594.3	5,263.9	9.8	36.0	258.7	289.7	1,649.5	3,139.7	474.7
1982	5,603.6	571.1	5,032.5	9.1	34.0	238.9	289.2	1,488.8	3,084.8	458.8
1983	5,175.0	537.7	4,637.4	8.3	33.7	216.5	279.2	1,337.7	2,868.9	430.8
1984	5,031.3	539.2	4,492.1	7.9	35.7	205.4	290.2	1,263.7	2,791.3	437.1
1985	5,207.1	556.6	4,650.5	7.9	37.1	208.5	302.9	1,287.3	2,901.2	462.0

1986	5,480.4	617.7	4,862.6	8.6	37.9	225.1	346.1	1,344.6	3,010.3	507.8
1987	5,550.0	609.7	4,940.3	8.3	37.4	212.7	351.3	1,329.6	3,081.3	529.4
1988	5,664.2	637.2	5,027.1	8.4	37.6	220.9	370.2	1,309.2	3,134.9	582.9
Percent change: rate per 100,000 inhabitants:										
1988/1987	+2.1	+4.5	+1.8	+1.2	+.5	+3.9	+5.4	−1.5	+1.7	+10.1
1988/1984	+12.6	+18.2	+11.9	+6.3	+5.3	+7.5	+27.6	+3.6	+12.3	+33.3
1988/1979	+1.8	+16.1	+.2	−13.4	+8.4	+1.1	+29.4	−13.4	+4.5	+15.3

[1] Populations are Bureau of the Census provisional estimates as of July 1, except April 1, 1980, preliminary census counts, and are subject to change.

[2] Because of rounding, the offenses may not add to totals. Although arson data are included in the trend and clearance tables, sufficient data are not available to estimate totals for this offense.

[3] Violent crimes are offenses of murder, forcible rape, robbery, and aggravated assault. Property crimes are offenses of burglary, larceny-theft, and motor vehicle theft. Data are not included for the property crime of arson.

All rates were calculated on the offenses before rounding.

Data for 1988 were not available for the States of Florida and Kentucky; therefore, it was necessary that their crime counts be estimated. See "Offense Estimation", page 3 for details.

Source: Federal Bureau of Investigation, *Uniform Crime Reports*, Table 1, p. 47, 1989, Washington, DC: U.S. Government Printing Office.

TABLE 2.2. Arrest, number and rate, population group, 1988.

[Rate: Number of arrests per 100,000 inhabitants]

		Cities								Counties		
Offense charged	Total (9,970 agencies; population 188,928,000)	Total cities (6,919 cities; population 129,469,000)	Group I (48 cities, 250,000 and over; population 36,742,000)	Group II (114 cities, 100,000 to 249,999; population 16,648,000)	Group III (269 cities 50,000 to 99,999; population 18,436,000)	Group IV (560 cities, 25,000 to 49,999; population 19,192,000)	Group V (1,311 cities, 10,000 to 24,999; population 20,777,000)	Group VI (4,617 cities under 10,000; population 17,674,000)	Suburban counties[1] (921 agencies; population 35,374,000)	Rural counties (2,130 agencies; population 24,085,000)	Suburban area[2] (4,656 agencies; population 75,593,000)
Total	10,138,830	7,928,566	2,903,162	1,095,055	955,717	996,239	1,032,130	946,263	1,372,807	837,457	3,282,456
Rate	5,366.5	6,123.9	7,901.5	6,577.6	5,183.9	5,190.9	4,967.8	5,354.0	3,880.9	3,477.1	4,342.3
Murder and nonnegligent manslaughter	16,326	12,575	7,838	1,649	1,193	813	618	464	2,290	1,461	3,471
Rate	8.6	9.7	21.3	9.9	6.5	4.2	3.0	2.6	6.5	6.1	4.6
Forcible rape	28,482	21,941	9,724	3,507	2,705	2,285	2,096	1,624	4,096	2,445	8,272
Rate	15.1	16.9	26.5	21.1	14.7	11.9	10.1	9.2	11.6	10.2	10.9
Robbery	111,344	99,438	60,394	13,383	10,402	7,254	5,207	2,798	9,475	2,431	21,082
Rate	58.9	76.8	164.4	80.4	56.4	37.8	25.1	15.8	26.8	10.1	27.9
Aggravated assault	304,490	240,212	106,220	36,036	30,778	26,540	21,548	19,090	41,526	22,752	86,709
Rate	161.2	185.5	289.1	216.5	166.9	138.3	103.7	108.0	117.4	94.5	114.7
Burglary	331,758	251,502	87,212	39,168	38,076	31,343	30,388	25,315	49,156	31,100	105,878
Rate	175.6	194.3	237.4	235.3	206.5	163.3	146.3	143.2	139.0	129.1	140.1
Larceny-theft	1,162,752	999,521	303,084	153,711	150,012	148,590	147,393	96,731	117,442	45,789	375,078
Rate	615.4	772.0	824.9	923.3	813.7	774.2	709.4	547.3	332.0	190.1	496.2
Motor vehicle theft	153,016	124,962	68,986	14,612	13,006	10,379	9,683	8,296	19,855	8,199	39,589
Rate	81.0	96.5	187.8	87.8	70.5	54.1	46.6	46.9	56.1	34.0	52.4

Arson	14,505	10,872	3,474	1,387	1,689	1,413	1,702	1,207	2,294	1,339	5,146
Rate	7.7	8.4	9.5	8.3	9.2	7.4	8.2	6.8	6.5	5.6	6.8
Violent crime[3]	460,642	374,166	184,176	54,575	45,078	36,892	29,469	23,976	57,387	29,089	119,534
Rate	243.8	289.0	501.3	327.8	244.5	192.2	141.8	135.7	162.2	120.8	158.1
Property crime[4]	1,662,031	1,386,857	462,756	208,878	202,783	191,725	189,166	131,549	188,747	86,427	525,691
Rate	879.7	1,071.2	1,259.5	1,254.7	1,099.9	999.0	910.5	744.3	533.6	358.8	695.4
Crime Index total[5]	2,122,673	1,761,023	646,932	263,453	247,861	228,617	218,635	155,525	246,134	115,516	645,225
Rate	1,123.5	1,360.2	1,760.7	1,582.5	1,344.4	1,191.2	1,052.3	880.0	695.8	479.6	853.6

[1] Includes only suburban county law enforcement agencies.
[2] Includes suburban city and county law enforcement agencies within metropolitan areas. Excludes central cities. Suburban cities and counties are also included in other groups.
[3] Violent crimes are offenses of murder, forcible rape, robbery, and aggravated assault.
[4] Property crimes are offenses of burglary, larceny-theft, motor vehicle theft, and arson.
[5] Includes arson. Population figures were rounded to the nearest thousand. All rates were calculated before rounding.
Source: Feder Bureau of Investigation, *Uniform Crime Reports*, table 26, p. 170, 1989. Washington, D.C.: U.S. Government Printing Office.

the threat of death was also important (Skogan, 1976; in Gove et al., 1985). Other studies indicate that a victim's claim that "the police could not be effective" or that the offending "was not serious enough" was an important consideration in decisions to report; some victims fear reprisal, while others feel that it is "a private matter." The reasons for failure to report also vary by the age of the victim and the nature of the offense.

Researchers have also shown variation in how respondents in victim surveys define crime. The case of assault is instructive, as summarized by Gove et al. (1985). While victimologists have assumed that assault victims are more commonly of lower status, as suggested in police reports, the results of victim surveys indicate the opposite: Assault victimization increases as education (a proxy for status) increases. This pattern of findings has been replicated in other countries. While there is evidence that better educated respondents give more complete information about assaults than less educated ones, this does not explain away the entire relationship. The other, perhaps more persuasive argument is that more educated persons more often define physically assaultive behavior as criminal than less educated persons.

Police decisions to arrest a suspect in reaction to a victim or witness complaint are also conditioned by a variety of factors. Few offenses are a result of direct police observation (Reiss, 1971); police are, as mentioned, mostly reactive to citizen complaint. Researchers have found that complainant preference is critical to decisions to arrest a defendant, along with offense seriousness, the relationship between the victim and offender, situational evidence, and other factors (Black & Reiss, 1970; Lundman, Sykes, & Clark, 1978). Piliavin and Briar's (1964) work also found that the demeanor of youth was important in explaining police action (although offense seriousness did not vary greatly in this study).

Another criticism is that police-based data are subject to fluctuations due to changes in official behavior (mentioned above) and not necessarily changes in the true crime level, which cannot likely be known. Improvements in police response time, the move toward professionalism in police work, policing "styles" (reactive or proactive), and "founding" practices, which can vary considerably by local jurisdiction, may greatly affect the statistics reported by police. Moreover, the public acceptance of various crimes changes over time, and legal codes are altered or added, which may also affect police statistics (Savitz, 1982, pp. 6–11).

Savitz's (1982, pp. 11–13) summary also offers 22 additional methodological limitations of the UCR, among them the exclusion of federal offenses, the inclusion of few white collar and victimless offenses, the questionable FBI practice of "estimating" total crime when agencies do not supply data (noted earlier), the difficulty of interjurisdictional comparability of statistics, the questionable use of overall population figures in calculating rates of offenses, and others.

Moreover, there are serious problems of crime classification: Only one crime classification is permitted for each event, even if such an event involves multiple offenses. The number of offenses recorded varies by what type of crime is involved—for violent crimes this is tied to the number of persons injured, whereas for property crimes the number of victims is not relevant. In addition, the Index of crimes is arbitrary. It is weighted by the more frequent but less serious offenses—larceny and auto theft—the latter of which is well reported (and relatively high) due to insurance reporting requirements. Larceny for relatively small monetary amounts is counted with equal weight in the Index as murder. Finally, the arbitrary identification of Index offenses as important has necessarily led police to focus attention on these rather than non-Index offenses. It is entirely unclear to what extent the reclassification of arson into an Index offense has led to increased police attention on this offense.

The Validity of UCR Arson Data

Despite the voluminous criticism of UCR data, researchers continue to use it because no alternatives are available for some research questions. Gove et al. (1985) have, in fact, recently argued that UCR Index-offense data, with some qualifications and excluding arson, are valid measures of crime.

In light of their conclusion, it is worth examining the validity of arson data, the most recent addition to the UCR's list of Index crimes. Research on the validity of arson data has only recently been attempted. Arson differs from other Index crimes in significant ways: Perhaps most important, it is an offense that does not fall under exclusive police jurisdiction. Moreover, it is unique in that it requires significant cooperation between fire and police officials. While exclusive fire or police jurisdiction does occur, sole police jurisdiction is quite rare; the most common pattern is combined fire and police jurisdiction. Finally, the manner in which arson comes to the attention of officials is substantially different than other Index offenses: In most instances, evidence for the offense is uncovered by officials; unlike other Index offenses, the official response to arson is therefore *not* reactive to citizen complaint.

To help ensure more accurate Index-offense data on arson, the UCR relaxed its hierarchy rule alluded to earlier. This means that, regardless of whether an attempted or completed arson occurs in conjunction with another Index crime, arsons will be recorded and reported separately. Using this procedure assures that an arson offense will not escape notice due to its commission in the context of another Index offense that may be more serious, such as when someone purposefully sets a fire as a murder coverup.

In light of these considerations, we can evaluate UCR arson data. A study on the quality of these data examined reported arsons from a random sample of fire departments in the United States (Jackson, 1988). The study found that arson Index-offense data suffer from a variety of deficiencies.

First, as of 1986, over 30% of local agencies failed to report *any* information on reported arsons to the FBI, which is substantially higher than non-reporting for the other Index offenses. Those agencies least likely to report were located in areas of less than 25,000 population, where arson was under exclusive fire department jurisdiction, where no arson unit existed, and in the South. Conversely, over 90% of fire departments located in areas with population greater than 70,000 reported arson data, as well as 80% of departments in the Western region, almost 77% of those jurisdictions with combined fire and police jurisdiction over arson, and about 84% of areas with a separate arson unit.

Moreover, those fire departments that do not report to the UCR have a greater overall volume of arson than those that do: Together they account for over 40% of the nation's arson.

Equally revealing of the study findings are those relating to the reported rate of arson per 100,000 population among those jurisdictions that report to the UCR. One might expect these data to be the most accurate of all, because the hierarchy rule has been relaxed for this offense. However, the overall rate of arson reported in the UCR is 50.3 per 100,000 population, while the rate reported by the reporting fire departments is slightly more than double this rate (104.6 per 100,000). The UCR undercounting of arson occurs in all regions of the country.

In summary, arson Index-offense data are not reported by nearly a third of local agencies; and those arsons reported in the UCR systematically underrepresent the rate of arson reported by fire departments. However, and most important, one would expect that the rates would be approximately equal, since *all* arsons are counted in the UCR. The reasons for the depressed UCR rate are unclear. Finally, the UCR does not include fires of suspicious origin, many of which are known to have been intentionally set (Moll, 1974).

Clearly, the optimistic statements of Gove et al. (1985) regarding the validity of UCR data should be tempered by the realization that all is not well with the UCR. Indeed, one of the most important criticisms of the UCR is that it does not capture unreported crimes. This is one reason given for the need to use alternative methods for measuring crime, discussed below, such as surveys of victims or potential offenders.

Asking Potential Victims: The National Crime Survey

Concern about the so-called "dark figure" of crime—the disparity between crime events and what comes to the attention of the police—led to the development of alternative procedures for estimating crime levels. The origin of the development of victimization surveys is found in the President's Commission on Law Enforcement and Administration of Justice, which pointed to the limited information about victims and the inaccuracies of the FBI's UCR data (Lehnen & Skogan, 1981).

The precursor to the NCS was begun in the mid-1960s in response to long-standing and widespread criticism that UCR data were invalid or biased. Initial victim survey projects focused on specific cities so as to test the available methods and procedures and to examine the effectiveness of various crime control programs. Since 1974, the NCS has been conducted on a nationwide basis, city-level studies have been discontinued, and now nationwide data are readily available for data analysis (U.S. Department of Justice, 1981). The NCS is presently a federal statistical program conducted by the U.S. Census Bureau under an interagency agreement with the Bureau of Justice Statistics. The NCS thus differs from the UCR in terms of the agency that conducts the research.

The NCS involves interviews with approximately 60,000 persons in households randomly selected in the United States. It employs a rotating panel design and bounded interviews similar to Census procedures that have been developed for the Census's population survey. The sample is divided into six rotation groups; each group is interviewed every 6 months over 3 years for a total of seven interviews per household. The initial interview data are not used; they only exist for "bounding" purposes—to fix a time reference period so that respondents will not duplicate prior crime reports to the NCS interviewer.

The NCS is intended to capture the crime experiences of both the respondent and others in the household who are 12 years of age or over, which totals approximately 120,000 individuals nationwide. The large sample of interviewees is necessary because at least some forms of victimization are, statistically speaking, infrequent and require large samples in order to make accurate nationwide estimates of the number and rate of crimes. (The actual sampling, interview procedures, and discussion of parameter estimation are more complex than suggested here. See the U.S. Department of Justice, 1981.)

Except for homicide and arson, the NCS attempts to measure offenses that are similar but not identical to those of the UCR's Index offenses (see Table 2.1). The NCS also does not count arson because of the apparent difficulty in measuring the offense using survey techniques. Both count attempted as well as completed crimes. However, the two data sources offer different portraits of crime since they have differing purposes and, most important, use different sources and procedures for gathering information about crime.

At the present time, the NCS is viewed as one of the most important sources of nationwide data about crime, in part because of the legitimacy it accrues from being collected by the U.S. Census (Maltz, 1977). It is also the second most used data source for studying crime (Gove, Hughes & Geerken, 1985, p. 491).

An example of NCS published data is shown in Table 2.3, which displays the number and rates of personal and household crimes in the United States (including the District of Columbia) for 1987. While these data do

TABLE 2.3. Number and rates of personal and household crimes[a] in the United States, 1987.

	Number of victimizations (in 1,000s)	Victimization rates[b]
Personal crimes	19,005	96.1
Crimes of violence	5,661	28.6
Rape	141	1.3[c]
Robbery	1,030	5.2
Aggravated assault	1,543	7.8
Simple assault	2,946	14.9
Crimes of theft	13,344	67.5
Personal larceny with contact	509	2.6
Personal larceny without contact	12,835	64.9
Household crimes	15,726	171.4
Household burglary	5,623	61.3
Household larceny	8,624	94.0
Motor vehicle theft	1,479	16.1

[a] Includes attempted and completed offenses.
[b] Victimization rates for personal crimes are defined as the number of victimizations per 1,000 persons age 12 or older. For household crimes, the rate is the number of victimizations per 1,000 households.
[c] The base for the computation of this rate is females only.
Source: Adapted from *Criminal Victimization 1987* (Tables 1 and 2, pages 14–15), by Bureau of Justice Statistics, 1988, Washington, DC: U.S. Department of Justice.

not employ the usual sample size that is generally used (as discussed above), the data are sufficient for the present discussion. The table indicates that there was a total of over 19 million personal crimes in 1987, which represents a rate of 96.1 per 1,000 persons. (Note that the base for computing the rate of personal crimes is per 1,000 persons age 12 or over.) Over two-thirds of this rate (67.5) is for crimes of theft, primarily larceny without contact, and the remainder for crimes of violence, particularly the less serious simple assaults (14.9). Rape is lowest at 1.3 per 1,000. It is of interest to note that the rate for rape, which only included females in the base, was in a footnote to the table. The original table included the overall rates for males and females age 12 and over, which was 0.7.

The number of household crimes (over 15 million) is more than 3 million less than personal crimes, but the rate of household victimization is substantially greater than that for personal crimes. An important reason for this is the size of the denominator used for computing the rate, which is the number of households rather than persons. The rate of household larceny

(94 per 1,000 households) is greatest, motor vehicle theft is the lowest (16.1), and household burglary is in between (61.3).

While it is not revealed in the table, there has been a steady decline in personal victimization rates since their peak in 1981. The small and statistically insignificant increase in the rate of personal victimizations from 1986 to 1987 ended a long-term decrease. However, rates of personal victimization have declined overall by over 23% since the first NCS in 1973. Rates of household victimization have continuously declined since 1979, and they rose only insignificantly from 1986 to 1987. Likewise, the rate of household victimization has decreased by over 21% from 1973 to 1987 (Bureau of Justice Statistics 1988, Table 3, p. 4). It is of some interest to note that during the period 1978 to 1987, rates of personal victimization decreased by 26.4% and of household crimes by 23.3%. It is worth noting that UCR data show substantial overall increases in both violent (a 22.5% increase) and property (a 6.4% increase) offenses during this same period (FBI, 1988, Table 1, p. 47). While the offense categories do not correspond exactly across the NCS and UCR, the general dissimilarity of the trends—in direction and strength—shown by the two sources of data is notable.

A small part of the differences in the two estimates of crime may be explained by changes in the level at which citizens reported offenses to the police, which has increased by 5%—to its highest level ever in the history of the NCS—from 32% of all crimes in 1973 to 37% in 1987. There continue to be differences in reporting by offense. In 1987, only 34% of all personal crimes were reported to the police, which includes 53% of all rapes, 56% of robberies, 60% of aggravated assaults, 40% of simple assaults, 33% of larcenies with contact, and only 27% of larcenies without contact. This compares with 41% of household crimes, which includes 52% of burglaries, 28% of larcenies, and fully 73% of vehicle thefts.

Despite warnings that NCS data are not directly comparable with UCR data, investigators frequently compare the nature and extent of the crime problem using the two sources of data (e.g., Hindelang, Hirschi and Weis 1979). We can make some simple comparisons between the UCR and NCS data for the offenses of rape, aggravated and simple assault, and motor vehicle theft in terms of the number of offenses/incidents (see Table 2.4). These data suggest that the number of offenses that do not appear in the UCR is greatest for assaults, where more than four times as many are reported by victims as appear in the UCR, and least for auto theft, where there is only a slight difference. About 1.5 as many rapes are reported by victims as are shown in the UCR, while the ratio for aggravated assaults is 1.8.

It should be noted that the reasons for the disparity in levels of crime determined by the two methods is complex and, presently, the subject of research inquires.[4] For example, on the one hand, NCS data may appear inflated because the police do not act as a filter for victim reports. On the other hand, the published NCS data do not include as crimes so-called

TABLE 2.4. Number and ratio of UCR[a] to NCS[b] offenses, 1987.

	UCR	NCS	NCS:UCR ratio
Rape	91,110	141,000	1.55:1
Aggravated assault	855,090	1,543,000	1.80:1
Assault*	671,938	2,946,000	4.38:1
Auto theft	1,288,700	1,479,000	1.15:1

* Includes UCR "all other assaults" and NCS "simple assaults". UCR "all other" assaults are not Index offenses.
[a] Uniform Crime Reports
[b] National Crime Survey
Sources: Federal Bureau of Investigation, Uniform Crime Reports, Table 1, p. 47, 1988a; and Bureau of Justice Statistics, Criminal Victimization 1987, Tables 1 and 2, pages 14–15, 1988.

"series incidents"—victimizations in which there are repeated incidents of offending that are more accurately described as enduring conditions than as a discrete event or discrete events and in which victims can not recall specific months in which incidents occurred. A series incident occurs, for example, when an offender repeatedly abuses a spouse or children. The most frequent kind of series incidents are occupation related, as among bus drivers and law enforcement officials, followed by violence between family, neighbors, and friends, then violence against children (mostly at school), and then all others (Dodge & Lentzner, 1978; in Skogan, 1981). Were all series events included in NCS estimates, the number of crimes would increase by fully 18% (Reiss, 1978).

Other major differences between the UCR and NCS that can affect crime counts include the following. The UCR counts all crimes excluding federal ones, whereas the NCS only counts those against persons age 12 or older and against their households. The UCR more conservatively counts multiple offenses, such as when a robbery offender steals a car to escape; the UCR would count the robbery, since it is the more serious of the two (given the hierarchy rule), but the NCS would count one as personal and the other as a household crime. The two methods also count some crimes differently, such as robbery. Each method also has its own particular problems, such as interviewer bias for the NCS and "unfounding" practices of the UCR. Finally, a direct comparison of published rates of crime across the two sources of data is not possible since the rates use differing bases: The UCR uses general population figures (i.e., for all ages) and the NCS either the population age 12 or over or the household. Thus, research that takes into account the differing denominators of the UCR and NCS when comparing the two sources of data, such as by expressing crime rates in terms of the number of offenses/incidents per 100,000 population, would likely give much more similar estimates of the nature or distribution of crime.

Asking Potential Offenders: The Self-Report Survey

An alternative to both police and victimization data is found in self-report surveys. These surveys are administered to samples of respondents using in-person interviews or questionnaires that may or may not be anonymous. Respondents who may or may not have had contact with legal agencies are asked about their participation in a variety of delinquent and criminal activities within a specified time frame, usually within 1 year or less. Such surveys permit researchers to estimate the prevalence and incidence of criminality or delinquency.[5] Moreover, this method permits researchers to ascertain the reasons why some offenders rather than others become a part of official statistics about crime.

Self-report surveys have been employed in a number of research investigations (for a summary, see Hindelang, Hirschi, & Weis, 1979).[6] Until the 1970s, samples were limited in size or in geographical location (e.g., Porterfield, 1946). Some significant criticisms of these studies are that their results are not generalizable, that they have excluded more serious but less frequent offenses, that they have a problem of response sets, and that they have used truncated response options that prevent the respondent from indicating the full extent of offending.

Only three major studies have used national probability samples, including the early work of Gold (Gold & Reimer, 1974), Bachman and colleagues' *Youth in Transition* studies (Bachman, Green, & Wirtanen, 1970, 1971; Bachman, D'Malley, & Johnson, 1978), and the more recent National Youth Survey (NYS) of Elliott and Ageton (1978). An annual self-report survey, *Monitoring the Future*, is also conducted on high school seniors (Bachman, 1987); youth in this study have recently been followed for a number of years (Osgood, O'Malley, Bachman, & Johnson, 1989). Other polls are taken on a nonregular basis, such as by Gallup, which are very restricted in the kinds of questions asked.

Data derived from self-report instruments have been found to be both valid and reliable, although certain specific subgroups have been shown to provide less reliable reports of offending (Hindelang, Hirschi, & Weis, 1979). Scales have been checked for reliability (e.g., Huizinga & Elliott, 1984), and cross-checks have been made between self-reported police contacts and official records (e.g., Hirschi, 1969).

The NYS went beyond earlier work by modifying self-report instruments to include offenses more-or-less comparable to those used by the UCR, by removing overlapping measures of delinquency, and by providing response options that captured the range of variation in delinquency offending. The study included a multicohort design intended to be representative of American youth born in 1959 through 1965. At the time of the first survey, conduct in 1976, youth were between 11 and 17 years of age. Interviewers collected data on youth involvement in delinquent behavior as well as information about parents. Five surveys of the same youth were conducted in successive years and a sixth in 1984. All surveys included a 1-year recall period except for year 1984, which included a 3- and a 2-year recall period.

Of the 2,360 eligible youth initially sampled, 73% agreed to participate, provided informed consent, and completed the initial survey. The survey was a confidential personal interview in the respondent's home unless this was deemed not appropriate. The characteristics of youth finally included in the study did not differ from those of the U.S. Census for the initial year on race, age, or sex. This suggests that the initial sample was representative of the United States population. The second survey of the same youth showed respondent mortality (due to inability to locate or refusal to participate) of only 4%. The third survey loss rate was a cumulative 6%, which rose to 10.6% for Survey 4 and 13.3% for Survey 6. Despite this mortality, the sample is still representative of the population in terms of such variables as age, race, sex, residence, and delinquency level.

NYS data have been used to estimate the prevalence and incidence of delinquency and crime and to examine the patterning of these as the youth have grown older. Elliott and Ageton (1978) have used the data to determine the relationship between social class and delinquency and have shown that UCR and self-report data are more similar than previously thought. However, more recently, Huizinga and Elliott (1987) have examined the correspondence between self-reported involvement in delinquency, criminality, and incarceration rates. They find that differences in rates of incarceration across racial groups cannot be explained on the basis of self-reported offending behavior.

The NYS researchers have compared NYS, UCR, and NCS data on UCR Index crimes (except homicide and arson) for the year 1979 among youth aged 14 to 20 (Huizinga & Elliott, 1984). Their analysis uses special data provided by the FBI as well as data taken from the incidents file of the NCS.[7] They attempted to adjust UCR, NCS, and NYS data sources so as to make their respective estimates of the true crime rate (which cannot be known) comparable. The results are of interest since they highlight the differing criminal incident estimates found by the three major sources of data used by criminologists.

As shown in Table 2.5, overall, UCR estimates of Index crimes are lowest, NCS estimates are higher, and NYS are the highest. The single exception shown in the table is for burglaries, in which NCS estimates are somewhat higher than the NYS. There are further exceptions to these general observations (too detailed to go into here) that Huizinga and Elliott (1984) found in breaking down the source of data estimates by race and sex.

The three data sources are closest for vehicle theft (UCR rate = 36, NCS = 44, NYS = 50) and burglary (rates = 101, 125, and 115, respectively), rape (rates = 1.24, 1.97, and 8.69, respectively), and robbery (rates = 19, 23, and 84, respectively). They differ most for larceny (rates = 374, 568, and 1,207, respectively) and aggravated assault

TABLE 2.5. Rate of offender-incidents per 1,000 persons age 14–20 by data source.

	UCR[a]	NCS[b]	NYS[c]
	Offender incidents	Offender incidents	Offender incidents[d]
Rape (males only)	1.24	1.97	8.69
Robbery	19.00	23.33	84.90
Aggravated assault	13.90	65.16	252.11
Burglary	100.94	124.70	114.71
Larceny	373.68	568.21	1206.74
Vehicle theft	36.46	44.25	49.90

[a] *Uniform Crime Reports*
[b] *National Crime Survey*
[c] *National Youth Survey*
[d] NYS incidents are adjusted for triviality.
Source: Huizinga and Elliot, *Self-reported measures of delinquency and crime: methodological issues and comparative findings.* (1984, p. 74, Table 3), with permission.

(rates = 14, 65, and 252, respectively). One can not help but note that the three estimates of Index offenses differ substantially. Whether this occurs because the data sources are actually tapping different dimensions of crime or because each data source has not been adjusted enough is unanswered in this study. The authors suspect that there is some truth in both interpretations.[8]

Concluding Remarks on UCR, NCS, and NYS Sources

The self-report method provides information about individual offender behavior, not crime events, and the information can be used to estimate incidence and prevalence rates and the characteristics of offenders. The method provides both valid and reliable results and indicates that delinquency/crime levels are higher for most offenses than are the levels found in either victim or (especially) official (police) data.

Police data, particularly on Index crimes (excluding arson) published in the UCR, are, like those obtained from the self-report method, offender based, but they are only useful for estimating incident rates and, when arrest occurs, contain only limited information about offender and victim personal characteristics. While this is not a necessary condition of police data, UCR arrest data cannot be used for estimating prevalence rates because they are not aggregated by person. A distinctive advantage of police data, however, is that they are ordered in time, whereas those obtained from the self-report technique are not (Huizinga & Elliott, 1984).

Victimization data, in contrast, are based upon self-reported information from potential victims of crime. Respondents are asked to describe any crime events that they may have experienced and to describe the offender, characteristics of the offense itself, and other information. Information about offenders is limited to crime events involving actual knowledge of the offender and by the victim's memory. Victimization data cannot be used to estimate offender prevalence, may be of limited use in estimating incidence rates of offending, and are especially limited for establishing the correlates of offending. Thus, the advantages and limitations of each source of data are defined in part by the nature of the information source noted above, aside from questions of the reliability and validity of each data source.

The advantages and limitations of each source are also defined by the crime events that are included within each. For example, neither victim surveys nor most self-report surveys ask questions about homicide. However, studies suggest that UCR data include fairly accurate information about criminal homicide (e.g., Hindelang, 1974; Cantor & Cohen, 1984). Moreover, no routinely collected victim or self-report source collects information about white collar crime or arson. The UCR has attempted to include information about arson, but reporting is not complete, and the data that are reported contain systematic errors (Jackson, 1988). In light of the foregoing, it bears repeating that the choice of a given data source importantly depends upon the interests of the investigator, including the question(s) being asked, the level of analysis, and a myriad of other issues. Existing data sources provide a wealth of choices for students of crime predisposed toward quantitative approaches. It bears repeating that investigators may well wish to consult the library of existing sources before attempting original data collection.

At present, efforts are under way to improve the quality of data generated by the NCS and UCR. The NCS has moved to expand the amount of information gained from victims (BJS, 1989, 1988). The major change, however, is in the UCR development of an *Incident-Based Reporting (IBR)* system, which is voluntary and will coexist with the UCR system (FBI, 1988b).

The most important difference between the anticipated IBR and the UCR is in the detail of information. Unlike the UCR, the IBR ties detailed offense information (about victims, offenders, offenses, and property) to any subsequent arrest(s) that occur. Moreover, the number of offenses for which such information is collected has been expanded to 22 groups of offenses (so-called "Group A offenses"). The Group A offenses are therefore "updated" if an arrest occurs for any of these 22 groups of offenses. The level of detail available is also revealed by the amount of information that can be included in a single Group A incident report: up to 10 types of offenses, 999 victims, 99 offenders and 99 arrestees, and 10 types of property. Another difference is that the *IBR* dispenses with the so-called "hierarchy" rule in those instances where there are multiple offenses; distinctions can be made between attempted and completed crimes; various offense definitions have been revised; and correlations between offenses, offenders, property, arrestees, and victims can be made. Whether these changes will alter the serious reporting problems presently associated with arson remains to be seen.

Institutional Statistics

Sources of data bearing upon the processing of offenders through agencies of social control deserve at least brief discussion since, among other reasons, they are frequently used to evaluate the effectiveness of the official response to crime—including that of both the police and the courts. When a high proportion of arrested defendants have their charges dismissed or significantly reduced at court,[9] the charge is frequently made that the judicial system is inefficient or experiencing a breakdown. However, it may also be that police make arrests that cannot withstand higher levels of scrutiny required for conviction. There is also the possibility that police may properly arrest someone whom a prosecutor may properly refuse to charge. Implicit in this reasoning is the idea that progressively higher standards of proof are required as the consequences attached to further actions increase (Feeney, Dill, & Weir, 1982).

The significance of tracking offenders as they pass in to and out of the criminal justice system was highlighted by the Wickersham Commission, which among other things published mortality tables of criminal defendants in Cincinnati. This study was followed by surveys in other cities and intense discussion of the meaning of attrition (nonconviction) of cases. Many of the issues and questions raised are still being grappled with today.

One of the primary difficulties facing data systems that track defendants through the criminal justice process is the lack of connection between the arrest offense and its disposition. UCR, victim, and self-report data are only of limited use in tracking arrestees through the court system.

Institutional-based data collection systems for tracking offenders share some of the same problems of the UCR, such as the manner in which offenses are recorded (i.e., the hierarchy rule) and in how subsequent dispositions are recorded. For example, *OBTS* and *Prosecutor Management Information Systems* (*PROMIS*) are defendant-based systems that are case based. If there is more than one offense involved, as frequently occurs, the case is usually defined by the most serious offense charged or filed against the defendant. The outcome of the defendant's "case" is then defined by a conviction on *any* offense in the case, regardless of whether it is the most serious or the least serious charge. This frequently means that (a) tracking frequently begins at filing charges at court, not arrest; in other words, arrest information may only be included when an arrest leads to some form of prosecutorial action, be it rejection, diversion filing of charges, and so forth and (b) a conviction on an offense less serious than the principal charge is counted as a *case* conviction.

In light of the decentralized system of arrest and charging practices in the United States, it should not be surprising that there is wide variation in the extent to which felony arrests, for example, actually enter into local defendant tracking systems. Among the 28 jurisdictions with tracking systems that were recently studied by Boland, Conly, Warner, Sones, and Martin

FIGURE 2.2. Outcomes of 100 "typical" arrests brought to the Superior Court of Washington, DC, in 1974.

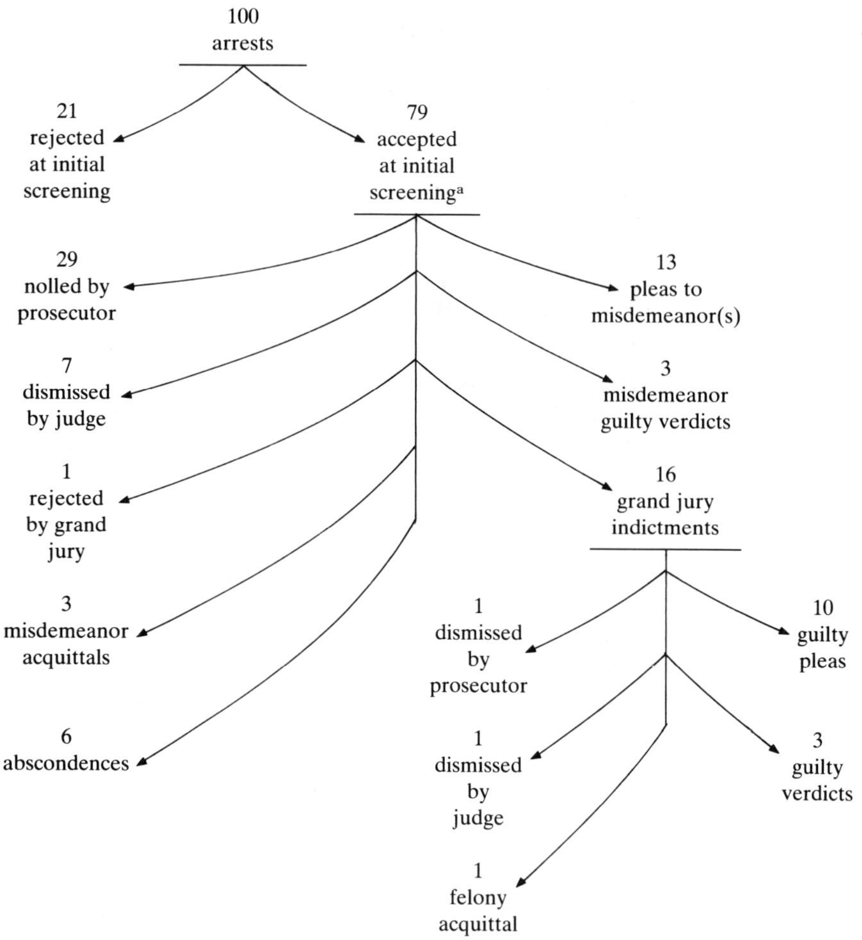

Note. Total does not agree due to rounding error.
Source: Brian Forst, Judith Lucianovic & Sarah J, Cox, *What Happens After Arrest?* Washington, D.C.: Institute for Law and Social Research, 1977, Exhibit 2.5, p. 17, with permission.

(1989), for example, the authors found that

. . . In some jurisdictions the definition of felony cases is all arrests; in others, cases filed; and in still others, cases indicted. . . Because of differing administrative arrangements for charging and weeding out cases prior to court filing, jurisdictions vary considerably in the fraction of felony arrests filed.

An earlier study by Forst, Lucianovic, and Cox (1977) that appears to begin at the point of arrest (regardless of whether a filing occurs) and tracks defendants using a case approach finds that the typical felony arrest follows the disposition indicated in Figure 2.2. Of 100 felony arrests, on the average 21 are rejected at initial screening, while 29 eventually result in a conviction through a plea of guilty or a trial.

Data obtained from the case approach does not necessarily lend itself to unqualified interpretation, however. The Vera Institute of Justice (1977) study of felony arrest dispositions, for example, found that the average number of charges per arrest was 2 and that it was necessary to classify cases in terms of the most serious charge. Outcomes are in turn discussed in terms of what happened to any offense in the case as a whole. Similar procedures may also have been used in Forst et al. (1977).

An alternative way of approaching the task of tracking defendants from arrest through disposition has been taken by Feeney et al. (1982). They tracked defendants in two cities whose principal charge at arrest was robbery, burglary, or assault. The outcome examined was conviction on the principal charge or a lesser included offense of the principal charge. However, a conviction on a wholly separate charge was not counted as a conviction on the principal charge. They compared the rates of conviction across the offenses and cities. Moreover, they also compared the results to that obtained by using the case approach. These data are shown in Table 2.6.

The table suggests that the case approach results in a higher percentage

TABLE 2.6. Conviction rates by principal charge and case (in percentage of persons arrested).

	Jacksonville		San Diego	
	Principal charge	Case	Principal charge	Case
Robbery	50	53	34	51
Burglary	70	72	43	57
Felony assault	47	48	46	49

Notes. (1) Data in this table for burglary are limited to burglaries of buildings and do not include auto burglaries and other nontraditional kinds of burglary. (2) Convictions for Jacksonville include adjudications withheld and pretrial intervention cases.
Source: *Arrests Without Conviction: How Often They Occur and Why* (p. 87, Table 10-1) by F.F. Feeney, F. Dill, and A. Weir, 1982, Washington, DC: National Institute of Justice.

of convictions. The effect of the case method of counting defendant dispositions is greatest in San Diego and particularly among the robberies and burglaries.

Clearly there are important differences in the way that institutional statistics track defendants. They differ in the unit of count, the manner in which charges are recorded, how outcomes are defined, and in a variety of ways too numerous to go into here (see, e.g., Boland et al., 1989; Feeney et al., 1982). Each nuance in decentralized data collection systems that exist in the United States may have substantial effects on the nature of defendant outcomes. Those who choose any given data source for study will profit by thoroughly examining procedures used in generating the data in question.

Other Sources

A variety of alternative quantitative sources of data are available for research purposes through the Inter-University Consortium on Political and Social Research.[10] One may obtain, for example, the census of United States jails and jail inmates, the national survey of prison inmates, and the national survey of probationers and parolees. Data from special projects commissioned or funded by the federal government can also be found through the consortium. These include studies that have coded historical data on violence to modern, randomized experiments in selected areas such as the prevention of spousal abuse programs or the reduction of crime among ex-offenders.

A Note on Qualitative Sources

While this survey has focused upon the limitations and advantages of varied sources of quantitative data, it should be recognized that criminological research using qualitative methodology could be subjected to scrutiny and evaluation as well. However, since the data or materials generated by the use of qualitative materials are as yet not readily accessible for secondary analysis by social scientists, consideration of them in this context would be premature.

Endnotes

1. For a recent discussion of the development of statistics for social science generally and in the study of crime, see Porter (1986).
2. They have, in addition, played an important role in the definition of new problems. This topic is not addressed in this paper.
3. No attempt at a definition of a crime event is offered here. For our purpose, it

is defined by the particular method or procedure used to obtain information about crime.

4. Past and current research on this topic takes one of two forms: It either compares *UCR* data with that obtained from cross-sectional surveys (e.g., Boothe, Johnson & Choldin, 1977; Cohen & Land, 1984; Decker, 1977; Jackson, 1988), or it compares the UCR and an alternative data source over time (e.g., O'Brien, 1985; Menard, 1987), or *both* (Messner, 1984; Menard & Covey, 1988).

5. Prevalence refers to the proportion of the population committing an offense during a given time period. One may examine the lifetime prevalence of crime or restrict it to a shorter time period, such as 1 year. Incidence refers to the number of offenses among a defined population for a particular time period. UCR data are generally only useful for estimating incidence rates, whereas the NYS is useful in specifying both prevalence and incidence. NCS data provide both prevalence and incidence rates for victims and, to a limited extent, may provide offender incidence rates.

6. A more up-to-date review on self-report studies that involve a test of control theory can be found in Kempf (1989).

7. These data, like the UCR, NYS, and others discussed below, can be obtained through the Inter-University Consortium for Political and Social Research.

8. For a more recent study that compares self-report crime or delinquency from the *Monitering the Future* study and arrest figures from the FBI, see Osgood et al. (1989).

9. Savitz (1982) suggests that only one-fifth of UCR arrests result in a conviction. The Wickersham Commission, and the surveys that followed it, discussed below, found that about half of all felony arrests result in conviction. See Feeney et al.'s (1982) summary of these studies.

10. See, for example, the Inter-University Consortium for Political and Social Research (1986) and National Institute of Justice (1987).

References

Bachman, G.G., Green, S., & Wirtanen, I.D. (1970). *Youth in transition: Vol. II.* Ann Arbor: University of Michigan, Institute for Social Research.

Bachman, G.G., Green, S., & Wirtanen, I.D. (1971). *Youth in transition: Vol. III.* Ann Arbor: University of Michigan, Institute for Social Research.

Bachman, G.G., O'Malley, P.M., & Johnston, J. (1978). *Youth in transition: Vol. IV.* Ann Arbor: University of Michigan, Institute for Social Research.

Bachman, G.G. (1987). *Monitoring the Future.* Ann Arbor: University of Michigan, Institute for Social Research.

Biderman, A.D., & Reiss, A., Jr. (1967). On exploring the "dark figure" of crime. *The Annals, 374,* 1–15.

Black, D., & Reiss, A., Jr. (1970). Police control of juveniles. *American Sociological Review, 35,* 63–77.

Blumstein, A., Cohen, J. Roth, J.A., & Vishor, C.A. (Eds.). (1988). *Criminal careers and "career criminals."* Washington, DC: National Academy Press.

Boland, B., Conly, C.H., Warner, L., Sones, R., & Martin, W. (1989). *The prosecution of felony arrests, 1986.* Washington, DC: Bureau of Justice Statistics.

Booth, A., Johnson, D.R., and Choldin H. (1977). Correlates of city crime rates:

Victimization surveys versus official statistics. *Sociological Quarterly*, 21, 391–401.

Bureau of Justice Statistics. (1988). *Criminal victimization 1987*. Washington, DC: U.S. Government Printing Office.

Bureau of Justice Statistics. (1989). *The redesigned National Crime Survey: Selected new data*. Washington, DC: U.S. Government Printing Office.

Cantor, D., & Cohen, L.E. (1984). Comparing measures of homicide trends: Methodological and substantive differences in the Vital Statistics and Uniform Crime Report Time Series (1933–1975). *Social Science Research*, 9, 121–145.

Decker, S.H. (1977). Official crime rates and victim surveys: An empirical comparison. *Criminal Justice*, 5, 47–54.

Dodge, R.W., & Lentzner, H.R. (1978, August 14–17). *Patterns of Personal Series Incidents in the National Crime Survey*. Paper presentd at the Annual Meeting of the American Statistical Association, San Diego, CA.

Elliott, D.S., & Ageton, S.S. (1978). Reconciling differences in estimates of delinquency. *American Sociological Review*, 45, 95–110.

Federal Bureau of Investigation. (1988a). *Uniform Crime Reports*. Washington, DC: U.S. Government Printing Office.

Federal Bureau of Investigation. (1988b). *Uniform crime reporting: National Incident-Based Reporting System. Volume I: Data collection guidelines*. Washington DC: U.S. Government Printing Office.

Federal Bureau of Investigation. (1989). *Uniform Crime Reports*. Washington, D.C.: U.S. Government Printing Office.

Feeney, F.F., Dill, F., & Weir, A. (1982). *Arrests without conviction: How often they occur and why*. Washington, DC: National Institute of Justice.

Forst, B., Lucianovic, J., & Cox, S.J. (1977). *What happens after arrest?* Washington, DC: Institute for Law and Social Research.

Gold, M., & Reimer, D.J. (1974). *Changing patterns of delinquent behavior among Americans 13 to 17 years old—1972. Report Number 1 of the National Survey of Youth, 1972*. Ann Arbor: University of Michigan, Institute for Social Research.

Gottfredson, M., & Gottfredson, D. (1988). *Decisionmaking in criminal justice* (2nd ed.). Cambridge, MA: Ballinger.

Gove, W.R., Hughes, M., & Geerken, M. (1985). Are Uniform Crime Reports a valid indicator of the Index crimes? An affirmative answer with minor qualifications. *Criminology*, 23, 451–501.

Hindelang, M.J. (1974). The Uniform Crime Reports revisited. *Journal of Criminal Justice*, 2, 1–17.

Hindelang, M.J., Hirschi, T., & Weis, J.G. (1979). Correlates of delinquency: The illusion of discrepancy between self-report and official measures. *American Sociological Review*, 44, 995–1014.

Hirschi, (1969). *Causes of Delinquency*. University of Calfornia Press.

Huizinga, D., & Elliott, D.S. (1984). *Self-reported measures of delinquency and crime: Methodological issues and comparative findings*. Boulder, CO: Behavioral Research Institute.

Huizinga, D., & Elliott, D.S. (1987). Juvenile offenders: Prevalence, offender incidence and arrest rates by race. *Crime and Delinquency*, 33, 206–223.

Inter-University Consortium for Political and Social Research. (1986). *Directory of criminal justice data collections in the United States*. Ann Arbor: Author.

Jackson, P.G. (1988). Assessing the validity of official data on arson. *Criminology*, 26, 181–195.

Kempf, K.L. (1989). *Hirschi's control theory: Is it fertile but not yet fecund?* Paper presented at the American Society of Criminology Meetings, Chicago.

Lehnen, R.G., & Skogan, W.G. (Eds.). (1981). *The National Crime Survey: Working papers. Volume I: Current and historical perspectives*. Washington, DC: U.S. Government Printing Office.

Lundman, R., Sykes, R., & Clark, J. (1978). Police control of juveniles: A replication. *Journal of Research on Crime and Delinquency*, 15, 74–91.

Maltz, M.D. (1977). Crime statistics: A historical perspective. *Crime and Delinquency*, 23, 32–40.

Menard, S. (1987). Short-term trends in crime and delinquency: A comparison of UCR, NCS and self-report data. *Justice Quarterly*, 4, 455–474.

Menard, S. (1988). UCR and NCD: Comparisons over space and time. *Journal of Criminal Justice*, 16, 371–384.

Messner, S.F. (1984). The "dark figure" and composite indexes of crime: Some empirical exploration of alternative data sources. *Journal of Criminal Justice*, 12, 435–444.

Moll, K.D. (1974). *Arson, vandalism and violence: Law enforcement problems affecting fire departments*. Washington, DC: U.S. Department of Justice.

National Commission on Law Observance and Enforcement. (1931). *Report on criminal statistics. Report No. 3*. Washington, DC: U.S. Government Printing Office.

National Institute of Justice. (1987). Data Resources of the National Institute of Justice. Washington, DC: U.S. Government Printing Office.

Nettler, G. (1989). *Criminology lessons*. Cincinatti, Ohio: Anderson Publishing Co.

O'Brien, R. (1985). *Crime and victimization data*. Beverly Hills, CA: Sage.

Osgood, D.W., O'Malley, P.M., Bachman, J.G., & Johnson, L.D. (1989). Time trends and age trends in arrests and self-reported illegal behavior. *Criminology*, 27, 389–418.

Piliavin, I., & Briar, S. (1964). Police encounters with juveniles. *American Journal of Sociology*, 70, 206–214.

Porter, T.M. (1986). *The rise of statistical thinking 1820–1900*. Princeton: Princeton University Press.

Porterfield, A. (1946). *Youth in trouble*. Fort Worth, TX: Leo Potishman Foundation.

Reiss, A.J., Jr. (1971). *The police and the public*. New Haven: Yale University Press.

Reiss, A.J., Jr. (1978). Final report for analytical studies of victimization in crime using National Crime Survey data. New Haven: Yale University, Institute for Policy Studies.

Savitz, L.D. (1982). Official statistics. In L.D. Savitz and N. Johnston (Eds.), *Contemporary criminology* (pp. 4–15). New York: Wiley.

Schwartz, I. (1988). *In-justice for juveniles: Rethinking the best interests of the child*. Lexington Books.

Sellin, T. (1951). The significance of records of crime. *The Law Quarterly Review*, 67, 489–504.

Skogan, W. (1976). Crime and crime rates. pp. 27–41. In W. Skogan (Ed.), *Sample surveys of victims of crime*. Cambridge, MA: Ballinger.
Skogan, W. (1981). Issues in the Measurement of Victimization. Washington, D.C.: U.S. Government Printing Office.
U.S. Department of Justice. (1981). *National Crime Surveys: National Sample, 1973–1979*. Inter-University Consortium for Political and Social Research. Ann Arbor.
U.S. Senate Subcommittee. (1978). Arson-for-Hire. *Proceedings of the 62nd Congress*. Washington, DC: U.S. Government Printing Office.
Vera Institute of Justice. (1977). *Felony arrests*: Their prosecution and disposition in New York City's courts (Monograph). New York: Author.

3
Prevalence, Incidence, Rates, and Other Descriptive Measures

PAUL E. TRACY, JR.

One of the most fundamental tasks that must be accomplished in the very beginning of any statistical analysis of research data is to specify and investigate the distribution of the particular phenomenon of interest in the study population or sample. In the most simple general terms, a researcher needs to know (a) how many persons in the study possess the trait being investigated and (b) how much of the trait these people have, or stated another way, how often these persons exhibit the trait. The former measure, which is qualitative and which concerns the classification of the population usually into two groups—those subjects that have the trait versus those persons that do not—is known as *prevalence*. The latter measurement, which is quantitative and which is concerned with counting the number of times that the trait is observed is known as *incidence*. These two measures, prevalence and incidence, are the fundamental raw material of any social science research involving human subjects, regardless of whether the research is testing a social science theory, evaluating a particular treatment program, or merely exploring and describing a set of data.

Although these concepts are very basic and must be examined before any sophisticated multivariate statistical procedures are applied to the data, it is surprising to see how often these concepts are confused or even neglected altogether. The problem surrounding prevalence and incidence is especially acute in criminal justice research, where the focus of the research concerns the criminal element in the population and the number of offenses committed by these persons or the number of arrests or convictions that they have. Because of the distributional nature of crime and criminals, we know that the prevalence of crime in a study population is often rare and will usually characterize only a small number of the subjects—most people have never been arrested or convicted of a crime. Likewise, the incidence of crime is usually skewed and unevenly distributed, thus indicating varying ciminal involvement levels among the subset of the population that is criminal—some offenders commit only one offense, others accumulate a few offenses, while still others commit many crimes.

This situation is further complicated by the fact that both prevalence and incidence measures in criminal justice are very often related to many sociodemographic characteristics of the subjects, such as sex, race, age, and social class. Thus, the extent to which there is variation in a study population in terms of sociodemographic factors (i.e., more males than females or more whites than nonwhites), there will be natural variation in the prevalence and incidence of crime that is directly related or attributable to these factors.

The goal of this chapter, then, is to elucidate the concepts of prevalence and incidence and to show why various types of descriptive statistical measures must be calculated in order to understand properly the group differences that are exhibited in the number of persons that can be classified as offenders and the frequency of criminal offenses committed by these offenders. In order to place the presentation in a real-life research context, all of the analyses will be based upon data that were collected from an actual research project that the author has been involved in for over 10 years. Thus, none of the results that are reported in tables or presented in figures have been orchestrated or constructed in order to support the issue being presented. The data being analyzed are real.

There are two types of statistical measures used by researchers, descriptive statistics and inferential statistics. Descriptive statistics are just what the name implies, a set of measures that describe a set of data in terms of frequency counts, percentages, rates, averages, and so forth. Inferential statistics, on the other hand, are concerned with making decisions about a population by studying data collected on a sample of the population. Inferential statistics thus require a concern about the statistical significance of sample results—could the sample results have occurred by chance, or do they indicate differences that would obtain if the entire population had been investigated? We will be concerned in this chapter only with the first type—descriptive statistics.

A particular style of analytical method will be employed throughout the presentation. This method, often referred to as *elaboration*, starts with a basic bivariate relationship of one independent variable and one dependent, or criterion, variable and then introduces other independent variables in a process designed to detect spurious relationships and interactive or contingent associations. At each step of the presentation, we will be concerned with the nature of the research issue before us, the reason for the particular analysis being conducted, and the effect of analyzing the data in a particular way.

The Data

The 1958 Philadelphia Birth Cohort[1] is a longitudinal research project that has been investigating the delinquency and adult criminal careers of a large group of subjects since 1977. Through the use of Philadelphia, Pennsylvania, public and parochial/private school records, a cohort of persons, born is 1958, who had continuous residence in Philadelphia at least from the ages of 10 through 17, was identified. A continuous residence restriction was used to ensure that each cohort member would be exposed to the same general environment at the same time and that all cohort members would confront the same period at risk for delinquent behavior. The 1958 birth cohort is composed of 27,160 subjects. The birth cohort contains 13,160 males and 14,000 females. The distributions by sex and race shows that 6,216 males and 6,637 females are white, while 6,944 males and 7,363 females are nonwhite. The measure of socioeconomic status (SES) that was used consisted of a factor analysis of Philadelphia census tract variables. For present purposes, we have dichotomized SES into low versus high, which produces the following breakdowns: for males—6,414 low SES and 6,746 high SES; for females—6,948 low SES and 7,052 high SES.

The delinquency data were collected from the Juvenile Aid Division of the Philadelphia Police Department and from the Juvenile Court Division of the Court of Common Pleas for Philadelphia. The juvenile offense data represent all police contacts experienced by a cohort member, whether or not the offense resulted in official arrest processing or whether the case was referred to the juvenile court. Thus, we have available for our analyses a series of delinquency measures: (a) offender status (delinquent vs. non-delinquent); (b) offender status by arrest category (e.g., onetime vs. recidivist); (c) number of offenses committed; (d) type of offenses committed; (e) age-at-onset of delinquency; and (f) age-at-offense for each delinquent act.

Prevalence

Our first task in the analysis of the delinquency data of the 1958 birth cohort is to investigate the prevalence of juvenile delinquency. Table 3.1 displays simple counts of the number of subjects that were not recorded as delinquent, the number that were classified as delinquent in the police files, and the total number of subjects. These data are given for females and males in the top portion of the table, and for males by race and SES in the bottom portion.[2]

When we examine just the frequency counts in Table 3.1, we note first that a total of 1,967 females in the cohort were delinquent compared to 4,315 males. On the basis of these counts, should we conclude that delinquency status was over twice as frequent for males as for females, thus indicating that males are more than twice as likely to be arrested as juveniles? On the other hand, suppose that we had half as many males in the study, say 6,580 instead of 13,160, and suppose further that this reduced number of males produced about half as many delinquents, around 2,100 instead of 4,315, should we now conclude that males with about 2,100 delinquents are only slightly more delinquent than females who showed

TABLE 3.1. Breakdown of nondelinquents, delinquents, and subjects by sex; and breakdown by race and socioeconomic status for males.

Category		Nondelinquents	Delinquents	Subjects
Females	No.	12,033	1,967	14,000
	%	86.9	14.1	100.0
Males	No.	8,845	4,315	13,160
	%	67.2	32.8	100.0
White males	No.	4,804	1,412	6,216
	%	77.3	22.7	100.0
Nonwhites males	No.	4,041	2,903	6,944
	%	58.2	41.8	100.0
Low SES males	No.	3,711	2,703	6,414
	%	57.9	42.1	100.0
High SES males	No.	5,134	1,612	6,746
	%	76.1	23.9	100.0

Note. Percentages are row percents.
Source: Tracy et al. (1985).

about 1967 delinquents? Similarly, concerning the delinquency data for males by race and by SES shown in the lower portion of Table 3.1, can we conclude that nonwhite males are more delinquent than white males, and can we conclude that low SES males are more delinquent than high SES males? We certainly should not reach any of these conclusions on the basis of frequency counts alone.

The essential problem with comparing the absolute frequencies of an observed trait or status is that such counts ignore the total number of cases in each group (e.g., males vs. females; whites vs. nonwhites) eligible to occupy the status or exhibit the particular trait. When the total number of cases in the comparison groups are equal, then the frequencies can be compared directly. When the comparison group differ in size, however, we need to take explicitly into account the size difference. Thus, in our example concerning delinquency prevalence, we need a general measure that takes into account the number of persons classified as delinquent *and* the number of persons at risk for delinquency. What we need simply is the *proportion* or *percentage* of delinquents in the two groups.

The proportion and the percentage are methods of standardizing a frequency distribution for the size of the groups being studied. The proportion is computed by dividing the frequency of delinquency by the number of persons at risk—(proportion = frequency of delinquents ÷ number of subjects). The percentage is perhaps a more familiar measure and is just another way of expressing the frequency occurrence of a status or trait per 100 cases of subjects. The percentage is computed by dividing the frequency of delinquency by the number of subjects and then multiplying by 100 (percentage = frequency of delinquents ÷ number of subjects × 100). Table 3.1 gives the appropriate percentages for the frequency counts of delinquency.

Table 3.1 indicates that about 14% of the females in the cohort compared to about 33% of the males were processed or recorded as delinquent by the Philadelphia police.[3] These are the appropriate prevalence measures for our purposes. They indicate, regardless of the size of the male and female groups, the relative prevalence of delinquency. Further, these measures are directly comparable and allow us to compute a male to female ratio, which indicates that males were 2.3 times more likely to be delinquent than their female counterparts.

Now that we have established the need to examine percentages, or proportions, rather than just frequency counts, we can begin our discussion of two of the major correlates of delinquency prevalence—race and socioeconomic status. These data are given in the bottom portion of Table 3.1 for the males in the 1958 cohort. The results shown pertain to two separate bivariate associations—race and delinquency status (i.e., nondelinquent vs. delinquent) and SES and delinquency status. When we first look at the data by race, we note that 1,412 cases or about 23% of the 6,216 white males were delinquent compared to 2,903 cases, or about 42% of the 6,944 nonwhite males. Similarly, we note that 42% of the low SES males were delinquent compared to about 24% of the high SES males.

The results displayed in Table 3.1 would seem to indicate that delinquency status is strongly related to both the race and the socioeconomic status of the cohort member. That is, nonwhites and low SES cohort subjects have a higher prevalence of delinquency. Before we accept the validity of these observations, however, we need to establish that the relationships are genuine and not spurious. That is, we need to know (a) whether nonwhites are more delinquent than whites not just because they also happen to be disproportionately of lower SES and (b) whether low SES persons in the cohort are more delinquent than their high SES counterparts not just because low status persons are more likely to be nonwhite. In effect, we need to know whether the race effect holds regardless of SES and whether the SES effects holds regardless of race.

In order to determine the proper inferences from the data, we need to consider all three variables at once—the two independent variables (race and SES) and the dependent variable (delinquency status)—in what is known as a multiway cross-tabulation, or contingency table. In such a table, we examine one of the independent variables while *holding constant* or *controlling for* the other. In order to do this, we examine the two levels of SES for each race category separately, and we examine the two race categories for each SES level separately. A basic layout of this approach is given in Table 3.2.

Table 3.2 presents the basic layout for an examination of the SES/

TABLE 3.2. Number and percentage of delinquents and nondelinquents by socioeconomic status controlling for race for males.

Category		Nondelinquents	Delinquents	Subjects
Males	No.	8,845	4,315	13,160
	%	67.2	32.8	100.0
White males				
Low SES	No.	881	437	1,318
	%	66.8	33.2	100.0
High SES	No.	3,923	975	4,898
	%	80.1	19.9	100.0
Nonwhite males				
Low SES	No.	2,830	2,226	5,096
	%	55.5	44.5	100.0
High SES	No.	1,211	637	1,848
	%	65.5	34.4	100.0

Note. Percentages are row percents.
Source: Tracy et al. (1985).

delinquency association controlling for race. These data indicate that among white males there is a moderate but definite SES effect—low SES subjects show a higher prevalence of delinquency than do high SES subjects (33.2% vs. 19.9%). Similarly, among nonwhite males, there is a weaker but definite SES effect, with low status (44.5%) showing a higher prevalence of delinquency than high status (34.4%).

If we were to focus instead on the race/delinquency relationship while controlling for SES, we would compare whites versus nonwhites at each SES level. These comparisons are as follows. Among low SES subjects, there is a moderate race effect—33% of whites were delinquent vs. 45% of nonwhites. At the level of high SES, there is a stronger race effect—20% of whites were delinquent versus 34% of nonwhites.

These particular results of our real-life analyses have indicated neither (a) a spurious relationship (between race and delinquency status, or between SES and delinquency status) nor (b) a conditional, or contingent, association. What would these particular results look like if they were present? We will briefly present these two hypothetical cases below.

First, considering a spurious relationship, the situation would appear as follows. We would have an initial relationship showing that nonwhites were more delinquent than whites (just like we have in Table 3.1). We suspect that the "race effect" is not really a function of race; rather, we believe the effect is due to the fact that low SES youngsters are more likely to get into trouble with the police, and since nonwhites are usually more likely to be low SES than are whites, the nonwhites receive the delinquency label more often than whites because of their low SES status. We would be able to detect this by examining a table like Table 3.2. In this hypothetical table, instead of the results we obtained before (where the race effect persisted for both SES levels), we would see instead that (a) there is no difference across SES levels in the percentage of whites versus nonwhites that were delinquent and (b) that a much higher proportion of nonwhites were low SES subjects compared to whites. These results would then indicate to us that the original race effect was spurious and was due to an extraneous SES effect.

Second, a conditional, or contingent, association is one in which a particular effect holds for a particular level of a control factor but not at other levels. Thus, in our original Table 3.2, we would find a contingent association if our original race effect existed for one level of SES but not the other, say the lower level of SES but not the higher. Here, unlike the spurious case discussed above, we would conclude that the race effect depends upon the SES level of the subject. Thus, it is not nonwhites overall who are arrested more often than whites; it is low SES nonwhites, in particular, that are more likely to be classified as delinquent. Contingent associations such as this would stimulate our thinking and analyses to determine why the low SES nonwhites were so different.

We did not obtain a spurious relationship or any contingent associations in our analysis. Thus, we may conclude that both race and SES are individually related to the prevalence of delinquency status regardless of the other factor. That is, through a process of "elaborating" the two bivariate relationships, we have found that the race effect holds regardless of SES and the SES effect holds regardless of race. This signifies that the relationships are genuine and not spurious. Also, however, we are able to conclude that the race effect represents the stronger association. By rank order from highest to lowest, the prevalence of delinquency was as follows: low SES nonwhites (44.5%), high SES nonwhites (34.4%), low SES whites (33.2%), and high SES whites (19.9%).

Thus far we have considered prevalence from the point of view of data that were presented or were displayed in tabular form. In this form, the frequencies and percentages of all categories of all variables are usually given. That is, it is customary to give complete data when using tables, but since we are primarily interested in the prevalence of delinquency, we should consider an alternative method of displaying our results. It is sometimes more effective to utilize figures rather than tables, because figures can immediately present and emphasize the results one is primarily interested in showing the reader.

Thus, for example, we might present our original male versus female prevalence data as shown in Figure 3.1. Figure 3.1 is known as a histogram or vertical bar chart. Along the vertical, or "y," axis is reported the percentage of cases that fall into the particular groups that are shown on the horizontal, or "x," axis. With the histogram, we can see quite immediately

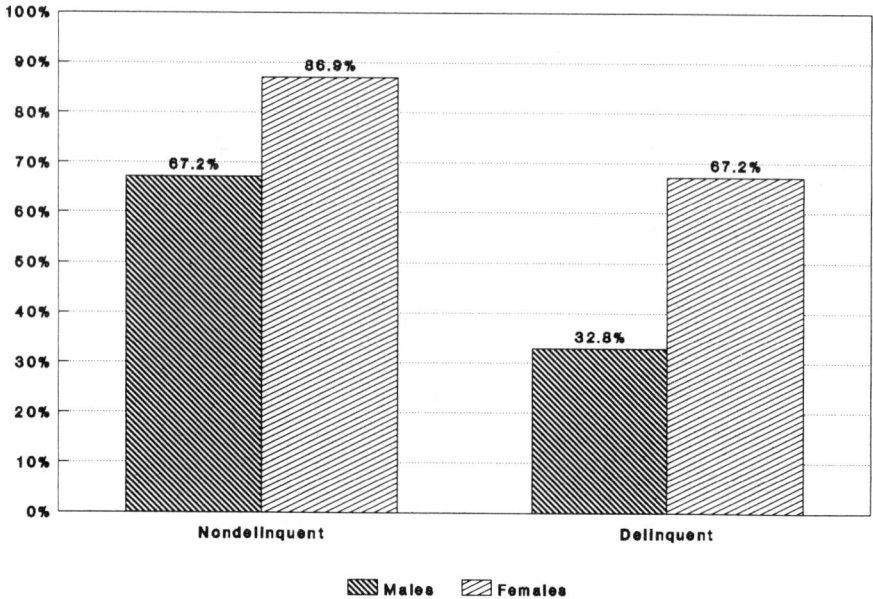

FIGURE 3.1. Delinquency status percentages by sex. (Tracy et al. [1985])

that the prevalence of delinquency varies considerably by sex. Males are much more likely to be delinquent, and females are much more likely to be nondelinquent.

In Figure 3.2 we turn to a histogram of our multiway cross-tabulation (Table 3.2). This figure portrays a comparison of the percentages of nondelinquents versus delinquents across our four combinations of race and SES. Just as in the previous diagram, Figure 3.2 allows us to observe quite clearly the effects that we discussed previously for the tabular data. That is, SES has an effect for both races—lower status subjects were more delinquent, and race has an effect for both SES levels—nonwhites were more often delinquent than whites. The value of the histogram as a presentation device is that the reader can immediately observe these results by looking at the heights of the respective vertical bars.

In this section, we have introduced the concept of prevalence, and in our particular research context, the prevalence of delinquency is properly taken to mean the component of a study population or the component of particular subgroups that are classified as juvenile delinquents. We have seen, in particular, that we cannot merely use the frequency counts of delinquents as the basic statistic for prevalence, because frequency counts ignore the total size of the underlying population or group that is eligible or available to be classified as delinquent. Thus, using frequency counts or absolute numbers would lead to incorrect conclusions regarding the rela-

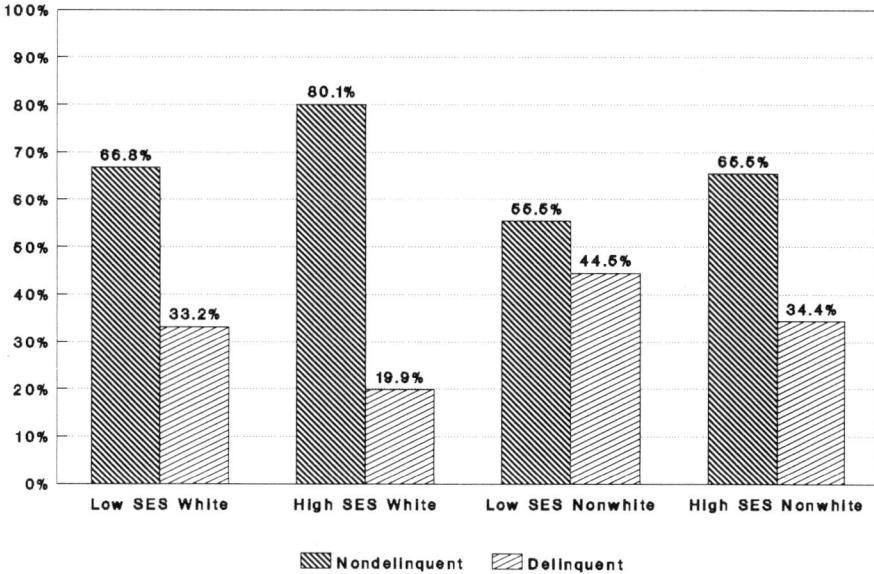

FIGURE 3.2. Delinquency status percentages for males by race and socioeconomic status. (Tracy et al. [1985])

tive prevalence of delinquency status across subgroups in a study population.

We have also shown that, because social science variables are related to one another and to the dependent or criterion variables of interest, we must examine the possible relationships, taking into account as many variables at the same time as we can. This process of elaborating a two variable association allows us to detect relationships that are not genuine or perhaps find relationships that hold for particular subject groups but not for others. In our case, we found that both race and socioeconomic status (or social class) were related to delinquency status separately, and more important, we found that when we examined the three-way association of race, SES, and delinquency, the associations held for all comparison groups.

Incidence

In this section, we turn to a discussion of the concept of the incidence of delinquency. We previously defined incidence as a quantitative measure that counts the number of times that offenders exhibit the trait of delinquency. In other words, regardless of the number of persons that occupy the status of delinquent, we need to investigate how many times offenders exhibit delinquent behaviors. This simple definition needs to be expanded now to reflect the two basic components of incidence—*extent* and the *character* of delinquency. The extent of delinquency pertains to the number, or frequency, of the sum total of delinquent acts committed by the offenders in the birth cohort. On the other hand, the character of delinquency incorporates a counting process, but it also includes first classifying or grouping offenses into meaningful categories and then counting them. We elucidate these concepts below.

There were a total of 15,248 delinquent acts charged to the 4,315 male delinquents in the cohort. These delinquency data are displayed by specific offense type and by race in Table 3.3. Our interest in analyzing these data is to compare the relative incidence of delinquency between nonwhites and whites. First, concerning the extent of delinquency, let us look at the two *N* columns, which show the number, or frequency, of offenses committed by each race group. We see, for example, that overall nonwhites committed 11,340 offenses compared to 3,908 for whites and we also see that the former committed 1,210 robberies compared to 80 for the latter. Can we just compare the numbers in these two columns to reveal the differences between whites and nonwhites? We cannot.

As we learned in our discussion above concerning prevalence, we cannot just compare frequency distributions directly, when the underlying sizes of the populations are different. Thus, nonwhites could have a greater extent of delinquency, not because the offenders were more delinquent, but rather, because (a) there were more subjects to become delinquent in the first place and (b) more delinquents did emerge among the nonwhite group.

In the case of prevalence we used percentages as the means of standardizing our frequency distributions. Can we do the same thing to compare the relative extent of delinquency for nonwhites versus whites? Table 3.3 gives the percentage of each offense type out of the total offenses for each race. We see that robbery accounts for 10.7% of nonwhite delinquencies (1,210 ÷ 11,340) and 2.1% of white delinquencies (80 ÷ 3,908). Here, the frequencies are very different with a ratio of about 15 to 1, and the percentages are very different but with a smaller ratio of about 5 to 1. Compare these results to the case of burglary which indicates that about 11% of nonwhite delinquencies were burglaries compared to 10.5% of white delinquencies being burglary crimes. Here, the frequencies are again very different (1,261 vs. 412) with a ratio of about 3:1, while the percentages are very similar (11.1% vs. 10.5%) and the ratio is approximately 1:1.

The problem with comparing the nonwhite and white percentages to reveal differences in the extent of delinquency is that the percentages do not remedy or remove differences in the size of the two subject groups, the number of offenders in each groups, and the vastly different total number of offenses committed by the offenders in the two groups. These percentages do not allow us to compare whites versus nonwhites in terms of the

TABLE 3.3. Number, percentage, and rate of delinquent offenses by race for males.

Offense	Nonwhites			Whites		
	N	%	Rate	N	%	Rate
Homicide	51	0.5	7.3	4	0.1	0.6
Rape	92	0.8	13.2	9	0.2	1.4
Robbery	1,210	10.7	174.3	80	2.1	12.9
Aggravated assault	458	4.0	66.0	103	2.6	16.6
Burglary	1,261	11.1	181.6	412	10.5	66.3
Larceny	1,304	11.5	187.8	367	9.4	59.0
Auto theft	458	4.0	66.0	182	4.7	29.3
Simple assault	504	4.4	72.6	194	4.9	31.2
Arson	27	0.2	3.9	15	0.4	2.4
Forgery	3	0.0	0.4	–	–	–
Fraud	4	0.0	0.6	2	0.1	0.3
Stolen property	41	0.4	5.9	28	0.7	4.5
Vandalism	528	4.7	76.0	285	7.3	45.8
Weapons	95	3.5	56.9	62	1.6	10.0
Prostitution	8	0.1	1.2	3	0.1	0.5
Sex offense	37	0.3	5.3	29	0.7	4.7
Drug offense	467	4.1	67.3	247	6.3	39.7
Gambling	7	0.1	1.0	1	0.0	0.2
Drunk driving	5	0.0	0.7	35	0.9	5.6
Liquor laws	77	0.7	11.1	134	3.4	21.6
Drunkeness	94	0.8	13.5	72	1.8	11.6
Disorderly	1,089	9.6	156.8	748	19.1	120.3
Vagrancy	27	0.2	3.9	8	0.2	1.3
Suspicious person	73	0.6	10.5	24	0.6	3.9
Traffic	39	0.3	5.6	30	0.8	4.8
Hospital cases	–	–	–	1	0.0	0.2
Investigations	33	0.3	4.8	9	0.2	1.4
Disturbance	3	0.0	0.4	1	0.0	0.2
Missing person	134	1.2	19.3	70	1.8	11.3
All others	2,911	25.7	419.2	753	19.3	121.1
Total offenses	11,340	100.0	1,633.1	3,908	100.0	628.7
UCR Index	4,834	42.6	696.2	1,157	29.6	186.1
UCR Non-index	6,506	57.4	936.9	2,751	70.4	442.6
UCR Violent	1,811	37.5	260.8	196	16.9	31.5
UCR Property	3,023	62.5	435.3	961	83.1	154.6

Note. Percentages are column percents. UCR = Uniform Crime Reports.
Source: Tracy et al. (1985).

extent of delinquency; they only permit us to compare the role that various offense types play for each group. Thus, using percentages we can suggest that robbery, with 10.7% for nonwhites vs. 2.1% for whites, is more characteristic of nonwhite delinquency than white delinquency. This, however, pertains to the character component of incidence and still does not address our need to investigate the relative extent of delinquency.

The answer to our problem is to compute delinquency *rate* statistics. Rates are widely used measures in social science research. We have all heard at one time or another reference to birth or death rates, unemployment rates, and especially crime rates. A rate is based on the number of actual cases of a phenomenon compared to the number of possible cases. A rate is also expressed in terms of some unit of population, like per capita (one person), per 1,000, per 10,000, or per 100,000. For our purposes, we will use 1,000 as the relevant unit of population because we have a cohort population that is in this unit rather than tens of thousands of subjects; we have 13,160 males divided into 6,944 nonwhite males and 6,216 white males. Then,

$$\text{delinquency rate} = \frac{\text{number of delinquent acts}}{\text{number of subjects in group}} \times (1,000)$$

Table 3.3 gives the various delinquency rates for nonwhites and whites in the cohort. With these rates, we can compare the two groups regarding the extent of delinquency for total offenses, specific offense types, and various offense classifications. We see that, overall, nonwhites have a delinquency rate of 1,633.1 offenses per 1,000 subjects which is about 2.6 times higher than the white offense rate of 628.7 delinquencies per 1,000 subjects. We note also that for all of the 30 specific offenses listed, the nonwhite delinquency rate is higher than the white rate except for three offenses—drunk driving, liquor laws, and hospital cases. Some of the nonwhite rates are very much higher than those for their white counterparts, while others are similar; but the point remains that the extent of delinquency is much greater for nonwhites than whites.

Another way to examine the extent component of incidence is to focus explicitly on the delinquent individuals in the nonwhite and white subgroups and the offenses they have committed. Although we cannot examine absolute frequencies or percentages, we can try to find a single measure that is typical of the nonwhite and white delinquency data. For this measure we need a statistic that incorporates the number of delinquents and the number of delinquencies into a measure that is comparable across groups. What we need is a measure of *central tendency*, and for quantitative data like offenses, what we need is the *arithmetic mean*. For us, the mean is simply the sum of the offenses committed by a particular group divided by the number of individuals responsible for these offenses, namely, the number of delinquents. These data are given in Table 3.4.

Table 3.4 indicates that the 11,340 nonwhite delinquencies were com-

TABLE 3.4. Number of offenders and offenses and mean number of offenses for select crimes by race for males.

	Nonwhites			Whites		
	Offenders	Offenses	Mean	Offenders	Offenses	Mean
All offenses	2,903	11,340	3.91	1,412	3,908	2.77
Homicide, rape, & aggravated assault	460	601	1.31	104	116	1.12
Robbery	724	1,210	1.67	67	80	1.19
Burglary	748	1,261	1.69	242	412	1.70
Larceny & vehicle theft	1,023	1,762	1.72	351	549	1.56
UCR Index	1,803	4,834	2.68	551	1,157	2.10
UCR Non-index	2,435	6,506	2.67	1,236	2,751	2.23

UCR = Uniform Crime Reports.
Source: Tracy et al. (1985).

mitted by 2,903 nonwhite delinquents, while the 3,903 white offenses were committed by 1,412 white offenders. These numbers produce a mean for nonwhites (3.91) that is greater than the mean for whites (2.77). We could also examine the mean number of offenses for specific groups of offenses, like violent crimes, or robbery, or burglary, or larceny/vehicle theft. Because the nonwhite means for these offense groups or types are higher than those for whites, we could conclude that, on average, nonwhite delinquents commit more offenses than their white counterparts, or we could say that nonwhite delinquency is more extensive than white delinquency.

Thus, in terms of the extent of delinquency we would use different measures of incidence depending upon our particular interest. We could use delinquency rates when we are interested in comparing across subgroups of our population, regardless of the size of the delinquent subgroup. We could use a measure of central tendency like the mean when we are interested in comparing the extent of delinquency across these specific delinquent subgroups.[4]

Thus far, we have ignored our other component of incidence—the character of delinquency. In order to focus on this concept, we need to examine particular offense types so that we can compare nonwhites and whites in terms of the type of delinquency they engage in. Let us turn back to Table 3.4 to see how we can properly use the percentage measure.

At the bottom of Table 3.3 we see the various offenses grouped according to the Federal Bureau of Investigation's *Uniform Crime Report* (UCR) index classification system that we are all familiar with. The offenses are grouped first into Index versus non-Index, and then only the Index offenses are separated into the violent Index crimes and the property Index crimes. We note that while UCR Index crimes account for 42.6% of the nonwhite delinquencies, they account for a smaller percentage (29.6%) of white delinquency. Whites predominate for non-Index crimes with 70.4% compared to 57.4% for nonwhites. Similarly, when we look at Index crimes, we find that even among this more serious set of crimes, nonwhites have a more serious character of delinquency. That is, violent Index crimes compose 37.5% of Index offenses for nonwhites but only 16.9% for whites. We could also examine the delinquency rates for these offense groups, and we would still find the same kind of results showing a more serious character of nonwhite delinquency.

In Table 3.4 we approach the character of delinquency question in much the same way. Overall, nonwhites commit an average of 3.91 offenses per offender, while whites commit 2.77 offenses per offender. When we turn to the serious offense categories, we find that for all types except burglary, the mean number of offenses for nonwhites is higher than for whites. Again, this suggests that the average nonwhite delinquent is more likely to repeat the serious offenses more often than his white counterpart.

In our foregoing discussion of incidence, we have referred to Tables 3.3 and 3.4 very frequently, and we have also referred to particular statistics given in these tables over and over again. We did this for the extent and we did this for the character of delinquency. Although our discussion here was to instruct and thus required this back and forth process, think of how confusing this can be for a reader when you are presenting your results in tabular form in a paper or a report. This is an excellent situation in which to show the value of graphic presentations of our results compared to tables.

Figure 3.3 is a *bar graph* that reports the extent of delinquency in terms of various delinquency rates per 1,000 subjects by race. Visually, it is quite apparent that, regardless of the offense group examined, the rate for nonwhites is substantially higher than the rate for whites. In fact, the relative size of the bars draws to our attention the fact that the offense rate for the serious set of UCR Index offenses for nonwhites (696.2) is greater than the total delinquency rate for whites (628.7). Thus, the graph also shows us something about the character and extent of delinquency in the two groups—namely, that nonwhites have committed more serious offenses per person than whites have committed any type of delinquency.

Figure 3.4 displays in bar graph form the mean number of offenses for select offense classifications by race. These results also show in a clear-cut fashion the fact that nonwhites have a greater average delinquency for all offenses except burglary. For burglary, the rates are virtually identical (1.7 vs. 1.69). Like Figure 3.3, this bar graph assists our presentation concerning the extent of overall delinquency (the total offenses bars), and it facilitates our awareness of the delinquency character differences for serious offenses committed by the two race groups.

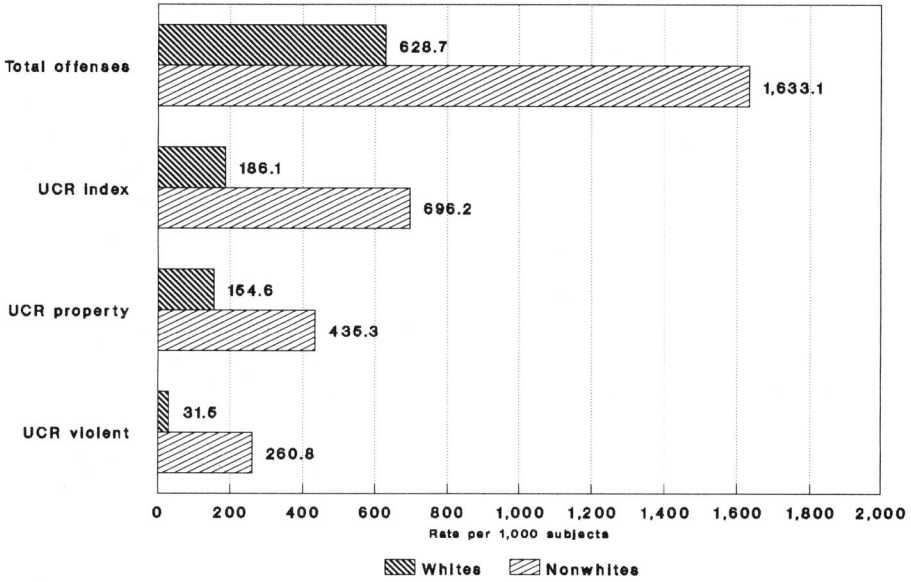

FIGURE 3.3. Delinquency rates by race for males. (Tracy et al. [1985])

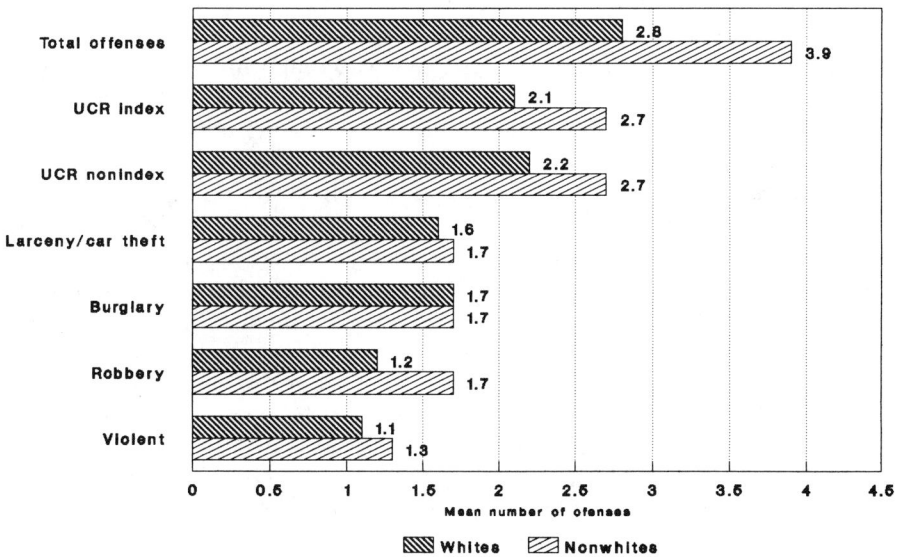

FIGURE 3.4. Mean number of select offenses by race for males. (Tracy et al. [1985])

Figure 3.5 returns to the histogram, or vertical bar chart, format and gives the percentage distribution of the various offense classifications. These results point out in a different way from the other figures the differences between nonwhites and whites concerning the type of offenses that were committed. Figure 3.5 shows that nonwhites have a greater percentage of serious offenses among their delinquencies (i.e., a higher percentage of Index crimes and violent Index crimes), while whites predominate for non-Index crimes and among property Index crimes as opposed to violent Index crimes. All of these differences are readily apparent from the relative height of the various bars in the chart.

All of the statistical results displayed in the figures are also readily available in the tables. However, the figures seem to highlight the significant differences by visually emphasizing the data in a way that is less possible with tabular data. Thus, figures are a decided advantage when the researcher is trying to describe or depict his or her results in the most convincing manner so that the reader will immediately grasp the nature and degree of relationship that is being presented.

Combining Prevalence and Incidence

Although essential in most respects, the data pertaining to the prevalence and incidence of delinquency in the birth cohort do not permit as precise a comparison as we might desire of the delinquent behavior across the two subgroups of whites and nonwhites. That is, comparing just the proportions of subjects who fall into the nondelinquent versus delinquent category ignores the fact that some delinquents commit one offense, while others commit two or three or more offenses. Thus, we need to focus on a more precise measure of delinquency status, which we shall call *delinquent subgroups*. Moreover, relying solely on the incidence of the delinquencies ignores the question of just what percentage of the delinquents are responsible for the various offenses. Thus, here, we need to focus on the incidence of delinquency across the various delinquent subgroups or categories.

In other words, what we will examine next are results that will take into account or combine both the various levels of delinquency prevalence and the frequency, or incidence, of the delinquencies committed. First, we will examine the classification of delinquents into three basic categories—one-time offenders, two-to-four-time recidivists (called nonchronic delinquents), and five-or-more-time recidivists (called chronic delinquents). Second, we will look at the number of offenses that can be attributable to these three levels, or categories, of delinquency status. With these two analyses, we will be better able to see any differences between whites and nonwhites in both the level of delinquency status and the degree of delinquency represented by these delinquent subgroups.

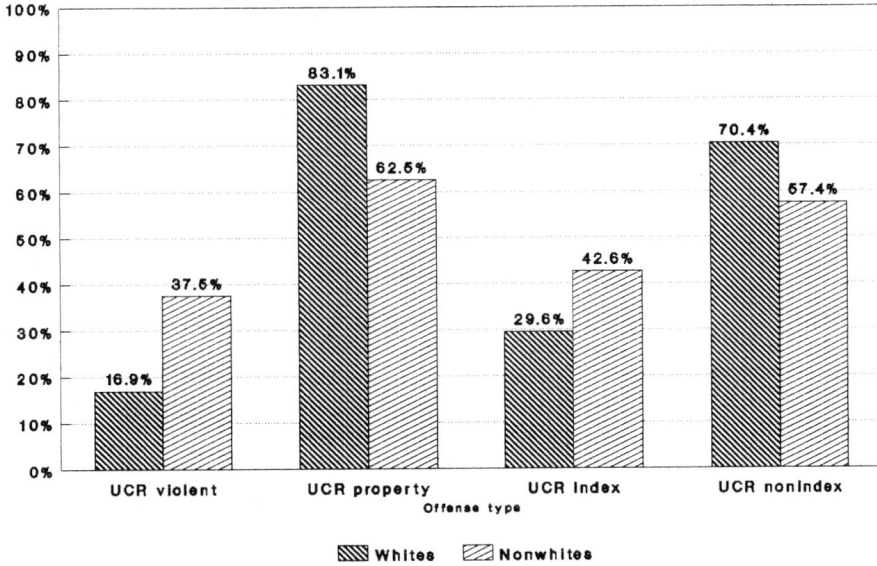

FIGURE 3.5. Percentages of offenses types by race for males. (Tracy et al. [1985])

TABLE 3.5. Number and percentage of delinquents by frequency category and race for males.

Delinquency Category		Nonwhite	White	Both
Delinquents	No.	2,903	1,412	4,315
Onetime offender	No.	1,071	733	1,804
	%	36.9	51.9	41.8
Two to four time recidivist	No.	1,059	470	1,529
	%	36.5	33.3	35.4
Five or more time recidivist	No.	773	209	982
	%	26.6	14.8	22.7
Recidivists	No.	1,832	679	2,511
Two to four time recidivist	No.	1,059	470	1,529
	%	57.8	69.2	60.9
Five or more time recidivist	No.	773	209	982
	%	42.2	30.8	39.1

Note. Percentages are column percents of the total number of delinquents and then the total number of recidivists.
Source: Tracy et al. (1985).

TABLE 3.6. Number and percentage of offenders and offenses by delinquency status and race for males.

	Nonwhites				Whites			
	Offenders		Offenses		Offenders		Offenses	
	No.	%	No.	%	No.	%	No.	%
Delinquents:	2,903	–	11,340	–	1,412	–	3,908	–
Onetime offender	1,071	36.9	1,071	9.4	733	51.9	733	18.8
Two to four time recidivist	1,059	36.5	2,944	26.0	470	33.3	1,260	32.2
Five or more time recidivist	773	26.6	7,325	64.6	209	14.8	1,953	49.0
Recidivists:	1,832	–	10,269	–	679	–	3,175	–
Two to four time recidivist	1,059	57.8	2,944	28.7	470	69.2	1,260	39.7
Five or more time recidivist	773	42.8	7,325	71.3	209	30.8	1,915	60.3

Note. Percentages are column percents of the total number of delinquents and then the total number of recidivists.
Source: Tracy et al. (1985).

Table 3.5 reports the delinquency status categories in two ways for non-whites and whites. In the top portion of the table with respect to total delinquents, we see that nonwhites are less likely than whites to be one-time offenders (37% vs. 52%), and they are more likely to be recidivists either with 2 to 4 offenses (37% vs. 33%) or with 5 or more offenses (27% vs. 15%). When we ignore the onetime offenders and use just the recidivists as the percentage base in the bottom of Table 3.5, we again see a distinct race effect. Among nonwhite recidivists, about 58% are classified as nonchronic, while about 42% are chronic. On the other hand, for whites, the percentage for nonchronic recidivists (69%) is higher and the percentage for chronic recidivists (31%) is lower than the nonwhite data.

In Table 3.5, therefore, we find that over one-quarter of nonwhite delinquents and about 4 out of 10 nonwhite recidivists may be classified as chronic delinquents by virtue of having committed five or more offenses.

The white percentages are much lower—15% of delinquents and 31% of recidivists were chronic delinquents. At this point, we need to examine the effect that this different proportion of chronic offenders has on nonwhite and white delinquency. By combining the delinquency status categories with the number of crimes committed, we see in Table 3.6 even more dramatically a chronic-offender effect for nonwhites.

Table 3.6 shows that the 773 nonwhite chronics account for 26.6% of the nonwhite delinquents, but more important, this group of chronic recidivists was responsible for 7,325 offenses, or about 65% of all the delinquencies committed by nonwhites. For whites, the 209 chronic delinquents make up 14.8% of all the delinquents and were responsible for 1,953 offenses, or 49% of all the white delinquency in the cohort. Thus, for both groups, the chronic delinquent represents the smallest group of delinquents but a group that was responsible for the greatest share of delinquency. This effect is most pronounced for nonwhites.

Figure 3.6 is a horizontal bar chart that displays the delinquent subgroup and offense data by race. The chart shows quite effectively the tabular results discussed above. In the top segment of the chart we note that non-white chronic delinquents represent 26.6% of the delinquents, but this chronic subgroup committed 64.6% of all the nonwhite delinquency. The white chronic subgroup represents a smaller percentage (14.8%), and con-

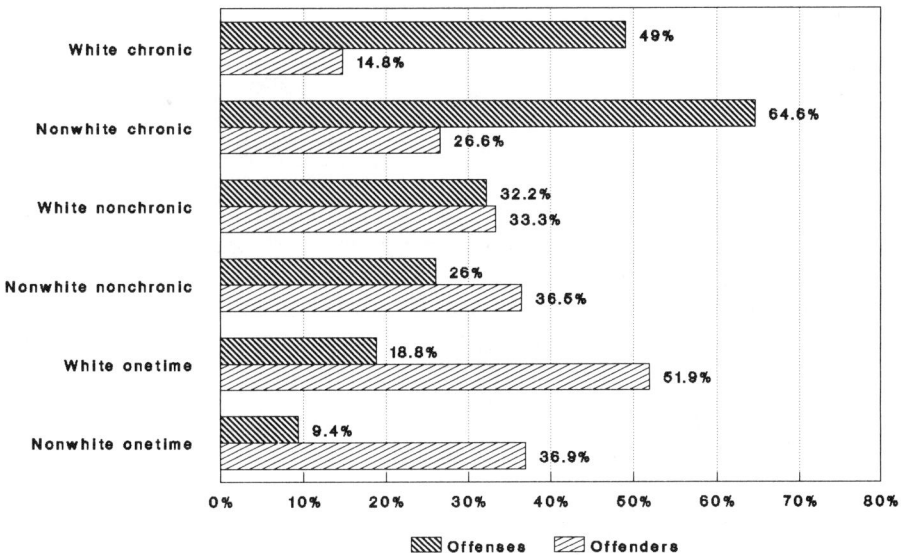

FIGURE 3.6. Percentage of offenders and offenses by race for males. (Tracy et al. [1985])

sequently, the share of white delinquency committed by the chronic subgroup (49%) is less than for nonwhites.

Turning to the other two subgroups, in the middle of the chart we see that nonchronic recidivism is characteristic of about one-third of the delinquents for both nonwhites (37%) and whites (33%) with a correspondingly close share of the offenses—26% for nonwhites and 32% for whites. In the bottom part of the chart we observe the clear result that more than half of the white delinquents (51.9%) were one-time offenders whose delinquency accounts for only 18.8% of the total, while about 37% of nonwhite delinquents committed only one delinquency, which amounts to only a 9.4% share of the total nonwhite crimes.

In this section we have seen, therefore, that using either prevalence or incidence separately to describe and compare the relative delinquency committed by whites and nonwhites does not portray the complete picture. Instead, we classified prevalence into three basic levels—onetime delinquents, nonchronic recidivists, and chronic recidivists—and examined the overall incidence data belonging to these delinquent subgroups. As before, we used simple percentages to reveal whether whites and nonwhites differ (a) in the distribution of delinquent subgroups and (b) in the share of overall delinquency committed by these subgroups. We used tables and a figure to display the fact that a chronic delinquent effect was evident in the data and that this effect was more pronounced for nonwhites than whites.

Age and Delinquency

Up to now, we have been analyzing data pertaining to the complete juvenile delinquency career. We have investigated overall prevalence, the extent and character (or severity) components of offense incidence, and a combination of prevalence and incidence. We have explored these topics for the complete juvenile career, regardless of the age at which the delinquency status began. Thus, we have been exclusively concerned with what might be called "career parameters." We have not looked at all at the delinquency data over time to investigate possible trends.

There is one last topic, therefore, that we should pursue. This topic concerns the natural relationship between age-at-onset and delinquency. Age-at-onset is an extremely important topic in relation to delinquency, because the point at which an offender starts his or her delinquency career forever establishes or fixes his or her career length owing to the fact that there is a statutory upper age boundary for delinquency in all states. Because the period at risk is thus set, the extent of career delinquency or even the character and severity of delinquency may be affected by an offender's age-at-onset. Thus, the basic question concerns whether offenders who begin committing delinquency early accumulate more offenses and more serious offenses than offenders who begin later in their juvenile years.

TABLE 3.7. Number and percentage of offenders and number and percentage of offenses by age-at-onset and race and males.

	Nonwhites				Whites			
Age-at-Onset	Offenders		Offenses		Offenders		Offenses	
	Number	%	Number	%	Number	%	Number	%
7	63	2.2	414	3.7	30	2.1	170	4.4
8	69	2.4	597	5.3	23	1.6	136	3.5
9	82	2.8	614	5.4	23	1.6	128	3.3
10	93	3.2	622	5.5	19	1.3	132	3.4
11	128	4.4	822	7.2	51	3.6	323	8.3
12	332	11.4	2,013	17.8	111	7.9	526	13.5
13	450	15.5	2,064	18.2	149	10.6	466	11.9
14	455	15.7	1,701	15.0	203	14.4	621	15.9
15	484	16.8	1,269	11.2	293	20.8	653	16.7
16	455	15.7	858	7.6	275	19.5	463	11.8
17	292	10.1	366	3.2	235	16.6	290	7.4
All	2,903	100.0	11,340	100.0	1,412	100.0	3,908	100.0

Note. Percentages are column percents and may not sum to 100.0% due to rounding error.
Source: Tracy et al. (1985).

An examination of delinquency data by age will allow us not only to explore these career trends in delinquency as our cohort ages toward adulthood (i.e., age 18 in Pennsylvania) but also to introduce a few different statistical measures, and a new kind of chart that are very useful for our purposes. We will begin our examination of age and delinquency by turning to Table 3.7.

Table 3.7 is the familiar tabular layout which contains separately by race (a) the number and percentage of offenders who began delinquency at ages from as early as 7 to a maximum of age 17 and (b) the number and percentage of career offenses accumulated by these offenders. The issue at hand is whether these types of data, and this particular form of presentation, are the most effective for our present purposes to analyze trends in delinquency over time. The answer, of course, is that these particular tabular data are not sufficient; we need some additional measures. Moreover, we shall also see below that figures are better than tables in presenting data that form trends over time.

Table 3.7 provides, for each age-at-onset category (ages 7 through 17), the number and percentage of offenders and offenses by race. These data thus allow us to examine the onset of delinquency year by year and the incidence of crime associated with the offenders who begin in a particular year. We can see that the data seem to indicate a trend of increasing delinquency with age for both races. The year with the greatest frequency of offenders, also known as the *mode*,[5] is age 15 for both nonwhites and whites. After age 15, the onset of delinquency declines. Table 3.7 also

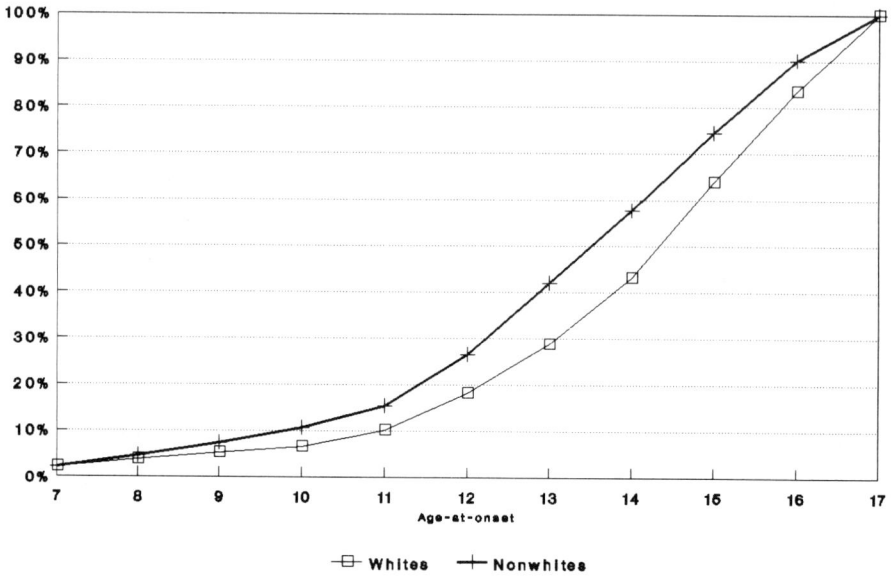

FIGURE 3.7. Cumulative percentage of offenders by age-at-onset and race for males.
(Tracy et al. [1985])

shows us that the onset group that committed the most offenses for nonwhites was age 13, while for whites the most delinquent group was offenders who started at age 15.

It should be clear that the standard descriptive data reported in Table 3.7
are not very suitable for demonstrating the trends in delinquency by age.
The year by year frequencies and percentages must be compared one by
one for nonwhites and whites to reveal differences. What we need is a
measure that will allow us to compare the relative race differences in the
ages at which offenders start their delinquency careers, regardless of the
fact that the pool of offenders is greater for nonwhites than for whites.
What we also need is a way to report these data so that the underlying
trend by age will be readily discernible.

Figure 3.7 utilizes such a measure, the *cumulative percentage*, and reports the data in a type of graph known as a *line chart*. The cumulative
percentage is a straightforward measure that represents the percentage of
cases that fall at a particular score or lower. Just like the simple percentage, the cumulative percentage standardizes frequency distributions
of unequal size.

In our case the cumulative percentage pertains to the percentage of cases
that fall at a particular age-at-onset or younger. By using the cumulative
percentage, we can compare the percentage of delinquents for nonwhites
and whites that have already entered the delinquency status at any particu-

Rate per 1,000 subjects

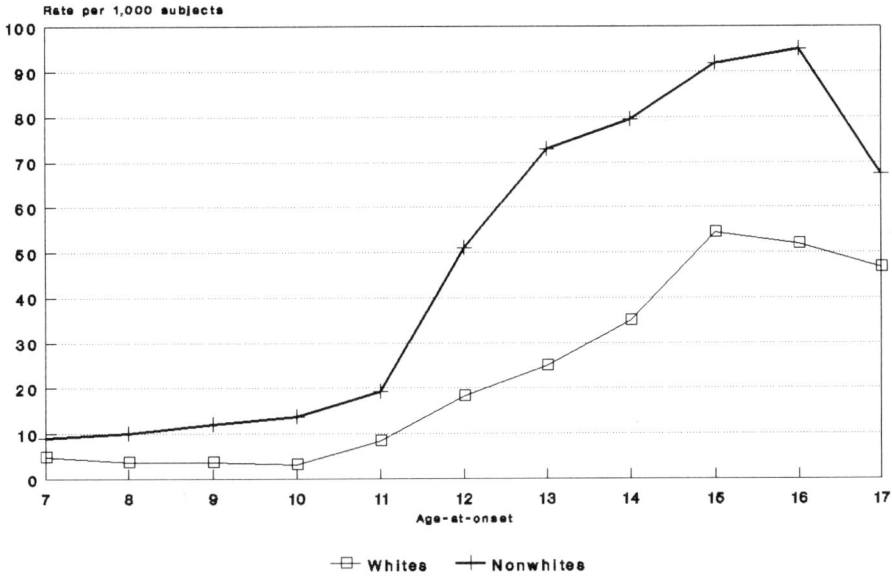

FIGURE 3.8. Offender rate by age-at-onset and race for males. (Tracy et al. [1985])

lar age. We have reported the results in a line chart, with the ages-at-onset on the "x," or horizontal, axis and the cumulative percentages on the "y," or vertical, axis. With this line chart, we can effectively display the shape or trend in the relationship with age.

Thus, Figure 3.7 shows that nonwhites and whites begin the onset of delinquency with virtually the same origin, about 2% at age 7. From age 8 through age 16, the nonwhite percentage is higher than that for whites at every age, and it is not until the final year of delinquency, age 17, that nonwhites and whites converge at 100%. The chart further shows that the cumulative onset of delinquency is gradual from ages 7 through 11, and then cumulative onset increases more sharply and continues to age 17.

If we were interested in any of the specific onset percentages for non-whites and whites, we could use the chart easily. For example, suppose we wanted to know that age at which 50% of the delinquents had begun their offenses. We would find the 50% increment on the "y" axis and then visualize a straight line across that intersects the two curves. For non-whites, we would find that 50% of the delinquents are accounted for at about age 13.25, while for whites, 50% occurs at about age 14.25.

In Figure 3.8 we turn to another line chart, but instead of the cumulative percentage, this chart is a graph of age-at-onset and the offender rates[6] for nonwhites and whites. We have discussed previously, with respect to offense incidence, that raw frequencies are not suitable when the compari-

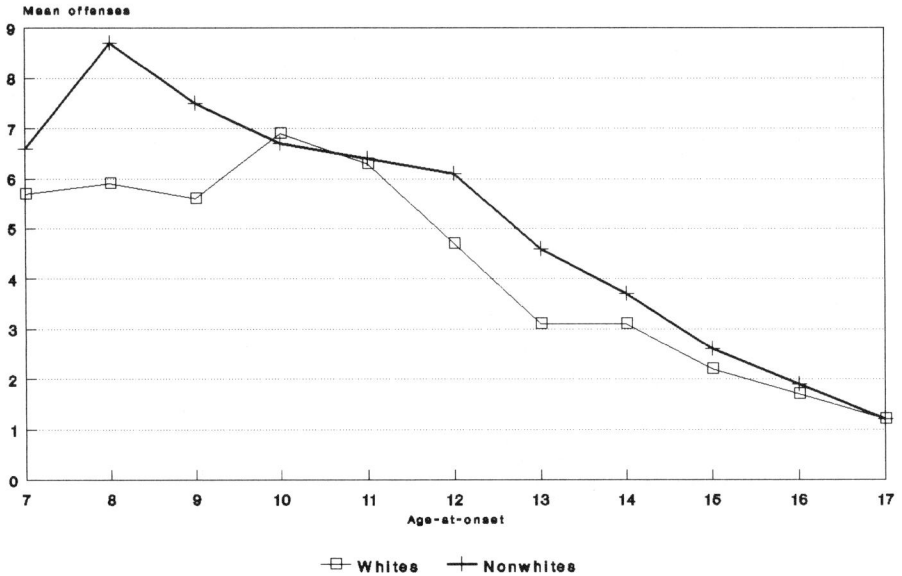

FIGURE 3.9. Mean number of offenses by age-at-onset and race for males. (Tracy et al. [1985])

son groups are of unequal size. By computing an offender rate, we again standardize the nonwhite and white frequency distributions as we did with the offense data.

Figure 3.8, through the use of an offender rate displayed in a line chart, is an effective way to demonstrate that the nonwhite offender rate is higher at all onset ages than the white rate. Further, the figure indicates quite well the age trend—that the nonwhite rate jumps sharply between ages 11 and 13 and continues to rise until age 16. The white rates are flat from ages 7 through 10 and then increase, but less sharply than nonwhites, between ages 11 and 15. It is unmistakable, therefore, from Figure 3.8, that the rate of nonwhite delinquency is higher than that for whites and shows a sharp increase with age.

We have thus far examined the ways that using either the cumulative onset percentage or age-based offender rates are effective in measuring the relationship over time between the various start points and delinquency. However, we still must examine how the ages-at-onset may be related to career offense accumulation. For this association we turn to Figure 3.9, which is the final chart that we will utilize in this chapter.

Figure 3.9 displays the relationship between the ages-at-onset and the mean or average number of career offenses. We can clearly see from the direction of the curves that age-at-onset is negatively related to delinquency for both races. That is, Figure 3.9 indicates that the earlier the age at which a delinquent begins, the greater the number of offenses that he will accumulate throughout his delinquency period. The decline in mean number of offenses as age increases is steep, thus suggesting that period at risk is significantly related to offense accumulation. This is not to say that offenders who begin their careers late in their juvenile years, say 14 or 15, will always commit fewer offenses than early starters. Rather, the mean tells us that, on average, an early starter will have a greater opportunity to accumulate offenses, and probably, this increased time to be delinquent will produce a higher number of offenses.

Summary

In this chapter we have examined two of the most basic descriptive concepts in criminal justice research—prevalence and incidence. We have explored the various descriptive measures that are necessary to describe properly the distribution of these concepts as we compare across the subgroups in our sample. We have also demonstrated that tables and graphs are not always interchangeable methods of presenting results. In some instances, a tabular presentation is better, while in other cases, a figure or chart is actually preferable. We may summarize our efforts as follows.

First, we have seen that prevalence in criminal justice research is a measure that pertains to the subgroup in a population or study sample that must be classified as delinquent or criminal by virtue of an arrest or conviction record or some other measurement of criminality. Thus, initially, prevalence is a qualitative variable that classifies subjects into the status of offender versus nonoffender.

Second, we have also learned that incidence pertains to a measurement of the offenses committed or the arrests or convictions recorded for the delinquent or criminal subgroup. Further, it was pointed out that the incidence concept subsumes two components—the extent of offenses and the character or seriousness of the offenses. Incidence, therefore, unlike prevalence, is primarily a quantitative concept that pertains to the frequency of offenses committed by offenders. in other words, incidence is the number of times that each subject may be classified as delinquent or criminal.

Third, we have further seen that, because the prevalence concept in criminal justice does not necessarily refer to only a dichotomous attribute of offender versus nonoffender, we must incorporate the concepts of prevalence and incidence into a more definitive measure that we called delinquent subgroups. The delinquent subgroup measure is a classification of offenders into frequency levels such as onetime, nonchronic recidivist, and chronic recidivist. By using a measure such as the delinquent subgroups, we are able to differentiate the presence of the high-rate offender across various subgroups of our study sample.

Throughout our discussions of statistical measures, we have emphasized the fact that it is not appropriate to just compare raw numbers or frequencies. Because the size of subgroups can be expected to differ in a study sample, the frequency distributions must be standardized so that the statistics will be comparable. We thus showed that the percentage, the rate, and the mean are simple descriptive measures that are easily computed and that allow the researcher to compare prevalence or incidence across subgroups such as males versus females or whites versus nonwhites.

Finally, we have demonstrated that both tables and figures have a place in the presentation of results. Tables are effective when more than one statistical measure is being reported or when sets of exact scores should be given. On the other hand, figures, such as histograms and bar charts, are very effective for displaying descriptive measures when the interest is in highlighting particular relationships, especially comparative differences across groups. Line charts are essential in depicting data trends over time.

In conclusion, one final cautionary note is necessary. There is a tendency in social science research today, especially with the availability of microcomputers and statistical software packages, to apply very sophisticated statistical models and multivariate analytical procedures to research data. In many instances, these highly advanced procedures are desirable, if not absolutely necessary. Despite this tendency, there is no substitute for a thorough descriptive analysis of one's data accompanied by a well-conceived presentation of tables and figures. The most simple analyses, effectively displayed, are often the most convincing and communicative to the reader.

Endnotes

1. For a complete discussion of this research project and the results, see Tracy, Wolfgang, and Figlio (1985, forthcoming) for the juvenile delinquency component, and see Tracy, Wolfgang, and Figlio (1989) for the adult offense component.

2. For the vast majority of the analyses to be presented, we will concentrate on the males in the cohort. There are many more male offenders and offenses for our analyses, and by restricting the presentation to a single gender group, the discussion will be much less confusing than going back and forth between males and females.

3. Note that the table also gives the number and percentage of nondelinquents. Since we are working with dichotomous measures (e.g., males vs. females or delinquents vs. nondelinquents), the frequencies across a row always add up to the total number of cases.

4. If we were going to test the statistical significance of the difference in means, in addition to comparing the means across subgroups, we would also have to examine the *standard deviation* or the *variance* of these data. However, these statistical measures are beyond the scope of this chapter. The reader should consult a statistics text for further information.

5. The *mode* is a measure of central tendency like the *mean* and the *median*. The mode refers to the most common, or frequent, value in a distribution. The median refers to the middlemost value in a distribution, the particular point at which there are fifty% of the cases above and below.

6. The offender rate is the number of offenders in each age-at-onset category per 1,000 cohort members. This is an actual rate of onset, because anyone that has started delinquency prior to a specific age is not counted in the eligible cohort population for any subsequent rate. The eligible population decreases with age.

References

Tracy, P.E., Wolfgang, M.E., & Figlio, R.M. (1985). *Delinquency in two birth cohorts*. Washington, DC: U.S. Government Printing Office.

Tracy, P.E., Wolfgang, M.E., & Figlio, R.M. (1989). *Patterns of Delinquency and Crime in the 1958 Philadelphia Birth Cohort*. Washington, DC: U.S. Government Printing Office, forthcoming.

Tracy, P.E., Wolfgang, M.E., & Figlio, R.M. (In Press). *Delinquency careers in two birth cohorts*. New York: Plenum Press, Inc.

4
Ethical Obligations and Social Research

SANDRA WEXLER*

Since the times of our earliest ancestors, people have tried to understand the world in which they live. While we no longer seek explanations from gods, as did our Athenian relatives, or metaphysics, as did our alchemist forefathers, our curiosity about and desire to gain mastery over our world remains strong. In contemporary society, research methods provide us with the principles and techniques to generate knowledge. Social science research allows us to go beyond our own experiences and gain insight into those different from ourselves as well as the factors that shape beliefs and behavior.

This chapter explores a particular aspect of the research enterprise: the ethical obligations of social science research and the methodological consequences of research ethics.[1] Whereas science is characterized as the pursuit of knowledge, ethical obligations can be seen as imposing constraints on this pursuit. As Yelaja (1982, p. 312) suggests: "When science takes man as its subject, tensions arise between two values basic to Western society: freedom of scientific inquiry and protection of individual inviolability."

Research that focuses on issues germane to criminologists often transverses areas of life deemed problematic, deviant, private, or embarrassing. The individuals or groups studied more often than not tend to be socially and/or economically disadvantaged, physically and/or psychologically impaired, or involved in some form of undesirable behavior. Of central interest, therefore, are those ethical considerations that emerge when we study such "sensitive" topics.

Yet there is no single or simple criterion for determining if a topic is sensitive. What constitutes a sensitive topic must be understood within a historical and cultural context. Almost all embody some form of stigma (Becker, 1970), although the degree of stigma associated with a forbidden

---

*I want to thank Kimberly Kempf, University of Missouri-St. Louis, and Lorraine Midanik, University of California, Berkeley, for their helpful comments on earlier drafts of this chapter.

78

act or idea is temporally bound. Thus, the "sensitivity" of a topic can be understood as a relativistic property.

Some sensitive topics involve law violating; some reflect acts or feelings that would be disapproved of or embarrassing if known. These may be considered as the "too personal" issues (e.g., terminal illness, heterosexual behavior, attempted suicide), while the former constitute those of "deviance" (e.g., criminality, drug use). And some topics manifest both of these traits (e.g., homosexuality, incest).

Typically, behaviors that are deemed deviant are construed as sensitive subjects for investigation (Becker, 1970). And as Becker (1973, p. 168) indicates: "It is not easy to study deviants." Drug use, adult or juvenile criminality, gambling, prostitution, and sexual "misbehavior" are issues that by virtue of their illegality are problematic to study (Becker, 1970, p. 168).

In the United States, sociocultural norms regarding the individual, privacy, and the distinction between public and private spheres also delimit appropriate, and conversely inappropriate, study topics. For example, questions about income or religion may be viewed as "threatening" (i.e., embarrassing, uncomfortable, or intrusive), and research texts (see, for example, Babbie, 1986; Kidder & Judd, 1986) offer a variety of suggestions for wording and locating such items. Issues involving race or ethnicity too may be deemed as sensitive depending upon the context. Similarly, sexual behaviors frequently are considered to be a private matter. While it is perhaps not as shocking to discuss these behaviors as it was when the Kinsey team (1948, 1953) initially undertook their exploration of sexual interactions in the late 1940s, they remain a sensitive topic for many (Pomeroy, 1966).

The family is thought to be one of the most personal and private institutions in our society (Gelles, 1978; Lasch, 1977). While social norms and public policies, such as child abuse reporting statutes, prescribe certain boundaries for familial interactions, family life in general occurs "behind closed doors" (Straus, Gelles & Steinmetz, 1980). As studies of family life move into areas deemed private (e.g., sexual relations) and/or norm violating (e.g., marital rape or violence), the sensitivity of investigation increases.

Ethical considerations represent one of the major dilemmas to be resolved in the study of sensitive issues. While ethical obligations are an important aspect of any social science inquiry, they hold particular sailence for criminologists because of the sensitivity of the topics under investigation. The vulnerability of those studied, as well as the potential vulnerability of those conducting such studies, calls for an understanding of the nuances and complexities of the ethical criteria of social research.

Moreover, criminological research does not just explore areas of social life deemed deviant but often does so in order to "do someting," whether that be informing policies or programs or attempting to predict future behavior. The applied nature of much of contemporary criminological research further confounds these ethical considerations. Kimmel (1988) argues that applied studies bring to the forefront concerns with norms and values because the information generated is used to change aspects of the social environment through the implementation of prevention, intervention, or rehabilitation strategies. Wolfgang (1982) highlights some of the ethical issues confronted by criminologists who are called upon to testify before governmental decision-making bodies and illustrates these points by citing his own experience presenting social science data at a federal court hearing. Given the possible uses to which applied research findings may be put, special care needs to be taken to ensure not just the methodological accuracy of the data obtained but their ethical integrity as well.

During the past 30 years, there has been a proliferation of professional and governmental codes of ethics for research. While these codifications differ in terms of their specificity and requirements, all reflects an interweaving of two underlying philosophical orientations. Attempts to balance these dual philosophical perspectives can be observed in various articulations of research ethics (Babbie, 1986; Gillespie, 1987; Kidder & Judd, 1986; Sherman, 1982; Yelaja, 1982).

On one hand, Kantian notions about the inviolability of the individual argue for the integrity and rights of man. According to this deontological perspective, researchers should treat participants as ends in themselves rather than as means (e.g., informational sources) to an end (Kimmel, 1988). Requirements of informed, voluntary participation are seen as a minimal prerequisite to ensure and protect this inviolability.

In contrast to Kantian preoccupations with the rights of the individual, utilitarian philosophy leads to an emphasis on the potential outcomes or "payoffs" of research. Within this framework, the end justifies the means. While treating research subjects solely as means to some greater end is not tenable, this position is given contemporary expression in risk/benefit assessment (Gillespie, 1987).

Ethical Obligations of Social Research

Attention to the ethical component of the research enterprise is a relatively recent historical development. Until well into this century, it appears, ethical issues were encapsulated within more general concerns for the ethos of the scientific method, or what Merton (1982) calls the four norms of science: universalism, communality, disinterestedness, and organized skepticism. That is, the practice of good science was seen as equivalent to ethical science.

Revelations after World War II of "criminal medical experiments . . . conducted as an integral part of the total war effort" (The Nuremberg Code, 1949, p. 181) sharply contradicted professional conceptions of the ethos of science and jolted popular beliefs in the altruistic, benign, and self-regulatory abilities of the professions involved in research with humans. The horrors of the Nazi medical experiments, which resulted in their classification as war crimes and crimes against humanity, precipitated formulation of one of the earliest codifications of ethical standards for research.

The Nuremberg Code set forth 10 principles for the permissible use of humans in medical experimentation. It established the concept of "voluntary consent" and offered an exposition of this principle as including the following: the legal capacity to give consent; the exercise of participant free choice; and the need to provide information sufficient to allow an "enlightened decision" by a potential participant (The Nuremberg Code, 1949, pp. 181–182). While concerned specifically with the ethical obligations of medical researchers, the Nuremberg Code has provided a model for developing and assessing ethical practices in the social and behavioral sciences.

Beginning in the late 1960s, publicity about research endeavors that harmed, or potentially harmed, participants spurred discussions about ethical issues in social science research. Reports about undertakings such as Project Camelot (Horowitz, 1967), Milgram's (1969) investigation of obedience to authority, and Humphreys's (1975) exploration of homosexuality touched off wide-ranging debates about the role of social science research in contemporary society and the potential intrusiveness and harmfulness of the methodologies employed in such efforts.

Social science research, however, was not the only form of investigation to capture public attention during this period. In 1972, newspaper accounts of the Tuskegee syphilis study, a project begun 30 years earlier under the auspice of the U.S. Public Health Service to document the effects of untreated tertiary syphilis among 400 poor, Black sharecroppers, gave rise to an outpouring of public indignation and outrage (Jones, 1981). The study, which purposefully withheld medical treatment, was compared by some to the medical experiments performed by the Nazis, and the negative publicity generated led to its termination.

During the same period, reports about the misuse of prisoners in medical experiments also surfaced. Prisoners at facilities across the nation were used for a wide variety of experimental purposes—for testing everything from the effects of radiation exposure, to the transmissibility of cancer cells, to new pharmaceuticals, to hand lotions and band-aids (Mills & Morris, 1974). In Maryland, for instance, inmates at the Maryland House of Corrections were routinely recruited to volunteer for infectious-disease experiments. In the first of its kind, a class action suit on behalf of the prisoners was filed in 1974 claiming that their participation in the experiments was not based on voluntary consent (Gilchrist, 1974).

Political events such as the Watergate break-in also focused public attention on issues of individual privacy and autonomy (Kimmel, 1988). Scandals in the political arena coupled with the exposure of several ethically questionable research studies gave rise to an environment of suspicion and disbelief. Within this context, concern mounted that the ability to conduct investigation might be severely constrained. To mitigate increasing public skepticism about biomedical and social science research, ethical codes were promulgated by numerous professional and governmental agencies.

According to Gillespie (1987), professional codes (see, for example, American Anthropological Association, 1971; American Psychological Association, 1981; American Sociological Association, 1981; National Association of Social Workers, 1979) have two characteristics that distinguish them from governmental regulations. First, they are inductively formulated on the basis of members' research experiences and, therefore, tend to be abstract. Second, they tend to emphasize individual responsibility for ensuring ethical practices. With respect to this second characteristic, it is interesting to note that penalties for violation often are not specified in professional codes; when indicated, expulsion from the professional organization typically is the remedy prescribed. Thus, it is proposed that such codes "seem to be a necessary but not sufficient condition of professional self-regulation" (Gillespie, 1987, p. 509).

In contrast to professional codes, ethical regulations developed by governmental entities provide explicit rules for the conduct of inquiry. Designed to protect the society and its members, governmental codes offer steps to the followed rather than guidelines for practice. Furthermore, a governmental agency, through its role as research funding agent, can exert its authority to ensure that ethical standards are met.[2]

The National Research Service Award Act (Public Law [PL] 93-348), signed into law in 1974, created the National Commission for the Protection of Human Subjects of Biomedical and Behavioral Research, which was charged in part with the development of ethical principles for research. Culminating a 4-year study of these issues, the Commission released the Belmont Report in September 1978 (*Belmont Report*, 1979). The Belmont Report, while not supplying specific rules, identifies three ethical for research—respect for persons, beneficence, and justice—and details their applications through procedures for informed consent, risk/benefit assessment, and subject selection.[3]

The ethical guidelines suggested by the *Belmont Report* were more specifically detailed in the 1980 regulations adopted by the U.S. Department of Health and Human Services (DHHS, formerly the Department of Health, Education, and Welfare), which have subsequently served as a model for federal and state departments (Gillespie, 1987). The DHHS regulations (*Code of Federal Regulations*, Title 45, Part 46, 1987 ed. [45 *CFR* 46]) make clear that no form of research involving humans in exempt simply on the basis of professional or sponsoring discipline. The regulations do exempt certain forms of inquiry, such as educational testing or the use of secondary or public data. Studies involving surveys, interviews, or observations of public behavior also are exempt unless (a) the information can be linked to and/or used to identify participants; (b) the information, if it became known, could place participants in legal or financial jeopardy or damage their work prospects; or (c) "the research deals with sensitive aspects of the subject's own behavior such as illegal conduct, drug use, sexual behavior, or use of alcohol" (45 *CFR* 46.101, p. 133, 1987).

The DHHS regulations offer explicit definitions and requirements. For example, section 46.116 details eight basic elements of informed consent, six additional elements, and six further requirements for local assurance. Methods of documenting informed consent are described in similar detail in section 46.117. Special requirements too are established for studies involving certain vulnerable populations, i.e., pregnant women, fetuses, prisoners, and children. Subpart C of the regulations (sections 46.301–46.306) governs all agency-sponsored behavioral and biomedical research involving prisoners and stipulates the types of investigation permitted. The need to afford such additional protection flows from the fact that "prisoners may be under constraints because of their incarceration which could affect their ability to make a truly voluntary and uncoerced decision whether or not to participate as subjects in research (45 *CFR* 46.302, p. 146, 1987). Similarly, Subpart D (sections 46.401–46.409) imposes additional rules regarding the use of children in research and establishes the need to acquire both parental consent and the child's positive assent.

In addition, the DHHS regulations specify the responsibilities of institutional review boards (IRBs), which resulted from PL 93-348 (National Research Service Award Act, 1974). As stipulated by the legislation, entities that conduct or sponsor research involving humans and seek DHHS funding must establish an IRB to assure that ethical standards and protocols are satisfactorily carried out. Further requirements regarding IRB composition and duties are imposed for studies involving prisoners (45 *CFR* 46.304–46.305). Thus, for example, at least one member of the IRB must be a prisoner or a prisoner representative, and the majority of those on the IRB should not be affiliated with the correctional institution involved in the research.

Gillespie (1987) suggests that the codification of ethical principles for research serves to delineate investigators' obligations. Researchers, he indicates, have responsibilities to participants in their studies, colleagues and professional audiences, and "sponsoring agencies, the public at large, or the society" (Gillespie, 1987, p. 503). Within each of these domains is the charge to minimize potential risks that may accrue through the conduct of investigation. Yet, although researchers have ethical responsibilities to all three sectors, attention and discussion have centered primarily on the ethics of human participation in research.[4] The remainder of this section addresses researchers' ethical obligations of informed, voluntary consent, anonymity and confidentiality, and risk/benefit assessment.[5]

Informed, Voluntary Consent

The phrase *informed, voluntary consent* implies several constituent elements. The researcher is obligated to explain the study, including possible risks, to potential participants in a manner that they can comprehend. The prospective participants must be capable of giving their authorization and must be allowed to make their own decisions in an environment that is free from explicit or implicit coercion. Unless exempt, the researcher must obtain written consent from prospective participants. The individuals also must understand that they have the right to withdraw consent to any point without jeopardy.

Although seemingly straightforward, these elements are fraught with controversial and problematic nuances. First, for instance, is the question of disclosure, i.e., how the study is explained. A full and thorough description of the purposes and nature of the research, it is believed, might bias subsequent responses. In fact, Macklin (cited in Kinard, 1985, p. 304) argues that "brutally frank disclosure" of selection criteria in investigations of sensitive issues might itself be unethical.

Partial or generalized disclosure frequently is employed. The true intent of the investigation is withheld, and a legitimate alternative or modified explanation of the study is offered. An investigation of child abuse may be couched as a study of emotional development (Kinard, 1985). In their study of family violence, Straus et al. (1980) report that the Conflict Tactics Scales were "presented in the context of disagreements and conflicts between members of the family and the ways in which such conflicts are resolved" (p. 257). In the Haney, Banks, and Zimbardo (1973) investigation of behavior in a simulated prison, volunteer "guards" were told that the intent of the study was to assess "prisoners" reactions, although the researchers were actually interested in documenting the behavior of both groups.

Similarly, Russell's (1986) initial contact letters indicated that her survey was about women's experiences of crime, rather than rape and sexual abuse. Interestingly, she reports that this designation was selected in order to "minimize the possibility that some husbands, fathers, and boyfriends might object on behalf of a potential respondent" (Russell, 1986, p. 26). Generalized disclosure, in this instance, appears to have been adopted as a way to protect prospective participants from the possible negative reactions of their significant others rather than as a strategy to mitigate participation refusals.

In contrast, Finkelhor (1979) provided a fairly explicit description of his study, which investigated child sexual abuse experiences among college students at six New England campuses. In the cover letter accompanying his questionnaire, the research was typified as a study of "the family and sexual behavior" and included an acknowledgment that some of the questions might be "personally embarrassing or painful" (Finkelhor, 1979,

p. 157). Potential participants also were informed that "some of the things you may be reporting in the questionnaire may be against the law" (Finkelhor, 1979, p. 157)

Regardless of how specifically the study is described, the researcher is obligated to present the information in a manner that is understandable to prospective participants. For consent to be informed, potential participants must comprehend what they are authorizing. Yet just as the argot of a specific group may seem like a new language to an investigator, the language of research well may be foreign to those from whom consent is being elicited. The need to ensure comprehension is particularly critical in studies involving vulnerable and/or disadvantaged individuals (i.e., racial or ethnic minorities, those with impairments or disabilities, the elderly, youth, or those incarcerated).

Not just the purpose but also the nature of the study needs to be described, and partial or generalized disclosure again may be employed to mask the true course of the study. The line between partial or generalized disclosure and actual deception, however, is fine. Milgram's (1969) study of obedience to authority, for example, has been criticized in part because participants were deceived as to the nature of the study and hence were placed at risk of psychological harm (Babbie, 1986). Binder and Geis (1983) suggest that Haney et al. (1973) deceived the volunteer participants by not accurately describing the purpose of their simulated prison study. Some argue (Hilbert, 1980; Kinard, 1985; Whyte, 1979), however, that deception may be appropriate in situations where there are no other ways of eliciting critical information and where possible harm is not involved. Others (Casal, 1980; Erikson, 1968) suggest that deceptive practices corrupt not only the ethics of the research undertaking but the methods and findings as well.

Certain forms of research also may contribute further complexities to the requirements of informed consent. Obtaining informed consent prior to the initiation of investigation may be particularly problematic in field studies or those using participant–observation methods. Wax (1980) describes the problems of trying to impose survey research models of informed consent procedures on fieldwork. He argues that in fieldwork "consent becomes a negotiated and lengthy process—of mutual learning and reciprocal exchanges—rather than a once-and-for-all event" (Wax, 1980, p. 275).

Covert participant–observation presents special ethical dilemmas within the tradition of field research. In these efforts, the investigator does not identify her- or himself as a researcher, and those under study are not aware of their participation (Casal, 1980; Kidder & Judd, 1986). Casal (1980) suggests that covert participant–observation violates the autonomy of individuals, changes the research interaction, and as a consequence, distorts the data obtained. She concludes that covert fieldwork "is unsound methodologically as well as morally" (Casal, 1980, p. 36). In contrast, Hilbert (1980), who conducted a covert participant-observation study of a teacher education program, argues that ethical objections to the method and the secrecy it entails are misplaced and should focus instead on whether or not individuals are hurt.

Qualitative studies of family life also give rise to unique ethical problems (LaRossa, Bennett, & Gelles, 1981). Because of the pervasiveness of family life, a wide range of topics, often unrelated to the initial thrust of the inquiry, may be discussed during an interview. The possibility of disclosing more than intended, or more than consent was obtained for, may be exacerbated by a number of factors. In addition to the inequality in power that generally exists between researcher and participant (Casal, 1980; LaRossa et al., 1981; Yelaja, 1982), the use of the participants' home as the research setting may introduce a degree of informality into the interaction that "may lull some families into disclosing more about themselves than they had originally planned" (LaRossa et al., 1981). In interviews involving multiple family members, no single individual can control what is said, and hence, more may be revealed than was intended. Finally, LaRossa et al. (1981) report that perceived parallels between qualitative family interviewing and therapeutic interactions create "role ambiguities" that may foster the disclosure of intimate details that otherwise would not mentioned (p. 308).

A second major facet of informed consent is that it is voluntarily given by an individual capable of making such a decision. The fact that certain populations (e.g., pregnant women, children, inmates) may be especially vulnerable to external pressures is recognized by the DHHS regulations. One characterization of the use of prisoners as research subjects illustrates both the rationale for their selection and the forces operating to constrain their free decision making:

Prisoners make splendid laboratory animals. Healthy, relatively free of alcohol and drugs, with regulated diets, they are captives, unlikely to wander off and be lost to both treatment and control groups, and they are under sufficient pressure of adversity to "volunteer." (Mills and Morris, 1974, p. 60)

If informed consent is to be voluntarily obtained, it must be elicited in an environment free of implicit or explicit coercion. Inducements that link participation to receipt of service, for instance, impinge upon the individual's right to free choice. Similarly, suggestions that benefits may be modified or withheld also contradict the notion of voluntary participation. Provision of better housing, food, or medical care as conditions of participation may easily sway the decisions of incarcerated individuals.

Financial incentives frequently are offered as a means of encouraging participation. For those experiencing financial difficulties, the possibility of monetary compensation may override other factors and unduly influence the decision to participate (Yelaja, 1982). For prisoners, even a few dollars compensation, given the low wages earned in prison employment, may be sufficient to induce their participation. For example, S. P., a prisoner who had participated in the Maryland infectious disease experiments, describes the rationale for his involvement:

. . . they pay two dollars ($2.00) a day, which I used to by items from the Institution Commissary. . . . I wasn't too interested in the voluntariness of the studies, only the fact that, [sic] the studies paid. . . . At this time I was assigned to the Institution Woodshop, and being paid fifty cents ($.50) a day. . . . (cited in Gilchrist, 1974, p. 84)

Moreover, an individual may be deterred from withdrawing consent if compensation is tied to completed participation in the research project. Thus, individuals may continue to be engaged in research projects because of economic pressures. Yelaja (1982) acknowledges the difficulties in formulating clear ethical guidelines about the use of financial incentives and urges that the amount of payment offered not be so great as to act as an undue inducement.

Yet these examples are almost too obvious; pressure to obtain consent may take many, more subtle forms. Being told that "everyone else said yes" or "you're the only one with questions" can sway an individual to act with the majority. Similarly, an agency staff member who contacts clients on behalf of a researcher may subtly influence their decisions. A client may agree in order to make a good impression on or court favor with the staff member or may consent because she or he feels that it is the expected response. Similarly, prisoners may agree to act as subjects in the belief that their participation will be viewed favorably in parole decisions, although DHHS regulations prohibit this (45 *CFR* 46.305). Strain and Chappell (1982) indicate that simply being a "client" may make one more acquiescent to research participation. Based on studies they conducted with the elderly in four different settings, they conclude that

Those who have been integrated into the service bureaucracy often accept unquestioningly another interviewer and another series of questions to answer. On the other hand, those who are . . . not part of the service bureaucracy are much more likely to decline. (Strain & Chappell, 1982, p. 527).

A third facet of informed, voluntary consent considerations involves methods of showing that consent has been obtained. According to DHHS regulations, written documentation of informed consent must be obtained by the researcher (45 *CFR* 46.117). A consent form, approved by an IRB and enumerating the elements of informed consent, is supposed to be read by, or to, the prospective participants and then signed by them.

The requirement of written consent may be waived if the consent form represents the only evidence linking the individual to the study and the principal risk of participation would result from the loss of confidentiality. In such situations, participants have the option of deciding whether or not they want to sign the consent form. Moreover, if the study presents minimal risks and involves procedures that in other spheres of life would not necessitate written authorization, the requirement of written consent may be waived.

Finally, the right to withdraw from a study without jeopardy is a fundamental aspect of informed, voluntary consent. Those giving consent must understand that they can exercise this right if they so choose. It must be clear that the availability of services or benefits is not contingent upon an individual's decision to terminate her or his participation in the research. Members of vulnerable populations may be especially reticent to exercise this right for fear of losing concrete assistance or being labeled as "uncooperative" or "bad."

Maltreated or institutionalized children, too, may be particularly reluctant to express such desires. Fear of opposing adult authority, be it that of an investigator, agency staff member, or parent, may keep them engaged in a research project long after they may wish. Kinard (1985) indicates that such children may be more likely to express their reluctance through body language and presentation rather than verbal statements.

Who Can Consent

Related to concerns regarding the voluntary nature of informed consent is the question of who can consent. Again this appears at face value to be a rather straightforward issue. Any individual who has reached the age of majority according to state law and who does not have significant cognitive or psychological impairments is believed to be capable of giving consent. For those considered to be minors by state law (i.e., typically under 18 years of age) and/or incapable of making their own decisions, consent can be obtained from either a parent or guardian.

Some of the complexities in obtaining informed, voluntary consent, however, become apparent when complex systems are the subject of inquiry. Closely connected groups of individuals, such as families or youth gangs, are common foci of investigation. Yet, for instance, can one member consent to the participation of "the family," or must all members agree? Decision making in families does not occur with full independence; the decision of one spouse may influence that of the other partner. One may question whether all members are truly exercising their freedom of choice in such circumstances or are simply following the lead of a more powerful or persuasive family member.

Parental consent on behalf of a child assumes a mutuality of interests (Frankel, 1978). However, personal reasons (e.g., selfishness or misguidedness) or economic or social pressures "may literally force parents into making choices of questionable value where their child's welfare is concerned" (Frankel, 1978, p. 104). Ferguson (1978) argues that parental consent establishes a necessary, but not a sufficient, condition for children's participation. Parental authorization must be complemented by the children's consent to achieve a condition sufficient for their involvement in research (Ferguson, 1978).

Just as parental interests may not reflect those of the child, so the interests of the child may not necessarily coincide with those of the parents. Wax (1980) cites an example of a researcher who wanted to study teen drug use. The investigator was told in this instance to obtain both parental and adolescent consent. Yet, "securing permission from parents would not only be awkward, expensive and time-consuming, it might also place the children in jeopardy if they were engaging in the use of illegal drugs or inhalants" (Wax, 1980, p. 280).

Complications and conflicts may occur in the eliciting of consent/assent for studies of child maltreatment (e.g., physical, emotional, or sexual abuse or neglect). Parental permission may be withheld if the abusing parent fears that the child may relate damaging information. Conflict over granting permission also may arise between the abusing and nonabusing parents (Kinard, 1985). A child's refusal to participate, where parental consent already is obtained, may further strain family interactions and may be interpreted by the family as "willful opposition to the parent" (Kinard, 1985, p. 304).

DHHS regulations stipulate "a waiver of the requirement for parental permission in certain areas of research, such as child abuse and neglect, where parents may fail to adequately protect their children" (Kinard, 1985, p. 302). The regulations do not, however, indicate who should act as a proxy or how this choice should be made. If parental rights are terminated and the child is made a ward of the state, consent can be given by an individual acting in a guardian role, most often a staff member of Child Protective Services. Yet this presumes that the individual knows the child well enough to accurately assess her or his best interest and does not base the decision on "personal or professional interests" (Kinard, 1985, p. 302). Kinard (1985) reviews a number of alternative, including the use of designated professionals, IRBs, and specially appointed advocates, and illustrates the strengths and limitations of each.

DHHS regulations necessitating acquisition of the child's assent appear to acknowledge both the personal rights of children and the potential for disagreement between parental and child views. There are not, however, clear guidelines or procedures for determining a youth's ability to assent. Chronological age has been suggested as one criterion, with the possibility of treating those over 14 as adults (Kinard, 1985). Ferguson (1978) argues for adopting a developmental perspective and identifies four broad categories—infants and toddlers, preschool and primary school age, preadolescents, and adolescents—which would require differing consent/assent procedures.

Whether and, if so, under what conditions an adolescent's consent may be sufficient to justify her or his participation in a research project is an important issue faced by those studying a variety of deviant or stigmatized behaviors. The Wax (1980) quote cited above illustrates how this dilemma unfolded in one attempt to study adolescent drug use. In that instance, it was decided that high school youths, who were living at home, needed parental permission before they could be interviewed by the researcher.

When youths are not living with their families, the issue of parental consent may present even more complexities. In Finkelhor's (1979) study of childhood sexual abuse experiences, for instance, college students, many of whom were not living with their parents, were instructed not to complete the questionnaire if they were under 18 years of age, thereby avoiding the issue altogether. Studies of runaway and homeless youths and adolescent prostitutes not infrequently confront the dilemma of parental consent requirements. In some instances, consent procedures used in child maltreatment research are applied because it can be argued that many of these youth either are "throwaways," i.e., abandoned or pushed out by their families, or have run away because of abusive home situations. Thus, consent on behalf of a youth is obtained from program staff instead of parents. Similar strategies have been employed in some delinquency studies, wherein participation was based on the adolescent's assent coupled with consent from institutional staff.

Anonymity and Confidentiality

In contemporary society, an individual's right to privacy is a social and legal norm (Yelaja, 1982). Informed, voluntary consent permits researchers to violate this right, to ask questions about or observe facets of an individual's private life. Anonymity and confidentiality procedures are used to mitigate possible risks asociated with having access to such information.

Babbie (1986) defines anonymity as the inability of the investigator to associate responses with individual participants. Accordingly, surveys in which there is no way of identifying who has and who has not responded afford participants' anonymity. Studies that rely on interviews, observations, data from identified records or files, or surveys that employ preassigned identification numbers do not mask the identity of the informational source vis-à-vis the researcher and, hence, are not anonymous.

Confidentiality, according to Babbie (1986), implies that although the researcher can link responses to an individual, she or he promises not to reveal the linkage publicly. Since many forms of research do not preserve anonymity, maintenance of confidentiality becomes vital. To ensure participants' confidentiality, results often are reported in aggregate statistical form.

In qualitative studies, pseudonyms or other devices (e.g., fictitious histories or global descriptions) are used to mask the identities of individuals or communities. These steps, however, do not guarantee that confidentiality will not be compromised. The publication of findings may contain information sufficient to allow those in the study community to identify the individuals described, thus violating the confidentiality that they had been assured. Furthermore, LaRossa et al. (1981) argue that qualitative family studies heighten confidentiality concerns because of the private nature of contemporary family life.

Trend (1980) notes that although researchers promise confidentiality, they cannot guarantee it legally, and some consent forms are now required to make this limitation explicit. Research information is not considered privileged, and data, notes, or records can be subject to subpoena. In addition, these materials can be accessed by the federal government under certain administrative laws, such as the Freedom of Information Act of 1966 (Public Law [PL] 89-554) or the Federal Property and Administrative Services Act of 1949 (Trend, 1980). Gelles (1978) acknowledges that in the absence of clear legal precedent

Researchers who engage in research that deals with illegal, sensitive, or taboo topics run the risks of being forced to turn over material they pledged would be kept confidential, of engaging in legal battles, or of spending time in jail for contempt of court. (p. 422)

Criminological research brings into relief a number of issues regarding the confidentiality of information. In addition to possible breaches through the subpoena of data, investigators may be faced with ethical dilemmas by virtue of their knowledge of illegal acts. Becker (1973) identifies this as one of the moral problems faced by researchers in studying deviance. Klockars (1979) terms these "dirty hands problems" (p. 264). Thus, for example, should a researcher "participate" in the possibly illegal activities of those being studied in order to gain an understanding of the deviant behavior of interest? Does the investigator become an "accomplice" or "accessory" in the illegal conduct described by participants?

Yelaja (1982) casts these questions in more general terms. For instance, one may inadvertently uncover, during the course of study, information about psychological states, illegal or dangerous behaviors, or drug or alcohol addiction that, in the view of the researcher, may place the participant or others at risk. Yelaja (1982) asserts that such situations place researchers in "a very difficult bind" where there are no clear guidelines for resolution (p. 331).

Investigations of child maltreatment, in particular, may engender confidentiality conflicts for the investigator. Since child abuse and neglect are reportable under state law, although researchers are not classified as mandated reporters, one must decide what to do if maltreatment is uncovered during the course of research. For example, in comparative studies it may be found that some of the control families abuse their children (Kinard, 1985). Analogously, studies of general populations, such as Straus et al.'s (1980) national survey, may reveal abusive and violent behaviors toward children. Kinard (1985), citing the logic of the Tarasoff decision (*Tarasoff v. Regents of the University of California*), asserts that researchers should "warn by reporting" suspected child abuse (p. 307).

Another facet of confidentiality dilemmas in child maltreatment research involves parental requests for information on the child's performance in the study (Kinard, 1985). Parents, because they have given permission for their child to participate, may feel that they have a right to their child's test scores or answers. Yet if the child was assured that her or his responses would not be shared, providing performance information to the parents would violate the confidentiality agreement established between the investigator and the child.

This last point, however, has more general implications. When access to study participants is dependent on the cooperation and/or authorization of a formal body, there may be an expectation that information on individual clients will be shared with the host agency. Brodsky (1980), for instance, depicts the tensions of trying to perform psychological consultation and research in correctional facilities. In attempting to balance the often-contradictory demands of serving two groups of clients (i.e., prisoners and prison administrators), Brodsky (1980) identifies the centrality of ethical standards for guiding such work.

Risk/Benefit Assessment

Whereas an objective of research is to build and refine knowledge, the means to achieving this end may entail risks. As discussed earlier, researchers have an obligation to minimize harms that may accrue to participants, as well as as those that may be experienced by other professionals and society more generally. Since the research enterprise cannot be made risk free, the question becomes one of tolerance—what kinds and degrees of risk are acceptable under what circumstances.

In the absence of certainty, risk/benefit assessment has been posited as a means for evaluating proposed studies with regard to ethics (Gillespie, 1987; Yelaja, 1982). In this model, the potential risks of implementing the study are weighed against the potential benefits of conducting it. If the benefits offset the risks involved, then the research is presumed to be worthwhile (Gillespie, 1987).

In the purest form of this model, the projected risks and benefits of an investigation should accrue to the study participants. Unfortunately, this often is not the case, and risks and benefits may accrue to different groups. Participants who are exposed to potential harms may not be the beneficiaries of the results. Other groups or society more generally may benefit from the findings (Gillespie, 1987).

In calculating this ratio, researchers should consider a wide range of potential risks. Most obviously are physical and/or psychological harms that may result directly from participation. In addition, there may be risks to the individual's social well-being (Yelaja, 1982). However, there are no clear criteria for rating risks or benefits. It is suggested that one function of an IRB review should be to safeguard against the vagaries that may occur in the rating of risks and benefits in the absence of explicit standards.

Threats to social well-being may be especially serious in studies of sensitive topics. Since such topics typically involve deviant and/or stigmatized behaviors or beliefs, identification of individuals simply as participants in the investigation, no less the information they provide, can have deleterious social consequences. For example, parents may speculate about the identities of the abusers when asked to take part in child abuse studies (Kinard, 1985). The suggestion that one is a child abuser, even if untrue, could seriously damage a parent's social and economic well-being.

The risk/benefit assessment model is not fail-safe. Numerous factors can impinge upon the calculations in this ratio. For instance, an investigator who is strongly committed to carrying out a study may overrate the expected benefits and underrate the risks involved. This sort of favorable weighting is not necessarily done with conscious intent but rather reflects the conflicting interests of the researcher (Gillespie, 1987).

Temporal considerations may affect these assessments as well. Yelaja (1982) indicates "the benefits of research may be long-term and yet short-term benefits do not provide any immediate hope or encouragement. Should these benefits be seen in the short-term or in the long-term?" (p. 325). Conversely, it is more difficult to project long-term risks, and most assessments tend to focus on short-term harms. Thus, comparison of benefits and risks may reflect unequal weighting over time.

Determining prospective benefits and risks also may be particularly problematic in certain forms of research. In field research, it is often difficult to identify specific and/or concrete risks or benefits because of the methodology employed and its purpose (Wax, 1980). Casal (1980, p. 31) suggests that the benefits of fieldwork involve "primarily the correction of misperceptions about various groups and the advancement of human knowledge," results that are not tangible and are difficult to value. Similarly, LaRossa et al. (1981) indicate that the "ad hoc character" of qualitative family research "makes calculating the risks and potential benefits of a project very difficult" (p. 304).

Most important, perhaps, such assessments are premised on the notion that risks and benefits can be identified and explicitly quantified and/or valued a priori. Yet much of the excitement of the practice of research derives from the unexpected, from the discovery of what is not anticipated. Just as outcomes or benefits of research cannot always be predicted, neither can risks. Participants may be exposed to unintended or unanticipated harms during the course of inquiry.

When unanticipated risks do occur, the researcher must assess their seriousness and, if necessary, terminate the study in order to protect participants from harm. This occurred in a study conducted at Stanford University in which volunteers assumed the roles of prisoners and guards in a simulated prison (Zimbardo, 1973). Prior to initiating the research, the investigators used psychological tests to guide their selection of participants. This precaution was employed as a way to minimize subsequent risks, and only those scoring within normal ranges were allowed to participate. The study, however, was prematurely ended when it was found that the volunteer prisoners were being subjected to continual physical and psychological abuses by the volunteer guards (Zimbardo, 1973). The obligation to terminate research when there are undue risks can be construed as the obverse of participants' rights to end their involvement.

Methodological Implications of Ethical Obligations

Clarification of researchers' ethical obligations leads to questions of how to put these requirements into practice and what their effects are for the conduct of inquiry. Risk/benefit assessment, from this perspective, may be the least troublesome of the ethical elements promulgated, because the researcher can maintain a relatively high degree of control over this evaluative process. Similarly, maintenance of anonymity and confidentiality are values long held in the research community and tend to become issues only when they are threatened. The use of subpoena to breach these promises is a possibility that must be considered. Such actions, however, are rare. Investigators also may consider breaching their confidentiality promises, as discussed in the previous section, to mitigate revealed harms. Although these are extremely difficult decisions to make, they, like risk/benefit assessments, occur within the researcher's domain.

The requirement of informed, voluntary consent, in contrast, calls into question the interaction of the researcher and the study participants. The investigator must decide the amount of information to be given to prospective participants, when it is to be given, and how. The researcher must justify these decisions in light of the principle that individuals have the right to determine their participation in research freely and with an understanding of the possible consequences of their choice. Not surprisingly, the requirement of informed, voluntary consent has been the most problematic and debated of the ethical standards promulgated.

The previous section described some of the dilemmas involved in eliciting informed consent in various forms of social science research. Sobal (1982) suggests that what constitutes informed consent in current practice exists along a continuum rather than as a dichotomy. This definitional variation occurs not just among different methods of investigation but within given methods as well.

Survey research is one of the most commonly used methods of contemporary investigation, encompassing diverse strategies of mail, telephone, and in-person interviews or self-administered questionnaires. Research texts (see, for example, Babbie, 1986; Kidder & Judd, 1986) and survey research literature (see, for example, Sudman & Bradburn, 1982) offer a variety of suggestions for how to handle survey introductions. One is typically advised to keep introductory statements brief and somewhat vague so as not to confuse, raise doubts, or taint results. Techniques to convince an individual to participate often are offered too. It is commonly assumed that individuals understand that their participation is voluntary, and this fact is, therefore, typically not mentioned in survey introductions (Sudman & Bradburn, 1982).

Many of the injunctions about how to introduce surveys reflect the accumulated wisdom of practitioners. The ways in which the concepts of "informed," "voluntary," and "consent" are defined and operationalized are influenced by the researcher's view of survey research practices in general and the dictates of her or his own study in particular. Development of informed, voluntary consent procedures thus have been cast to a large extent against a backdrop of survey methodology "folklore" (Sobal, 1982, p. 349).

Yet, whether and how ethics regulations affect the efficiency and effectiveness of survey methods are rightfully questions for exploration. A few studies from the early 1970s touch on some of these issues. Hauck and Cox (1974), for instance, found that fuller study descriptions resulted in fewer refusals in telephone interviewing. In contrast, Blumberg, Fuller, and Hare (1974), in a mail survey study, found that more extensive information appeared to antagonize prospective participants. Their study also found that promises of confidentiality and anonymity had no effect on response rates (Blumberg et al., 1974). Moreover, the quality of mail survey data was found not to be significantly affected by confidentiality and anonymity assurances (Becker & Bakal, 1970; Fuller, 1974; King, 1970).

Singer (1978) alleges that the "debate . . . has been conducted, largely without benefit of empirical evidence, between those who champion the new rules on ethical grounds . . . and those who oppose them in the belief that they will destroy the possibility of doing needed research" (p. 144). In the decade since Singer's comment, some additional evidence has been accumulated that can inform this debate. The remainder of this chapter reviews the methodological implications of ethical criteria for survey research.

Response-Rate Effects

Singer (1978) conducted what is perhaps one of the earliest and most detailed explorations of the consequences of informed consent procedures on participation and response rates and response quality. Three elements of informed consent were manipulated: the amount of detail given in the description of the study's content (e.g., short vs. long description); the degree of confidentiality promised (e.g., absolute vs. partial vs. no mention); and the documentation of consent (e.g., before the interview vs. after vs. no mention). The resulting 2 × 3 × 3 factorial design yielded 18 different introductions that were randomly tested in face-to-face interviews with a national probability sample of 2,084 individuals.

Singer (1978) found that the amount of information about the survey and the degree of confidentiality promised had no effect on whether or not individuals refused to participate. The documentation of consent, however, was significantly associated. Those from whom signed consent was requested before the interview were more likely to refuse than those not asked to document their consent. She concludes that since documenting consent by asking for a signature was the only condition that affected overall participation rates, the conventional widsom that brief and vague introductions are better is not supported. Rather, there does not appear to be a substantial "response-rate cost" associated with implementing at least these two dimensions of informed consent (Singer, 1978, p. 150).

In a modified replication of Singer's (1978) study, Singer and Frankel (1982) developed a 2 × 2 factorial design to assess the consequences of informed consent procedures on telephone survey participation response rates. Four introductory conditions were created: long content description and statement of purpose; long content description and no statement of purpose; short content description and statement of purpose; and short content description and no statement of purpose, a conventional survey introduction. Although differences in participation rates related to the four conditions did not achieve statistical significance, highest participation rates (or conversely, lowest refusal rates) were found among those who received the long content description and statement of purpose. This statistical finding of "no difference" again supports the contention that there are not substantial methodological costs associated with the provision of greater information in survey introductions.

Sobal (1982) also assessed the effects of introductory disclosure on survey refusals for in-person interviews. Approximately 200 individuals, selected by a quota sampling plan, were randomly assigned to two groups and read one of two introductory statements: a longer, "fuller disclosure introduction" and a briefer, "lesser disclosure introduction," similar to a typical survey introduction (Sobal, 1982, pp. 352–353). As with Singer (1978), Sobal (1982) found no difference in the proportion of interviews refused related to the amount of introductory information provided.

In the course of the study, however, it was observed that "the crucial point of many refusals . . . was the statement that the interview would take about twenty minutes" (Sobal, 1982, p. 352). A second field test was undertaken to explore the influence of this time element on refusals. The two introductory statements (i.e., fuller and lesser disclosures), modified by the addition of two time lengths, were used to approach 169 prospective participants, half of whom were told that the interview would take about 20 minutes and half told that it would take about 5 minutes. The amount of information disclosed again exhibited no relationship to interview refusals. The amount of time, however, had a significant association: Those told that the interview would take 20 minutes were twice as likely to refuse to participate as those told that it would take 5 minutes. This effect remained when the amount of information disclosed was controlled. Sobal (1982) also found an interaction effect, "with fewer refusals in the five-minute condition and more refusals with nondisclosure" (p. 353). Sobal (1982) interprets the findings of these two community studies as "supporting greater disclosure" in survey introductions (p. 357).

Ethical regulations necessitating parental consent on behalf of minor children have been viewed as placing substantial restrictions and burdens on surveys attemtping to access youth through their schools. Some suggest that these requirements have led student samples to diminish by almost 50% (Thompson, 1984). Lueptow, Mueller, Hammes, and Master (1977), reporting on a 1975 study of graduating high school seniors, found that the "use of volunteer participants resulted in a substantial loss of cases" (p. 187). They achieved an overall participation rate of almost 60%, less than two-thirds of what had been obtained by them in a comparable study a decade earlier. The total 1975 participation rate was then disaggregated in terms of consent source: adult students (i.e., those at least 18 years of age) versus parents of minors. Where the students could consent for themselves, approximately 70% agreed to participate. In contrast, parental authorization was granted for only 42% of the minor students.

In a Seattle school-based program evaluation conducted by Kearney, Hopkins, Mauss, and Weisheit (1983), parental consent for elementary and secondary school children was elicited through a form letter, documented by a postcard, and followed up by two additional mailings. Overall, about a third of the parents did not respond. Of those who did, 78% consented to their child's participation (or 51% of those eligible). The participation of only about half of the eligible students is similar to the Lueptow et al. (1977) finding and provides support for the suggestion that response rates in student surveys have declined sharply with the advent of explicit informed, voluntary consent procedures necessitating parental approval.

In light of findings showing substantial declines in students' involvement in school-based surveys, Thompson (1984) investigated four methods for increasing the participation of elementary grade children. The strategies tested included (a) offering an incentive to the child; (b) offering an incentive to the parents; (c) communicating directly with the child; and (d) communicating directly with parents. A fifth, or control, condition consisted of a follow-up letter to the parents.

Direct communication with the parent proved to be the most effective way of promoting consent (96% consent rate overall). This finding held for both Caucasian and Black parents, whose children represented about 30% of those enrolled. The next most successful method was the use of an incentive for the child, although this was slightly less effective among Blacks (80% overall; 82% Caucasian vs. 79% Black). However, the use of children to obtain parental consent can raise ethical problems in itself and should be approached with caution (Thompson, 1984). It is worth noting that the use of a follow-up letter alone, which is one of the more common mechanisms for enhancing response rates, was the least successful of the methods tested, yielding an overall consent rate of only 37%.

Thompson's (1984) study illustrates the variety of innovations that can be introduced to improve parental consent rates. In addition to increasing the number of cases available for analysis, such innovations could minimize the possibility of biased results due to the use of voluntary student samples. Lueptow et al. (1977) define "bias" as "the departure of an estimate based on the sample of participants from the population value" and contrast this with what they term "difference," which they define "as the difference between participants and nonparticipants" (p. 193).

Lueptow et al. (1977) found few statistical or substantive differences between participating and nonparticipating students in terms of grade point averages and intelligence test scores. Similarly, participants did not significantly or substantively differ on these indicators from the student population as a whole. They conclude that the "amount of bias . . . introduced by the informed consent procedures in minor . . . these results have positive implications for the representativeness of the participant group on other educationally relevant variables" (p. 197).

Kearney et al. (1983) also investigated bias and difference as functions of response rates. No differences were found when participants' reading and vocabulary test scores were compared with those of the population, suggesting little bias in these educational variables as a result of the consent procedures. Test score differences between participants and nonparticipants, however, indicated the "potential 'bias' . . . to be of more substantive significance" (Kearney et al., 1983, p. 101). Important differences were found in relation to race, with minority children being greatly underrepresented among participants. They conclude that "research concerning variables which differ greatly among the various racial/ethnic groups is likely to yield biased results if the explicit consent procedure must be used" (Kearney et al., 1983, p. 101).

Item-Response Effects

The Singer (1978) in-person interview study contained eight classes of questions, ranging from nonsensitive, general, attitude items to sensitive, survey-specific, factual ones (see Table 13, pp. 157–158). Sensitive, survey-specific, factual items were indicators of behaviors commonly viewed as private, stigmatized, and/or deviant (e.g., frequencies of masturbation, intercourse, marijuana smoking, drinking). Singer (1978) was thus able to investigate the effects of the 18 introductory conditions on response rates for these different types of questions.

Overall, the study had a fairly low item nonresponse rate, with only two questions, one about income and one about masturbation, obtaining nonresponse rates of 10% or more. The effects of the introductory conditions were assessed in relation to 12 items, 11 of which involved sensitive behaviors, that had individual nonresponse rates of at least 3%. Singer (1978) found that the degree of study description did not have a consistent or statistically significant relationship to nonresponse rates for these items. The confidentiality conditions, in contrast, did exhibit a relationship. Those promised absolute confidentiality had the lowest nonresponse rates for these questions, with 5 of the 12 comparisons achieving statistical significance.

In examining the effects of consent documentation, Singer (1978) found that those who signed the consent form prior to the interview had slightly lower item nonresponse rates than those asked to sign afterward or not asked to sign at all. Individuals who refused to sign the consent form but were willing to be interviewed were retained in the study, allowing for analysis of item response rates for these "nonsigners," who differed from other participants in terms of their education (e.g., either less than high school or a college degree or more) and age (e.g., older).

Requests for signed consent prior to the interview more often met with a refusal than did postinterview requests (10% vs. 7%). Those who refused to sign the consent form also were found to be more likely to refuse to answer individual items. The greatest differences in item nonresponse rates were found between these nonsigners and those in the other three consent documentation conditions. These differences led Singer (1978) to speculate "whether refusers are a distinct group, inclined to say 'no' to questions which they construe as sensitive, or whether . . . asking respondents to sign a consent form ahead of time had sensitized them to the content of the interview, so that they were more likely to refuse to answer particular questions" (pp. 151–152). A comparison of item nonresponse rates for those who refused to sign the consent form before versus after the interview found few differences, suggesting that "refusers are a distinct group . . . signing the consent form appears to function simply as another sensitive question, so that those who refuse the questions, refuse to sign, and vice versa" (Singer, 1978, p. 152).

Singer and Frankel (1982) also found few statistical differences in item nonresponse rates, including those for sensitive questions, related to the amount of information provided in the telephone survey introduction. Of those comparisons reaching statistical significance, "most indicate an advantage for the more detailed, rather than for the vague introduction" (Singer and Frankel, 1982, p. 422). No statistical differences were found in relation to the two purpose conditions; nor were differences in item nonresponse rates observed for the interaction of content and purpose conditions. Introductory conditions did not appear to be associated with response quality either.

Sobal (1982), in his community interview study, defined cooperation as the willingness of respondents to provide information. Interview questions asked about attitudes and, to a more limited extent, behaviors that may be deemed private but not necessarily sensitive. He found that those in the fuller disclosure condition were more likely to respond to individual items and to provide fuller responses than those in the lesser disclosure condition (Sobal, 1982). Although this appeared to be a consistent pattern, differences in item nonresponse rates did not achieve statistical significance.

Reamer (1979) investigated the effects of confidentiality assurances on the apprehension levels, response rates, and response quality of interview information obtained from 505 adolescents charged with status offenses. Youths were randomly assigned to experimental and control conditions. Those in the experimental group were told that their answers would be kept anonymous and confidential and were given a certificate to this effect signed by the lead researcher. This introduction was specifically "designed to reduce apprehension" (Reamer, 1979, p. 499). The other group received a brief, informal introduction; issues of confidentiality and anonymity were not mentioned.

Of the 121 items in the interview schedule, only 36 had nonresponse rates above 3%. Reamer (1979) found that nonresponse rates for these 36 items were not associated with the introductory conditions. Thus, in contrast to Singer's (1978) general population findings, assurances of confidentiality did not enhance the response likelihood of these vulnerable youths.

Response-Quality Effects

Determination of the quality, or truthfulness and accuracy, of responses is often a difficult task. Data triangulation, which entails comparison of study and external indicators, has been proposed as one method to enhance convergent validation (Campbell & Fiske, 1959).[6] In the absence of external measures, it is suggested, more reporting on sensitive questions and less reporting on nonthreatening questions reflects better reporting (Sudman & Bradburn, 1982; Singer, 1978).

Singer (1978) examined the quality of responses obtained in the face-to-face interviews in relation to the 18 introductory conditions established. All sensitive attitude and behavior items and a sample of nonsensitive ones were selected for analysis, for a total of 43 items. The amount of information provided in the introduction did not result in a consistent substantive or statistical pattern. Of the five comparisons that achieved statistical significance, the brief, vague introduction was associated with better reporting for two sensitive attitude items, and the longer, more detailed introduction yielded better reporting for three sensitive behavior questions.

Response quality did not vary significantly with respect to confidentiality conditions either. Only 3 of the 43 comparisons were statistically significant. A substantively interesting pattern, however, did emerge in terms of the more sensitive behavioral items. In these instances, the promise of unconditional confidentiality appeared to be related to the acquisition of better quality information.

Finally, few of the item quality contracts based on consent documentation conditions (excluding nonsigners) reached statistical significance. In the five statistically significant comparisons, all involving sensitive behavior items, greater response quality was associated with signing the consent form. Those who signed the consent form after the interview gave higher reports on these indicators than those signing before or not signing at all. Singer (1978) concluded that "asking for a signature before the interview has a sensitization effect. Respondents asked to sign . . . before the interview are more likely to underestimate socially undesirable behavior than if they had not been asked to sign at all, or if they had been asked to sign afterwards" (pp. 157–158).

Reamer's (1979) study of youths in the juvenile justice system found that the experimental "apprehension reduction" introduction was not associated with lower mean scores on an eight-item apprehension questionnaire. Indeed, Reamer (1979) reports that the experimental introduction "appears . . . to have slightly increased the youth's concerns" (p. 503). Comparisons of the quality of responses given for the 121 interview items identified only nine statistically significant relationships, a result that may have occurred by chance. Thus, although the experimental introduction may have unintentionally heightened apprehension in the experimental youths, it did not appear to affect the quality of individual responses given in the interviews.

While more comprehensive research in this area is still needed, the studies reviewed in this section do point to the relative compatibility of ethical considerations and survey research requirements. In light of the lack of association observed between the amount of introductory information provided and participation and item response effects, there does not appear to be strong methodological grounds for restricting such information. Confidentiality assurances either were found to exhibit no effect (Reamer, 1979; Singer & Frankel, 1982) or appeared to have somewhat positive influence on response quality (Singer, 1978). Documenting consent via signature prior to an interview may distort subsequent responses to sensitive questions (Singer, 1978); however, the task of developing alternative ways of documenting consent, when such documentation is needed, is not insurmountable.

Conclusions

Investigating topics of interest to criminologists presents a myriad of unique research difficulties. Because the beliefs or acts under exploration are deemed sensitive to public discourse and scrutiny, they are typically hidden, undertaken in private or among small circles of other like-minded individuals. To gain information about these issues requires that the shields surrounding them be pierced.

The conduct of inquiry in these areas, as well as in others, has been influenced by societal concerns about the use of humans in research. Attention to the ethical aspects of research was stimulated in the late 1940s by revelations of Nazi atrocities committed under the guise of medical experimentation. Ethical codes, stipulating norms of conduct, were first developed for those engaged in medical research. In the late 1960s and 1970s, debates resulting from several highly publicized social science and biomedical projects, as well as political events such as the Watergate break-in, prompted the expansion of ethical standards to include all investigations involving humans. The ethical regulations promulgated by DHHS are perhaps the best known current standards and provide explicit rules to be followed when humans are used in research, regardless of a study's disciplinary sponsorship.

Contemporary ethical obligations of researchers to elicit informed, voluntary consent, to mitigate potential risks, and to assure that the prospective benefits of the research outweigh potential risks reflect a reconciliation of competing philosophic stances. Kantian notions about the inviolability of man and utilitarian emphases on outcomes are brought together in a series of criteria by which the ethical soundness of a research proposal can be judged. The meaning, operationalization, and implementation of these criteria, particularly the requirement of informed, voluntary consent, have been the subjects of debate.

Research into sensitive issues may engender special ethical considerations. Individuals whose beliefs or behaviors are stigmatized may experience substantial harm if exposed and are therefore considered to be vulnerable populations for study. The maintenance of data confidentiality may be threatened, for example, by agents of the state attempting to obtain information on criminal activities or by parental requests in the case of child participants. Conversely, the investigator who discovers that participants are at risk of harm must decide for her- or himself whether or not to breach confidentiality promises.

To the extent that these requirements are seen as impinging upon the practice of research, ethical obligations have been posited in competition to methodological standards. Yet studies of the effects of informed consent practices on survey research suggest that methodological rigor is not sacrificed when ethical obligations are fulfilled. Contrary to practitioner wisdom, providing prospective participants with fuller study information does not appear to compromise survey participation, item response rates, or informational quality, including that for sensitive questions. Similarly, confidentiality assurances were found to have either no effect or a somewhat positive effect on these three dimensions. Obtaining signed documentation of consent before conducting an interview, however, may entail methodological costs. This does not, however, necessarily present a substantial obstacle to fulfilling ethical obligations.

The apparent compatibility of ethical and methodological requirements should be positively greeted by criminologists. Incorporating the requirements of research ethics may pose some challenges, but surmounting such dilemmas will only enliven and strengthen the field. Perhaps the greatest benefit of an ethical pursuit of knowledge will be to enhance the applicability of our findings. In the end, however, it is up to each of us as researchers to decide for her- or himself that this advantage is worth pursuing, since all the codes and regulations in the world cannot force one to behave ethically.

Endnotes

1. Ethical considerations in research involve a wide range of divergent issues and problems. This chapter addresses just one set of these concerns—the ethical obligations of researchers to those they are studying. As important to consider are the ethical implications of research design selection and publication decisions. For more discussion of these topics see, for example, Diener and Crandall (1978), Kimmel (1988), Reynolds (1982).
2. The role of the funding agent in research itself raises a number of complex and involved questions. At times, the "strings" attached to research funding by public and private sponsors can present their own ethical dilemmas. For a further discussion of these issues see, for example, Wolfgang (1982).
3. For more complete discussions of the National Commission for the Protection of Human Subjects and the Belmont Report, see Gray (1979) and O'Connor (1979).
4. For dicussions of the implications of research ethics for the professions and society see, for example, Ben-Yehuda (1985), Broad and Wade (1983), Diener and Crandall (1978), and Horowitz (1967).
5. While the following discussion focuses on individuals as participants, the ethical issues described apply as well to studies focusing on groups or organizations.
6. Statistically based methods, such as the randomized response technique, have been proposed as means of eliciting sensitive information. For a more complete discussion of this approach, see, for example, Bradburn, Sudman, and Associates (1979), Fox and Tracy (1986), Orwin and Boruch (1982).

References

American Anthropological Association. (1971). *Principles of professional responsibility*. Washington, DC: Author.
American Psychological Association. (1981). *Ethical principles of psychologists*. Washington, DC: Author.
American Sociological Association. (1981). *Code of ethics*. Washington, DC: Author.
Babbie, E.R. (1986). *The practice of social research* (4th ed.). Belmont, CA.: Wadsworth.

Becker, G., & Bakal, D.A. (1970). Subject anonymity and motivational distortion in self-report data. *Journal of Clinical Psychology, 26*, 207–209.

Becker, H.S. (1970). Practitioners of vice and crime. In R.W. Habenstein (Ed.), *Pathways to data* (pp. 30–49). Chicago: Aldine.

Becker, H.S. (1973). *Outsiders: Studies in the sociology of deviance.* New York: Free Press.

Belmont Report. (1979). Washington, DC: U.S. Department of Health, Education, and Welfare, National Institutes of Health.

Ben-Yehuda, N. (1985). *Deviance and moral boundaries* (Chap. 5, pp. 168–207). Chicago: University of Chicago Press.

Binder, A., & Geis, G. (1983). *Methods of research in criminology and criminal justice.* New York: McGraw-Hill.

Blumberg, H.H., Fuller, C., & Hare, A.P. (1974). Anticipating informed consent: An empirical approach. *American Psychologist, 28*, 913–925.

Bradburn, N.M., Sudman, S., & Associates. (1979). *Improving interview method and questionnaire design.* San Francisco: Jossey-Bass.

Broad, W., & Wade, N. (1983). *Betrayers of the truth: Fraud and deceit in the halls of science.* New York: Simon & Schuster.

Brodsky, S.L. (1980). Ethical issues for psychologists in corrections. In J. Monahan (Ed.), *Who is the client: The ethics of psychological intervention in the criminal justice system.* Washington, DC: American Psychological Association.

Campbell, D.T., & Fiske, D.W. (1959). Convergent and discriminant validation by the multitrait-multimethod matrix. *Psychological Bulletin, 56*, 81–105.

Casal, J. (1980). Ethical principles for conducting fieldwork. *American Anthropologist, 82*, 28–41.

Code of Federal Regulations. Title 45-Public Welfare. Part 46—Protection of Human Subjects. (1987 ed.). Washington, DC: U.S. Department of Health and Human Services, National Institutes of Health.

Diener, E., & Crandall, R. (1978). *Ethics in social and behavioral research.* Chicago: University of Chicago Press.

Erikson, K. (1968). On the ethics of disguised observation—A reply to Denzin. *Social Problems, 27*, 505–506.

Federal Property and Adminstrative Services Act of 1949. 288 U.S. C. 63 Stat. 377.

Ferguson, L.R. (1978). The competence and freedom of children to make choices regarding participation in research: A statement. *Journal of Social Issues, 34*, 114–121.

Finkelhor, D. (1979). *Sexually victimized children.* New York: Free Press.

Fox, J.A., & Tracy, P.E. (1986). *Randomized response: A method for sensitive surveys.* Beverly Hills, CA: Sage.

Frankel, M.S. (1978). Social, legal, and political responses to ethical issues in the use of children as experimental subjects. *Journal of Social Issues, 34*, 101–113.

Freedom of Information Act of 1966 (PL 89-554) U.S. C. 1982, Title 5, § 552.

Fuller, C. (1974). Effect of anonymity on return rate and response bias in a mail survey. *Journal of Applied Psychology, 59*, 292–296.

Gelles, R.J. (1978). Methods for studying sensitive family topics. *American Journal of Orthopsychiatry, 48*, 408–424.

Gilchrist, I. (Ed.). 1974. *Medical experimentation on prisoners must stop: Documents generated during the course of a struggle.* College Park, MD: Urban Information Interpreters.

Gillespie, D. (1987). Ethical issues in research. In *Encyclopedia of social work* (18th ed., pp. 503–512). Washington, DC: National Association of Social Workers.

Gray, B.H., (1979). The regulatory context of social research: The work of the National Commission for the Protection of Human Subjects. In C.B. Klockars & F.W. O'Connor (Eds.), *Deviance and decency: The ethics of research with human subjects* (pp. 197–223). Beverly Hills, CA: Sage.

Haney, C., Banks, W.C., & Zimbardo, P. (1973). Interpersonal dynamics in a simulated prison. *International Journal of Criminology and Penology*, *1*, 69–73.

Hauck, M., & Cox, M. (1974). Locating a sample by random digit dialing. *Public Opinion Quarterly*, *38*, 253–256.

Hilbert, R.A. (1980). Covert participant observation. *Urban Life*, *9*, 51–78.

Horowitz, I. (Ed.). (1967). *The rise and fall of Project Camelot: Studies in the relationship between social science and practical politics*. Cambridge, MA: MIT Press.

Humphreys, L. (1975). *The tearoom trade: Impersonal sex in public places* (enl. ed. with retrospect on ethical issues). Chicago: Aldine.

Jones, H.H. (1981). Bad blood: The Tuskegee syphilis experiment—A tragedy of race and medicine. New York: Free Press.

Kearney, K.A., Hopkins, R.H., Mauss, A.L., & Weisheit, R.A. (1983). Sample bias resulting from a requirement for written parental consent. *Public Opinion quarterly*, *47*, 96–102.

Kidder, L.H., & Judd, C.M. (1986). *Research methods in social relations* (5th ed.). New York: Holt, Rinehart and Winston.

Kimmel, A.J. (1988). *Ethics and values in applied social research*. Beverly Hills, CA: Sage.

Kinard, E.M. (1985). Ethical issues in research with abused children. *Child Abuse and Neglect*, *9*, 301–311.

King, F.W. (1970). Anonymous versus identifiable questionnaires in drug usage surveys. *American Psychologist*, *25*, 982–985.

Kinsey, A., Pomeroy, W., & Martin, C. (1948). Sexual behavior in the human male. Philadelphia: Saunders.

Kinsey, A., Pomeroy, W., Martin, C., & Gebhard, D. (1953). Sexual behavior in the human female. Philadelphia: Saunders.

Klockars, C.B. (1979). Dirty hands and deviant subjects. In C.B. Klockars & F.W. O'Connor (Eds.), *Deviance and decency: The ethics of research with human subjects* (pp. 261–282). Beverly Hills, CA: Sage.

LaRossa, R., Bennett, L.A., & Gelles, R.J. (1981). Ethical dilemmas in qualitative family research. *Journal of Marriage and the Family*, *43*, 303–313.

Lasch, C. (1977). *Haven in a heartless world: The family besieged*. New York: Basic Books.

Lueptow, L., Mueller, S.A., Hammes, R.R., & Master, L. (1977). The impact of informed consent regulations on response rate and response bias. *Sociological Methods and Research*, *6*, 183–204.

Merton, R.K. (1982). *Social research and the practicing professions*. Cambridge, MA: Abt.

Milgram, S. (1969). *Obedience to authority*. New York: Harper Colophon.

Mills, M., & Morris, N. (9174). Prisoners as laboratory animals. *Society*, *11*(5), 60–65.

National Association of Social Workers. (1979). *Code of ethics*. Silver Spring, MD: Author.

National Research Service Award Act of 1974 (PL 93-348). U.S. C. 1982. Title 42, §§ 241, 242a, 282, 286a, 286b, 287a, 287b, 287d, 288a, 289c, 289c-1, 289k, 289L, 289L-1, 289L-2, 289d.

Nuremberg Code, The. (1949). *Trials of war criminals before the Nuremberg military tribunals under control council law no. 10* (Vol. 2, Appendix 3, pp. 181–182). Washington, DC: U.S. Government Printing Office.

O'Connor, F.W. (1979). The ethical demands of the *Belmont Report*. In C.B. Klockars & F.W. O'Connor (Eds.), *Deviance and decency: The ethics of research with human subjects* (pp. 225–258). Beverly Hills, CA: Sage.

Orwin, R.G., & Boruch, R.F. (1982). RRT meets RDD: Statistical strategies for assuring response privacy in telephone surveys. *Public Opinion Quarterly, 46,* 560–571.

Pomeroy, W.B. (1966). Human sexual behavior. In N.L. Faberow (Ed.), *Taboo topics* (pp. 22–32). New York: Atheling.

Reamer, F.G. (1979). Protecting research subjects and unintended consequences: The effect of guarantees of confidentiality. *Public Opinion Quarterly, 43,* 497–506.

Reynolds, P.D. (1982). *Ethics and social science research*. Englewood Cliffs, NJ: Prentice-Hall.

Russell, D.E.H. (1986). *The secret trauma: Incest in the lives of girls and women*. New York: Basic Books.

Sherman, L.W. (1982). *Ethics in criminal justice education*. Hastings-on-Hudson, NY: The Hastings Center.

Singer, E. (1978). Informed consent: Consequences for response rate and response quality in social surveys. *American Sociological Review, 43,* 144–162.

Singer, E., & Frankel, M.R. (1982). Informed consent procedures in telephone interviews. *American Sociological Review, 47,* 416–427.

Sobal, J. (1982). Disclosing information in interview introductions: Methodological consequences of informed consent. *Sociology and Social Research, 66,* 348–361.

Strain, L.A., & Chappell, N.L. (1982). Problems and strategies Ethical concerns in survey research with the elderly. *The Gerontologist, 22,* 526–531.

Straus, M.A., Gelles, R.J., & Steinmetz, S.K. (1980). *Behind closed doors: Violence in the American family*. Garden City, NY: Anchor.

Sudman, S., & Bradburn, N.M. (1982). *Asking questions: A practical guide to questionnaire design*. San Francisco: Jossey-Bass.

Tarasoff v. Regents of the University of California, 17 Cal. 3d 425, 131 Cal. Rptr. 14, 551 P. 2d 334 (1976).

Thompson, T.L. (1984). A comparison of methods of increasing parental consent rates in social research. *Public Opinion Quarterly, 48,* 779–787.

Trend, M.G. (1980). Applied social research and the government: Notes on the limits of confidentiality. *Social Problems, 27,* 330–349.

Wax, M.L. (1980). Paradoxes of "consent" to the practice of fieldwork. *Social Problems 27,* 272–283.

Whyte, W.F. (1979). On making the most of participant observation. *The American Sociologist, 14,* 56–66.

Wolfgang, M.E. (1982). Ethics and research. In F. Elliston & N. Bowie (Eds.),

Ethics, public policy, and criminal justice (pp. 391–418). Cambridge, MA: Oelgeschlager, Gunn & Hain.

Yelaja, S.A. (1982). Human subjects for research and experimentation. In S.A. Yelaja (Ed.), *Ethical issues in social work* (pp. 312–337). Springfield, IL: Thomas.

Zimbardo, P. (1973). On the ethics of intervention in human psychological research: With special reference to the Stanford prison study. *Cognition, 22,* 243–246.

5
Natural Experiments in Criminal Justice

JEFFREY A. FAGAN*

Experiments with Social Policy and Reform

Experimentation in criminal justice has become both philosophy and policy in recent years. Campbell (1969) first proposed an explicit link between social reforms and experimental methods and challenged the United States to become an "experimenting society." The inferential persuasiveness of experimental results has contributed to the design of early childhood education programs, income maintenance policies, work and job training programs, regulatory law, and environmental conservation strategies. In general, these efforts illustrated conditions where experimental methods could be moved from the laboratory traditions of the natural and behavioral sciences to the uncertain conditions of social policy. Despite an uneven history of experimental research in social policy reform and program development, a recent manifesto on social policy experimentation called for a "marriage between experimental methods and assessments of public policy" (Berk, Boruch, Chambers, Rossi, & Witte, 1985, p. 389) and an explicit link between social policy change and experimentation.

The history of policy experiments in criminal justice also has evolved over a relatively brief period. Before 1970, criminal justice experiments were rare events, but the lack of experimental evidence had profound effects on policy. For example, the absence of conclusive evidence on the effectiveness of correctional programs led critics to attack rehabilitation as ineffective or posing greater risk to the public (Lipton, Martinson, & Wilks, 1975; Logan, 1972; Robison & Smith, 1971). The 1970s saw a rapid increase in the number of experiments on criminal justice policies and programs. These experiments occurred in parallel with the growth of social policy experiments by foundations and government agencies to inform public

*The author is grateful to Ronald Clarke and Don Gottfredson for their comments on the chapter.

policy and funding decisions (see Berk et al., 1985, for a brief history of social experimentation and Farrington, Ohlin, & Wilson, 1986, and Rezmovic, 1979, for reviews of criminal justice experiments).

Experiments in criminal justice have been influential in shaping policy and practice in community and institutional treatment, crime prevention, police responses, and court decision making. Experiments with larger units, such as institutions or areas, also have been successfully implemented with widespread acceptance of their policy implications. The National Institute of Justice currently is supporting two dozen field experiments in such diverse criminal justice policy areas as policing, prosecution, victim services, bail guidelines, sentencing guidelines, collection of fines, and probation and parole strategies (Garner & Visher, 1988). The National Academy of Sciences has endorsed the use of experimental designs as an appropriate and effective mechanism for developing informed public policy on crime control (Lempert & Visher, 1988).

Cook and Campbell (1979) described several circumstances that are conducive to social experimentation in field settings and that specifically avoid the problems of nonequivalence and intergroup contamination that may damage validity. For example, when lotteries are planned or ties must be broken, when subjects express no preference, or when demand outstrips supply, randomization is a reasonable way to distribute people or study units. When a planned innovation cannot be implemented in all units at once or when experimental units can be isolated temporarily, randomization may guide the implementation of experimental conditions. Another circumstance involves planned change when several alternatives are considered but none is preferable. In this case, the assignment of options to organizational units can occur randomly.

When Experiments Are Constrained

Experiments are systematic efforts to test hypotheses about the effects of variation of an independent variable on a dependent variable. Criminal justice experimentation provides evidence to determine what a rule of law does or does not accomplish. Investigators control the independent variable and the experimental situation. By using randomization, investigators can ensure that every eligible person or group has the same probability of receiving any level of the independent variable. Thus, differences between equivalent groups on the dependent variable are attributable to variation in the independent variable and not to differences between the groups or to the conditions of the experiment. In turn, investigators can make causal inferences about the effects of the independent variable.

However, there are situations where independent manipulation of a policy or treatment cannot occur. Sometimes, true experiments encounter obstacles from the law, especially in the concept of equality before the law or denial of constitutional rights of procedure. At other times, practical and political considerations may prohibit experimentation with certain subjects or constrain the range of the independent variable. For example, researchers in New York City were unable to randomize preventive detention for juvenile offenders or pretrial release of certain types of drug offenders. Thus, predictions of pretrial dangerousness were unfalsifiable for these groups, and the accuracy of judicial predictions was not verified empirically. Farrington et al. (1986) found that existing criminological experiments involved manipulations of the independent variable that were relatively weak or unimportant. Moreover, there have been very few experiments that included a truly "untreated" control group, thus limiting the generalizability of results to absolute (not relative) effects of intervention. More typically, experiments compare alternative policies or interventions to the *status quo*.

Ethical concerns also limit experimentation. Again, both exclusion of subjects and limitations on the range of the independent variable may constrain experimental conditions. Conditions that would pose risks to subjects often are prohibited by ethical concerns and the objective review of institutional review boards in universities (see Wexler, this volume). For example, an experiment on the specific deterrent effects of arrest for wife assault (Sherman & Berk, 1984) excluded felony cases from the randomization of police response conditions. Officers responding to domestic disturbances also exercised their option to override the randomization decision if they judged that a response other than arrest would place the victim at risk for further violence and injury.[1] Klockars (1979) provides examples of several moral dilemmas where researchers must "do wrong" to accurately observe the range of the independent variable. Thus, a valid study of police corruption would require investigators to vary the amount of money offered to police officer to induce hypothesized responses. Klockars terms these "dirty hands" problems.

Politics, both within agencies implementing experiments and through external pressures, also may limit experimentation. There are many examples of contaminated randomization processes (see, for example, Lerman, 1975), or "cold feet" by judges or decision makers (Empey & Erickson, 1972) where exclusions to randomization occurred despite prior agreements. Other times, contamination is well hidden and discovered only after the fact through re-analysis or replication. For example, Fienberg, Singer, and Tanur (1985) reviewed data from the Kansas City preventive patrol experiment (Kelling, Pate, Dieckman, & Brown, 1976), and found that it was unlikely that beats were randomly assigned. Kelling et al. confirmed that finding, stating that the police selected the configuration of beats that best suited the department's operational concerns.

There also are practical difficulties in implementing randomization. Differential attrition of subjects may result in groups that initially were equivalent but that are found significantly different on the initial variables later, when results are compared. Shifts in the pool of eligible participants or overrides of randomization decisions also may change the nature and outcome of an experiment. These shifts are likely to occur when referral sources (for example, judges or corrections staff) may wish to prevent the assignment of a particular youth to any of the experimental or control conditions. Clarke and Cornish (1972) noted declines over time in the referrals of boys to a school hosting an experiment where boys were randomly assigned. They attributed the decline to concerns by referral sources that boys may be assigned to an inappropriate treatment. Differences in pool and group composition over time may interact with staff characteristics or an intervention planned for a specific group, confounding the experiment.

Several other limitations of experiments also are evident. Correctional treatments are especially vulnerable to implementation problems, where the independent variable is only partially implemented or varies in strength across subjects (Sechrest, White, & Brown, 1979). In a study of correctional treatment for violent juvenile offenders, Fagan and Hartstone (1986) found that elements of an experimental correctional treatment actually were stronger in the control conditions than the experimental programs! Clarke and Cornish (1972) noted substantial changes in treatment methods over the duration of an experimental test of a therapeutic community for boys in England. They also noted several forms of staff reactivity, including Hawthorne effects (Roethlisberger & Dickson, 1939), ethical reservations about the randomization procedures, doubts raised among staff about their own abilities given the implementation of the new treatment method, and self-selection of staff for the innovative experimental treatment.

Not only are manipulations of the independent variable at times trivial but, also, experiments often are conducted under a narrow range of sampling conditions and artifactual settings. Stapleton and Teitelbaum (1972) found that experimental results can differ by setting and boundary conditions; Clarke and Cornish (1972) question generalizations of experimental results from one setting to the next. Both costs and time pose further obstacles to experimentation. Legislators will frown if an elaborate and costly experiment runs into unforeseen complications and ends inconclusively after a few years.

Accordingly, the defining characteristics of a true experiment are the presence of an independent variable that is manipulated by an experimenter and the establishment of experimental conditions and selection and assignment of subjects randomly to these conditions. However, there are several constraints on experiments in operational settings that limit their implementation and, in turn, the generalization of results. There remain conditions and circumstances when the independent variable is not free to vary or to interact with setting and context. Where practical or ethical constraints prevent experimentation on questions of policy and theory, their assumptions remain both untested and unfalsifiable—that is, since they cannot be tested experimentally, they cannot be disproven. In these situations, other conditions must be present to provide valid tests of policy, theory, and practice.

Natural Experiments

Legal and practical constraints on experiments in sensitive criminal justice areas may be overcome through modifications of experimental procedure. In *indirect* experiments, control over the experimental variable is removed from the investigator while the controlled character of the experiment remains. For example, the Manhattan Bail Project was an indirect experiment where the information to guide the bail decision was manipulated by the experimenters, but the decision whether or not to release a defendant on bail was left to the judge (Zeisel, 1973). Random assignment of cases to conditions of pretrial information remained in the domain of the experimenter, but the uses of the information remained at the discretion of the judge. The cost to experimental rigor was the exclusion of direct measures of the effects of bail release decisions on pretrial behavior, since these decisions were mediated by judicial discretion—that is, the experiment measured only the judges' use of information and its effects on pretrial decisions.[2]

When natural events intervene to create unique conditions, however, *direct* experiments in sensitive areas also are possible. Even assumptions thought to be unfalsifiable may be tested experimentally when natural events produce conditions that cannot otherwise be created. Boruch (1975, p. 35) suggests that "it is intuitively appealing to regard some processes as naturally random, and to capitalize on the intuition to develop procedural approximations to true experiments." When laws change or court actions alter criminal justice practices, when services are eliminated due to the end of funding or administrative decisions, or when other special circumstances create unusual conditions or practices, experiments may be created naturally rather than through the intervention of an experimenter. Also, when manipulation of independent variables is neither politically nor ethically feasible, natural experiments may be the only acceptable alternative.

In some instances, natural experiments actually may be preferable to experiments where researchers manipulate the conditions of intervention. For example, when interventions actually encompass several variables, it may be wise to allow them to vary in their natural combinations rather than try to estimate their relative contributions through complex designs. In complex social interventions, it is difficult to isolate single variables from an array of factors that compose treatment and that may covary and interact with staff characteristics. Natural variation across several institutions may more accurately capture the relative contributions of each dimension of intervention (Sinclair & Clarke, 1981). Or, when the effects of the experimenter on the research setting introduce controls or influences that otherwise would not exist, natural experiments can minimize these arti-factual research effects.

This chapter describes the unique contributions of natural experiments to tests of policy and theory. Distinctions between natural and "true" ex-periments are analyzed, and their strengths and weaknesses are assessed relative to experimental and quasi-experimental designs. Three case studies of recent natural experiments in criminology and criminal justice are analyzed. The chapter concludes with a discussion of the methodo-logical issues inherent in natural experiments.

Natural Experiments in Criminology and Criminal Justice

Opportunities to conduct experimental research often may occur in the absence of a planned experiment. In some instances, natural events may result in subject assignment to interventions on a random basis (Rezmovic, 1979). In other cases, natural conditions may produce changes in policy that create interventions that otherwise are not possible (Rossi & Free-man, 1985). In a natural experiment, researchers sample these situations rather than produce them (Anderson, 1975). Accordingly, researchers in natural experiments do not manipulate interventions, nor do they assign subjects to the conditions. They observe and measure differences in natur-ally occurring intervention conditions and in the criterion behaviors among subjects in these conditions.

Natural Experiments Defined

The natural experiment is a procedural approximation to the true experi-ment that uses a natural methodology to assign subjects to conditions or to produce experimental conditions. As in true experiments, equivalent groups are established through random assignment or other inherently natural processes or as a result of natural forces that create distinct condi-tions of policy or practice. In true experiments, a predetermined random methodology is the basis for assigning subjects to experimental or control groups, and the independent variable is manipulated by the experimenter while other variables are controlled. Differences in outcomes can be attri-buted to differences solely in the independent variable, since all other fac-tors are assumed to be distributed randomly among subjects. This enables the investigator to consider the groups equivalent while the experimental conditions differ on the critical factor.

In the natural experiment, the independent variable occurs as part of a natural process, where neither the setting nor the randomization proce-dures are controlled. This affords a unique advantage to the natural experi-ment: Because the experimental setting is not artificially configured to isolate all possible effects other than the independent variable, it is not contrived. Thus, the "true" magnitudes of experimental effects are estimated since they occur within their natural context, rather than in conditions produced specifically for the experimental test. Although confounding may occur with "third" factors in the natural context, these factors are part of the context where the experimental effects occur and may be viewed as part of the natural configuration of the independent variable. Variables that may produce large effects in a controlled setting may be relatively unimportant in a natural setting, because influential factors inherent in the context may have been controlled or eliminated in the natural setting. Natural experiments also reduce confounding produced by subject reactivity with the experimental setting (Rezmovic, 1979), and they minimize researcher influence.

Natural experiments are particularly suitable for criminal justice applications where policies and practices are subject to diverse contextual influences and where researcher influences may alter the nature of the experiment. Consider the following brief example. A new treatment program is planned in a camp for youthful offenders. However, due to delays in staff hiring, the experimental program is implemented in only one of the two residential units of the camp for 6 months. The natural variation in these circumstances creates a unique opportunity for program comparisons. Unlike a planned experiment, where the researchers would train staff and oversee a randomization procedure as well as ensuring therapeutic integrity in the experimental unit, the experimental effort is randomly assigned to one of the two residential units, and implementation occurs through natural organizational processes. Researchers then observe the relative differences in counseling services and compare behaviors accordingly.

Another example of an inherently natural processes also illustrates the unique contributions of natural experiments. Court-ordered releases of an offender cohort due to prison overcrowding offer opportunities for randomzation of sentence length that are unattainable under sentencing policy or practice. The contention that sentence length influences recidivism is an unfalsifiable premise, since sentence length is not likely to be tested experimentally except under the most unique circumstances. The release of a randomly selected cohort of offenders creates such conditions that permit experimental tests of otherwise unfalsifiable claims. Moreover, since such releases are not anticipated, reactivity by both corrections staff and inmates are avoided.

Another genre of natural experiments involves changes in environmental contingencies that support criminal or deviant behavior. Mayhew, Clarke, and Elliott (1989) observed dramatic changes in the rates of motorcycle theft in the Federal Republic of Germany when a mandatory helmet law went into effect. The absence of displacement of motorcycle thefts by thefts of other types of vehicles (automobiles or bicycles) supported the efficacy of situational crime prevention. In this case, the natural experiment involved changes in the choice structuring properties of motorcycle theft at a sufficiently broad environmental level to encompass accurate measures of displacement.

Another natural experiment was reported by Clarke and Mayhew (1988) on the effects of the detoxification of domestic gas on suicides in England and Wales. Prior to detoxification efforts, suicides by domestic gas accounted for almost 50% of all suicides. As the carbon dioxide content of domestic gas was steadily reduced over a 20-year period, suicides by domestic gas were nearly eliminated. Since there was little increase in suicides by other methods, displacement away from gas to other methods was not evident. These natural experiments in prevention address the opportunity structure for specific behaviors. Their designs are akin to experimental methods in the natural sciences, such as oceanography or geology, where large ecological changes present immediate opportunities for observation of environmental change.

The Comparative Strengths and Weaknesses of Natural and True Experiments

There is disagreement on the comparative rigor of "true" and natural experiments. True experiments isolate a single variable and can make unambiguous claims of its relationship to a dependent variable. They provide the most conclusive and least fallible tests of intervention effects. In the true experiment, all variables are controlled, and variation is introduced one variable at a time. True experiments thus represent one end of a continuum of rigor in assessing the effects of policies or practices.

In natural experiments, all variables that compose the experimental condition are free to vary simultaneously; controls are introduced (where possible) one at a time and, often, only through statistical methods. Some confounding is likely in natural experiments, since factors present in the context are covarying with the experimental variable. The problem of confounding actually is the problem of the presence of a third factor in the natural setting that may be a simultaneous influence on the relationship between the independent and dependent variables. Accordingly, while true experiments yield causal information, the relationships analyzed in natural experiments may more accurately be termed "predictive" information (Anderson, 1975). Nevertheless, the threats to validity are minimized in natural experiments because the essential elements of randomness of subject participation and independence of interventions are preserved. This becomes evident when natural experiments are compared to nonexperimental designs.

Quasi-experimental designs that use nonequivalent control groups risk several threats to validity. For example, when randomization is not feasible, matching techniques frequently are employed. The matching criteria are presumed to be related to outcome in an attempt to eliminate all possible influences other than the independent variable. The investigator must determine factors that render groups equivalent, factors that should approximate a random pattern. However, designs that use matched samples are limited by the assumptions that guide the selection of matching factors. Rarely are these factors known a priori, and the matching procedure itself may introduce regression effects into the results. That is, the groups will be nonequivalent since some factor not included in the matching procedure is likely to be related to the outcome variable, and the two groups will differ in their probabilistic associations with the dependent variable. Eventually, the investigator must adjust for nonrandomness in the distribution of matching criteria by introducing controls for factors related both to subject variability and to the presumed differences between conditions. Nevertheless, this procedure is preferable to not using any type of control group. Interactions between unmatched factors and criterion variables also may be stronger for one group than another, further confounding the experiment.

Other quasi-experimental techniques also may approximate true experiments. Multiple interrupted time series designs can address validity problems with history when one series serves as a control series. Validity threats are present, however, from coincidental influences of context and external events that may confound the effects of the independent variable. A thorough knowledge of the context and setting is necessary if an investigator is to address these potential validity issues. Campbell and Stanley (1966, p. 57) refer to recurrent institutional cycle designs as an "inelegant accumulation of precautionary checks . . . [that] approaches experimentation." The technique requires that several nonequivalent groups be patched together in a study design to rule out various specific validity threats. Although the strategy gains in inferential strength through multiple comparisons, it is based on the accumulation of several pieces of evidence, each of which by itself may be inadequate. Although this strategy may produce a convincing argument, it appears that its overall strength will be limited by its weakest single piece of evidence.

Finally, regression-discontinuity designs are appropriate for situations where a specific group is selected for an intervention based on some quantification of dimensions of antecedent behaviors and classification of cases based on a threshold index of the antecedents. When outcome variables are plotted, there should be a (significant) discountinuity at the cutting point in regression curves for persons who receive the intervention compared to those who do not. This powerful design is limited primarily by the validity of the classification measures and the selection of the cutting point (Campbell, 1969), as well as selection-maturation interactions between pretest and posttest measurements (Cook and Campbell, 1979). The integrity of the classification procedure also directly affects internal validity;

deviance from the classification criteria alters the fundamental assumption of the technique. There are other potential troubles in this design, however. The method works best with linear regressions, but curvilinear models can lead to different interpretations. Cook and Campbell (1979) suggest that when one of the regressions is not linear, spurious intercepts may emerge.

Thus, on a continuum of rigor and certainty in research design, natural experiments closely approximate true experiments in attributing causality to one or more variables in a field setting. Natural experiments may provide greater confidence in the randomness of sampling and integrity of the independent variable than the variety of quasi-experimental designs. Yet, because they encompass an experimental condition *in situ*, rather than a single independent variable, natural experiments do not provide the certainty of a true experiment in discounting one variable as a possible cause of change in another. Nevertheless, they may offer conclusive evidence that group differences are not attributable to subject differences, although the locus of effect in the natural setting is less precise than in an experiment.

Three Case Studies

In this section, three case studies illustrate the promises and conundrums of natural experiments.

Preventive Detention: Predicting Pretrial Dangerousness for Adolescents

The preventive detention of allegedly dangerous but unconvicted offenders is designed both to ensure defendants' future court appearances and to protect the community from crimes they might commit during the pretrial period. Traditionally, the setting of high bail effectuated the pretrial detention of many defendants thought to be dangerous or risks for not returning to court.[3] Beginning with the Federal Bail Reform Act of 1966 (P.L. 89-465, 80 Stat. 214) and the District of Columbia Court Reform Act of 1970 (D.C. Code Ann. 23-1321–1332), 34 states and the District of Columbia enacted preventive detention statutes that provide for the denial of bail and pretrial incarceration of individuals based on judicial predictions of "dangerousness" (Goldkamp, 1985).[4] Yet the accuracy of danger predictions for adults or juveniles has been inconclusive and limited by a variety of methodological shortcomings (Shannon, 1985).

In 1981, after declaring New York's preventive detention law for juveniles unconstitutional in what became known eventually as *Schall v. Martin* (1984), the U.S. District Court for the Southern District of New York issued an injunction prohibiting the detention of juveniles based on a judicial determination that the youth would commit a serious crime before the next court date. However, many judges continued to order juveniles into detention under the New York Family Court Act, 739 (a)(ii). The injunction was directed at the Commissioner of Juvenile Justice to not accept youth into detention, rather than at judges to not render such determinations. Experimental conditions were created by the court order that were politically not feasible for the researcher to negotiate.

These events provided a unique opportunity to test experimentally the validity of preventive detention for juveniles based on predictive models of subsequent juvenile and adult criminality. Preventive detention is predicated on assumptions that previously were unfalsifiable: Defendants are detained on the basis of anticipated crimes or danger that they never have the opportunity to commit because they are confined. Accordingly, the opportunity to pose the anticipated danger is removed. The injunction temporarily restored the opportunity to commit the acts they were predicted to commit. An experimental condition was created that previously was politically infeasible: the release of a cohort of defendants predicted to be dangerous.

Study Design

Research to examine the accuracy of judicial predictions of dangerousness unfortunately began well after the injunction expired (Fagan & Guggenheim, 1987, 1988). Between 1981 and 1984, while the injunction was in effect, 75 juveniles were remanded to detention under the Family Court provisions for preventive detention. Prosecutors moved that the youths be detained preventively, and judges ruled on the motion. However, youths remanded to preventive detention were released within hours of the detention order pursuant to the injunction. To certify that these in fact were preventive detention cases, defense attorneys consulted with the prosecutors to assess the intent and statutory basis of their motion. Legal counsel for the Department of Juvenile Justice, the agency that operated the detention facility, ordered the release of youths based on this joint communication from defense counsel and prosecutors. These youths became known as *Schall* youths, named after the Commissioner of Juvenile Justice who was a defendant in the lawsuit.

The control group was a random sample of youths not ordered into detention, either under the preventive detention provisions of the Family Court Act or on other grounds. A supplemental comparison group was selected who matched the *Schall* cases on classifications of age, race, committing offense, and prior record. The comparison groups were drawn from three time periods: 1981 to 1984 (when the *Schall* injunction was in effect) and periods both preceding and following the *Schall* injunction. By selecting cases from the periods both preceding *and* following the injunction, controls for possible period effects were introduced. Since the supplemental group was selected from a randomly sampled population of non-detained youths, the supplemental sample was used as the basis for comparison of the accuracy of judicial predictions of dangerousness.

The rates and severity of criminal behavior of *Schall* and control youths were compiled from information on the juvenile and criminal court histories for 68 of the 75 *Schall* defendants and 69 juveniles in the comparison group.[5] Data collection ended in October 1987; the follow-up interval ranged from 3 to 6 years. The study examined two specific dimensions "dangerousness": (1) the time to the first rearrest for any offense and for offenses that matched the statutory description of "danger" and (2) the total rearrests for any offense and "dangerous" offenses. "Dangerousness" was operationally defined as an arrest for felony violence, based on the general consensus in definitions in states that permit preventive detention (Goldkamp, 1985).

The failure rate analysis was particularly concerned with rearrests that occurred within the time period when the *Schall* youths would have been detained had the injunction not been effect. In the New York City Family Courts, over 90% of detained youths are released from detention within 17 days after apprehension, when the probable cause hearing occurs. If detention is continued beyond the probable cause hearing, the median stay is 120 days, the expected duration of a case that is tried before a Family Court judge.

Results

Schall defendants were rearrested earlier than the control group, for both violent or other offenses. Among the *Schall* youths, 21.7% were not rearrested at all, compared to 27% of the control youths. Within the crucial 17-day period, 8.6% of the *Schall* youths were rearrested, 2.8% for a violent offense. Among the comparison group, only 1.6% were rearrested at all during the 17-day period, none for a violent offense. Within 120 days, nearly half of the *Schall* youths (46.3%) were rearrested for any offense but only 11.2% of the comparison group. For violent offenses, 18.8% of the *Schall* youths were rearrested versus 6.2% of the control group. Over 50% of the *Schall* youths and 60% of the controls were never arrested for violent offenses during the follow-up period. These differences were significant for all arrests but were not significant for violent offenses.

The results suggest that judges accurately selected juvenile defendants for preventive detention who were more likely than other defendants to be rearrested within the critical 17- and 120-day periods. However, they were not able to identify defendants more likely to pose "danger" to the community within those intervals, based on the *charged* offense.[6] Although the marginal gain in predictive efficacy was significant for rearrests that did not meet the evaluative criteria for "dangerousness," false positives still were far greater than accurate predictions.[7] More than 9 in 10 *Schall* youths were not rearrested at all in the 17-day period, and 97.2% did not pose the danger to the community that was inherent in their designation as a *Schall* defendant.

Conclusions

The *Schall* v. *Martin* (104 S. Ct. at 2410, 1984) decision reaffirmed the New York juvenile detention law permitting preventive detention on the basis of anticipated future crime. The U.S. Supreme Court strongly supported the community protection aims of preventive detention decisions. The court accepted the constitutionality of prevention of future crimes based on a record of unproven past acts or anticipated future conduct for the many. However, this study suggests that the theoretical goals of preventive detention may be only partially achieved at the expense of due process measures in pretrial decision making (von Hirsch, 1972). Although aggregate social benefits may accrue from such predictions, there are significant violations of the obligations to individualized justice.

Methadone Treatment: A Study of a County Policy Change

Despite the popularity of methadone maintenance as a treatment modality for heroin addiction, numerous questions have been raised about its effectiveness in reducing opiate and polydrug abuse, alcoholism, and unproductive life-styles (Brown, Jansen, & Benn, 1975). Methadone originally was defined as an indefinite, long-term (perhaps lifetime) treatment modality. However, diminishing public resources, inconclusive evidence of methadone's positive effects, and a changing political climate regarding substance abuse have changed public conceptions about methadone. As a result, methadone policy and treatment goals have envolved from lifetime maintenance to viewing methadone as an interim step toward detoxification and abstinence (Dole & Nyswander, 1976; Newman, 1977).

Accordingly, controversy over methadone treatment has centered on the inability of methadone users to "detach" from methadone maintenance and the wisdom of indefinite methadone treatment. In turn, policies were developed in California that advocated a limited duration of methadone treatment (McGlothlin & Anglin, 1981). In Alameda County (Oakland), California, health officials adopted a policy to limit the duration of subsidized methadone maintenance to 2 years. Effective October 1, 1984, the county withdrew funding for methadone maintenance for individuals who had occupied county-funded methadone maintenance slots for 2 years or longer. Over 300 patients in three county-funded clinics were affected. The patients had the option of transferring to private programs, where they would be required to pay $200 per month for treatment, or detoxifying.

The sudden policy shift created a unique opportunity to study the effects of varying lengths of methadone maintenance, as well as the effects of the withdrawal of methadone treatment from methadone-dependent patients. Historically, few methadone patients terminated their treatment except under adverse social or medical circumstances. Medical protocols, opposition from treatment providers, and ethical considerations prevented systematic research on varying lengths of methadone treatment or the withdrawal of methadone (Anglin & McGlothlin, 1982; Ben-Yehuda, 1982). The precipitous cutoff created natural variation in the length of methadone treatment among those affected, with a minimum of 2 years. It also created the unprecedented opportunity to examine the effects of withdrawal of methadone maintenance from dependent patients.

Study Design

Researchers responded to the advance notice of the policy change by obtaining support from the National Institute of Drug Abuse for a longitudinal study of the methadone patients affected by the study (Rosenbaum, 1984). The study cohort included half of the 300 methadone patients for a 30-month follow-up study, selected to reflect the demographic makeup of the general methadone population in the county. Six waves of interviews were planned: an initial interview upon termination from subsidized methadone and five follow-up interviews at 6-month intervals. The research examined the effects of methadone withdrawal on their social well being, physical health, substance abuse, and criminal behaviors. Subjects were recruited from the clinics during the period immediately preceding their cutoff from eligibility for county-funded treatment.

The research design relied on qualitative methods to assess the impacts of the policy on methadone patients. These methods had been used widely in substance abuse research and were viewed as appropriate for this study. Quantitative data were collected on drug use, work history, family makeup, and criminal behavior. Qualitative methods were used to assess patients' interpretations of their experiences during the confusing and difficult months following withdrawal from methadone, or their struggles to pay for treatment for those who elected to transfer to unsubsidized methadone slots. Since there had been few studies of the social psychological processes of withdrawl from methadone, these methods were appropriate for the tasks of theory development and interpretation.

Results

After 315 follow-up interviews over 2 years, patterns emerged that were evident throughout the study. One in 4 patients (24%) elected to continue methadone maintenance at a $200 monthly cost. To circumvent the rule, a few (9%) moved to another county with no restrictions. The remainder struggled to detoxify, remain free of substance use, and construct new lives away from the "heroin life."

Opiate use among terminated patients varied extensively: 40% were still addicted after the first 6 months, 30% reported occasional heroin use but not addiction, and 30% reported no heroin use. However, illicit drug use continued for many former methadone patients: 1 in 3 avoided drug use, but over half (54%) reported some drug use, while 12% reported habitual use of illicit drugs including opiates. Even among patients continuing methadone treatment in paying slots, nearly 60% continued using heroin. Many others reported increased criminality to pay for their clinic fees. Other problems were reported, as well: 60% reported that they had committed serious crimes, and 30% had been jailed within 6 months. Most clients (68%) remained unemployed, and many of these were receiving public assistance.

In analyses of the posttreatment experiences, Murphy and Rosenbaum (1988) found some unintended consequences among the former methadone patients. "Successful" clients often had homes, jobs, families and material possessions. Although they had stopped using opiates and stayed out of the heroin life, they continued in methadone treatment and experienced financial difficulties in paying for it. In turn, these difficulties created family tensions, particularly around child rearing. For some, the difficult economic choices brought on by clinic fees motivated a return to crime to finance continued methadone treatment.

Other former patients adapted to the policy by using acute-care mental health facilities between maintenance periods, financing their continued use of methadone by selling methadone to others obtained through "take home" privileges, or making chronically late or only partial payment of fees. For a few "model" patients, detoxification from methadone proceeded smoothly, through the use of social and financial support systems that were intact during their time in treatment. Finally, there were few distinctions in these groups by time-in-treatment prior to their withdrawal from subsidized treatment. Patients who were aware of the 2-year limitation well in advance did not fare better in making posttreatment adjustments than others who were more precipitously terminated.

Conclusions

The 2-year rule was instituted to balance decreasing county treatment budgets among drug-free residential programs and methadone maintenance programs. However, for many former methadone patients, the rule's effects were counterproductive. Many methadone patients were destabilized from methadone by the rule, while few were able to successfully detoxify and maintain productive lives without methadone maintenance (Rosenbaum, Irwin, & Murphy, 1988). The rule contradicted empirical evidence of the natural history of heroin addiction and previous experiences with methadone withdrawal in other California counties. Premature detoxification from methadone contributed to increased heroin use and criminality. The economic circumstances of some former patients created a Hobbesian choice of returning to crime to support clinic fees or returning to heroin use. Moreover, the relationship between the 2-year rule and AIDS risks was not anticipated by policy makers. The researchers concluded that premature, involuntary detoxification from methadone returned many patients to intravenous heroin use and its attendant needle-sharing practices that expose users to HIV infection.

The Validity of Psychiatric Judgements About Violence

Psychiatrists are often called upon to judge whether an individual is "dangerous." This decision is a critical aspect of the process of involuntary hospitalization of patients diagnosed as "mentally ill" or "dangerous" to oneself or others, their length of stay, and the timing of their release. In the criminal justice system, psychiatric recommendations are extremely influential in the decision to acquit on the basis of insanity or to release incarcerated offenders diagnosed as mentally ill.

Psychiatristis' judgments are presumed to be reliable and valid (Ennis & Litwack, 1974). However, there is considerable dispute over the accuracy of such predictions, especially for predictions of violence. Critics cite research that shows no special ability among psychiatrists or mental health professionals to make accurate predictions in more than 1 case in 3 and consistent evidence of unacceptably high rates of false positives (Bottoms & Brownsword, 1983; Monahan, 1981; Steadman & Cocozza, 1974; cf. *Barefoot v. Estelle*, 1983; Litwack & Schlesinger, 1987). Also, violence is especially difficult to predict because it is a low-base-rate, context-bound behavior with multiple definitions (Megargee, 1981).

However, many of the studies critical of psychiatric prediction are flawed by sampling and selection artifacts. The paradigms for studying the accuracy of predictions have been release cohorts and the use of prediction instruments. But released patients often were not representative of those predicted to be violent (e.g., Kozol, Boucher, & Garofalo, 1972). Other studies used predictions based on behaviors that occurred long before the prediction was made (e.g., Wenk, Robison, & Smith, 1972). Virtually no studies examined predictions based on recent history of repeated violence (Litwack & Schlesinger, 1987). The predicting professionals themselves have been a variable in prediction research. Thornberry and Jacoby (1979) reported "political predictions" where the psychiatrists are not representative of their profession or even other mental health professionals.

Until 1966, there were no experimental studies to test the validity of predictions of "dangerousness" among either inmates or patients hospitalized based on psychiatric diagnoses. For obvious reasons, there has been no research that examined the behaviors of hospitalized or incarcerated inmates pursuant to a psychiatric diagnosis of "dangerousness." Nor had conditions occurred where a cohort of such inmates was randomly selected for release following the prediction. In 1966, the U.S. Supreme Court in *Baxstrom v. Herold* (1966) ordered the release of 969 prisoner-patients in New York State Department of Corrections hospitals whose terms had expired. These inmates had been detained beyond the expiration of their prison sentences because psychiatrists had determined that they were too "dangerous" for release or transfer to civil facilities. A natural experiment had been created where a cohort of incarcerated offenders predicted by psychiatrists to be dangerous was released from secure confinement.

Study Design and Results

The release cohort ($N = 969$) was studied by various researchers who examined their institutional and community adjustments (Hunt & Wiley, 1968; Steadman & Cocozza, 1980; Steadman & Keveles, 1972). Within the first year, 24 patients had died, 10 had transferred, 62 were convalescents in medical hospitals, and 24 others had miscellaneous dispositions. Of the remaining 849 patients who were transferred to civil mental hospitals, 147 had been discharged to the community within 1 year. The 702 who remained experienced no incidents of intrainstitutional violence. Only 7 patients were recommitted to a Department of Corrections hospital within the first year (Hunt & Wiley, 1968). By 1970, 4 years after the court order, 27% of the patients were living in the community, only 9% had been convicted of a crime (only 4% for felonies), and 3% were in either a correctional facility or a hospital for the criminally insane (Steadman & Keveles, 1972).

Evidently, the psychiatric predictions of danger were inaccurate for the vast majority of the *Baxstrom* patients. The false positive rates were well in excess of the "two in three" barometer cited by Ennis and Litwack (1974), among others. However, criticisms of the *Baxstrom* study give caution to its conclusions. Many of the inmates were elderly and physically limited in their violence potential. The "predictions" have been characterized as "global assessments," rather than careful individualized diagnoses (Steadman & Cocozza, 1980). Whether the predictions were made in good faith has been disputed by Litwack and Schlesinger (1987), who cited the tendency of psychiatrists to recommend retention of chronically ill patients. This criticism was rejected by Monahan (1981), who suggested that such bureaucratic pressures often translate into a social reality and prophecy. The studies illustrated the complex interactions of predispositions among predicting professionals, information on patient behaviors and characteristics, and the inexact science of psychiatry.

Conclusions

Psychiatric predictions of violence evidently are inaccurate, but the extent of overprediction remains in dispute. The *Baxstrom* study illustrates the diversity of factors that influence the accuracy of predictions. Ennis and Litwack (1974) concluded that the validity of psychiatric predictions of "dangerousness" for mental patients, as for juvenile defendants, is less valid than predictions based on the flip of a coin.

Designing Natural Experiments

The case studies offer a cross section of natural experiments in criminal justice. However, the circumstances that produce natural experiments are more varied than those illustrated in the case studies. Recognizing the inherently natural processes that produce experimental conditions is the task of the researcher. Keeping abreast of events in one's areas of interest and specialization should provide advance notice of the development of experimental conditions. Even if one becomes aware after natural experimental conditions develop, researchers can move quickly to implement research designs to provide conclusive evidence on the relevant policy or theoretical questions. In any natural experiment, researchers will face many of the same challenges that confront investigators in laboratory or field experiments. They also face some unique challenges. Strategies to maximize the validity of natural experiments are described below.

Research Design

The research design of a natural experiment is likely to be governed by the conditions that produce the experiment. Campbell and Stanley (1966) identified three experimental designs that maximize internal validity, although there remain limitations on external validity in these designs. The pretest-posttest control-group design and Solomon four-group designs are less likely to be used in natural experiments, since the development of the experiment often occurs with short notice and few options. This naturally leads to limitations on pretest measurement. These designs also require extensive involvement of the researcher in manipulation of the independent variable.

The researcher in a natural experiment is most likely to use a posttest-only control group design. In the *Baxstrom* and *Schall* examples above, this design was the only available design, since the experimental conditions resulted precipitously. In the methadone study, the researchers were able to conduct interviews with methadone clients before they were terminated by the 2-year rule. The posttest-only design always leaves the researcher wondering whether the control and experimental groups actually were equivalent before the intervention, even under rigorous randomization procedures. Campbell and Stanley (1966) recommend that where appropriate antecedent measures are available (e.g., prior criminal records), they should be used as covariates to test for interactions between the intervention and pretest behaviors. This strategy also broadens the generalizability of the findings with greater care.

Another design useful in some natural experiments is the prospective longitudinal cohort study, where there is natural variation on the independent variable. Regardless of the specific experimental design, the researcher still must rigorously maintain and verify the conditions of randomization of subjects, and the independence of the groups or conditions.

Special Issues About Control Groups

Strategies for the construction of control groups should be evident from the conditions that create the natural experiment. However, issues about control groups may surface in some natural experiments. In studies of prison release cohorts, for example, natural variation is created in sentence length, the independent variable; control groups thus are present in the study population. But there are situations when judgment is required in accepting subjects as valid controls.

In the *Schall* study, for example, the youths remanded to preventive detention were not representative of all youths in juvenile court nor other youths detained under other statutory criteria. They were remanded for preventive detention because they were deemed "dangerous" by judges; adequate controls could not be identified simply by sampling randomly from the juvenile court population. *Schall* youths probably were at the extremes of the distribution of important factors in detention decision making such as prior record and severity of current offense. Youths preventively detained before and after the injunction did not experience the conditions of freedom that the *Schall* youths did and, therefore, were not a valid test of the marginal gain in predictive efficacy. Accordingly, the selection of controls for this study required decisions beyond simply selecting a table of random numbers.

Thus, the strategy for sampling controls may not be readily apparent in some natural experiments. In some cases, there may be no natural control group. Alternatives, such as the use of matched controls, may reduce the validity of an experiment (Cook & Campbell, 1979; Rezmovic, 1979). In the *Schall* study, the researchers elected to sample randomly from within a segment of the control population. Although the control sample did not differ statistically from the *Schall* youths, important subjective criteria in detention decision making were not controlled: the youth's demeanor and appearance and the appearance of a parent at the detention hearing, for example (Fagan & Guggenheim, 1988). In this case, the researchers chose to proscribe the universe of controls based on criteria derived from statutory language that governed the preventive detention decision.

There is no simple answer to such challenges. Researchers should understand the hierarchy of research designs that are available and consider the weaknesses of control-group strategies that vary from rigorous randomization procedures. Appropriate disaggregation of analyses and analysis of covariate effects can provide statistical controls that may restore the power of a true experimental design.

Measurement Issues

Selection of measurement approaches also may be dictated by circumstance. The researchers in the methadone experiment were able to develop and use a qualitative research instrument for two reasons. First, they had advance notice of the creation of the experiment. Second, they did not specify hypotheses regarding the effects of the rule change and instead opted for research using grounded theory. Researchers who must implement designs with little notice or preparation obviously will not have the option of careful development and pretesting unique measures and instruments.

Thus, it is likely that researchers in natural experiments will select measurement strategies already developed and validated. Their appropriateness for the subjects, conditions, and hypotheses of the natural experiment should be carefully assessed. For example, using a general self-reported crime scale (with trivial or global crime items) may be less useful for a prison population than using a scale that emphasizes more serious items. Standardized scales also should be carefully reviewed regarding the populations on which they were normed. Researchers using official records should be aware of their strengths and limitations and the possible exogenous factors that may determine their relevance. For example, parole officers use wide discretion in responding to technical violations by parolees. The decision to formally or informally respond to such violations varies by region and even by local parole offices within regions. Local custom, therefore, may influence reincarceration rates and recidivism measures as much as offender behaviors.

Moreover, not all natural experiments may be amenable to systematic research. For example, studies with hard-to-locate populations (e.g., an experiment randomizing drug enforcement against street-level dealers) may not be amenable to interview procedures to assess the specific deterrent effects. Costs and other factors also will influence the selection of measures. Lengthy interview schedules require a cadre of skilled and trained interviewers. Researchers should determine if funds and time are available to create those measurement conditions. In general, the decisions involved in measurement should reflect many of the same criteria as in field experiments or other sound research designs.

Assessing the Strength and Integrity of the Independent Variable

Natural experiments are vulnerable to the problem of variability over time and subjects in the strength and integrity of the independent variable.

Earlier, the strength of interventions was discussed. The integrity of an intervention refers to its consistency over time and among staff or the organizational units involved, its fealty to the theories underlying the policy or intervention, and whether it is perceived by participants as intended by planners or staff. Accordingly, natural experiments require more than careful measurement of dependent variables or vigilance over randomization. The generalizability of "X" requires equally careful measurement of the independent variable. Its strength and integrity are other sources of variability in all experiments, whether they be field, natural, or laboratory experiments. Interventions may more accurately be conceived of as vectors than dichotomous or unidimensional variables.

The risks of dichotomous or "black box" approaches to characterizing the independent variable have been well documented (Fagan & Hartstone, 1986; Rezmovic, 1979; Sechrest et al., 1979). Interventions should be conceptualized in measurable terms and data collected on the independent variable itself. For example, in a treatment intervention, contact hours and types of services can be charted. Data from both staff and participants can be collected to see if differences in interventions that were evident to the researchers were perceived by subjects in the situations. It is possible that there are elements of an experimental intervention present in a control situation; the distinctions between conditions would then be measurable as ordinal or interval measures of some dimension(s) of the intervention, rather than as nominal categories. This measurement strategy also has implications for data analysis and assessment of intervention-subject interactions.

This question has taken on new importance in recent years as researchers have recognized the importance of therapeutic integrity on the outcomes of treatment experiments. It also has implications for the interpretation and generalizability of the conditions that were created by natural processes. As a source of variability and a threat to or reinforcer of external validity, attention to the measurement of the independent variable is a critical factor in the conduct of natural experiments.

Sources of Error in Natural Experiments

The unique strengths of the natural experiment lie in its simultaneous operation of two or more variables that compose an intervention or policy. Often, these combinations are difficult to achieve in field or laboratory experiments, particularly in criminal justice applications such as correctional interventions or legal decision making. Manipulation of several variables simultaneously is expensive and time consuming and depends on large numbers of subjects and complicated strategies to control other influences.

Natural experiments address these problems but with possible sacrifice in both internal and external validity. True experiments randomize all potential sources of error associated with these variables (Anderson, 1975). The possibility of constant error remains in a natural experiment, just as in a true experiment. Constant error may enter the relationship between the dependent and independent variables in a natural experiment precisely because of the simultaneous influence of several independent variables and their interaction with the setting and each other. Natural experiments are vulnerable to many of the other same internal and external validity problems that threaten true and quasi-experiments, such as history, maturation, instrumentation, and mortality. In this section, several major sources of constant error in a natural experiment are examined.

Sampling Error

Researchers can generalize confidently from experimental results when observations are repeated on an adequate number of members randomly sampled from a population. In an experiment, *sample variables* refer to the characteristics of the objects studied, whether they are chemical samples, tissue samples from animals, or defendants in a criminal proceeding. However, only a limited number of the subjects to which we may wish to generalize usually are included in the experiment itself. Their characteristics thus become sample variables, regardless of whether these characteristics are randomly distributed among experimental conditions.[8]

Since natural experiments capitalize on inherently natural processes to assure equivalence, the experimenter often must rely on the samples that are present when the events occur to create the experimental condition. In a field or laboratory experiment, the researcher may re-create the experimental variable with a range of sample variables to ensure its generalizability. Researchers in natural experiments are not likely to be able to sample more than once in a unique experimental condition.

Sample variables therefore represent one source of error in a natural experiment. The unique contexts of natural experiments limit their sampling conditions and suggest caution about the generalizations that confidently can be made. Criminal justice researchers should be aware of the sample variables present in a natural experiment and their relationship to other offender or general populations. Researchers should recognize that large experimental effects observed in a natural experiment may not be evident with other samples where their importance may be mitigated by the effects of sample variables.

Regression to the Mean

Regression artifacts in quasi-experimental designs have been well documented as a source of error and ultimately false interpretation (see Campbell & Stanley, 1966; Cook & Campbell, 1979; Maltz, Gordon, McDowall, & McCleary, 1980). Experiments with criminal justice populations are especially vulnerable to problems of statistical regression, since offenders often may enter the criminal justice system during an interval of relatively high-rate offending when the likelihood of official detection is greatest. Similarly, new policies may be adopted when some phenomenon—such as violent crime—has increased to a relatively high rate (Campbell, 1969).

In its simplest form, statistical regression occurs when a population is selected for some intervention precisely because this group represents the extremities of the behaviors of interest, such as offending rates or educational deficiencies. When their subsequent behaviors reflect improvement, it is falsely attributed to an experimental intervention, when in fact it more likely reflects the imperfect correlation between observations conducted with the same individual at two different times. The decrease in values of a series could have been predicted with or without the intervention. Or, as Campbell and Stanley (1966, p. 11) stated: "the more deviant the score, the more measurement error it probably contained."

Although true experiments control for regression artifacts through randomization procedures, natural experiments in criminal justice may be more vulnerable to them. Recall that in natural experiments, the researcher samples situations rather than produces them. However, the situations themselves may reflect the conditions of extremity that produce regression artifacts rather than naturally occurring variation. For example, the behaviors of prisoners released from overcrowded facilities may reflect the extreme conditions of imprisonment and may not be generalizable to prisoners released from overcrowded facilities.

Especially when there are a small number of observations and a small number of extreme pretest scores among either of the experimental conditions, regression artifacts may supplement or explain actual between-group differences. Sample error also may lead to significant pretest differences between groups in these situations, creating possible selection biases or a group with deviant scores. Such occurrences are more likely in natural experiments involving short time periods or small organizational units where events create new interventions. Typically, however, these sources of error are rare in natural experiments and can be compensated by adjunct sampling strategies to add greater precision to "natural" randomization.

Period Effects

Research designs are inherently vulnerable to period effects, regardless of whether they are true, natural or quasi-experiments. Period effects may occur in several ways: season, time of day, historical era, or temporal proximity to specific exogenous events. Period effects threaten internal validity by potentially confounding the effects of an independent variable with sample variables—that is, the reactivity of subjects to specific temporal influences. In criminal justice experiments, this suggests that specific forms of crime may be more susceptible to interventions in some seasons than others or at some times of the day than others. For example, homicide, domestic violence, and drug selling vary seasonally as well as by time of the day—the effects of interventions in any of these areas are likely to interact with the base rates of those behaviors disaggregated by season and time.

Researchers using experimental designs can adjust for these influences in several ways. Experimental conditions can be replicated at different times of the day or in different seasons. If an experiment occurs over a more limited time period, controls may estimate seasonal or other temporal effects. Period effects that reflect historical influences are less easily addressed. For example, efforts to mobilize neighborhood residents to organize patrols against neighborhood drug selling are likely to be more effective in this decade than they may have been in the past decade.

In natural experiments, variables that may be of considerable importance in nature are difficult to control. When inherently natural processes occur, they are beyond the temporal control of the researcher. They also are not likely to be repeated often. If they recur, it is unlikely that temporal variation will be available or that they will recur within an interval short enough to minimize historical influences. Researcher in natural experiments should be aware of this important source of error and avoid the false interpretations that may result.

The Generalizability of "X"

The effects of factors that influence internal validity might be misinterpreted as effects of the independent variables. In true experiments, these factors are randomly distributed among subjects in both control and experimental conditions. However, other factors may influence the independent variable, rather than subjects, and accordingly may limit the generalizability of the results beyond the groups studied. Researchers in true experiments may address these effects through careful and precise manipulation of sample variables and experimental conditions.[9] Natural experiments are limited in this regard, since the confluence of events producing the experiments often occurs serendipitously, with little regard to external validity. However, natural experiments have a major advantage over true experiments in their proximity to the conditions of application of the results.

There are several influences on the generalizability of effects observed in a natural experiment. First, interventions actually are the product of interactions among complex variables. Their integrity in a natural setting may vary over time, as may the events in the control setting. For example, members of a prison release cohort resulting from a court order are likely to have experienced prison in a variety of ways as conditions in the facility varied over time and worsened with overcrowding. There are not likely to be repetitions of the events that produce this experiment. Thus, in addition to period effects, the natural experiment is limited by the conditions that serendipity or natural processes provide.

Second, natural experiments are limited in terms of sample variables. Since the experiments is unlikely to be replicated often, artifacts of sample selection may interact with the experimental variable to limit generalizability. In a true experiment, the researcher can manipulate sample variables; researchers in natural experiments are constrained in this regard. In the *Schall v. Martin* case study described previously, for example, the predictive validity of preventive detention could only be tested for those juveniles remanded to preventive detention. It may be a false generalization for judges to confidently remand other youths preventively given the restricted range of the *Schall* sample.

The more complex and politically sensitive the natural experiment, the more unlikely it is to be repeated with other subjects. Accordingly, the possibility remains in both true and natural experiments that the effects hold true only for the unique population with which the experiment occurred. If the effects of an independent variable are more salient for some samples than others, interactions between selection and the independent variable also may limit generalizability and mask the true results of the experiment. Although replication is recommended, it is more difficult to re-create the experimental conditions that were produced by natural processes, limiting the opportunities for replication.

Third, factors that threaten internal validity also may interact with the independent variable. Researchers in true experiments face these problems as well. Again, the limited opportunities to manipulate sample and independent variables in natural experiments increased the likelihood of these effects. The interactions of testing, maturation, and history (Campbell & Stanley, 1966) with sample variables may present sources of error that cannot be corrected through supplementary sampling or measurement approaches.

Despite these limitations, the natural experiment offers unique opportunities to measure effects that cannot be measured in criminal justice settings and to test assumptions thought to be unfalsifiable within the boundaries of true experiments. This discussion shows the potential limitations that researchers must acknowledge in conducting research within the natural setting and their implications for interpretation and generalization of results.

Conclusions

Natural experiments have an important place in criminal justice research. Many of the limitations of field or laboratory experiments are strengths of the natural experiment. When conditions are created by inherently natural processes that otherwise are not feasible, assumptions and practices can be tested through systematic research to provide conclusive evidence of their impacts. Whether researchers can capitalize on natural events that create experiments requires a quick response, often with entrepreneurial skills, to recognize the development of natural experiments and mount systematic data collection efforts. Limitations on resources may be an initial barrier in designing research to study natural events, but flexibility in research strategies can still yield valid and conclusive results. Ongoing relations and collaboration with agencies where natural events may lead to experiments are a prerequisite to effective research on policy changes or innovations.

Endnotes

1. In some instances, offenders who were ordered to leave refused to do so or even assaulted the police officer. The officer was likely to arrest the offender, even if the randomization procedure called for a nonarrest experimental condition.
2. Nevertheless, the experiment has had dramatic effects over the past 25 years. The interviewing and recommendation procedures have been institutionalized as a permanent feature of the criminal justice system and widely replicated in jurisdictions throughout the country.
3. But defendants with sufficient funds could post even high money bail, avoiding the intentions of the court that they remain incarcerated pending adjudication (Goldkamp, 1985).
4. Preventive detention has been formally used in juvenile justice for many years. Such detention has been recognized to serve the traditional twin *parens patriae* aims of the juvenile court by "protecting both the juvenile and society from the hazards of pretrial crime" (*Schall v. Martin*, 104 S. Ct. at 2415). The statutes described danger as a risk that the juvenile would commit a crime in the pretrial period. In effect, the New York law opted for the pretrial incapacitation of juveniles based on judicial predictions of their future threat to the community.
5. Although there were no rearrests recorded for seven of the *Schall* youths, their records could not be located in the Family Court to determine the outcomes of their cases. They were excluded from the analyses.
6. Measurement error with official crime data is another source of error in criminal justice experiments. Arrest charges are a function of both the behavior of the accused and the response of the criminal justice system. See Jackson this volume.
7. Goldkamp's (1985) review of research on assessment of pretrial decision making found similar rates of false identification of "dangerous" defendants, with a margin of error of 10 inappropriate confinements for each appropriate confinement.
8. For example, geologists may examine the effects of volcanic emissions only on the natural minerals present in the areas surrounding an eruption; re-creating the experiment on minerals present in another area must await an eruption in that area.
9. Campbell and Stanley (1966) suggest that external validity problems may be most efficiently overcome by moving randomization to a larger contextual unit—in the case of educational research, the classroom.

References

Anderson, B.F. (1975). The experiment. In G.H. Lewis (ed.), *Fistfights in the kitchen*. Pacific Palisades, CA: Goodyear, pp. 169–176.

Anglin, M.D., McGlothlin, W.H. (1982). Methadone maintenance in California: A decade's experience. In L. Brill & C. Winick (Eds.), *The yearbook of substance use and abuse*. New York: Human Sciences, pp. 219–280.

Barefoot v. Estelle, 77 L. Ed. 2d 1090 (1983).

Baxstrom v. Herold, 383 U.S. S.Ct. 107 (1966).

Ben-Yehuda, N. (1982). Private practice, competition, and methadone maintenance. *The International Journal of the Addictions*, *17*, 329–341.

Berk, R.A., Boruch, R.F., Chambers, D.L., Rossi, P.H., & Witte, A.D. (1985). Social policy experimentation. *Evaluation Review*, *9*(4), 387–430.

Boruch, R.F. (1975). Coupling randomized experiments and approximations to experiments in social program evaluation. *Sociological Methods and Research*, *4*: 31–53.

Bottoms, A.E., & Brownsword, R. (1983). Dangerousness and rights. In J.W. Hinton (Ed.), *Dangerousness: Problems of assessment and prediction*. London: George Allen and Unwin, pp. 9–22.

Brown, B.S., Jansen, D.R., & Benn, G.J. (1975). Changes in attitudes toward methadone. *Archives of General Psychiatry*, *32*, 214–218.

Campbell, D.T. (1969). Reforms as experiments. *American Psychologist*, *24*, 409–429.

Campbell, D.T., & Stanley, J.C. (1966). *Experimental and quasi-experimental designs for research*. Chicago: Rand McNally.

Clarke, R.V.G., & Cornish, D.B. (1972). *The controlled trial in institutional research: Paradigm or pitfall for evaluators?* (Home Office Research Studies Report No. 15). London: Home Office Research Unit.

Clarke, R.V., & Mayhew, P. (1988). The British gas suicide story and its criminological implications. In N. Morris & M. Tonry (Eds.), *Crime and justice: An annual review of research, Volume 10*. Chicago: University of Chicago Press, pp. 79–116.

Cook, T.D., & Campbell, D.T. (1979). *Quasi-experimentation: Design and analysis issues for field settings*. Boston: Houghton-Mifflin.

District of Columbia, Court Reform Act of 1970 (D.C. Code Ann. 23: 1321–1332).

Dole, P., & Nyswander, M.E. (1976). Methadone maintenance treatment: A ten year perspective. *Journal of the American Medical Association*, *235*, 2117–2119.

Empey, L.T., & Erickson, M.L. (1972). *The Provo Experiment*. Lexington, MA: Lexington Books.

Ennis, B.J., & Litwack, T.R. (1974). Psychiatry and the presumption of expertise: Flipping coins in the courtroom. *California Law Review, 62*, 693–752.

Fagan, J., & Guggenheim, M. (1987, November). *The predictive validity of judicial determinations of dangerousness: Preventive detention of juvenile offenders in the* Schall v. Martin *case*. Paper presented at the Annual Meeting of the American Society of Criminology, Montreal.

Fagan, J., & Guggenheim, M. (1988, November). *The prediction of pretrial danger among juvenile offenders: The case for preventive detention*. Paper presented at the Fortunoff Colloquium Series, New York University School of Law, New York.

Fagan, J.A., & Hartstone, E.C. (1986). *Innovation and experimentation in juvenile corrections: The implementation of treatment interventions for violent juvenile offenders. Final Report, The Violent Juvenile Offender Research and Development Program, Volume I* (Grant 85-MU-CX-0001, Office of Juvenile Justice and Delinquency Prevention). Washington, DC: U.S. Department of Justice.

Farrington, D.P., Ohlin, L.E., & Wilson, J.Q. (1986). *Understanding and controlling crime.* New York: Springer-Verlag.

Fienberg, S.B., Singer, B., & Tanur, J.M. (1985). Large-scale social experimentation in the United States. In A.C. Atkinson & S.B. Fienberg (Eds.), *A celebration of statistics.* New York: Springer-Verlag, pp. 287–326.

Federal Bail Reform Act. P.L. 89-465, So Stat. 214, 1966.

Garner, J.A., & Visher, C.A. (1988). Policy experiments come of age. *NIJ Reports, No. 21.* Washington, DC: U.S. Department of Justice, National Institute of Justice.

Goldkamp, J. (1985). Danger and detention: A second generation of bail reform. *Journal of Criminal Law and Criminology, 76,* 1–74.

Hunt, R.C., & Wiley, E.D. (1968). Operation Baxstrom after one year. *American Journal of Psychiatry, 124,* 974.

Kelling, G.L., Pate, T., Dieckman, D., & Brown, C.E. (1976). The Kansas City preventive patrol experiment: A summary report. In G.V. Glass (Ed.), *Evaluation studies review annual, volume I.* Beverly Hills, CA: Sage, pp. 605–657.

Klockars, C.B. (1979). Dirty hands and deviant subjects. In C.B. Klockars & F. O'Connor (Eds.), *Deviance and decency: The Ethics of research with human subjects.* Beverly Hills, CA: Sage, pp. 261–282.

Kozol, H.L., Boucher, R.J., & Garofalo, R.J. (1972). The diagnosis and treatment of dangerousness. *Crime and Delinquency, 19,* 371–392.

Lempert, R.O., & Visher, C.A. (1988). Randomized field experiments in criminal justice agencies. *Research in Action.* Washington, DC: U.S. Department of Justice, National Institute of Justice.

Lerman, P. (1975). *Community treatment and social control.* Chicago: University of Chicago Press.

Lipton, D. Martinson, R., & Wilks, J. (1975). *The effectiveness of correctional treatment: A survey of treatment effectiveness studies.* New York: Praeger.

Litwack, T.R., & Schlesinger, L.B. (1987) Assessing and predicting violence: Research, law and applications. In I.B. Weiner & A.B. Hess (Eds.), *Handbook of forensic psychology.* New York: Wiley, pp. 205–257.

Logan, C.H. (1972). Evaluation research in crime and delinquency: A reappraisal. *Journal of Criminal Law, Criminology and Police Science, 63,* 378–387.

Maltz, M.D., Gordon, A.C., McDowall, D., & McCleary, R. (1980). An artifact in pretest-posttest designs: How it can mistakenly make delinquency programs look effective. *Evaluation Review, 4,* 225–240.

Mayhew, P., Clarke, R.V., & Elliott, D. (1989). Motorcycle theft, helmet legislation, and displacement. *The Howard Journal, 28(1),* 1–8.

McGlothin, W.H., & Anglin, M.D. (1981). Shutting off methadone: Costs and benefits. *Archives of General Psychiatry, 38,* 885–892.

Megargee, E.I. (1981). Methodological problems in the prediction of violence. In J.R. Hays, T.R. Roberts, & K.S. Solway (Eds.), *Violence and the violent individual.* New York: Spectrum, pp. 179–191.

Monahan, J. (1981). *Predicting violent behavior: An assessment of clinical techniques.* Beverly Hills, CA: Sage.

Murphy, S., & Rosenbaum, M. (1988). Money for methadone II: Preliminary findings from a study of Alameda County's new maintenance policy. *Journal of Psychoactive Drug, 20*, 397–402.

Newman, R.G. (1977). *Methadone treatment in narcotic addiction.* New York: Academic.

Rezmovic, E.L. (1979). Methodological considerations in evaluating correctional effectiveness: Issues and chronic problems. In L. Sechrest, S.O. White, & E.D. Brown (Eds.), *The rehabilitation of criminal offenders: Problems and prospects.* Washington, DC: National Academy Press, National Academy of Sciences, pp. 163–209.

Robison, J., & Smith, G. (1971). The effectiveness of correctional programs. *Crime and Delinquency, 17*, 67–80.

Roethlisberger, F.J., & Dickson, W.F. (1939). *Management and the worker.* Cambridge, MA: Harvard University Press.

Rosenbaum, M. (1984). Methadone treatment: A study of a county policy change (Grant 1-R01-DA 03804-01, National Institute of Drug Abuse). Rockville, MD: U.S. Department of Health and Human Services, Alcohol, Drug Abuse and Mental Health Administration.

Rosenbaum, M., Irwin, J., & Murphy, S. (1988). De facto destabilization as policy: The impact of short-term methadone maintenance. *Contemporary Drug Problems, 15*, 491–518.

Rossi, P.H., & Freeman, H.E. (1985). *Evaluation: A systematic approach (3rd ed.).* Beverly Hills, CA: Sage.

Schall v. Martin. 104 U.S. S. Ct. 2403 (1984).

Sechrest, L., White, S.O., & Brown, E.D. (1979). Report of the Panel. In L. Sechrest, S.O. White, & E.D. Brown (Eds.), *the rehabilitation of criminal offenders: Problems and Prospects.* Washington, DC: National Academy Press, National Academy of Sciences, pp. 3–118.

Shannon, L. (1985). Risk assessment vs. real prediction: The prediction and public trust. *Journal of Quantitative Criminology, 1*, 159–184.

Sherman, L.W., & Berk, R.A. (1984). The specific deterrent effects of arrests for domestic assault. *American Sociological Review, 49*, 261–280.

Sinclair, I., & Clarke, R.V. (1981). Cross institutional designs. In E.M. Goldberg & N. Connelly (Eds.), *Evaluative research in social care*, pp. 101–113. London: Heinemann.

Stapleton, W.V., & Teitlebaum, L.E. (1972). *In defense of youth.* New York: Russell Sage Foundation.

Steadman, H.J., & Cocozza, J. (1974). *Careers of the criminally insane.* Lexington, MA: D.C. Heath.

Steadman, H.J., & Cocozza. J. (1980). The prediction of dangerousness—Baxstrom: A case study. In G. Cooke (Ed.), *The Role of the forensic psychologist.* Springfield, IL: Thomas, pp. 204–215.

Steadman, H.J., & Keveles, G. The community adjustment and criminal activity of the Baxstrom patients: 1966–70. *American Journal of Psychiatry, 129*, 304–310.

Thornberry, T.P., & Jacoby, J.E. (1979). *The criminally insane: A community follow up of mentally ill offenders.* Chicago: University of Chicago Press.

von Hirsch, A. (1972). Prediction of criminal conduct and preventive confinement of convicted persons. *University of Buffalo Law Review, 21*, 717–725.

Wenk, E.A., Robison, J.O., & Smith, G.W. (1972). Can violence be predicted? *Crime and Delinquency, 18*, 393–402.

Zeisel, H. (1973). Reflections on experimental techniques in the law. *Journal of Legal Studies, 2*(1), 107–124.

6
Exploring the Offender's Perspective: Observing and Interviewing Criminals*

RICHARD WRIGHT and TREVOR BENNETT

The offender's perspective is perhaps the most neglected area of criminological inquiry (see, for example, Walker, 1984). This perspective, however, is of crucial importance to the formulation of both theory and policy. In regard to theory, for example, the factors often observed to be associated with crime must be linked to criminality through the perceptions and decision making of offenders. As Glueck (quoted in Bovet, 1951 p. 20) has suggested, "A factor cannot be a cause before it is a motive." Somewhat similarly, Toch (1987 p. 152) has argued that "criminology can benefit by illuminating the 'black box' (offender perspectives) that intervenes between conventional independent variables (criminogenic influences) and dependent variables (antisocial behavior)." And Walker (1984) has gone so far as to maintain that criminological theorists are "wasting their time" (p. viii) if they do not consider what he calls the "states of mind" (p. viii) that lead up to criminal offenses.

Criminal justice policy-making, much of which is based on specific assumptions about the perceptions of criminals, also requires an understanding of the offender's perspective. Indeed, this perspective can be thought of as an important intervening variable that can determine, independently, the effectiveness of a crime prevention strategy. The traditional policy of deterrence, for instance, rests squarely on the notion that offenders are rational, weighing the potential costs and rewards of their anticipated actions. The policy attempts to increase the perceived costs of crime (by enhancing the chances of the offender's being apprehended or receiving more severe penalties) and thereby "tip the balance" towards nonoffending. Similarly, situational crime prevention strategies—things like

---

*Prepared, in part, under Grant No. 89-IJ-CX-0046 from the National Institute of Justice, Office of Justice Programs, U.S. Department of Justice. Points of view or opinions expressed in this document are those of the authors and do not necessarily represent the official position or policies of the U.S. Department of Justice. The authors wish to thank Allison Redfern for her help in preparation of this manuscript.

property marking and lock installation campaigns—assume that offenders are influenced by the factors being manipulated. They seek to alter these factors in such a way that potential offenders decide an offense is too risky, too unrewarding, or too difficult to commit. Little research attention, however, has been paid to the way in which criminals perceive and make decisions in relation to (1) the threat of apprehension and official penalties (Beyleveld, 1980; Henshel & Carey, 1975) or (2) the alteration of situational cues and features (Mayhew, 1979; Mayhew et al., 1979). Lamenting this state of affairs, Feeney (1986 p. 68) has noted: "If headway ever is to be made in dealing with crime, we must access the information that offenders have. . . ." And Bennett and Wright (1983 p. 20) echo his sentiments: "In the absence of this kind of research, there is a danger of wasting public money on crime prevention projects which may ultimately reduce the quality of life more than opportunities for crime."

The reasons for the neglect of the offender's perspective are not difficult to discern. Tapping into that perspective calls for the use of a research design that allows offenders to "speak for themselves" (Bennett & Wright, 1984a; Toch, 1987). Positivism, which has dominated American criminology for decades, traditionally has rejected such designs as "soft" or "unscientific" (Toch, 1987). What is more, these approaches often require that researchers deal directly with offenders "in the field"—something that many criminologists have been reluctant to do (Chambliss, 1975; Polsky, 1969). Recently, however, positivism has become more amenable to the offender's perspective (Gottfredson & Hirschi, 1987). And researchers, especially those with crime prevention policy concerns, have shown increased interest in the perceptions and decision making of lawbreakers (see, for example, Bennett & Wright, 1984a; 1984b; Feeney, 1986; Rengert & Wasilchick, 1985).

In the following pages, two direct, field-based approaches to exploring the offender's perspective will be considered. The first is participant observation, while the second relies on interviewing. Each approach yields a different type of data (see McCall, 1978), and as Glassner and Carpenter (1985) have observed, "They supplement one another and provide flexibility [in designing a research plan]."

Participant Observation

Participant observation, as the term implies, requires the researcher to observe subjects in their natural surroundings. More precisely, McCall (1978 p. 2) defines participant observation as the "collection of empirical data concerning behavior, interaction, or social organization through more or less disciplined processes of looking at and listening to the conduct of relevant organisms within the context of their indigenous settings." Calls for criminological researchers to adopt this strategy have been heard for years. More than two decades ago, Polsky (1969), in a stinging indictment of criminologists who rely solely on data obtained from incarcerated criminals, pointed out:

Animal behavior has a narrower range of determinants than human behavior, is much less complex and variable. And yet, in recent years, animal ecologists have demonstrated that when you undertake "free-ranging" study of an animal in his natural habitat, you discover important things about him that are simply not discoverable when he is behind bars. Obviously we can no longer afford the convenient fiction that in studying criminals in their natural habitat, we would discover nothing really important that could not be discovered from criminals behind bars. What is true for studying the gorilla zoology is likely to be even truer for studying the gorilla of criminology. (p. 116)

In spite of such observations, few criminologists have opted for studying criminals, so to speak, in the wild. Their reluctance to do so undoubtedly is attributable to a variety of factors. Walker (1984 p. viii), for instance, has observed that there simply is "easier game" for criminological researchers to go after, namely official data and the agencies of criminal justice. Probably the most important reason for their reluctance, however, is a longstanding belief that this type of research is impractical (see, for example, Sutherland & Cressey, 1974).

The entrenched notion that participant-observation research involving criminals is unworkable has been challenged by Chambliss (1975 p. 39), who argues: "The data on organized crime and professional theft as well as other presumably difficult-to-study events are much more available than we usually think. All we really have to do is to get out of our offices and onto the street. The data are there; the problem is that too often sociologists are not."

A study of "urban danger" by Merry (1981) provides evidence that the participant-observation approach to studying crime and criminals is feasible. As part of the study, which centered on a residential housing complex, she managed successfully to spend several months "lounging with the group of local black youths who are involved in crime, talking to both males and females and participating in their activities" (p. 11). In doing so, Merry was able to learn about the strategies of robbery and burglary as well as techniques for handling the police.

The participant-observation method has the advantage of capturing criminal events as they unfold, rather than relying on after-the-fact accounts of what transpired. Retrospective accounts may be distorted, either wittingly or unwittingly. Offenders have obvious reasons for being circumspect in recounting their activities. Moreover, they may not recall accurately all of the relevant information. In fact, they may never have been aware of some of the important factors surrounding their crimes (Glassner & Carpenter, 1985). After all, offenders are preoccupied with successfully completing the offense, rather than with analyzing the environmental or social context in which it occurs.

The participant observation of criminals, of course, also has drawbacks. Perhaps the most important of these are the ethical and legal problems presented by directly observing criminal events. In light of these problems, Glassner and Carpenter (1985) recommend that researchers studying property offending avoid directly observing offenses, being present only during the planning stages and after the crime has been carried out. Their advice, of course, would equally be applicable to violent crime, perhaps more so. Others also have suggested that there is no need for researchers to observe directly the commission of crimes or other dangerous activities. Irwin (1972 p. 118), for instance, maintains that it is a "false notion that in order to study a group you must observe all aspects of the lives of its members." He goes on to argue that most of the material needed for a study of the offender's perspective can be collected through interviews and conversations without actually observing crimes. Certainly, a great deal of valuable data can be obtained in this way. However, some important information concerning offenses is unlikely to surface in conversations, especially the presence or absence of situational factors that the offenders may not have noticed (McCall, 1978).

Bennett and Wright (1984a), in their study of decision making and target selection among British residential burglars, adopted an alternative approach to this problem. They had offenders serving probation reenact offenses for which they already had been convicted (absent, obviously, the actual breaking and entering). This is not a fully satisfactory solution in that, by their nature, reenactments are somewhat unrealistic (e.g., Carroll & Weaver, 1986) and may be distorted for a variety of reasons. At the same time, this approach does allow for direct observation of the crime scene and may furnish valuable insights into the various factors that contribute to the commission of offenses. A particular strength of this procedure is that it may help to refresh the offender's memory. In the following quotation, taken from a tape recording of one of these reenactments, this can be seen clearly:

The more I think about it, the more it comes back to me. We'll have to go back along this road because I'm sure that's where the house was. It's coming up. That's the house I done! Now you can see why I done it, can't you. One, there's a bloody great wall right round it so, obviously, once you are in there you are screened well. It's mainly the cover around the house. (p. 187)

In addition to the ethical dilemmas posed by the participant observation of criminals, the technique suffers from a couple of methodological drawbacks. First, it is restricted to the here and now; past activities cannot be observed (McCall, 1978). Second, the meanings and beliefs attached to the activities under scrutiny may not be apparent (Glassner & Carpenter,

1985). Observing burglars, for example, might provide valuable clues regarding the way in which they go about offenses but reveal little about why they choose to commit burglaries in the first place. Such drawbacks, however, can be reduced significantly through the skillful use of interviewing.

Interviewing

The term *interviewing* covers a broad range of research strategies in that interviews can vary greatly in length, in the degree to which they are structured, and so on (Glassner & Carpenter, 1985). In studying the offender's perspective, however, an open-ended, semistructured interview typically is called for (at least initially) in order to avoid imposing artificial concepts and categories on subjects, thereby letting them speak freely using their own terminology.

There are two basic types of interviewing. In practice, though, both often are employed during the course of a single interview. The first, the informant interview, treats the subject as a witness who can report on the events being studied. As McCall (1978 p. 5) has noted, the informant in this sort of research is treated esssentially as a "surrogate observer." Steffensmeier (1986) draws on this method of interviewing in his study of "fencing," that is, dealing in stolen goods. In the following quote, for example, Sam Goodman, Steffensmeier's informant, observes that the fences he associated with typically were marginal characters:

I wouldn't say that many fences had been burglars or thieves before, like it was for me. But most will be shady in one way or another. If not into crime, on the edge of it. Maybe their old man or an uncle was into fencing. Some of the main fences I knew were into gambling, counterfeiting, in the rackets, and different things that weren't above board. (pp. 22–23)

The informant interview represents an efficient way of learning about the general characteristics of the offender's world; it provides an "offender's eye view" of the way in which that world is organized (McCall, 1978). On the other hand, this type of interview does not yield information on the attitudes and feelings of specific offenders. For collecting those sorts of data, the second type of interview—the respondent interview—is more appropriate.

The respondent interview seeks information from subjects concerning their own thoughts and experiences. In other words, the interviewees are asked to report on themselves. Much of the recent work in criminology on offender's perceptions of targets and sanctions has been based on this approach (see, among others, Feeney, 1986; Rengert & Wasilchick, 1985). Bennett and Wright (1983; 1984a; 1984b) used respondent interviewing extensively in their study of burglars. In exploring whether such offenders ever worried about getting caught, for instance, they went to the offenders themselves. The comments of three of these offenders are set out below:

I worry about it once I'm caught, saying "What a bloody mug I am," but I wasn't worried when I was actually doing things. (pp. 127–128)

I was drunk all the time. That's why I think a lot of things didn't bother me. I wasn't worried about going into a place or how much noise I made. I just didn't give a damn. (p. 129)

It used to worry me, the actual getting caught. I'd got caught twice before. Both times it was a bad experience. (p. 127)

Although, on the face of it, the interviewing of criminals may appear ethically "safer" than direct participant observation, this is somewhat illusory. During such interviews, researchers may well learn the details of past crimes or, worse yet, plans concerning future ones. This can create two problems for researchers. First, it makes them vulnerable to police pressure and perhaps even arrest (e.g., McCall, 1978; Polsky, 1969). Second, it presents them with an ethical dilemma; do their loyalties rest with the study subjects or the victims, past or intended, of these subjects? There is no fully satisfactory answer to these problems, though various steps can be taken to minimize them. Certainly, researchers should decide beforehand on what sorts of information they are willing to hold in confidence (Hagan, 1982) and make it clear to offenders that anything beyond this might be divulged to authorities. Offenders understand that revealing certain details, such as those relating to offenses they have gotten away with, place them at increased risk and put researchers in an ethical bind. Therefore, such "ground rules" need not undermine the confidence of subjects and, indeed, may enhance it (see, for example, Klockars, 1977). Of course, researchers simply may elect not to ask offenders about specific criminal incidents, though this does not preclude the possibility that such information will be volunteered. In her study of urban delinquents, Merry (1981) dealt with this problem by refraining "from cataloging in any detail the past activities of these youths" (p. 17).

Sample Selection and Strategy

In most social science research, the ideal subject sample will be representative of the total population under study. As Glassner and Carpenter (1985) have noted, however, such a sample often is impossible to obtain in research on criminals where the parameters of the population are unknown. A sample of prisoners, for example, will not even be representative of all convicted offenders, let alone the total population of criminals. And representativeness is particularly problematic in field-based studies, because direct access to offenders is limited by the fact that their activities are clandestine (Glassner & Carpenter, 1985). This means that, practically speaking, sample selection often will be determined by "opportunities and resources at the researcher's disposal" (McCall, 1978 p. 9). No doubt this explains why much of the recent work on the offender's perspective has been based on the study of prisoners (e.g., Rengert & Wasilchick, 1985).

Research using prisoners can contribute greatly to understanding the perceptions and decision making of criminals (Irwin, 1972). Incarcerated offenders can be interviewed, even if they cannot be observed directly in their "natural habitat." Bennett and Wright (1983; 1984a; 1984b), for instance, based much of their burglary work on interviews conducted with prisoners.

As already noted, a prison sample is not representative of the population of offenders as a whole, and it is particularly unrepresentative if all of the subjects are drawn from a single facility. Offenders typically are not assigned to one prison or another randomly but, rather, according to certain criteria. Sampling from a single institution, therefore, restricts the type of offender included in the research. This is true even when one is studying a distinct category of offenders, such as burglars. In an attempt to minimize this problem, Bennett and Wright drew their sample of offenders from several different sorts of penal institutions. Their goal was to encompass the diversity of views found among the population of incarcerated burglars.

Although prisons often are characterized as providing a "ready source of criminals," gaining access to prisoners can be time consuming and frustrating as researchers attempt to negotiate a plethora of bureaucratic obstacles. In some cases, at least, it actually may be simpler to research offenders at large in the community. Observing and interviewing criminals in the community, however, virtually rules out the use of a random selection procedure, unless the focus is limited to those on some form of probation or parole. Locating currently active offenders typically calls for the use of a "snowball" sampling strategy, whereby an initial subject is contacted and asked to recommend further subjects. This process continues until a suitable sample has been "built." While the resulting sample clearly is not random, this does not mean that of necessity it is unrepresentative. Glassner and Carpenter (1985 p. 39), for example, note that the representativeness of a sample of active property offenders could be assessed by checking "whether every relevant role is included . . . and by the level of knowledge the subjects have within those roles. . . ." They suggest that researchers

should be able to use their informants to reconstruct particular crime events. For example, one could take the end product of a burglary—an item that has been fenced—and use the pool of subjects to trace the item in other directions. In so doing, one is able to determine gaps in one's subject pool; for instance, if one is unable to ascertain through interviews or observations, who originally initiated the burglary, one can then conduct additional queries among informants to discover where the gap exists in the fieldworker's information chain, and which additional subjects need to be located. (p. 39)

Probably the most difficult aspect of researching offenders in the community using a "snowball" sampling technique is locating an initial contact or two. Various ways of doing so have been suggested. McCall (1978), for example, recommends using a "chain of referrals":

If a researcher wants to make contact with, say, a bootlegger, he thinks of the person he knows who is closest in the social structure to bootlegging. Perhaps this person will be a police officer, a judge, a liquor store owner, a crime reporter, or a recently arrived Southern migrant. If he doesn't personally know a judge or a crime reporter, he surely knows someone (his own lawyer or a circulation clerk) who does and who would be willing to introduce him. By means of a very short chain of such referrals, the researcher can obtain an introduction to virtually any type of criminal. (p. 31)

This strategy can be enhanced where the researcher already has access to imprisoned offenders (Glassner & Carpenter, 1985) or, better yet, to those on probation or parole. Such persons may well know criminals in the community and be willing to provide some sort of introduction. (However, researchers must exercise caution in making use of these referrals, as those on probation or parole typically are prohibited from associating with other offenders.) Other researchers (e.g., Chambliss, 1975; Polsky, 1969) suggest that it is possible to make initial contacts in the field by frequenting locales favored by offenders. Needless to say, this does not mean entering a tavern saying, "I'm looking for a burglar," but, rather, becoming a "familiar face" so that such contacts evolve naturally. Polsky (1969) notes that having interests in common with the offenders facilitates this process:

. . . one excellent way of establishing contact involves a small bit of fakery at the beginning, in that you can get to know a criminal on the basis of common leisure pursuits and then let him know of your research interest in him. (But, this latter should be done quite soon, after the first meeting or two.) Where and how you start depends, other things being equal, on what you do best that criminals are also likely to be interested in. (p. 125)

There are, of course, additional ways in which offenders in the community possibly could be contacted. For instance, advertisements might be run in a local underground newspaper or letters sent to suspects identified in newspaper stories. Depending on the circumstances (e.g., offense type), such strategies may be highly successful.

Field Relations

The success of field research on criminals, whether carried out in a prison or a community setting, is dependent on the ability of the researcher to convince potential subjects to participate in the study. This can be a delicate task, as offenders, understandably, may be deeply suspicious of outsiders. Nevertheless, a number of successful field studies have demonstrated that it is possible to gain the confidence and cooperation of criminals (see, among others, Miller, 1986; Shover, 1973; West, 1978).

There are several keys to becoming trusted by offenders. The first is that researchers simply must be willing to spend a great deal of time in the research setting. Familiarity, after all, is a key to gaining acceptance in any social situation (Hammersley & Atkinson, 1983). Giallombardo (1966), for example, notes in regard to studying the prison community:

. . . I do not think it can be emphasized too strongly that continuous presence in the institution day after day for the first five or six months . . . is essential, not only for the researcher to adjust to the routine of the prison world, but, also, in order for him to achieve acceptance by the members of this community. (p. 324)

This observation applies equally to research involving currently active offenders. As McCall (1978) has pointed out, however, it can be very difficult for researchers to maintain regular contact with criminals in informal settings owing to the fact that (1) most criminals have chaotic lives and (2) they tend not to gather socially on a routine basis. It should be possible, though, to keep in touch with one or two offenders leading fairly stable lives (Irwin, 1972) and, in doing so, gradually build up a rapport with their criminal acquaintances.

A second, somewhat related, key to gaining acceptance involves "fitting in" by dressing appropriately and, more important, learning the distinctive terminology, phrasing, and so on used by the offenders. Several commentators have stressed that researchers should modify their dress and language to accommodate those they are studying (Irwin, 1972; McCall, 1978; Polsky, 1969). Certainly this takes time, but it need not be an onerous task. The acquisition of such skills is part and parcel of learning to blend into any social setting and often is accomplished almost unconsciously. Polsky (1969), writing about participant observation, offers some advice on getting started:

. . . initially, keep your eyes and ears open *but keep your mouth shut.* At first, try to ask no questions whatsoever. Before you can ask questions, or even speak much at all other than when spoken to, you should get the "feel" of their world by extensive and attentive listening—get some sense of what pleases them and what bugs them, some sense of their frame of reference and some sense of *their* sense of language (not only their special argot, as is often mistakenly assumed, but also how they use ordinary language). (p. 121)

A third key to being accepted by offenders requires researchers to give as well as take. Researchers, after all, expect subjects to answer their questions frankly and, therefore, must be prepared to reciprocate. Criminals, whether in prison or the community, almost certainly will have questions about how the information will be used, who will have access to it, and so on. They also may want to ask researchers about *their* criminal activities. These questions must be answered honestly; otherwise, there is a risk of being labeled as "phony" (Irwin, 1972; Polsky, 1969). Further, researchers should be willing to honor offenders' requests for various forms of assistance. As McCall (1978) has observed, criminals tend to lead problematic lives and frequently require help of one kind or another. Provided that the help requested is not illegal and falls within the general set "of norms governing the exchange of money and other kinds of favors" (Berk & Adams, 1970 p. 112), the researcher may be well served by offering it. (It may be worth noting that, although requests for aid typically are associated with offenders in the community, they also may be made by prisoners [Jacobs, 1977], e.g., "Could you phone my wife?")

A fourth, and final, key to gaining and keeping the confidence of criminals requires researchers to demonstrate trustworthiness by remaining "close-mouthed in regard to potentially harmful information" (Irwin, 1972, p. 125). Understandably, offenders are concerned that researchers not divulge data that are incriminating or otherwise confidential. To reassure themselves, they often will test researchers by, for example, asking them what a criminal associate said about a particular matter. Offenders also might provide researchers with a small amount of minimally incriminating information and wait to see if there are any "comebacks"—that is, negative consequences—before cooperating further. In both cases, of course, it is important that researchers protect the informant's confidence (for ethical as well as practical reasons).

Although much has been written about the necessity for researchers to appear able to stand up to official coercion (see, for example, Irwin, 1972; McCall, 1978; Polsky, 1969), such coercion is seldom forthcoming. Much more likely are subtler forms of questioning by criminal justice officials along the lines of "Did John have anything interesting to say?" Here again, researchers must avoid disclosing confidential information if they are to be accepted by offenders as "all right square[s]" (Irwin, 1972 p. 123) who can be trusted.

Validity and Reliability

The two approaches to investigating the offender's perspective outlined above—participant observation and interviewing (both informant and respondent)—are direct methods. In other words, these approaches allow for the collection of "first order data (or data one step removed from the mind of the actor)" (Frazier, 1978 p. 128). The information obtained through either of these methods, therefore, can be expected to be highly valid, that is, it should reflect what is going on in the offender's mind with considerable accuracy. As Lofland and Lofland (1984 p. 12) have noted, the face-to-face interaction that is part and parcel of collecting this information represents "the fullest condition of participating in the mind of another human being." What is more, participant observation and interviewing, when used in conjunction, can enhance the validity of each other. Putting it simply, interviews can be used to assess the validity of observations, and observations can be used to assess the validity of data obtained through interviews (see, for example, Glassner & Carpenter, 1985).

Glassner and Carpenter (1985 p. 48), among others, have identified two questions regarding the validity of data obtained through participant observation and interview-based research on criminals: "(1) Given the illegality of their activities, how do we know the subjects are telling the truth about what they do and why they do it? (2) To what extent does the presence of the researcher change the 'natural' environment they are studying?" The question of truthfulness, of course, bears primarily on the validity of the interviewing approach. It is worth noting in this context that a well-known study comparing the responses of offenders to official records revealed close agreement between the two (West & Farrington, 1977). Given that such responses are voluntary (as they typically are in the research interview; see Benney & Hughes, 1956), this should not be surprising. Lying seems pointless when the subjects simply could have declined to be interviewed in the first place (Ianni, 1972). What is more, the interview situation itself often provides opportunities for assessing the veracity of offenders' accounts through checking for, and questioning, inconsistent responses (e.g., Bennett & Wright, 1984c).

The question of whether the researcher's presence alters the environment relates predominantly (though not exclusively) to the participant-observation approach. Certainly, the presence of an observer initially affects the way in which subjects conduct themselves. Provided that the researcher is able to "fit in," however, this effect should diminish over time (Hammersley & Atkinson, 1983; Schwartz & Schwartz, 1969). In any case, the problem of observer effects "comes with the turf" in participant-observation studies. Researchers must recognize this fact and take care to note situations that have been distorted by their presence (Pelto & Pelto, 1973).

The reliability of participant observation and interviewing (particularly open-ended, semistructured interviewing), that is, "the extent to which [these methods] yield a consistent result when used on more than one occasion or by different people" (Bulmer, 1977 p. 30), often is limited. As Glassner and Carpenter (1985 p. 50) have noted, ". . . the multiplicity of types of observation and questioning make replication across subjects, sites or studies difficult." Although not truly based on a participant-observation approach, a field-based pilot study by Bennett and Wright (1984a) nevertheless demonstrates the near impossibility of replication in a "real world" setting. This study, which was aimed at obtaining as realistic an assessment as possible of the ways in which burglars perceived the environment of potential crimes, involved walking through the same neighborhood with a number of different burglars while they described favorable and unfavorable aspects of possible targets. During the conduct of the project, however, it became apparent that taking offenders around the same route (sometimes just minutes apart) offered only limited comparability, because the environment kept changing—cars were moved, lights went on or off, children came out to play, and so on.

This same study, however, also demonstrated one of the particular strengths of participant-observation-like approaches, namely, their ability to generate hypotheses and open up new areas of investigation. Recognizing that the information they were getting was not highly reliable, Bennett and Wright abandoned the idea of using the same area for each offender and opted instead for allowing subjects to choose neighborhoods where they actually had committed offenses. Doing so, of course, undermined reliability still further, but it also allowed for a highly realistic assessment of the perceptions and decision making of burglars. The leads developed during these "walkabouts" subsequently were investigated using more systematic and standardized (and therefore more reliable) procedures (see Bennett & Wright, 1984a; 1984b).

Conclusion

Exploring the offender's perspective, by its very nature, presents researchers with numerous difficulties. As Walker (1984 p. viii) has observed, "States of mind are less easy to ascertain . . . than many other kinds of data." Participant observation and interviewing represent two of the most promising methods of addressing this issue. Given the growing awareness within criminology that a convincing explanation of criminal behavior must incorporate the offender's perspective (e.g., Kobrin, 1982; Toch, 1987; Walker, 1984), it seems likely that more researchers will adopt such approaches. To the extent that they do, both criminological theory and criminal justice policy-making will be enriched.

References

Bennett, T., & Wright, R. (1983). Offenders' perception of targets, Home Office Research Bulletin, Vol. 15, London: Home Office Research and Planning Unit, pp. 18–20.

Bennett, T., & Wright, R. (1984a). *Burglars on burglary: Prevention and the offender*. Aldershot: Gower.

Bennett, T., & Wright, R. (1984b). Constraints to burglary: The offender's perspective. In R. Clarke & T. Hope (Eds.), *Coping with burglary*, Boston: Kluwer-Nijhoff, (pp. 181–200).

Bennett, T., & Wright, R. (1984c). The relationship between alcohol use and burglary. *British Journal of Addiction*, 79(4), pp. 431–437.

Benney, M., & Hughes, E. (1956). Of sociology and the interview. *American Journal of Sociology*, 62(2), pp. 137–142.

Berk, R., & Adams, J. (1970). Establishing rapport with deviant groups. *Social Problems*, *18*(1), pp. 102–117.

Beyleveld, D. (1980). *A Bibliography on general deterrence research*. Farnborough: Saxon House.

Bovet, L. (1951). *Psychiatric aspects of juvenile delinquency*. Geneva: World Health Organization.

Bulmer, M. (1977). Introduction: Problems, theories and methods in sociology— (How) do they interrelate? In M. Bulmer (Ed.), *Sociological research methods*. London: Macmillan, pp. 1–33.

Carroll, J., & Weaver, F. (1986). Shoplifters' perceptions of crime opportunities. In D. Cornish & R. Clarke (Eds.), *The reasoning criminal*. New York: Springer-Verlag, pp. 19–38.

Chambliss, W. (1975). On the paucity of original research on organized crime: A footnote to Galliher and Cain. *American Sociologist*, *10*(1), pp. 36–39.

Feeney, F. (1986). Robbers as decision-makers. In D. Cornish & R. Clarke (Eds.), *The reasoning criminal*. New York: Springer-Verlag, pp. 51–71.

Frazier, C. (1978). The use of life histories in testing theories of criminal behavior. *Qualitative Sociology*, *1*, pp. 122–142.

Giallombardo, R. (1966). Interviewing in the prison community. *Journal of Criminal Law, Criminology and Police Science*, *57*, pp. 318–324.

Glassner, B., & Carpenter, C. (1985). *The feasibility of an ethnographic study of property offenders: A report prepared for the National Institute of Justice*, Mimeo., Washington, D.C.: National Institute of Justice.

Gottfredson, M., & Hirschi, T. (1987). The positive tradition. In M. Gottfredson & T. Hirschi (Eds.), *Positive criminology*. Beverly Hills, CA: Sage, pp. 9–22.

Hagan, F. (1982). *Research methods in criminal justice and criminology*. New York: Macmillan.

Hammersley, M., & Atkinson, P. (1983). *Ethnography: Principles in practice*. London: Tavistock.

Henshel, R., & Carey, S. (1975). Deviance, deterrence, and knowledge of sanctions. In R. Henshel & R. Silverman (Eds.), *Perception in criminology*. New York: Columbia University Press, pp. 54–73.

Ianni, F. (1972). *A family business: Kinship and social control in organized crime*. New York: Russell Sage Foundation.

Irwin, J. (1972). Participant observation of criminals. In J. Douglas (Ed.), *Research on deviance*. New York: Random House, pp. 117–137.

Jacobs, J. (1977). *Stateville: The penitentiary in mass society*. Chicago: University of Chicago Press.

Klockars, C. (1977). Field ethics for the life history. In R. Weppner (Ed.), *Street ethnography*. Beverly Hills, CA: Sage, pp. 201–226.

Kobrin, S. (1982). The uses of the life history document for the development of delinquency theory. In J. Roller & J. Snodgrass. *The Jack Roller at seventy*. Lexington, MA: Heath, pp. 153–165.

Lofland, J., & Lofland, L. (1984). *Analyzing social settings: A Guide to qualitative observation and analysis*. Belmont, CA: Wadsworth.

Mayhew, P. (1979). Defensible space: The current status of a crime prevention theory. *The Howard Journal*, *81*, pp. 150–159.

Mayhew, pp., Clarke, R., Burrows, J., Hough, M., & Winchesten, S. (1979). *Crime in Public View*. London: Her Majesty's Stationary Office.

McCall, G. (1978). *Observing the law*. New York: Free Press.

Merry, S. (1981). *Urban danger: Life in a neighborhood of strangers*. Philadelphia: Temple University Press.

Miller, E. (1986). *Street woman*. Philadelphia: Temple University Press.

Pelto, P., & Pelto, G. (1973). Ethnography: The fieldwork enterprise. In J. Honigmann (Ed.), *Handbook of social and cultural anthropology*. Chicago: Rand McNally, pp. 241–288.

Polsky, N. (1969). *Hustlers, beats, and others*. Garden City, NY: Anchor.

Rengert, G., & Wasilchick, J. (1985). *Suburban burglary: A time and a place for everything*. Springfield, Ill: Thomas.

Schwartz, M., & Schwartz, C. (1955). Problems in participant observation. *American Journal of Sociology, 60*, pp. 343–353.

Shover, N. (1973). The social organization of burglary. *Social Problems, 20*, pp. 499–514.

Steffensmeier, D. (1986). *The fence*. Totowa, NJ: Rowman and Littlefield.

Sutherland, E., & Cressey, D. (1974). *Criminology–9th Ed*. Philadelphia: Lippincott.

Toch, H. (1987). Supplementing the positivistic perspective. In M. Gottfredson & T. Hirschi (Eds.), *Positive criminology*. Beverly Hills, CA: Sage, pp. 138–153.

Walker, N. (1984). Foreword. In T. Bennett & R. Wright, *Burglars on burglary: Prevention and the offender*. Aldershot: Gower.

West, D., & Farrington, D. (1977). *The delinquent way of life*. London: Heinemann.

West, W. (1978). The short term careers of serious thieves. *Canadian Journal of Criminology, 20*, pp. 169–190.

7
Longitudinal Research Designs

ELIZABETH PIPER DESCHENES

Introduction

The major goals and objectives of longitudinal research are the following: to quantify trends in human behavior, to describe the progression of life events, to identify patterns of behavioral change, to test theory, and to justify interventions to prevent human and societal ills. The primary use of longitudinal research has been to study the development and natural history of events in the life course. This type of design is often regarded as superior to a cross-sectional design because it enables processes and causes of change within individuals and among individuals to be identified. Longitudinal research is useful in testing theory because it allows the examination of causal hypotheses. For example, the researcher can examine the relationship between school failure and delinquency rates and determine if those who fail are more likely to be delinquent than those who succeed in school. Longitudinal research is also useful in describing the progression of life events, such as the effect of marriage or becoming unemployed on offending. Does unemployment lead to an increase in criminal behavior? Is there a greater likelihood of desistance from crime after one is married? These questions are just two of the many that are best answered with a longitudinal design.

There is also a demand for longitudinal research designs in order to justify interventions for societal ills such as criminality and delinquency. Longitudinal research is needed not only to identify predictors of delinquency and criminal behavior but also to evaluate the effectiveness of various interventions and to identify determinants of desistance. Studying only those already involved in a problem behavior (such as delinquency or mental illness) makes it impossible to separate the antecedents of that behavior from other possible explanations for the behavior. Thus, it is necessary to start with an entire population and follow the life course of events that lead to various outcomes. If certain characteristics can be identified as precursors of delinquency, it may then be possible to select those likely to be delinquent in another population and provide certain prevention measures or, at least, design effective intervention techniques.

Definition of Longitudinal Research Design

In comparison to cross-sectional designs, which measure subjects at one point in time, longitudinal research designs, by definition, involve repeated measurement over time of one or more groups of subjects. The major advantage of a longitudinal research design is the ability to study the natural history and course of development of a phenomenon. Longitudinal research can also provide information about the time ordering of different events, which can be useful in determining causal relationships between variables.

In criminology research, for example, the study of criminal careers demands a longitudinal design, because it is necessary to measure patterns of behavior in the beginning, progression, and cessation of delinquency or crime. It is also possible to measure the prevalence (number of delinquents or criminals in a given population) and the incidence (number of offenses committed by a group of individuals) of offending. Different stages in the criminal career and patterns of seriousness and diversity can be studied. The real strength of longitudinal design is the ability to measure the patterns and parameters of delinquent and criminal behavior, which allows examination of causal effects.

Types of Designs

There are four types of longitudinal designs: trend studies, cohort studies, panel designs, and time-series designs. The different types of designs are characterized by the group that is sampled, the length of time under study, and the number of measurements obtained.

Trend studies are employed to examine the changes over time among samples that are representative of a general population. For example, the Drug Use Forecasting studies of drug use among arrestees (Wish, 1987) are trend studies sponsored by the National Institute of Justice that measure changes in type and quantity of drug use over 4 quarters within 1 year and from 1 year to the next.

Panel designs involve two or more waves of data collection using the same measures on the same sample. The National Youth Survey Project (NYS) by Elliott, Ageton, Huizinga, Knowles, and Canter (1983) is a good example of a multi-wave panel study of delinquency. In this project, a series of annual surveys were conducted with a representative national sample of American youth ages 11 to 17 in 1976. The sample was drawn from 2,360 youths representative of the population of youths 11 to 17 in 1976 according to geographical area, population size within that area, households, and dwelling units according to age, sex, and race. Each year from 1976 and 1980, the youths answered the same questions about self-reported delinquency. The NYS allowed measurement of prevalence and incidence rates of delinquent behavior among the sample and estimation of national prevalence and incidence rates based on that sample.

A cohort design is defined by membership in a particular group, such as a "birth" cohort (all those born in a given year), a "school entry" cohort, an "arrested" cohort, or a "prison" cohort. The same population is studied each time data are collected, even though the sample may differ from one time to the next. The Philadelphia Cohort Study (Wolfgang, Figlio, & Sellin, 1972) is a well-known example of a birth cohort study. In this study, all youths born in Philadelphia in 1945 who lived in the city from the ages of 10 to 17 were identified retrospectively from school records according to their date of birth. Data were then collected from secondary sources, including school records and police arrest records and investigative reports. By using this technique, Wolfgang et al. (1972) were able to determine the onset, prevalence, and incidence of delinquency in a population of youths born in Philadelphia in 1945. It is also possible to study multiple cohorts, as has been done by Shannon (1981) in the study of 1942, 1949, and 1955 cohorts, selected to allow simultaneous measurement of the cohorts at various ages (6 to 11, 12 to 17).

An example of a prison cohort study is explained by Farrington, Ohlin, and Wilson (1986, p. 166). They propose drawing a sample of all those beginning their first prison sentences from a specific geographical area among persons ages 18 to 24. Data could be collected from the prisoners themselves and from the guards, employers, and families of the prisoners. The study could be used to determine the effects of imprisonment on in-prison and post-prison behavior.

The time-series design involves a series of measurements at periodic intervals, usually to measure the impact of a specific change that occurs at some point during those measurements. One example of a multiple time-series design is the evaluation of the Connecticut crackdown on highway speeding (Campbell & Ross, 1980). The number of traffic fatalities were recorded before and after the police initiated a crackdown on speeding to determine if the crackdown was effective in reducing fatalities.

Issues in Research Design

Sample Versus Population

Choosing between the different types of longitudinal designs, panel versus cohort, or trend versus time-series, involves making a decision about whether to study the same population over time, a sample from that population, or samples from a more general population. The advantage to a cohort design that studies the same population over time is the lack of sampling error. In addition, each individual acts as his own control, which reduces the problem of selection bias. If a sample of the population is selected without random procedures, the subjects may not be representative of the larger population, thereby making it impossible to generalize the results of the study to other populations.

Prospective Versus Retrospective

Longitudinal design can be prospective or retrospective. In the former, a group of subjects is selected and studied as time passes, whereas in the latter, the past behaviors of a selected group of subjects are studied. There are greater advantages to prospective studies than retrospective longitudinal designs. Prospective studies can be used to test hypotheses, because data collection instruments can be designed in advance. In addition, prospective studies need not rely upon official records, and interviews can be used. On the other hand, retrospective interviews may face problems of memory recall or telescoping, e.g., individuals may not be able to remember their part accurately and may attribute specific events to the wrong time period.

However, prospective studies also have their limitations. In order to conduct a prospective longitudinal study, it may be necessary to wait several years before analyzing the collected data. Longitudinal research can also be very expensive if one attempts to track the life course of individuals and obtain information on them at frequent intervals, such as annually.

The issues of selecting a retrospective versus a prospective design involve primarily time and money. It is costly to fund studies while waiting for data collection, analyses, and results. In addition, subjects may drop out of the study, which creates loss of data, otherwise known as attrition. By using a retrospective design, researchers often find it possible to collect similar information in a much shorter time period without the problem of attrition. However, there may be a problem of maturation, which refers to the inability to determine whether the dependent variable (for example, cessation of delinquency), is an artifact of the research design. Because subjects mature during the time period studied, it is difficult to say if any changes are due to maturation or to actual events. There may also be an effect due to history; for example, the reported changes or patterns may be due to the passing of time or historical events.

Data Sources

Numerous data sources exist for measuring the extent of crime and delinquency, and a decision needs to be made regarding the use of primary versus secondary data. For example, in measuring crime and delinquency, it is possible to interview respondents and inquire about their past behavior or to collect information from archival record sources, such as police or court records. The best solution is usually to do both.

Collecting data from secondary sources is often cheaper and quicker than interviewing subjects, but the type of information that can be gathered is limited. It is necessary to use interviews in order to collect information on people's attitudes. However, repeated interviewing might lead to a "testing" effect. Because prospective longitudinal designs involve repeated measurements, it is difficult to determine if changes are real or due to the repeated testing of individuals. Having been interviewed previously, respondents may give similar answers because they have learned a response pattern. Instrumentation effects may also occur if there have been changes in the production of data.

Correlation Versus Causation

The correlational design is used most often in a cross-sectional study. In this type of research, the two groups (experimental and control, such as delinquent and nondelinquent) are compared statistically. This may involve matching the samples of delinquents and nondelinquents according to specific background characteristics. The correlational design can be misleading as relationships of association are often confused with causality. For example, a correlational study may show that more delinquents than nondelinquents are raised in single-parent households. However, it would be wrong to say that being raised in single-parent households causes children to become delinquents. Despite these problems with misinterpreting results as causal effects, the correlational design can be used effectively in exploring relationships between independent and dependent variables.

Causal effects can be tested only by a longitudinal research design. This type of design allows the researcher to control for the effects of other factors and to determine the temporal order of various phenomena. This is important because selection of the most appropriate strategies for preventing delinquency is dependent upon establishing causal order. For example, in a prospective longitudinal study, one could increase the amount of parental supervision among one group of youths and examine the impact on delinquency rates, while holding constant the effects of other factors such as peer pressure, religion, or education. Examining causal effects is also important in determining factors that predict the cessation of delinquency and crime.

The Use of Longitudinal Research in Criminology

While examples of each type of longitudinal design can be found in criminology, for the past two decades longitudinal research has focused on criminal careers, investigated primarily through cohort and panel designs.

The following section discusses some of the problems found in previous research studies.

Sample Versus Population

The limitations of using a matched sample rather than a population are illustrated in the comparison of research by Sheldon and Eleanor Glueck (1934, 1940, 1950), Powers and Witmer (1951), and McCord (1979) to the cohort studies conducted by Wolfgang et al. (1972), Tracy, Wolfgang, and Figlio (1985), West and Farrington (1973), and Farrington and West (1979).

The research studies conducted by the Gluecks and the Cambridge Somerville study (McCord, 1979; Powers & Witmer, 1951) are limited by the fact that they used nonrandom samples of delinquents and then matched them to nondelinquents. Neither the results from the Gluecks' first study of 1,000 delinquents (1934, 1940) nor those from a later survey of 500 delinquents in correctional schools matched to 500 nondelinquents (1950) can be generalized to the total population. In the Cambridge Somerville study, 650 boys were selected initially on the basis of their "difficult" behavior in schools. One half of the sample was to receive services from social workers for a period of 5 years, and the other half was to receive no special services. In a 30-year follow-up, McCord (1979) found that those who had received the social work services had higher rates of delinquency than the control group. The results of the Cambridge Somerville study are ambiguous, however, because they cannot be generalized to a larger population.

In comparison, some cohort studies gathered information on populations. For example, in the 1945 Philadelphia cohort study, Wolfgang et al. (1972) obtained official police records for all males born in 1945 and residing in Philadelphia between the ages of 10 and 17. They found that one-third of all subjects had a record of delinquency by the time they were 18, e.g., a prevalence rate of 33%. They also found that a small number of subjects, 6.3% of the cohort, were chronic recidivists (committed five or more offenses) and accounted for 62% of all the offenses and a majority of the violent and serious offenses. The second Philadelphia cohort study selected a cohort of males and females born in 1958. In replicating the earlier analyses, Tracy et al. (1985) found similar incidence and prevalence rates for the 1958 cohort as the 1945. However, in the 1958 cohort, drug use was more prevalent, as were violent and serious offenses. Similar to the Philadelphia study, Farrington (1983a) found that one-third of his London cohort were convicted for a criminal offense by their 25th birthday, and the peak age of conviction was 17. The peak age of onset was between 13 and 15, but the average conviction career length was longest for those first convicted between the ages of 10 and 12. The results of these cohort studies describe the situation for a population; so there is no need to make inference beyond the research subjects.

Prospective Versus Retrospective

The differences between retrospective and prospective studies are perhaps best illustrated in the London cohort studies of Farrington and West (1979) and West and Farrington (1973) and the Philadelphia cohort studies by Wolfgang et al. (1972) and Tracy et al. (1985). The delinquency study by Farrington and West (1979) and West and Farrington (1973) used a prospective design, in that boys were repeatedly interviewed over a number of years. Farrington (1983b) reported that 6% of the sample accounted for 40% of all convictions up to their 25th birthday. In comparison, in the Philadelphia cohort studies (Tracy et al., 1985; Wolfgang et al., 1972), information about the delinquent behavior of individuals was gathered retrospectively from official police records. These two Philadelphia cohort studies are limited due to the retrospective nature of the data collection and the type of data collected. Few variables were collected that could be used for causal analysis to predict onset of delinquency. Nevertheless, both studies found similar results in measures of onset, prevalence, and incidence of delinquency.

Data Sources

There has been some controversy as to the use to official records versus self-reports. It is often argued that official records only measure police behavior; so self-reports should be used. However, there are many methodological problems with self-report delinquency scales. Studies that have used interviews or surveys, such as the studies by the Gluecks (1934, 1950) and by Farrington and West (1979) and the RAND Inmate surveys (Petersilia, Greenwood, & Lavin, 1978; Peterson, Braiker, & Polich, 1981), can often collect a greater amount of information on individual characteristics than studies that use official records, such as the two Philadelphia cohort studies. An advantage of the London cohort study was the use of self-report as well as official records of criminality. For example, Farrington (1977) found that those convicted of offenses significantly increased their offending in comparison to those not convicted of offenses.

Correlation Versus Causation

In their follow-up study of 1,000 delinquents, the Gluecks (1934) found that the best predictors of recidivism were paternal discipline, maternal discipline, school retardation, school misconduct, and the age of the first known behavior disorder. The Gluecks used this information to develop prediction tables. However, their methods of constructing the prediction tables have been criticized, because they measured only correlates of criminal behavior and had no information on nondelinquents. In addition, the Gluecks did not make use of the longitudinal nature of their data in the last survey and relied upon correlational methods to analyze the data, pointing out differences between delinquents and nondelinquents in body type, temperament, attitude, psychological makeup, and sociocultural background (1950).

Similar to the Gluecks, McCord (1979) also used measures of family patterns to predict types of crimes. She found that property offenses could be predicted by maternal supervision, maternal affection, and parental deviance, whereas violent offenses could be predicted by maternal supervision, parental conflict, and parental aggression. McCord found that 47% of those convicted of serious crimes as juveniles and 18% of those not convicted as juveniles were convicted of serious crimes as adults. These findings, however, are limited in their generalizability, and the causes of crime are difficult to disentangle.

Predictors of future delinquency and correlates of crime were also investigated in both the London and Philadelphia cohort studies. In all of these studies, West and Farrington (1973), and Farrington and West (1979), and Wolfgang et al. (1972), and Tracy et al. (1985) found a lack of offense specialization and a greater probability of chronicity given an earlier age at onset. West and Farrington (1973) found that future convictions were predicted by troublesome behavior in elementary school, low family income, large family size, low IQ, convicted parents, and poor parental child-rearing behavior. In attempting to predict the termination of careers, Knight and West (1975) and Osborn and West (1978, 1980) found that "terminators" were less likely to come from large low-income families and to have convicted parents. Other findings of the 1945 Philadelphia cohort study were (1) an earlier onset of delinquency predicted a longer and more chronic criminal career, (2) there was no specialization in type of offense when examined by transitions, and (3) offenses appeared to escalate in seriousness over the criminal career. Wolfgang et al. (1972) also examined the probabilities of recidivism. Whereas the probability of a first offense was 33%, this increased to 54% for a second offense and up to 80% for subsequent offenses. Because recidivism appeared to be quite high after the fifth offense and the majority of offenders quit after one or two, usually trivial, offenses, Wolfgang et al. (1972) concluded that juvenile justice policy should focus on the recidivists. As these examples illustrate, longitudinal research designs are thus best suited for examining causality of crime.

The Recent Controversy

The choice of longitudinal versus cross-sectional research design in criminological research has been under debate since 1983. A key factor in this debate appears to be the continued emphasis by government funding sources, such as the National Institute of Justice and the Office of Juvenile Justice and Delinquency Prevention, on the need for longitudinal studies.

Opponents of longitudinal design, led by Hirschi and Gottfredson (1983), and Gottfredson and Hirschi (1986, 1987, 1988) argue that longitudinal research is unnecessary. They give three reasons: (1) cross-sectional research shows the relationship between age and crime is invariant, and so there is no need for longitudinal research, (2) findings from cross-sectional research achieve the same results as longitudinal studies with less cost in terms of time and expense, and (3) the proponents of a longitudinal design are theoretically biased towards selective incapacitation, and their research is focused on career criminals. In response, advocates for longitudinal research design, led by Blumstein, Cohen, and Farrington (1988a, 1988b) have pointed out the inconsistencies and flaws in the opponents' criticisms (Farrington, 1986; Greenberg, 1985).

Hirschi and Gottfredson's Point of View

Hirschi and Gottfredson's opening argument states that the relationship between age and crime is invariant (1983). Using data from the Uniform Crime Reports (UCR), they show that crime rates reach a peak in the middle to late teens and then decline. Furthermore, they argue, this relationship between age and crime does not vary over time or with race, gender, or type of offense. They conclude that cross-sectional research is sufficient to specify the time course of criminal careers, because the causes of crime at one age are the same as those at any other age.

Gottfredson and Hirschi (1986) continue to question the need for longitudinal research in a later article with respect, in particular, to selective incapacitation and "career criminals." They propose that the focus on selective incapacitation by scholars is an attempt to convince policymakers to continue the resources for this type of study. Examining data from the Gluecks' longitudinal study of 1,000 delinquents, Gottfredson and Hirschi show that the age distribution of specific crimes is similar to that of the UCR. Gottfredson and Hirschi also use data from Farrington's (1983a, 1983b) longitudinal research to calculate the crime rate, or incidence rate, by age. They conclude that the crime rate does not vary by age, and consequently, it is not necessary to conduct longitudinal research on "career criminals."

The argument continues in Gottfredson and Hirschi's 1987 article, which questions the methodological adequacy of longitudinal research. They contend that the widespread view of the superiority of longitudinal research designs is based on the alleged methodological advantages of longitudinal research in solving causal questions and the alleged substantive superiority that "the facts of crime and criminality require a longitudinal design for their explication" (Gottfredson & Hirschi, 1987, p. 583). Gottfredson and Hirschi support their position by claiming that longitudinal research has only confirmed the results of earlier cross-sectional research as regards age, period, and cohort effects, standard causal relationships, the effects of life course events, and criminal justice interventions. In addition, it is suggested that the theoretical point of view espoused by advocates of longitudinal design is the very reason they use this type of design.

The Criminal Career Approach: Why Longitudinal Studies Are Necessary

In their rebuttal, Blumstein et al. (1988a) maintain that Gottfredson and Hirschi (1986) confuse the terminology of career criminals and criminal careers and do not understand the concepts of lambda, prevalence, and incidence. Blumstein et al. (1988a) point out that it is the age-crime invariance, discussed by Hirschi and Gottfredson (1983) and Gottfredson and Hirschi (1986), that should be studied using longitudinal research. Furthermore, they provide evidence that refutes the position by Gottfredson and Hirschi (1986). First, the relationship between age and crime is not invariant; second, the relationship obtained in cross-sectional data is different from that obtained longitudinally (Farrington, 1979, 1986); third, the age-crime relationship is different for different kinds of offenses (Cline, 1980); and fourth, there are different relationships at different ages (Cline, 1980; Farrington, 1986; West, 1982).

Blumstein et al. (1988a) state that the criminal career approach is based on this construct, which refers to the longitudinal sequence of offenses committed by an offender. The criminal career differs from a career criminal, which can be defined as an offender who makes a livelihood out of crime. The criminal career approach, which depends on a longitudinal research design, has specific key parameters—lambda, prevalence, incidence, onset, and desistance. Prevalence refers to participation in crime by a proportion of a population. Gottfredson and Hirschi (1986) do not accept the idea that participation can vary with time. The frequency of offending, lambda, is an individual crime rate per unit of time, not an aggregate population crime rate. Gottfredson and Hirschi (1986) mistake incidence rates for lambdas in their article. Criminal career knowledge does not presuppose a belief in selective incapacitation but can be applied to any policy. In conclusion, Blumstein et al. (1988b) note that while causal inferences are better drawn from longitudinal surveys, which control for extraneous variables and allow determination of temporal order, longitudinal research designs are also superior to cross-sectional designs because they permit description of the natural history and course of development of a phenomenon, measurement of developmental sequences, and possible prediction of events.

A Second Look at Lambda

New light has been shed upon this argument in a study by Loeber and Snyder (1990). Using juvenile court archival case records to construct a longitudinal data base of multiple birth cohorts, they analyze the relationship between age at onset, age at offense, and lambda. The results of their analyses provide support for Hirschi and Gottfredson (1983) and Gottfredson and Hirschi's (1986, 1988) position of the invariance of the age-crime curve by showing that, even when controlling for the age at onset and age at desistance, lambda increases with the age at offense. The fact that previous research found an increase in lambda with an earlier age at onset is explained by the lower average rates of offending at the lower ages. Thus, the article by Loeber and Snyder again questions the need for longitudinal research. The fact that these authors used longitudinal data in order to prove the position of Gottfredson and Hirschi (1986, 1988) regarding the invariance of age and crime and consequently the lack of justification for longitudinal design, suggests they may not actually be in agreement with the need for longitudinal design. In addition, these authors only focus on one parameter of criminal career research—lambda; they have overlooked the value of longitudinal and criminal career research in the definition of the parameters of participation and desistance and the exploration of the patterns of change and constancy over time.

What We Have Learned from Longitudinal Research

We have learned a great deal about the prevalence and incidence of delinquency and the patterns of criminal careers. For example, about one-third of all males are likely to have a police record by the time they are 18. However, only a small proportion (6%) continue to offend and are responsible for the majority of offenses. Of those arrested as juveniles, between 40 and 50% are arrested as adults. Furthermore, those who begin their criminal careers at an early age have longer and more serious criminal careers than those who begin later. Recidivism rates increase with the number of prior offenses, and seriousness of offenses increases with age, but the type of offense can not be predicted. Delinquency can be predicted by poor parental supervision and discipline, parental criminality, and large, low-income families. Similar factors predict the persistence of offending into adulthood. Although longitudinal research has made significant progress in specifying some of the key parameters of criminal careers, still more longitudinal research is needed to examine further the patterns of onset, duration, and termination of criminal careers, as well as the effects of the criminal justice system.

Summary

In this chapter, we have examined the strengths and weaknesses of longitudinal research designs. Longitudinal designs are best suited for causal development because they involve repeated measurements and allow analysis of patterns of change. As stated by Blumstein et al. (1988a):

Longitudinal data are most clearly superior to cross-sectional data in testing causal hypotheses, for two main reasons. One is that the time ordering of events can be determined more precisely in prospective than in retrospective longitudinal data, which makes it easier to resolve problems of causal order. The second is that there is better control of extraneous variables in longitudinal data, because each person acts as his own control. Hence, changes within subjects as well as variations between subjects can be investigated in longitudinal data. (p. 29)

Longitudinal designs, however, are quite expensive and time consuming. Furthermore, it can be difficult to control for testing, instrumentation, and maturation effects, as well as attrition. The results also may be biased due to lack of representativeness or to history effects. On the other hand, cross-sectional designs are particularly useful and preferable in exploratory research to investigate correlations between variables.

There are two possible solutions to the controversy over cross-sectional versus longitudinal design. First, a multiple cohort technique can be used. This cohort analytic technique simultaneously compares two or more cohorts in a combined longitudinal/cross-sectional analysis (Lab, 1988, p. 2). An example of this type of design is Shannon's study of three birth cohorts, with birth years of 1942, 1949, and 1955 (Shannon, 1981). Simultaneous measurement of the cohorts at various ages (6 to 11, 12 to 17) allows comparison across groups, i.e., between the 1942 and 1949 cohorts and the 1949 and 1955 cohorts. As Lab (1988) points out, by using the cohort analytic technique one can identify age, period, and cohort effects and disentangle longitudinal, cross-sectional, and time-lag differences. There are some problems with the technique, however, including potential lack of generalizability and the possibility of a dominant cohort effect, in which the effects of one cohort outweigh all other factors.

A possible second solution to the debate over cross-sectional versus longitudinal design is to formulate a different conceptualization of criminal behavior, one which employs a different methodology (Hagan & Palloni, 1988). If criminal events are viewed as a part of the life course, it is possible to use the methods of event history analysis. This "new etiology" focuses on the causes and consequences of criminal behavior:

The point of a life-course perspective is to emphasize that social events that are called delinquent or criminal are linked into life trajectories of broader significance, whether those trajectories are criminal or noncriminal in form. (Hagan & Palloni, 1988, p. 90)

The advantage of the life course perspective is the ability to study the effects of different events on behavior. Not only is it possible to compare delinquents to nondelinquents in terms of onset of criminal behavior but it also is possible to examine the causes of desistance from criminal behavior. The best research designs for event history analysis are retrospective histories or prospective longitudinal data. However, this does not preclude the use of cross-sectional research designs. As noted by Blumstein et al. (1988b), these two methods are not mutually exclusive and have different strengths and limitations and should be used to complement each other. In closing, Blumstein et al. (1988b) state:

While longitudinal surveys are superior in drawing causal inferences when variables vary within subjects, longitudinal surveys are no better than cross-sectional ones in establishing causal effects of facts (such as sex or race) that can only vary between subjects. However, to the extent that the relation between such factors and offending is mediated by factors (such as parental supervision) that do vary within subjects, this interaction could be addressed more effectively by longitudinal surveys. (p. 72)

The real decision in determining which type of research design to use is up to the researcher. He or she must carefully consider the purposes of the study and the broader conceptual framework. It should be evident that the longitudinal research design is superior for testing causal hypotheses; however, this does not preclude the use of a cross-sectional design for other purposes. The advantages and disadvantages of each method must be weighed with regard to the objectives of the proposed research.

References

Blumstein, A., Cohen, J., & Farrington, D.P. (1988a). Criminal career research: Its value for criminology." *Criminology*, 26(1), 1–35.
Blumstein, A., Cohen, J., & Farrington, D.P. (1988b). Longitudinal and criminal career research: Further clarifications. *Criminology*, 26(1), 57–74.
Campbell, D.T., & Ross, H.L. (1980). The Connecticut crackdown on speeding: Time-series data in quasi-experimental analysis. In S.M. Talarico (Ed.), *Criminal justice research* (pp. 70–88). Cincinnati: Anderson Publishing.
Cline, H.F. (1980). Criminal behavior over the life span. In O.G. Brim & J. Dagan (Eds.), *Constancy and change in human development* (pp. 641–674). Cambridge, MA: Harvard University Press.
Elliott, D.S., Ageton, S.S., Huizinga, D., Knowles, B.A., & Canter, R.J. (1983). *The prevalence and incidence of delinquent behavior: 1976–1980*. Boulder, CO: Behavioral Research Institute.
Farrington, D. (1977). The effects of public labeling. *British Journal of Criminology*, 17, 112–125.
Farrington, D. (1979). Longitudinal research on crime and delinquency. In N. Morris & M. Tonry (Eds.), *Crime and justice: An annual review of research* (Vol. 1, pp. 289–348). Chicago: University of Chicago Press.
Farrington, D. (1983a). *Further analyses of a longitudinal survey of crime and delinquency*. Final Report to the National Institute of Justice. Washington, DC: National Institute of Justice.
Farrington, D. (1983b). Offending from 10 to 25 years of age. In K.T. Van Dusen & S.A. Mednick (Eds.), *Prospective studies of crime and delinquency* (pp. 17–37). Boston: Kluwer-Nijhoff.
Farrington, D. (1986). Age and crime. In N. Morris & M. Tonry (Eds.), *Crime and justice: An annual review of research* (Vol. 7, pp. 29–90). Chicago: University of Chicago Press.

Farrington, D., & West, D.J. (1979). The Cambridge study in delinquent development. In S.A. Mednick & A.E. Baert (Eds.), *Prospective longitudinal research in Europe: An empirical basis for primary prevention*, pp. 137–145. New York: Oxford University Press.

Farrington, D., Ohlin, L.E., & Wilson, J.Q. (1986). *Understanding and controlling crime: Toward a new research strategy*. New York: Springer-Verlag.

Glueck, S., & Glueck, E.T. (1934). *One thousand juvenile delinquents*. Cambridge, MA: Harvard University Press.

Glueck, S., & Glueck, E.T. (1940). *Juvenile delinquents grown up*. New York: Commonwealth Fund.

Glueck, S., & Glueck, E.T. (1950). *Unraveling juvenile delinquency*. Cambridge, MA: Harvard University Press.

Gottfredson, M., & Hirschi, T. (1986). The true value of lambda would appear to be zero: An essay on career criminals, criminal careers, selective incapacitation, cohort studies, and related topics. *Criminology, 24*(2), 213–234.

Gottfredson, M., & Hirschi, T. (1987). The methodological adequacy of longitudinal research on crime. *Criminology, 25*(3), 581–614.

Gottfredson, M., & Hirschi, T. (1988). Science, public policy, and the career paradigm. *Criminology, 26*(1), 37–55.

Greenberg, D. (1985). Age, crime, and social explanation. *American Journal of Sociology, 91*, 1–21.

Hagan, J., & Palloni, A. (1988). Crimes as social events in the life course: Reconceiving a criminological controversy. *Criminology, 26*(1), 87–100.

Hirschi, T., & Gottfredson, N. (1983). Age and the explanation of crime. *American Journal of Sociology, 89*, 552–584.

Knight, B.J., & West, D.J. (1975). Temporary and continuing delinquency. *British Journal of Criminology, 15*, 43–50.

Lab, S.P. (1988). Analyzing change in crime and delinquency rates: The case for cohort analysis. *Criminal Justice Research Bulletin, 3*(10), 1–7.

Loeber, R. & Snyder, H.N. (1990). Rate of offending in juvenile careers: Findings of constancy and change in lambda. *Criminology, 28*(1), 97–109.

McCord, J. (1979). Some child-rearing antecedents of criminal behavior in adult men. *Journal of Personality and Social Psychology, 37*, 1477–1486.

Osborn, S.G., & West, D.J. (1978). The effectiveness of various predictors of criminal careers. *Journal of Adolescence, 1*, 101–117.

Osborn, S.G., & West, D.J. (1980). Do young delinquents really reform? *Journal of Adolescence, 3*, 99–114.

Petersilia, J., Greenwood, P., & Lavin, M. (1978). *Criminal careers of habitual felons*. Washington, DC: U.S. Department of Justice.

Peterson, M., Braiker, H.B., & Polich, S.M. (1981). *Who commits crime?* Cambridge, MA: Oelgeschlager, Gunn & Hain.

Powers, E., & Witmer, H. (1951). *An experiment in the prevention of delinquency*. New York: Columbia University Press.

Shannon, L.W. (1981). *Assessing the relationship of adult criminal careers to juvenile careers*. Iowa City: The University of Iowa, Iowa Urban Community Research Center.

Tracy, P.E., Wolfgang, M.E., & Figlio, R.M. (1985). *Delinquency in two birth cohorts*. Washington, DC: National Institute for Juvenile Justice and Delinquency Prevention.

West, D.J. (1982). *Delinquency: Its roots, careers, and prospects.* London: Heine-mann.

West, D.J., & Farrington, D. (1973). *Who becomes delinquent?* London: Heine-mann.

Wish, E.D. (1987). Identification of drug abusing offenders: A guide for practition-ers. *Prosecutors Perspective, 1*(2), 2–3.

Wolfgang, M.E., Figlio, R.M., & Sellin, T. (1972). *Delinquency in a birth cohort.* Chicago: University of Chicago Press.

8
Issues in Legal-Impact Research

JULIE HORNEY AND CASSIA SPOHN

Policy analysis has been defined as "finding out what governments do, why they do it, and what difference it makes" (Dye, 1976, p. 1). It involves determining the causes and consequences of public policies. Legal-impact research is a type of policy analysis that focuses on the consquences of legal changes. It poses questions concerning the impact of statutory changes, court-ordered reforms, and appellate court rulings. Did statutory changes in rape laws make arrest, prosecution, and conviction for rape more likely? Did restrictive drunk driving laws lead to a decline in the number of crash-related injuries or fatalities? In asking questions such as these, legal-impact research attempts to delineate the social, economic, and political effects of legal changes.

Legal-impact research is not a special kind of research with a unique methodology. Standard methodological procedures—survey research, experimentation, time-series analysis, and sampling—are used by researchers examining the impact of legal changes. This type of research does, however, have its own methodological issues and problems. In this chapter, we summarize four studies of legal impact and then use these studies and others to illustrate the methodological issues confronting the researcher who wants to evaluate the impact of statutory changes and legal decisions. We focus our discussion on changes affecting the criminal justice system.

Four Studies of Legal Impact

Rape Reform Legislation

The first study we will describe is our own evaluation of rape law reform (Horney & Spohn, 1989). During the 1970s, most states made changes in their rape laws. The most common changes were redefining rape as gender-neutral sexual assault; replacing the single crime of rape with a series of graded offenses defined by the presence or absence of specified aggravating

167

circumstances; modifying or eliminating requirements that the victim resist and that her testimony be corroborated; and placing restrictions on the use of evidence of the victim's prior sexual relationships. These changes were designed to improve the treatment of rape victims; to encourage victims to report rapes to the police; and to make arrest, prosecution, and conviction for rape more likely.

Our study was a multijurisdiction study evaluating the effect of the legal changes on reports of rape and on the processing of rape cases. We chose six jurisdictions to represent different types of reforms: Detroit, Michigan; Cook County (Chicago), Illinois; Philadelphia County (Philadelphia), Pennsylvania; Harris County (Houston), Texas; Fulton County (Atlanta), Georgia; and Washington, D.C. In each jurisdiction we collected data from court records on all rape cases indicted between 1970 and 1985. For each case we recorded the original and final charges, the type of disposition, and the sentence. From the Federal Bureau of Investigation (FBI) *Uniform Crime Reports (UCR)*, we obtained monthly data on reports of rape. To aid us in interpreting the data and to provide information about case processing practices, we also conducted interviews with judges, prosecutors, defense attorneys, police officers, and rape crisis center personnel.

We used an interrupted time-series-design *analysis* to test for the impact of the legal changes on reports of rape and on indictments, convictions, and sentences for rape. We found the types of effects anticipated by reformers only in the jurisdiction (Detroit) with strong and comprehensive changes; there the reforms produced increases in the number of reports (Figure 8.1), and in the indictment rate (Figure 8.2). Figures 8.3 and 8.4 show reports of rape and the indictment rate in Washington, D.C., where, as in the other jurisdictions, the law had no impact.

The results of the *analyses* led us to conclude that the ability of rape reform legislation to affect case processing is limited; this type of impact will be confined primarily to jurisdictions that enact strong and comprehensive changes. We also concluded, however, that the reforms may have had positive effects on the attitudes of criminal justice officials. Interviews in the six jurisdictions revealed that criminal justice officials approve of the legal changes, which they believe have resulted in more appropriate treatment of men accused of rape and more humane treatment of their victims. On the other hand, the interviews also provided evidence that officials had failed to comply with some of the substantive and procedural restrictions contained in the laws.

Deterrence and Drinking and Driving

A second example of legal-impact research is an evaluation of a law in France designed to deter drinking and driving (Ross, McCleary, & Epperlein, 1981–82). The new law allowed law enforcement officials to set up

No. of reports

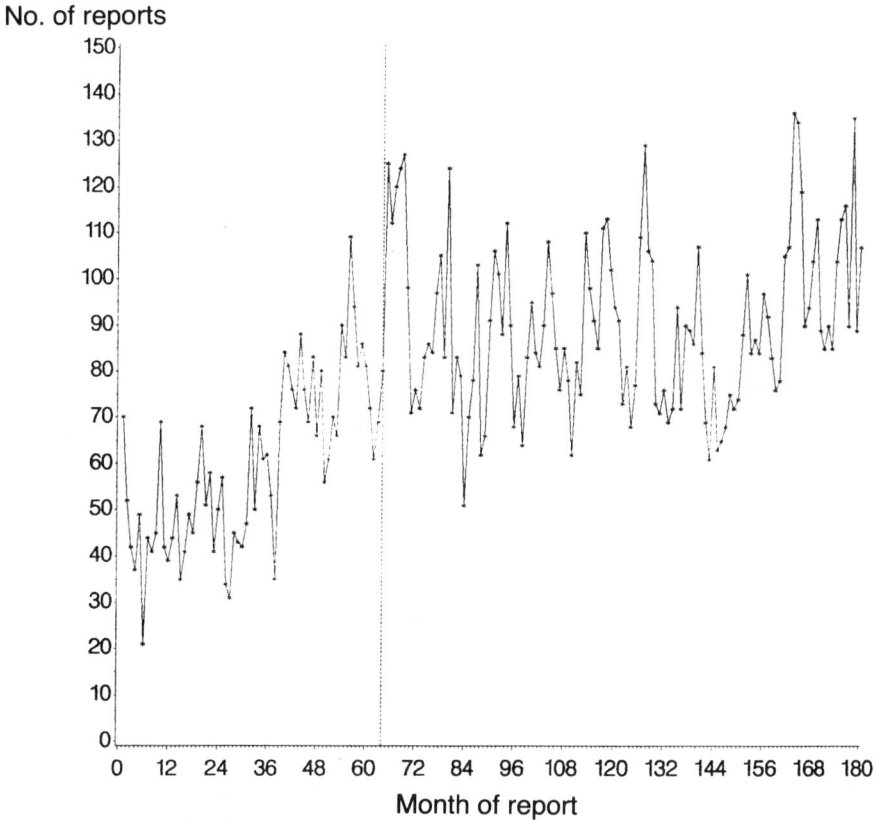

FIGURE 8.1. Monthly reports of rape; Detroit, Michigan, 1970–1984. Note: Broken line indicates date reforms implemented. Source: The Impact of Rape Reform Legislation by J. Horney and C. Spohn, 1989, Final report to the National Institute of Justice and the National Science Foundation, p. 79.

roadblocks and test drivers for blood alcohol. Those found guilty of driving with a certain level of blood alcohol faced possible revocation of their driver's license. Revocation was mandatory under certain specified circumstances, and the offender could not apply for a new license for up to 3 years.

The new law went into effect in 1978. The authors used an interrupted time-series design to analyze its impact on crash-related injuries and crash-related fatalities in France from 1973 through 1980. They found that the law had statistically significant effects on both variables; there was a decline of 12.5% in crash-related injuries (Figure 8.5) and a drop of 13.9% in crash-related fatalities (Figure 8.6). Both effects, however, were temporary. The effect on injuries lasted only 8.4 months, the effect on fatalities only 12.9 months.

% Indicted

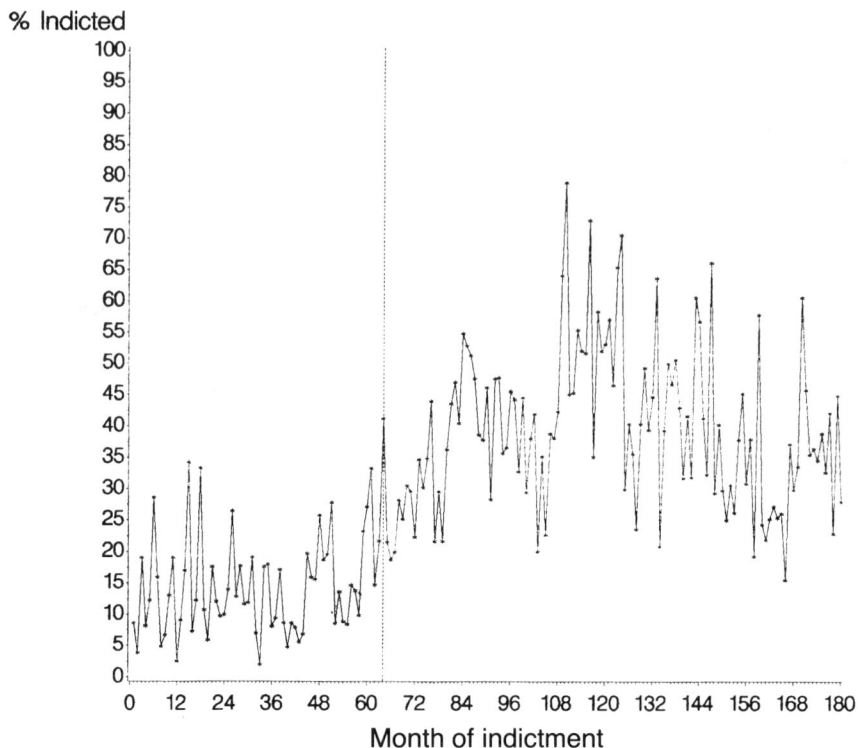

Month of indictment

FIGURE 8.2. Percentage indicted monthly for rape, sodomy, gross indecency, and 1st or 3rd-degree criminal sexual conduct; Detroit, Michigan, 1970–1984. Note: Broken line indicates date reforms implemented. Source: The Impact of Rape Reform Legislation by J. Horney and C. Spohn, 1989, Final Report to the National Institute of Justice and the National Science Foundation, p. 80.

The authors also conducted separate analyses of crash-related injuries and fatalities that occurred on weekend nights and that occurred Tuesday through Thursday. Previous research had shown that accidents involving alcohol were more common on weekend nights. Their analysis revealed that the law had an even larger impact or injuries and fatalities on weekend nights; it produced a drop of 34.9% in crash-related injuries and a decline of 35.2% in crash-related fatalities. Again, however, both effects had dissipated in less than 1 year. This confirmed the overall interpretation that the law had a significant, although temporary, effect.

Court-Ordered Reforms in a Texas Penitentiary

The two studies described above examined the impact of statutory changes. The study described in this section evaluated the effect of court-

No. of reports

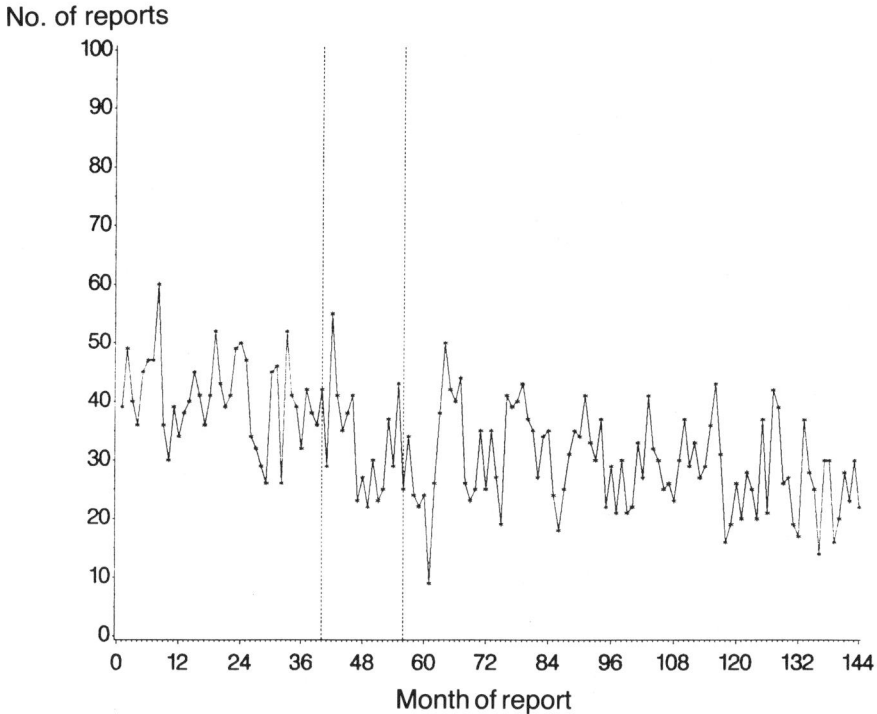

FIGURE 8.3. Monthly reports of rape; Washington, DC, 1973–1984. Note: Broken lines indicate dates of court rulings. Month 40 = Corroboration, Month 56 = Shield. Source: The Impact of Rape Reform Legislation by J. Horney and C. Spohn, 1989, Final report to the National Institute of Justice and the National Science Foundation, p. 101.

ordered reforms on a Texas penitentiary (Marquart & Crouch, 1985). In 1980, a legal decree against the Texas Department of Corrections was de-livered as a result of a suit in federal court. Marquart and Crouch focused on a central feature of *Ruiz v. Estelle* (1980), which ordered the Depart-ment of Corrections to abandon certain methods of prisoner control, and evaluated the impact of the court order on one particular prison.

In *Ruiz v. Estelle*, the judge ordered prison officials to reduce the use of force by prison personnel, to remove and reassign inmates known as "building tenders" (BTs), who apparently were controlling other inmates, to hire more guards, and to develop a more extensive inmate classification plan. Marquart and Crouch studied a maximum security Texas prison before, during, and after the reform measures were implemented. In conducting the analysis, they used participant observation, interviews with guards and inmates, documents and inmate records, and informal con-versations resulting from the participant observation.

% Indicted

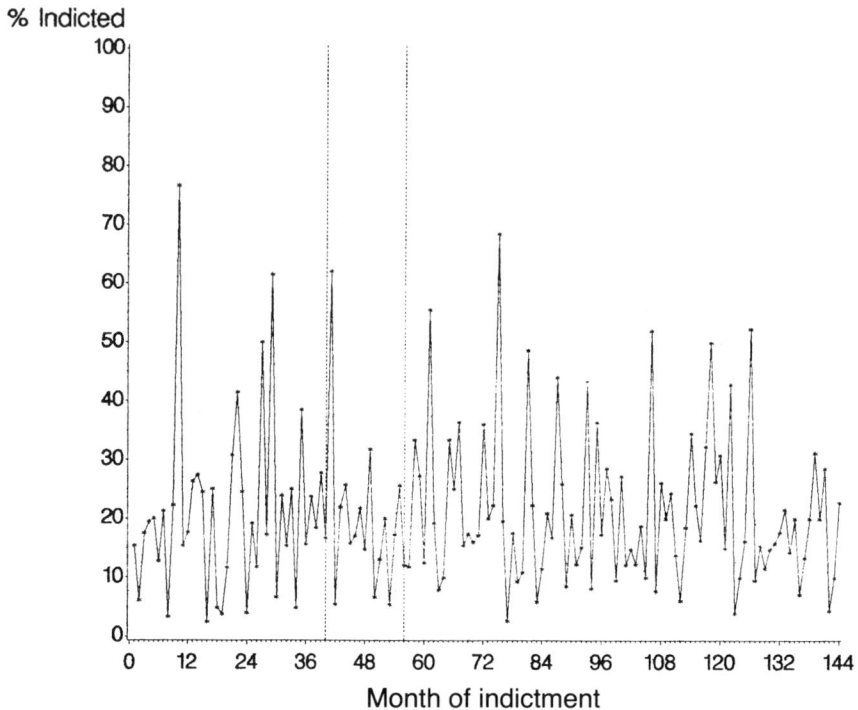

FIGURE 8.4. Percent indicted for rape by month; Washington, DC, 1973–1984. Note: Broken lines indicate dates of court rulings. Month 40 = Corroboration, Month 56 = Shield. Source: The Impact of Rape Reform Legislation, by J. Horney and C. Spohn, 1989, Final report to the National Institute of Justice and the National Science Foundation, p. 102.

Marquart and Crouch used participant observation for 19 months before implementation of the court-ordered reforms. One of the authors entered the prison as a guard and collected data on social control and order. Through observation and interviews with informants, he learned how prison staff co-opted certain inmates with special privileges in return for help in controlling the rest of the inmate population. These "building tenders" were expected to inform on other inmates, socialize new inmates, protect guards from attacks by inmates, and discipline other inmates through physical punishment. The observer also learned how staff unofficially used threats of physical force as well as actual physical force to control inmate behavior.

To comply with the court order, prison administrators reassigned the BTs to ordinary jobs and took away their former power and duties. Guards were told they would be fired for using unnecessary force with inmates. Court-appointed monitors regularly observed the process in order to insure compliance.

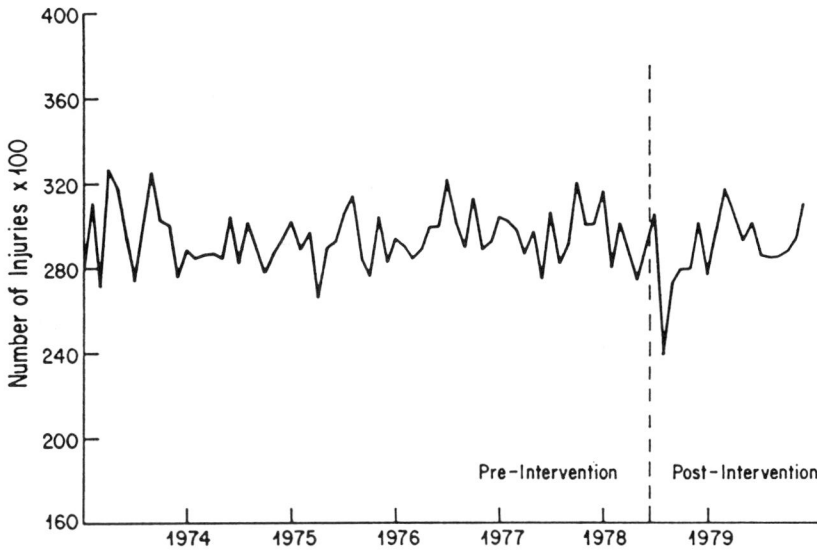

FIGURE 8.5. Crash-related injuries in France, seasonal variation removed. Source: "Deterrence of Drinking and Driving in France: An Evaluation of the Law of July 12, 1978" by H.L. Ross, R. McCleary, and T. Epperlein, 1981–1982, *Law and Society Review, 14,* p. 356. Reprinted by permission of the Law and Society Association.

After implementation of the reforms, Marquart and Crouch studied the impact on interpersonal relations between guards and inmates. They returned to the prison to collect additional observation data and to conduct structured interviews with guards and inmates. Table 8.1 shows changes over time of disciplinary cases resulting in solitary confinement for inmates who challenged authority. As fear of physical reprisals from guards and BTs was eliminated, inmate challenges to guards' authority increased. There was also a rise in serious violence between inmates, as documented in Table 8.2. Marquart and Crouch (1985) concluded that "although court intervention has made Eastham's operations more consistent with constitutional requirements of fairness and due process, the fact remains that life for the inmates and guards at Eastham is far less orderly than it was before. Authority has eroded, and the cell blocks and halls are clearly more dangerous" (p. 584).

A Mandatory Gun Law

On January 1, 1977, the Michigan Felony Firearm Statute went into effect. This law mandated a 2-year "flat-time" sentence for those convicted of

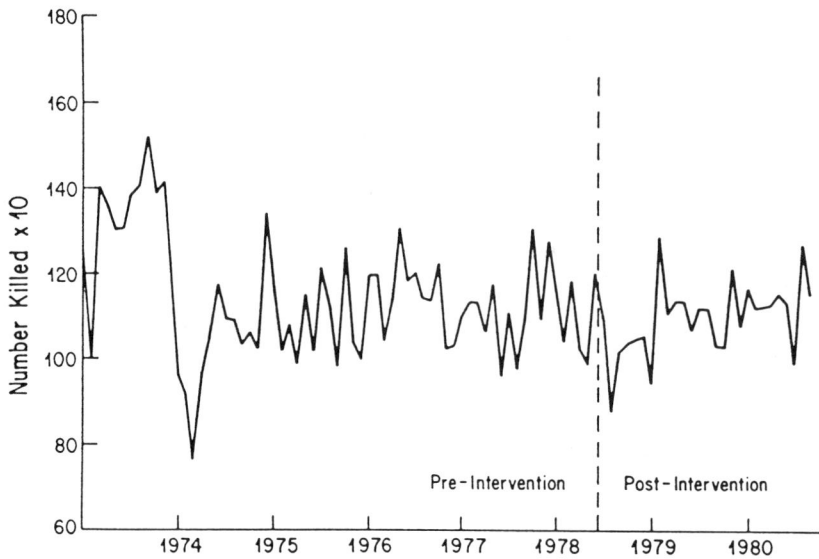

FIGURE 8.6. Crash-related deaths in France, seasonal variation removed. Source: "Deterrence of Drinking and Driving in France: An Evaluation of the Law of of July 12, 1978" by H.L. Ross, R. McCleary, and T. Epperlein, 1981–1982, *Law and Society Review, 16,* p. 357.

TABLE 8.1. Selected disciplinary cases resulting in solitary confinement: Direct challenges to authority from 1981 to 1984*.

	1981	1982	1983	1984
1. Striking and Officer	4	21	38	129
	(1.3)	(6.5)	(12.0)	(49.4)
2. Attempting to strike an officer	7	9	18	21
	(2.3)	(2.7)	(5.7)	(8.0)
3. Threatening an officer	4	5	38	109
	(1.3)	(1.5)	(12.0)	(41.8)
4. Refusing or failing to obey an order	90	65	72	213
	(30.6)	(20.1)	(22.8)	(81.7)
5. Use of indecent/vulgar language	11	14	89	94
(cursing an officer)	(3.7)	(4.3)	(28.2)	(36.0)
Total	116	114	225	556
Population levels	2,938	3,224	3,150	2,607

*Numbers in parentheses indicate the rate per 1,000 imates. The population figures are based on the average monthly population at Eastham.
Source: "Judicial Reform and Prisoner Control" by J.W. Marquart and B.M. Crouch, 1985, *Law and Society Review, 19,* p. 573. Reprinted by permission of the Law and Society Association.

TABLE 8.2. Selected inmate-inmate offenses resulting in solitary confinement: Weapons offenses, 1981–1984.

	1981	1982	1983	1984
1. Fighting with a weapon	25	31	46	31
	(8.5)	(9.6)	(14.6)	(11.8)
2. Striking an inmate with a weapon	21	25	40	57
	(7.1)	(7.7)	(12.6)	(21.8)
3. Possession of a weapon	40	25	59	134
	(13.6)	(7.7)	(18.7)	(51.4)
4. Homicide	0	1	0	3
	(0)	(.3)	(0)	(1.1)
Total	86	82	145	225
Population levels	2,938	3,224	3,150	2,607

Source: "Judicial Reform and Prisoner Control" by J.W. Marquart and B.M. Crouch, 1985, *Law and Society Review*, *19*, p. 575. Reprinted by permission of the Law and Society Association.

possessing firearms while committing felonies. The 2-year sentence is added to the sentence for the main felony, and the two sentences must be served consecutively. Loftin, Heumann, and McDowall (1983) evaluated the impact of this law on the treatment of defendants charged with possession of firearms and on the crime rate. The authors collected data on all cases disposed of by Detroit Recorders Court during 1976, 1977, and 1978 in which the original charge was one of six violent felonies: murder, first degree criminal sexual assault, armed robbery, assault with intent to commit murder, assault with intent to commit great bodily harm, and felonious assault. They also interviewed judges, prosecutors, and defense attorneys in Detroit.

To determine the law's impact on sentencing of offenders, Loftin and his colleagues calculated a measure called *expected minimum sentence* (EMS), which corresponded to the length of time to first possible release. Loftin et al. (1983) calculated the average EMS for four categories of cases, defined by whether the offense was committed with a gun or not and whether it was committed before or after the law went into effect. Figure 8.7, which presents data on armed robberies, reveals that gun offenses received longer sentences than nongun offenses but that the distribution of sentences in the pre- and postreform periods was not very different. Statistical analyses of the EMS before and after the law went into effect indicated that the gun law did not produce an across-the-board increase in sentences. The only significant effects were found for felonious assault and assault with intent to commit murder.

Loftin et al. (1983) also examined the impact of the law on likelihood of

GUN OFFENSE, PRE 1977

GUN OFFENSE, POST 1977

OFFENSE WITHOUT GUN, PRE 1977

OFFENSE WITHOUT GUN, POST 1977

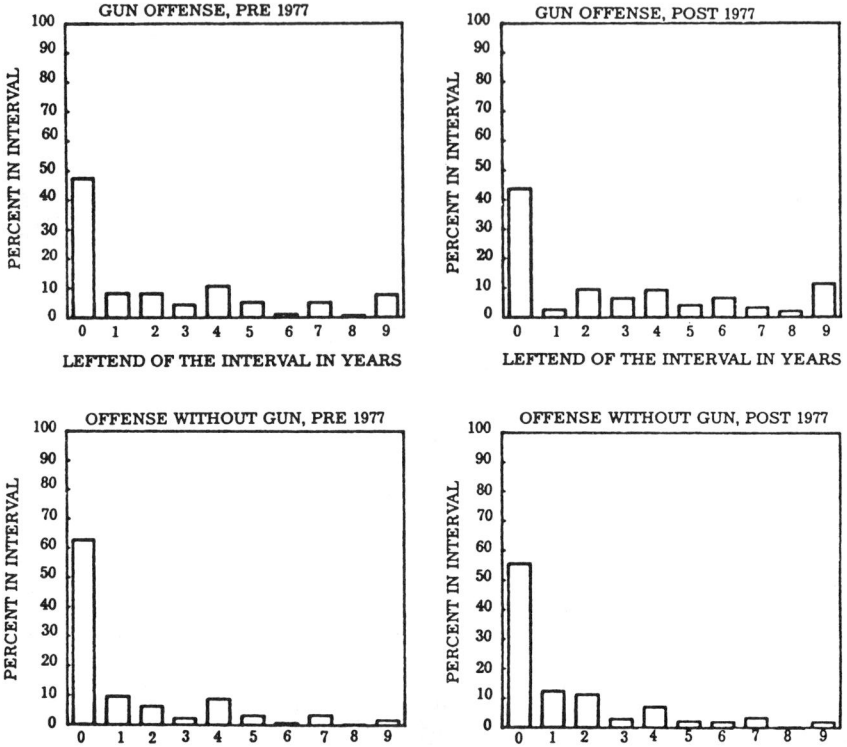

FIGURE 8.7. Expected minimum sentence for armed robbery in days by weapon and time period. Source: "Mandatory Sentencing and Firearms Violence: Evaluating an Alternative to Gun Control" by C. Loftin, M. Heumann, and D. McDowall, 1983, *Law and Society Review, 17,* p. 292. Reprinted by permission of the Law and Society Association.

conviction, likelihood of incarceration if convicted, and length of sentence if incarcerated. They found that the gun law apparently reduced the probability of conviction for felonious assault and perhaps armed robbery. For those convicted, it increased the likelihood of incarceration for felonious assault only. For those incarcerated, the sentence length was increased for armed robbery, assault with intent to commit murder, assault with intent to commit great bodily harm, and felonious assault. Loftin et al. (1983) concluded that all the data taken together indicate that "the Gun Law had a consistent and clear impact only in the case of felonious assault" (p. 297). Interviews with judges, prosecutors, and defense attorneys provided an explanation for the lack of impact on sentences. Apparently, there was an

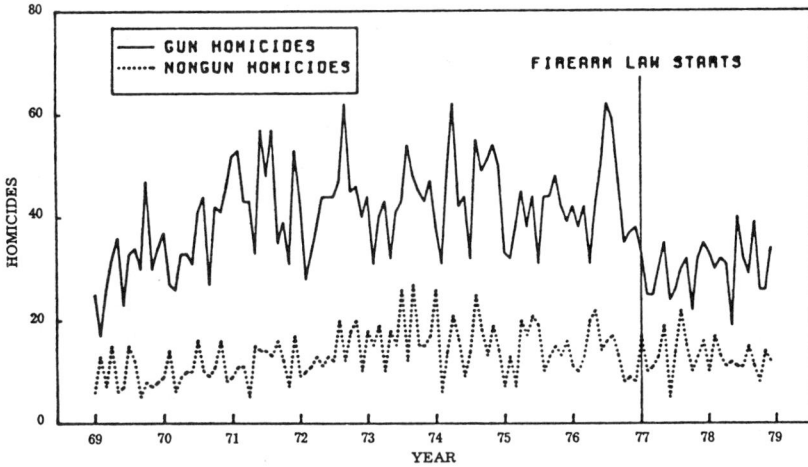

FIGURE 8.8. Detroit homicides (1969–1978). Source: "Mandatory Sentencing and Firearms Violence: Evaluating an Alternative to Gun Control" by C. Loftin, M. Heumann, and D. McDowall, 1983, *Law and Society Review*, *17*, p. 306. Reprinted by permission of the Law and Society Association.

agreed-upon "going rate"—a typical sentence—for stereotypical felonies. Even though under the new law judges were required to impose the additional 2 years when a gun was involved, they were able to adjust the sentence for the main felony so that the total time to be served did not deviate significantly from the going rate.

To assess the impact of the mandatory gun law on crime rates, Loftin et al. (1983) used an interrupted time-series design to analyze police records of monthly crime rates. The only crime to show a statistically significant decline in the postreform period was homicide with a gun (Figure 8.8). The authors then divided homicides into three categories based on the relationship between the offender and victim. They reasoned that if the gun law was responsible for the decline in gun homicides, the effects should show up among premeditated homicides involving strangers rather than among "crime of passion" homicides involving nonstrangers. The analysis, however, indicated that the decline was the same when the offender and victim were strangers, acquaintances, or relatives or close friends. Based on this, Loftin et al. (1983) concluded that the gun law probably was not responsible for the decline in gun homicides and thus "did not have a discernible effect on the level or the pattern or violent crime in Detroit" (p. 309).

The Nature of Legal-Impact Research

As noted above, legal-impact research focuses on the consequences of statutory changes, court-ordered reforms, and appellate court rulings. Like evaluation research, which attempts to determine whether a *program* produced the desired results, legal-impact research focuses on the intended consequences of legal changes. It involves measuring the effects of a legal change in terms of its goals and outcomes. It involves, in other words, specifying the goals of the legal change; operationalizing these goals in terms of measurable outcomes; formulating an appropriate research strategy; collecting data on the individuals, groups, or institutions targeted by the legal change; and assessing the degree to which the goals have been realized. While this sounds like a relatively simple and straightforward process, each of these steps is fraught with unexpected difficulties. We dicuss several of these problems in the sections that follow.

Specifying Goals and Outcomes

In order to assess the impact of a legal change, the researcher must first determine what the law or court ruling is trying to accomplish. The researcher must first specify the goals of the legal change "in terms that are clear, specific, and measurable" (Weiss, 1972, p. 26). Before she can assess the degree to which changes in the rape laws have been effective, in other words, the researcher must spell out the intended consequences of the reforms. To do this, she must decide whom the law targets. She must also recognize the importance of considering manifest and latent goals, proximate and ultimate goals, and process as well as outcome measures.

Determining the Law's Target

In specifying the goals of a legal change, a useful first step is to examine the law closely to determine whom or what the law targets. Some laws aim to produce changes in the attitudes or behavior of individuals. Criminal justice researchers often analyze laws that are designed to have a general deterrent effect and that target the behavior of criminal offenders or would-be offenders. A major goal of the Michigan Felony Firearm Statute (1977), for example, was to reduce the number of crimes committed with guns; legislators expected that the mandatory 2-year prison term would deter offenders from using guns during the commission of felonies. Similarly, the French law on drinking and driving was aimed at deterring citizens from driving with unsafe levels of blood alcohol.

Criminal justice reforms may also target the attitudes or behavior of officials within the criminal justice system. Those who championed rape reform legislation argued that the legal changes would reduce both the skepticism of criminal justice officials toward the claims of rape victims and their reliance on legally irrelevant assessments of the victim's status and character in decision making. Ultimately, the reforms were expected to affect the behavior of criminal justice officials, making it more likely that police officers would arrests, prosecutors would charge, and judges or juries would convict. The *Ruiz v. Estelle* court order was directed at corrections administrators and was designed to change their treatment of prison inmates. The Michigan gun law could be thought of as directed at judges who sentence offenders who use guns; it was intended to limit their discretion in exercising sentencing options.

Legal changes within the criminal justice system might also seek to alter public values or attitudes. One could argue, for example, that a goal of laws mandating license revocation or jail terms for drunk driving is to foster public disapproval of drinking and driving. Similarly, rape reform legislation might be viewed as an attempt to counteract negative views of rape and rape victims among the general public. Changes in the rape laws also were designed to encourage victims to report rapes to the police; thus, these changes could be seen as specifically targeting rape victims.

Other criminal justice reforms focus not on the attitudes or behavior of individuals but on the responsiveness or operating procedures or institutions. While the reforms generally produce institutional effects by altering the behavior of individuals within the system, the ultimate target is the institution itself. Many states, for example, enacted rape shield laws that restrict the use of evidence of the victim's past sexual history and that mandate *in camera* hearings to determine the relevance of potentially admissible evidence. The reforms, in other words, sought to alter the procedures and standards used to determine the relevance of this type of evidence. Similarly, speedy trial laws were designed to reduce delay in the processing of court cases, bail reforms sought to reduce or increase the percentage of defendants detained prior to trial, and laws authorizing the use of six-person juries were designed to produce monetary and/or time savings for court systems.

Specification of the persons or institutions targeted by the legal reform is an important and necessary first step in devising outcome measures. Clearly, appropriate outcome measures depend upon program intent. If the legal change targets individuals, measures of attitudes, knowledge, values, and behavior can be used. If, on the other hand, the reform is aimed at altering the "behavior" of the institution, the indicators of impact will be measures of institutional characteristics: the number of *in camera* hearings; the average length of time between arrest and disposition; the percentage of defendants detained prior to trial, and so on.

Manifest and Latent Goals

To evaluate the impact—that is, the success or failure—of a legal change, the researcher must first be able to specify the goals of the statute or court ruling. This is not an easy task; frequently the objectives of the policy are unclear, diffuse, disparate, or even conflicting. When this is the case, "determining the extent to which they have been attained becomes a difficult and frustrating task" (Anderson, 1979, p. 157).

Information about a policy's goals can be gleaned from the statute itself or from legislative debate about the issue. Congressional debate concerning the 1984 Bail Reform Act, for example, included the following statement:

> Many of the changes in the Bail Reform Act incorporated in this bill reflect the committee's determination that federal bail laws must address the alarming problem of crimes committed by persons on release and must give the courts adequate authority to make release decisions that give appropriate recognition to the danger a person may pose to others if released. (98th Congress, 1st Sess. 8, at 3 [1983])

From this it appears that the goals of the Bail Reform Act are twofold: to reduce the number of crimes committed by persons on release and to ensure the safety of citizens. A policy's objectives might also be found in public statements made by key supporters of the change. Those who advocated reform of the Illinois rape laws stated publicly that the new laws would lower "psychological barriers which discouraged victims from testifying" and cause conviction rates to go up ("Rape convictions soar with new laws", 1985).

Examining public documents or public pronouncements about the legal change, on the other hand, may not tell the whole story. As Casper and Brereton (1984) point out, a policy or legal change may have both latent and manifest goals. They note that "there may be a significant gap . . . between the actual policy goals of those who help formulate or adopt an innovation and the goals that are 'self-evident' from the face of the legal documents or in the public discussion" (p. 123). Thus, a determinate sentencing law seemingly designed to ensure equality in sentencing (the manifest goal) may in reality be formulated to encourage judges to send more offenders to prison (the latent goal).

Legal reforms can also have symbolic goals. Faced with a vocal constituency demanding action, decision makers might adopt a policy primarily to provide "symbolic reassurance that needs are being attended to, problems are being solved, help is on the way" (Casper & Brereton, 1984, p. 124). Policymakers might placate constituents by enacting a very weak version of the legal change being sought. In Georgia, for example, the supporters of rape law reform introduced a bill that specified that evidence of the victim's past sexual conduct is inadmissible unless the court finds that the evidence concerns behavior with the accused *and* supports an inference that the accused reasonably could have believed the victim consented. Defense attorneys in the legislature successfully lobbied to change the *and* to an *or*; this greatly weakened the bill by opening up the possibility of allowing evidence concerning sexual relations with persons other than the defendant. In fact, prosecutors in Fulton County reported that the new law made the situation worse, because previous case law clearly excluded evidence related to third parties.

Policymakers might also appease vocal interest groups by passing legislation that is not intended to meet its stated or manifest goals. Some laws requiring mandatory minimum sentences fall into this category. Casper and Brereton (1984) refer to this as the "'bark' and 'bite' sentencing policy" (p. 125). That is, legislators specify long terms or mandatory minimum terms (the bark), "knowing full well that the actual 'bite' will be substantially reduced by the activities of judges, parole authorities, and others." (p. 125). In this way, policymakers respond to the fears of constituents concerned about crime without having to worry about the effects of the sentencing scheme.

The Michigan Felony Firearm Statute (1977) was intended to add two years to the sentences of offenders convicted of possessing a firearm while committing a felony. Contrary to reformers' expectations, sentences did not increase in the postreform period; instead, judges adjusted the sentence for the main felony so that the additional 2 years made no difference (Loftin et al., 1983). Similarly, an analysis of the impact of laws mandating jail terms for repeat-offender drunk drivers found that judges often did not impose the mandated sentence and that jail officials interpreted the statute in such a way that jail terms were reduced (Ross & Foley, 1987). The authors conclude that the evidence "suggests that a principal motive for shielding a substantial number of recidivist drunk drivers from mandatory imprisonment lies in the view of justice system personnel that drunk driving is not the serious matter the statute presumes" (p. 320).

The legal-impact researcher should be attuned to the presence of both latent and symbolic objectives and should attempt to determine if official documents or statements misrepresent the policy's actual intent. It clearly would be misleading to evaluate a legal change in terms of its manifest goals if it was not intended to achieve those goals.

Proximate and Ultimate Goals

A third issue confronting the legal-impact researcher concerns proximate and ultimate goals. As Weiss (1972) points out, often the ultimate goals of the legal changes "lie far in the future and are not so much 'goals' as unanalyzed pious hopes" (p. 37). Many criminal justice reforms have as their ultimate goal the deterrence of criminal behavior. Advocates of rape reform legislation, for example, hope that the reforms will affect the conviction rate for rape, thereby deterring would-be rapists and ultimately leading to a decline in the number of rapes. Those who support gun control legislation expect that the restrictions will reduce the number of guns in circulation and eventually lead to a decline in the number of crimes committed with guns. And those who lobby for stricter drunken driving laws expect that the laws will deter drinking and driving and thus lead to a reduction in the number of alcohol-related injuries and fatalities.

Since it may take years, even decades, to test a reform's success in achieving its ultimate goals, researchers often use measures "that are germane to more immediate goals and presumably linked to desired ultimate outcomes" (Weiss, 1972, p. 37). A legal change, in other words, may produce a series of interconnected short-term effects leading (presumably) to the ultimate goal. In measuring the reform's effectiveness against these short-term goals, the researcher assumes that achievement of the proximate goals is an indicator of progress toward meeting the ultimate goal. Evidence that a restrictive gun control law resulted in a significant decrease in the number of handguns sold, for example, might be viewed as an indicator of progress toward achieving the reform's ultimate goal of reducing the number of crimes involving handguns.

Our study of the impact of rape reform legislation also involved both proximate and ultimate goals. The most obvious proximate goal of the rape shield laws was to make it more difficult for defense attorneys to introduce evidence of a victim's prior sexual relations. But reformers also hoped that a number of other outcomes would follow. They hoped that the reform would make it more likely that victims would report rapes to the police, that police would make an arrest, that prosecutors would fully prosecute, and that judges or juries would convict. They hoped that ultimately the reform would have a deterrent effect leading to a decline in the number of rapes.

In contrast to many studies, in which it is easier to measure proximate than ultimate goals, in our study it was not possible to measure impact in terms of the proximate goal of reducing the use of evidence concerning the victim's sexual past. In the jurisdictions we studied, court administrators did not keep adequate records of the use of *in camera* hearings or the introduction of evidence of the victim's prior sexual behavior. Through our interviews we obtained estimates of the number of *in camera* hearings being held and, also, anecdotal evidence that sexual history evidence was being introduced less frequently, but we were not able to measure these outcomes objectively. On the other hand, we were able to measure some of the long-term goals; we obtained data on reports of rape and on indictments, convictions, and sentences for rape. Because we did not have a reliable measure of the proximate goal, however, we could not establish a direct link between changes in the use of evidence of the victim's past sexual history and the achievement of any of these long-term goals.

In conducting legal-impact research, the investigator should be cognizant of the fact that legal changes can have both proximate and ultimate goals, and she should attempt to specify, operationalize, and measure both types of outcomes. If the time period between implementation of the reform and attainment of long-term objectives precludes assessment of the reform's impact on ultimate goals, the researcher may have to focus exclusively on proximate goals. This may be problematic if previous research has not shown that the short- and long-term goals are causally linked. It is not entirely clear, for example, that a decline in sales of handguns will lead to a reduction in the number of crimes committed with guns. The researcher must demonstrate that the attainment of proximate goals is an indicator of the eventual achievement of the ultimate goal.

Outcome and Process Measures

In evaluating a legal change, a researcher typically asks, "Did the change produce the intended consequences?" The researcher focuses, in other words, on outcome measures: Did the French drinking and driving law lead to a reduction in crash-related fatalities and injuries? Did rape reform legislation produce an increase in the indictment or conviction rate? Did the Michigan gun law result in longer sentences for those convicted of using guns to commit crimes?

An equally important question concerns the implementation process itself. The investigator should ask not only whether the legal change produced the intended outcomes but also whether the reform was effectively implemented. The researcher should attempt to determine, in other words, whether officials affected by the reform complied with its substantive and procedural components. If not, there is little point in speculating about the impact of the reform on outcome measures.

This is an especially important question to ask with respect to a system, like the criminal justice system, where participants have vast amounts of discretion and are often required to interpret broad and ambiguous statutes. If participants disagree with the law in principle or feel that its implementation will interfere with the smooth and efficient operation of the criminal justice system, they may find ways to avoid compliance.

The legal-impact literature is rife with examples of noncompliance. Our study of rape reform legislation found that the procedural requirements of the rape shield laws were being circumvented in all of the jurisdictions. Instead of holding *in camera* hearings to determine the relevance of sexual history evidence, as required by the statutes, judges in each jurisdiction were permitting certain types of evidence to be admitted without a ruling on relevance. This clearly weakened the potential impact of the shield law and helped account for the lack of impact in most of the jurisdictions.

Ross and Foley (1987, p. 320) found that both jailers and judges "avoided applying the apparently firm mandates of the drunk-driving laws" enacted in two states. They suggested that this lack of compliance reflected participants' beliefs that drunk driving was not the serious crime the statutes presumed, as well as judges' resentment of "the law's intrusions on their traditional discretion" (p. 320). Loftin et al.'s (1983) study of the Michigan gun law also produced evidence of subtle noncompliance; judges there imposed the required mandatory term for using a gun to commit the crime but reduced the sentence for the main felony, so that the total time to be served did not differ significantly in the pre- and postreform periods.

In evaluating legal changes, the researcher should not assume that police officers, prosecutors, and judges will comply with the formal requirements of the law. In fact, it is probably more appropriate to assume that criminal justice officials will ". . . engage in adaptive behavior designed to serve their own goals and institutional or personal needs" (Casper & Brereton, 1984, p. 123).

Measurement Issues

Once the goals of the legal change have been ascertained, the investigator must operationalize the goals. That is, the investigator must decide how to measure the goals. As with all research projects, this involves specifying an indicator or set of indicators that will validly and reliably measure the variables (outcomes) and identifying appropriate sources of data. In accomplishing this, the legal-impact researcher may be confronted with several problems.

Interviews versus Statistics

One major decision in the measurement of legal impact is whether to collect data through interviews with officials familiar with the legal changes and the operation of the system or to gather statistics from archival sources. Although frequently the best approach is to do both, it is important to understand the strengths and limitations of each data gathering technique.

Many legal-impact studies require objective statistical data. Questions about the impact of rape law reforms on indictments or convictions for rape or about the impact of a mandatory gun law on the number of offenses committed with guns cannot be answered without solid statistics on these outcome measures. Although officials in the justice system may have opinions about these issues, they often do not know the answers to these questions. And while police departments or prosecutors' offices may keep records of the cases they process, they seldom organize or analyze their data in a way that lets them answer these questions objectively. Thus, the anwers the researcher would get in interviews with these officials would be based on subjective impressions subject to many different biases. For example, those who were instrumental in changing the law will expect positive results; those who opposed the changes will expect either no impact or negative results.

On the other hand, interviews can fill in the gaps left by "cold, hard statistics." If, for example, the researcher wants to understand the mechanism of legal impact or to explain the lack of impact, interviews with persons closely involved in implementation and enforcement of the law can provide valuable insights. Statistics can demonstrate the Michigan's mandatory gun law did not result in a decrease in offenses committed with guns, but they cannot explain why there was no decrease. Similarly, statistics can show that the tough drinking and driving law enacted in France had a temporary impact on accidents and fatalities, but they cannot explain why the impact did not last.

In the study of the Michigan gun law (Loftin et al., 1983), interviews were critical to understanding the lack of impact on sentencing. Interviews confirmed the notion of a "going rate" and revealed that judges made adjustments in sentences to accommodate the mandatory sentence while still maintaining the going rate for certain crimes.

In our study of rape law reform, we collected statistical data on the processing of rape cases and also interviewed officials familiar with the reforms. Analysis of the statistical data revealed few changes in case processing, even in jurisdictions that enacted strong rape shield laws. This result was somewhat puzzling, since reformers had predicted the shield laws would have an important impact on the processing and disposition of sexual assault cases. Interviews with judges, prosecutors, and defense attorneys suggested several explanations for the lack of impact. In talking with officials in each jurisdiction, we discovered that prior court rulings already had begun to restrict the use of sexual history evidence; that there was substantial noncompliance with the procedural restrictions contained in the laws; and that judges and procescutors tended to believe, the law notwithstanding, that certain types of sexual history evidence were relevant and therefore should be admitted. The information gleaned from the interviews, in other words, allowed us to interpret the statistical data and explain the lack of impact.

Interview data can also be used in studies examining how attitudes have been affected by a change in the law or by a court ruling. Although statistics from police or court records can provide indirect evidence of attitudinal change, the best way to find out what people think is to ask them. In our study of rape reform legislation, we wanted to know whether judges, prosecutors, and defense attorneys approved of the legal reforms. We also wanted to know how they would handle rape cases in the postreform period. We asked them directly about many aspects of the law. We also asked them to respond to a series of hypothetical cases in which evidence of the victim's past sexual history was at issue.

Researchers who use interview data must be careful not to confuse attitudes and behavior. If we want to know whether criminal justice officials favor the legal reforms, we should ask them. If we want to know whether, as a result of these attitudes, they process cases differently, we should consult court records. We cannot assume that attitudes will be translated into behavior, leading to attainment of the reform's objectives. There are many extraneous factors and constraints that make a close correspondence between attitudes and behavior unlikely. In our study, for example, we found much evidence of positive attitudes toward the reforms but little evidence of changes in case processing.

Whenever possible, it will be beneficial to use multiple outcome measures. No measure is perfect; each indicator will have its own strengths and weaknesses. An approach that balances the weaknesses of one measure with the strengths of another will provide the greatest confidence in the results. Therefore, the researcher will often want to include both attitude and behavior measures; both self-report and records data; both subjective and objective assessments of impact.

Archival Data

One obviously important source of data for legal-impact studies is archives or written records. As Lempert (1966) stated:

The United States federal system of government has furnished the experimenter with 50 states which, in the words of the Supreme Court, are 'natural laboratories.' Much of the behavioral output of these laboratories with respect to particular laws is reported in relatively available and uniform statistical form. Where such information exists it is usually available over an extended period of time. (p. 131)

In criminal justice research we rely heavily on periodically produced records such as the UCR, police reports, court records, and prison records. Each of the studies described above used archival sources to obtain data on outcome measures. Horney and Spohn (1989) used court record data on indictments, prosecutions, and sentences for rape to assess the impact of rape reform legislation. Ross et al. (1981–82) relied on government records of automobile accidents to determine whether the French law deterred drinking and driving. Marquart and Crouch (1985) analyzed prison records of disciplinary reports to determine the impact of court-ordered changes on inmate challenges to authority and on violence among inmates. And Loftin and his colleagues (1983) used court record data on sentences and police records of reported crimes to assess the impact of the Michigan felony firearm law. Because of the importance of archival data sources to legal-impact research, we discuss below several issues pertaining to the use of these records.

Access to Records

Some archival data sources are defined by law as public records. One important example is court records. In two of the jurisdictions in which we collected data on rape cases, the clerk of the court maintained huge docket books containing basic information on charges and dispositions for every case bound over to the court of general jurisdiction. In other jurisdictions, the docket books contained only the case identification number, the defendant's name, and the charge; data collectors had to request the actual court file to obtain the additional data. Both types of records were generally available to the public.

Prosecutors also maintain files on criminal cases. Although the information in these files is typically more detailed than the information contained in court files, it is not legally defined as public data. This means that the investigator will have to obtain special permission to gain access to these records. It also means there are no clear rules regarding the maintenance of the records. Instead, decisions as to how long to keep case files, which case files to keep, and in what form to keep them are discretionary. As a result, these decisions are often arbitrary and reflect the needs of the prosecutor's office rather than the rational and objective factors considered important by researchers. For example, the prosecutor may decide to throw out all case files after 5 years. Similarly, a prosecutor who tries a particularly difficult or important case may keep the records of the case in her own personal file; the researcher searching for the case file may simply be told that the file is "missing."

In our rape study, we originally intended to use prosecutors' files, but we ran into trouble in the first jurisdiction we visited. Because there was no index to the prosecutors' files, we needed to use cards filled in by the intake staff that listed both the charges and the case docket number. We found those cards for 5 of the years we needed, but could not locate the ones for the other 10 years. Staff members told us that the card file had been cleaned out when the prosecutor moved into a new office 2 years earlier; they believed the missing cards were stored in the basement. After a full morning in a basement room stacked floor to ceiling with boxes of all shapes and sizes, some marked and some not, we gave up on the search.

Even when records are defined as public, the kind of access a researcher needs is not always simple. Again, our study of rape reform laws is illustrative. In the jurisdictions that maintained court records in docket books with handwritten entries, they were usually kept in a room in the clerk of court's office. Any member of the public could walk into the office and pull a docket book off the shelf to examine the contents. Thus, physical access to the records was no problem. Collecting the data we needed was another matter, however, because neither of these jurisdictions had a useful index to the docket books. We wanted to code data on every rape case between 1970 and 1985; in order to do this, our data collectors had to turn page by page through the books, examining every felony case bound over during that period until they came across a case in which a rape charge was filed. Needless to say, it was a very time-consuming process.

Other problems can also plague researchers using public data. In one jurisdiction, the records we needed for 2-year period seemed at first to be missing. Diligent staff in the clerk of court's office eventually tracked them down for us. The records had been tossed into boxes in no particular order and then stored in a basement room that later flooded. The moldly, rat-nibbled pages were not a pleasure to work with. In Chicago, many of the files we needed had been confiscated by the federal government for its Operation Greylord investigation into corruption in the Chicago courts. We had to go through a special procedure for requesting the individual files as we needed them.

Access to records defined as public may also be limited by privacy and confidentiality laws. In one of our original jurisdictions, for example, we found that the law restricted access to case information on defendants who had been acquitted of the charges or for whom charges had been dismissed. The only people allowed access to those files were court employees. Even though we did not intend to record the defendant's name or other identifying information, we were not allowed to examine the files. The limited-access status of the files meant it was not even possible to determine if rape charges had been filed in those cases. Thus, we were not even able to obtain an accurate count of the number of rape cases prosecuted.

Most privacy laws include exceptions for valid research purposes, and researchers who agree to protect the confidentiality of the records carefully can be given access. In this particular jurisdiction, the legislature had included such an exception in the case of juvenile records but had neglected to do so for adult records—the exact reverse of what is done in most privacy laws. We proposed several alternatives for gathering the data in compliance with law—such as paying court employees to code data for us on their own time so that only those people entitled to access under the law would ever see the names of defendants in those cases—but all to no avail. The chief judge of the jurisdiction interpreted the law strictly; he had previously even denied access to federal tax court judges because they were not court employees in that jurisdiction. Because of these problems, we eventually had to select another jurisdiction for our study.

Standardization of Records

A researcher initially approaching the task of evaluating the impact of rape law reforms across the country might assume that measuring impact on prosecutions, convictions, and sentences would be a fairly simple task. She might assume there would be sources at the state level that could provide annual figures on the number of rape cases prosecuted and on the outcomes of those cases. In fact, very few states maintain such statewide statistics. It is therefore necessary to go to the local jurisdictions—to the county or judicial district—to obtain these data. These jurisdictions often operate independently or with very little oversight from any state agency. As a result, records and record-keeping procedures are not standardized either within or across states. Differing types and amounts of information will be kept, different formats will be used, different terms and definitions will be used, stages of the prosecution process will differ, and so on.

The FBI's *UCR* represent one attempt at standardization at the national level. In order to determine the amount of crime occurring, the FBI has provided standard definitions for certain crimes and standard formats for reporting by local law enforcement agencies around the country. In spite of these standards, however, there are problems. In our study of rape law reform, we relied on *UCR* data to measure reports of rape. In one jurisdiction, the data were not available for a 2-year period because they did not comply with the FBI's standards for reporting.

Unfortunately, there is no similar nationwide reporting system for court or correctional system statistics. Researchers studying multiple jurisdictions will find tremendous variation in the kind and quality of data maintained by these jurisdictions. We found, for example, that the records in one jurisdictions did not include the date of indictment, while those in another county did not indicate if the defendant was tried by a judge or jury. Ross and Foley (1987) studied the impact of laws mandating 48-hour jail terms for drunk drivers. They had serious difficulties adequately measuring terms actually served because the records kept by different jails varied dramatically. Some entered the dates of incarceration and release but not the times, making it impossible to detrmine whether a person actually spent 48 hours in jail. Some used unusual filing systems, such as filing cases according to whether or not fines had been paid. Some of the jails maintained computerized records, while others kept records in inexpensive notebooks. One of the jails actually kept no records at all.

Validity of Records Data

All records are subject to errors in entries, but these are usually infrequent and random and will not seriously bias a study of legal impact. Other kinds of errors may raise questions about the validity of the data. As mentioned earlier, even standarized records such as the *UCR* sometimes have problems.

The Illinois Department of Law Enforcement is responsible for administering the Uniform Crime Reporting Program for Illinois. Each year they publish a report on crime in Illinois. In *Crime in Illinois, 1982* (Illinois Department of Law Enforcement, 1983), the statistics for Chicago are published separately from those for the rest of the state; the Introduction to the presentation of Chicago data explains the reason:

"Killing Crime: A Police Cop Out," a series of reports aired in late 1982 and early 1983 by a Chicago investigative news team, alleged that the Chicago Police Department incorrectly classified (killed) reports of major crime, resulting in lower crime statistics and inflated clearance rates. A major focus of the news reports centered on the high rate of cases classified as "unfounded" (false or baseless complaint). Preliminary analysis of state and national crime statistics indicated Chicago exhibited an extremely high unfounded rate for major crimes (21.4%), compared to the average (1.5%) of the 31 cities with populations over 250,000.

The rate of unfounded cases caused concern within the Chicago Police Department and the Illinois Department of Law Enforcement. Incorrect reporting practices of the Chicago Police Department could seriously impact state crime trends.

For these reasons, the Chicago Police Department's 1982 criminal offense data are presented as a separate section of *Crime in Illinois, 1982*. The data have not been adjusted and do not account for incorrect reporting practices. Caution is advised in any analysis of these data. (p. 151)

The researcher must be aware of problems such as these; records data cannot always be taken at face value.

Computerized Records

The era of computers certainly holds great promise for research on legal impact. As more and more court systems, corrections systems, and law enforcement agencies computerize their records, many measures of legal impact have become, in principle at least, much easier to collect and analyze.

The advantages of computerized records, however, quickly become disadvantages when researchers are denied access to the records. Some agencies are willing and able to share their computerized data base and will use their own programmers to generate the data needed for a research project. Other agencies have decided not to use their resources for such efforts. If this is the case, access to the data can be more limited than it was when handwritten records were kept.

In our rape study, we encountered one court system that had computerized all its records but would not provide listings of rape cases, even for a fee. Since they no longer kept docket books, the only publicly available records were the actual court files. The clerk of the court informed us that we had a right to see any file we wanted; all we had to do to obtain a file was provide the docket number. Unfortunately, the list of docket numbers that we needed to use to identify rape cases was the computerized list that the clerk would not provide for us. In effect, then, in that jurisdiction court records are public, but they are available as the books in a library would be available if there were no card catalogue and if books were filed in the order in which they were acquired by the library!

In this juridiction, we eventually were saved by gaining access to the prosecutor's computerized list of cases. We were able to use this list to obtain the docket numbers of rape cases, which we then used to obtain the court files. Ironically, because the prosecutor's records were not defined as public records, to obtain the records we had to go through complex procedures for insuring confidentiality, all in order to be able to use the court files, which were public records.

Some jurisdictions with computerized records would be willing to share their data, but they lack the resources to do so. They enter a tremendous amount of information into the computer, but their programmers have provided for only one basic report to be produced from the data. If they do not have adequate staff for programming, they are not able to retrieve information needed by the agency, much less information requested by an outside researcher. In one jurisdiction we visited, for example, the clerk of court was not even able to determine how many felony trials had been held during the previous year.

Issues in Research Design

Researchers will almost never be able to use true experimental designs to study legal impact. Statutes and court decisions are never applied to a randomly assigned group of the population, with a control group exempt from their mandates. Usually the most appropriate designs for legal-impact research are the quasi-experimental designs, which approximate the logic of true experiments. Unlike true experiments, quasi-experiments do not randomly assign subjects to treatment and control groups; instead, the researcher compares nonequivalent groups that may differ from one another in a number of ways. Cook and Campbell (1979) have described several quasi-experimental designs that can be quite powerful when used properly. The one best suited to and most widely used in legal-impact research is the multiple time-series design described in chapter 9 of this book. Lempert (1966, p. 130) called this the "design *par excellence*" for impact theory experimentation. In the sections that follow, we discuss several issues concerning the use of the interrupted time-series design in legal-impact research.

Controls for History

The most serious threat to the internal validity of the interrupted time-series design is the threat Campbell and Stanley (1966) have called the "history" threat. This refers to the possibility that external events occurring at about the time of the treatment might have been responsible for the changes measured. In the study of the French drinking and driving law, a hypothetical example of a history threat would be the possibility that a new tax on liquor coincident with the new law reduced alcohol consumption and therefore led to fewer crash-related injuries and fatalities. With no controls for history, the design does not allow the researcher to separate the effects of the treatment (the implementation of the drinking and driving law) from other events such as the tax.

Several kinds of controls may be used with the interrupted time-series design. When we think of controls, we usually think of a control group that does not receive the treatment but is otherwise identical to the experimental group. In legal-impact research, the investigator does not have a randomly assigned control group that is equivalent to the experimental group. Instead, the researcher uses the logic of the true experiment to choose similar controls that did not receive the treatment, i.e., that were not subject to the law being studied. In a study of the effects of a crackdown on speeding drivers in Connecticut, for example, researchers compared Connecticut to neighboring states (Campbell & Ross, 1968). The rationale for using the neighboring states as controls was that they were similar to Connecticut in weather, driving conditions, driving patterns, and so on. By measuring traffic fatalities in these neighboring states, the researchers controlled for the possibility that the decrease in traffic fatalities in Connecticut was due to drier weather or changes in car safety; if these factors were responsible for the change, the drop in fatalities would have shown up in Connecticut's neighbors as well. Campbell and Stanley (1966) named the design a multiple time-series design.

In our study of rape law reform, we were concerned about the possible history threat of national efforts on the part of women's groups and the media to sensitize the public to the seriousness of the crime of rape and to problems in the treatment of rape victims. We were aware that this national publicity might have led to changes in the processing of rape cases even in the absence of specific legislative changes. We therefore selected Washington, D.C., the only jurisdiction in the country that had not enacted some type of statutory change in its rape laws, as a control jurisdiction. We felt that if we found changes in the reform jurisdictions but not in Washington, we could be more confident that the effects were in fact due to changes in the laws. Unfortunately for our research design, we discovered that case law in Washington had resulted in changes similar to the changes enacted by statute in other jurisdictions. Thus, Washington, D.C., was not the perfect control we had envisioned.

In our study we also used a second type of control for the threat of history. Since we did not have equivalent jurisdictions without rape law reforms, we chose jurisdictions that implemented reforms at different times. We reasoned that if changes in case processing occurred as a result of national publicity focused on the crime of rape, we would see the impact at about the same time in all of the jurisdictions. On the other hand, if the legislative changes produced the effects on case processing, we would see changes at different times—at times coincident with the implementation of the reforms. We might think of our design as a multiple time-series design with staggered interventions.

Another approach to controlling for history is to use a multiple time-series design for which differential predictions of impact are made based on previous knowledge of the variables being studied. In the study of deterrence of drinking and driving, Ross et al. (1981–82) analyzed separately the time series of injuries and fatalities occurring on weekend nights and occurring Tuesday through Thursday. Because of previous research showing that accidents involving alcohol were more common on weekend nights, these authors reasoned that any deterrent effect of the new law would have its greatest impact at those times. As they predicted, they found the drop in injuries and fatalities greater for the weekend nights than for the Tuesday through Thursday period.

Ross et al. (1981–82) also compared changes in injury-producing crashes in northern France and in southern France. Studies had shown that problems involving the use of alcohol were more common in northern France than in southern France. Therefore, they compared the two regions, not because one region was subject to the new law and one was not, but because patterns of alcohol use would predict differential effects of the new law on the two regions. Their analysis showed a significant drop in serious crashes in the northern region but no statistically significant change in the southern region, thus confirming their prediction.

In a similar study of new laws on drinking and driving in Great Britain, Campbell, Ross, and Glass (1970) compared injuries and fatalities on weekend nights with statistics for commuting hours, when the British pubs were closed. They, also, found a dramatic impact for weekend nights but not for commuting hours. In both studies, if factors such as weather conditions, improved roads, or new safety features on cars had been responsible for the reduction in injuries and fatalities, similar results should have been found for both time periods. The multiple time-series design successfully controlled for these history threats, because those other factors could not account for the different pattern of results.

In studying the impact of the Michigan gun law, Loftin et al. (1983) used similar logic. To control for other factors that could have resulted in changes in sentencing patterns in general (such as public outcry or new sentencing guidelines), they looked separately at sentencing for offenses committed with and without guns. Although gun offenses received longer sentences than nongun offenses, the pattern was not very different before and after passage of the gun law.

They also examined the impact of the law on crime rates. When they found the only change in crime rates to be for homicide with a gun, they were not certain whether that drop was due to the gun law or to other factors. To control for history, they divided homicides into three categories based on the relationship between the offender and victim. The rationale was that if the gun law was responsible for the decline in homicides, the effects were more likely to show up among premeditated homicides involving strangers than among homicides involving nonstrangers, because the latter homicides were more likely to be "crimes of passion." When they found instead that the same patterns of decline occurred regardless of whether the offender and victim were strangers, acquaintances, or relatives or close friends, they concluded that something other than the gun law must have caused the decrease in homicides committed with a gun.

Threat of Instrumentation

Another threat to the internal validity of the interrupted time-series design is intrumentation. According to Campbell and Stanley (1966), instrumentation is a problem when a change in the measurement process itself coincides with the treatment or intervention being studied. The investigator must be cognizant of changes in the method of collecting or managing data that might confound the results of the evaluation. One of the jurisdictions we studied, for example, switched from docket books to a computerized record-keeping system about a year after the legal changes went into effect. Thus, for the first 6 years of the period, cases were selected by data collectors who paged through the docket books; for the last 9 years, they were selected by the computer. Had we discovered an increased in the number of rape cases coincident with this change in record keeping, we might have attributed at least some of the increase to the greater efficiency of the computerized case selection procedures.

Instrumentation poses an even more serious problem for legal-impact research when the legislation being studied includes changes in the definitions of the variables being measured. We encountered a classic example of this problem in a jurisdiction that redefined the crime of rape at the same time that it eliminated corroboration and resistance requirements and enacted a rape shield statute. We were using the interrupted time-series design to examine the impact of the legal changes on the number of reported rapes and on the number of indictments, convictions, and incarcerations for rape. The problem was that after the law changed, there was no longer any such crime as rape. The old crime of rape had been replaced with four degrees of criminal sexual conduct, which included acts and persons not covered under the old law. Thus, it was not possible to have exactly comparable crimes before and after the reform. Although we did the best we could at matching offenses, adding some crimes to the prereform measure and subtracting others from the postreform measure, we were concerned that the observed increases in our dependent variables might be due in part to the greater inclusiveness of the postreform offense definitions.

Postintervention Time

One problem with many studies of legal impact is the time frame for measuring impact. If the measurement period following the implementation of the new law is too short, there are two major errors of interpretation that may occur. First, the study may miss real impact that is gradual in nature. Casper and Brereton (1984), for example, discuss the changing patterns of compliance with the U.S. Supreme Court's Court's *Miranda* (1966) decision mandating preinterrogation warnings for criminal suspects. Early studies on the impact of *Miranda* (Medalie, Zeitz, & Alexander, 1968; Wald, Ayres, Hess, Schantz, & Whitebread, 1967) indicated that in many cases police were not giving full warnings or were giving them in a manner such that they would not be taken seriously. Some authors interpreted these early results as a sign that *Miranda* would never be effectively implemented. Over time, however, the warnings have become a routine part of policing. The early studies simply missed these gradual effects.

Ross and Foley (1987), in their study of mandatory jail sentences for driving under the influence, concluded that there was a lack of compliance with the law's requirement that a minimum of 5 days be spent in jail, with at least 48 hours served consecutively. They acknowledged, however, that there may have been a gradual process of compliance with the law because a second study in one of the sites indicated less noncompliance in the second year after the law was enacted. Some changes may thus take years to realize their full impact, and an implementation study done immediately after the law's introduction, when the gradual change has just begun, may inappropriately conclude that there has been little or no impact.

The opposite problem occurs when a study measures only the initial reaction to a new law, which may be seen as significant impact, but is not extended long enough to determine that the impact is transitory. Many of the studies on laws designed to deter drinking and driving have found fairly dramatic initial effects followed by a return to the preintervention baseline (Ross, 1981). The study of the French law, for example, found that the reduction in injuries lasted 8.4 months, the reduction in fatalities 12.9 months. Ross et al.'s (1981–82) explanation of "why deterrent effect was lost is that the threat was not fulfilled and that people gradually learned this fact" (p. 366). The risk of being tested at a roadblock was very low, the officers operating the roadblocks were lenient in reading the alcohol tests, and judicial discretion led to suspended or mitigated sentences for many of those who were convicted. Thus, "a well-publicized and controversial threatening rule may have deterrent effects because its threat is exaggerated in the perception of the subject population. If, however, the perception rests on an unrealistic basis, the learning process will undermine it . . . " (Ross et al., 1981–82, p. 368).

Casper and Brereton (1984) point out that there is an eagerness to evaluate the impact of new laws or policies very soon after implementation and that funding sources, which are interested in assessing impact, are part of the problem. Their "desire for quick answers . . . usually means that funding sources want the evaluation to begin almost as soon as the innovation has begun" (p. 141). Because of this perspective, their own study of the 1977 California Uniform Determinate Sentencing Law (Casper, Brereton, & Neal, 1982) focused on what happened during only the first year after implementation. The lack of data on what happened after the first year prevented them from concluding that the results they found were, in fact, due to the law. Longer time perspectives are critical to good legal-impact research.

Conclusion

We have tried to demonstrate that the seemingly simple and straight-forward procedures involved in evaluating the impact of legal changes are in reality neither simple nor straightforward. In order to determine if a legal change has produced the intended consequences, one must be able to specify and measure those consequences. These tasks become complicated when the goals of a law or court ruling are unclear, conflicting, or symbolic. Even when the goals of the change are clear, measuring them is no easy task; one must decide whether to collect data from official records or from interviews with criminal justice officials and then must obtain access to those records or officials. One must also take care to construct a research design that is capable of detecting subtle and gradual effects but that does not mistake coincidental effects for real effects. In evaluating the impact of legal changes, the researcher should be cognizant of these special problems.

References

Anderson, J.E. (1979). *Public policy-making* (2nd ed.). New York: Holt, Rinehart and Winston.

Campbell, D.T., & Ross, H.L. (1968). The Connecticut crackdown on speeding. *Law and Society Review, 3*, 33–53.

Campbell, D.T., & Stanley, J.C., (1966). *Experimental and quasi-experimental designs for research*. Chicago: Rand McNally.

Casper, J.D., & Brereton, D. (1984). Evaluating criminal justice reforms. *Law and Society Review, 18*, 121–144.

Casper, J.D., Brereton, D., & Neal, D. (1982). *The implementation of the California Determinate Sentencing Law* (U.S. Department of Justice). Washington, DC: U.S. Government Printing Office.

Cook, T.D., & Campbell, D.T. (1979). *Quasi-experimentation: Design and Analysis for field settings*. Chicago: Rand McNally.

Dye, T.R. (1976). *Policy analysis*. University, AL: University of Alabama Press.

Horney, J., & Spohn, C. (1989). *The impact of rape reform legislation*. Final Report to the National Institute of Justice and the National Science Foundation.

Illinois Department of Law Enforcement (1983), *Crime in Illinois, 1982*. Springfield, IL: State of Illinois.

Lempert, R. (1966). Strategies of research design in the legal impact study. *Law and Society Review, 1*, 111.

Loftin, C., Heumann, M., & McDowall, D. (1983). Mandatory sentencing and firearms violence: Evaluating an alternative to gun control. *Law and Society Review*, *17*, 287–318.

Marquart, J.W., & Crouch, B.M. (1985). Judicial reform and prisoner control. *Law and Society Review*, *19*, 557–586.

Medalie, R.J., Zeitz, L., & Alexander, P. (1968). Custodial police interrogation in our nation's capital: The attempt to implement Miranda. *Michigan Law Review*, *66*, 1347–1422.

Mich. Comp. Laws Ann. § 750, 227 b.

Miranda V. Arizona, 384 U.S. 436, 470 (1966).

Rape convictions soar with new laws. (1985, November 29). *Chicago Tribune*, p. 20.

Ross, H.L. (1981). *Deterrence of the drinking driver: An international survey* (Technical Report DOT HS-805 820). Washington, DC: U.S. Department of Transportation, National Highway Traffic Safety Administration.

Ross, H.L., Campbell, O.T., & Glass, G.V. (1970). Determining the social effects of a legal reform. *American Behavioral Scientist*, *13*, 493–509.

Ross, H.L., & Foley, J.P. (1987). Judicial disobedience of the mandate to imprison drunk drivers. *Law and Society Review*, *21*, 315–323.

Ross, H.L., McCleary, R., & Epperlein, T. (1981–82). Deterrence of drinking and driving in France: An evaluation of the law of July 12, 1978. *Law and Society Review*, *16*, 345–374.

Ruiz v. Estelle, 503 F. Supp. 1265 (S.D. Texas 1980).

Wald, M., Ayres, R., Hess, D., Schantz, M., Whitebread II, C. (1967). Interrogations in New Haven: The impact of Miranda. *Yale Law Journal*, *76*, 1519–1648.

Weiss, C.H. (1972). Evaluation research. Englewood Cliffs, NJ: Prentice-Hall.

9
Time Series, Panel Design, and Criminal Justice: A Multi-State, Multi-Wave Design

Carol W. Kohfeld and Scott H. Decker

Introduction

Finding the right analysis for research questions is a difficult chore. Frequently, researchers are faced with a situation where the data are not suitable for the type of analysis they would like to carry out. In other circumstances, the data are not available for the appropriate analysis. This chapter presents a view to the kind of analysis that can be performed under a variety of circumstances. We present the approach to a time-series analysis, concluding with a specific application of this technique.

Time-series or panel studies examine a number of measures over a period of time. The length of the time trend, the number of variables used, and the inclusion of the impact of a lag structure add to the strength of this approach. These considerations allow the researcher to consider the effect of a variable over several different time periods, as well as to more effectively specify the effect of a specific variable. This is particularly true for variables whose effect may best be seen in subsequent time periods. The use of time-series analysis has been a hallmark of the criminological enterprise. Such analyses have been implemented in the works of Wolfgang, Figlio, and Sellin (1972), McCleary, Nienstedt, and Erven (1982), and Elliott, Huizinga, and Ageton (1982). It is a technique best suited to capturing the impact of variables whose effect on outcome measures is likely to change over time. In addition, this technique allows the researcher to examine the growth and progression of variables related to the dependent variable. Frequently, this approach can more accurately control for potentially spurious effects better than other techniques. While it is often used to address causal questions relating to criminal or delinquent behavior, it is also well suited to address changes in policy or law.

Sequence, Change, and Cross Sections

Two generic questions underlie technical scientific investigation of crime rates and processes that impact them: How much? How fast? The question

198

of quantity is answered by some measure usually referred to as a change score, and an answer to the question of speed furnishes a metric for that change. At the most fundamental level, processess are characterized with the joint concepts of change and sequence. In typical applications, the time units are provided by the way in which observations come to the investigator, and if he or she is sufficiently fortunate, it will be possible to interpret the measures of change as quantities. Even if the change is purely qualitative, however, some analysis is possible, and if, in addition, purely qualitative events can be aggregated in time or space or both, then conversion to a useful metric is immediate. In what follows, we assume that the processes we are concerned with are organized in calendar time but recognize that this sets aside some important theoretical issues. We also assume that repeated measures of some kind at different time points are available to describe the process of interest. In criminology the most ubiquitous examples are found in the reports of annual crime rates and their graphic display for a series of years.

If change is our most common intuition of time and time series, it nevertheless presents subtleties in analysis even at the simple level of secular change or trends. A common practice when one is confronted with some systematic time series is to inquire what the overall change in the data are, i.e., to ask whether or not these data exhibit a trend of some kind. The most obvious technical attack on this question is to plot the series against time and perhaps fit a line in an attempt to determine the trend. Obvious and simple as this tactic appears, it contains dangers. Most fitting will be done by minimizing the squared error around the line of best fit, and that line, in the case of a simple trend on time, has one extraordinarily bad property—it greatly exaggerates the arbitrary beginning and ending points of the time series (McCleary & Hay, 1980, pp. 32–36). Since the beginning point is likely to be selected precisely because something special was happening at the time and since the end point is likely to be determined by running the series up to the most recent measurements, such a fitting procedure is doubly suspect. The reader can quickly convince herself or himself of this danger by recalling that the scatter plot of a time series is identical to the time plot of the series and then recognizing that the observations farthest from the mean will receive the maximum (squared) weight in locating the line. There are alternative, perhaps more technically satisfactory, procedures with which to model the trend, of course, but even in this simple case, it is easily seen that one must be careful. We use yearly unemployment data below to give some empirical examples.

A conceptual empirical exercise may easily be constructed from monthly data on unemployment. We know, a priori, that such data have a seasonal component and, also, longer run components driven by the business cycle and political events (most notably wars). Suppose we were ignorant of this prior knowledge. If unemployment is higher in winter (for seasonal reasons) and lower in summer (for similar seasonal reasons) and if the other components of fluctuation are ignored, then it would be easy to obtain either an upward trend or a downward trend for 6-month periods depending on the choice of starting and ending observations. Clearly, under these hypotheses, if one starts in February and trends through July, the movement will be downward, whereas starting in August and trending through January will produce an upward movement. A potential cure for this arbitrariness is obvious: Increase the time period of observation to extend over a year or, better yet, over several years, and perhaps, aggregate months up to years to hide the short-run seasonal variation. The point to be made, however, is that the arbitrariness of starting and stopping points is an important rationale for choosing the length of the series, i.e., to capture known fluctuations. Furthermore, the prospect of more observations is frequently not available realistically to the social scientist as a methodological fix.

Nevertheless, simple time trends may be useful if they are done with care and if the rationale for carrying them out is natural. After all, it is of some interest to all of us to know whether murder rates are going up or down. And what about robbery? Or burglary? Such questions are not insignificant, although they may be difficult to answer satisfactorily.

To say that time series may present difficult questions of analysis is not to say that analyses in the cross section are superior. Indeed, it is almost certainly the case that cross-sectional causal models are misspecified in a quite precise sense—their parameters are not identified because the rate parameters of the dynamic processes driving the cross-section components are not known (Sprague, 1980). A simple example may suffice to show this.

Suppose that a policeman's skill level, Y, is learned or enhanced by training, X, but in the absence of training, the policeman's skill declines through natural decay (intervention of other learning, laziness, aging processes, or whatever). Let those assumptions specify a dynamic process in discrete time. A simple representation, ignoring random error, then might be written as

$$Y_t = Y_{t-1} - aY_{t-1} + bX_t \tag{1}$$

In words, the skill level at time t results from the accumulated (learned) skill level at time $t - 1$, from decay of that skill level at the rate a during the period $t - 1$ to t, and from skill acquisition from training in the interval $t - 1$ to t at the rate b. Now, if a large number of policemen are measured on skill level and training at a fixed point in time, a cross section, the observations may be pooled, and some relationship between skill and training may be estimated, ignoring all technical issues concerning pooling. Notice that there is no measure of decay, and presumably none is possible, since all observations are taken at one point in time. On its face, the cross section must be flawed at least in regard to decay since it is nowhere measured in the cross section. The traditional answer to this dilemma is to assert that the problem is solved if the processes are at equilibrium. However, it turns out that this answer is no answer at all. If the processes are *not* at equilibrium, then surely the cross section is not justified. On the other hand, if the processes *are* at equilibrium, is the problem solved? The answer is negative, which is easily seen when one examines the equilibrium condition for equation 1. At equilibrium, Y_t equals Y_{t-1} and hence the equation may be rewritten, after trivial algebra, as

$$Y_t = (b/a)X_t \qquad (2)$$

The difficulty is immediate. If equation 2 is used for estimation, what can be estimated is the ratio (b/a) and not either parameter alone. In short, the traditional answer, that everything is correct with cross-sectional analysis if the processes are at equilibrium, is wrong! The force of this example is extraordinary. We do not wish to push the methodological morals too far, but clearly, there is no easy road to methodological salvation in either cross-sectional or time-series analyses. Of the two strategies, we tend to the opinion that time-series analyses, when executed with care, are likely to be less misleading.

This discussion brings us to the beginning of this chapter and the possibilities and dangers of time-series analyses, to which we now turn.

Modes of Time-Series Analysis

It is convenient to organize a discussion of time-series analysis into broad categories that may be fuzzy at the edges but that nevertheless do discriminate among styles of analysis and modes of quantitative treatment. We distinguish the analysis of time trends as perhaps the oldest and the most widespread of all forms of time-series analysis. This is true not only in criminology but also in many other social sciences where, for example, in economics the price of wheat over several centuries has furnished a standard textbook example. Increasingly important in contemporary criminology are panel studies, where a population of special interest and perhaps also a control group are identified, measured repeatedly, and followed over a period of years. Of classic significance have been attempts to assess the significance of particular public policies by means of before/after quasi-experimental designs. Less common are studies applying mathematically and technically sophisticated models to time-series data but without explicit causal structure. More usual and perhaps in the central mode of contemporary time-series analysis in criminology are approaches through regression that have trend components and pooling components and that draw heavily on the writing of econometricians in the handling of statistical problems. These latter efforts are characterized by a strong causal structure to the arguments that underlie the quantitative work. The examples given below fall in this more usual category. There are, of course, variants of these approaches, for example, the line of analysis known as Granger causality, which combines causal arguments with noncausal statistical modeling in a hybrid approach. Our focus will be on practical issues in the analysis of trends and an extensive empirical example utilizing a regression approach.

Trends

In sharp contrast with the natural sciences, social scientists are usually stuck with a single realization of the processes of interest to them. A natural scientist may repeat his experiment or, in a perhaps better analogy, repeat his observations. Especially in attempting to determine periodicity, natural scientists can frequently step up the rate at which they sample the object of study. Such alternatives are not usually available to the social scientist. However, the criminologist has better opportunities here than many social scientists. Statistics on the phenomena of interest to criminologists are gathered in many jurisdictions over long periods of time and provide a potentially rich source for time-series analyses. This advantage is partially offset by the fact that such information is gathered by others—usually nonscientists—for nonscientific purposes. As a consequence, the analyses of trends using such data bases require special care in guarding against systematic biases arising from the motives of the original data collectors or the structure of the data gathering processes.

Such cautions were perhaps first expressed most vividly by the muckraker Lincoln Steffens in his autobiography (1931), where he describes how, as a beginning reporter, he created a crime wave. (Steffens's secret: While on the police beat, he simply started reporting almost everything.) Some have argued that improvements in reporting, simple changes in accuracy and procedures of reporting, underlie some of the secular change in crime presumably observed starting in the 1960s. If that is true, then in any real scientific sense, there was nothing to either observe or explain in any case. The National Crime Surveys and Central Cities Survey at a somewhat later date have provided convincing evidence that the frequency of victimization is radically underestimated by almost all official statistics. These differences should not be decisive against the use of officially collected information but, rather, should signal the reader to be aware of the dangers and the different purposes for which each data source is collected. In some illustrative analyses below an official crime report which contains very little reporting error, and which cannot be evaluated with victimization surveys, is used as the data base-murder.

Perhaps the most important conceptual distinction in this area is that between the short run and the long run. A typical short-run trend might be the fluctuation between winter and summer in certain kinds of crime. An example of trends of the somewhat longer run might be the rise of crime rates in most felony categories in the 1960s to middle 1970s. Such longer term changes have furnished the occasion for much policy debate and much serious scientific work in the attempt to find the causes of these secular trends.

Yearly data on unemployment can be used to illustrate some of the problems and possibilities in simple trend estimation. Unemployment may influence crime rates, a matter of some controversy and importance as a policy matter (Jenks, 1987; Kohfeld & Sprague, 1988) and an issue that has received a great deal of scientific attention (see review by Long & Witte, 1981). We use black male unemployment rates, expressed as a percentage of the black male work force, for the years 1948 through 1984 for illustration. The black male rates are convenient since they exhibit considerable variation over that time period. Similar results hold for total unemployment and the obvious subgroups of black females, white females, and white males. The differences lie in the levels or magnitudes of the phenomena in the differing groups and the rapidity of their response to short-run changes in economic conditions. The time patterns for all these categories are quite comparable.

Figure 9.1 gives a plot of black male unemployment on year. The points have been connected to emphasize the notion of sequence between them. The pattern would have been altered somewhat, but not too dramatically, if the time periods had been aggregated in 12-month periods from August through July. There is no magic in the calendar year, and different periods of time aggregation will in general produce different patterns. It is also worth noting that if monthly data, rather than yearly data, were plotted, the line connecting the points would not be as smooth. It would exhibit more short-run noise, evidenced by an increased irregularity in the line display.

A slightly different perception of exactly the same set of observations can be induced by not connecting the points in time and superimposing the simple trend line estimated by least squares. That display is set out in Figure 9.2. It is immediately obvious from the display that some long-run patterns are present in the data. They manifest themselves as an intuitive snakelike pattern around the line. It is easy to get a fairly good estimate of the time trend slope with the naked eye. With the run from 1970 to 1980 as a base, the rise of the line in that interval is from approximately 11 to 13, or 2 percentage points. Hence the slope is approximately 0.2, and on average for the period, unemployment has increased 1% every 5 years. Is that a good representation of the data? Clearly not. We know that unemployment has turned around and declined in recent years. A good rule of thumb with time series data is—interpolate, yes, extrapolate, no. But this elementary series also be used to illustrate the pitfalls of end point sensitivity when one uses least squares in this context.

In Table 9.1, a series of slopes for different yearly periods of the black male unemployment series are set out. As advertised, the straight line slope for the entire period is about 0.2. If the arbitrary 11-year period 1964 through 1974 is estimated separately, the slope is nearly identical to the

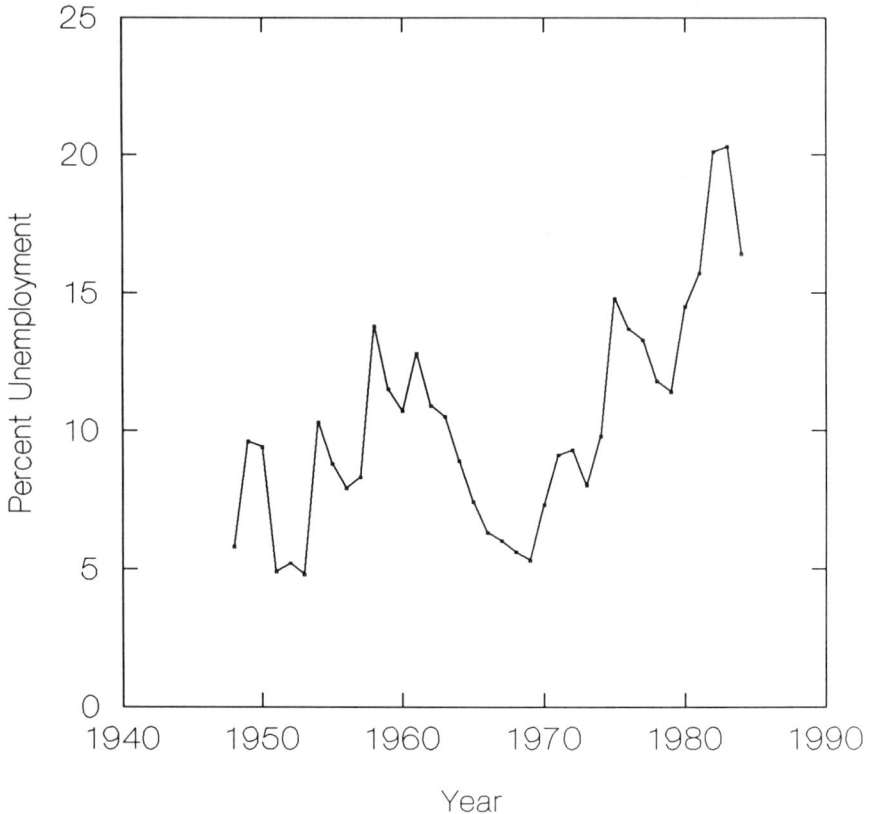

FIGURE 9.1. Yearly black male unemployment rates, U.S. data.

overall slope. Note, if the data had not been plotted, analyst at this point might be tempted to make strong, and clearly unjustified, assertions.

Table 9.1 also illustrates the sensitivity to starting and ending points of simple time trends estimated by least squares. The positive slope of the 11-year-period 1965 through 1975 (.62) is cut to one third (.22) simply by moving this 11-year-window back in time 1 year at both ends. If the window is moved back one more year, the trend goes to zero and clearly, with a few more moves back in time, becomes markedly negative. In this case, such behavior could easily have been anticipated, because we have knowledge of a longer series encompassing these shorter time periods and we have seen the pattern of longer run economic conditions in Figures 9.1 and 9.2. But if one did not have this additional information, the 1960 to 1975 period would perhaps appear very curious to investigator. The data in this table underscore the importance of seeing a trend of several years.

The essential difficulties that Table 9.1, Figure 9.1, and Figure 9.2 point

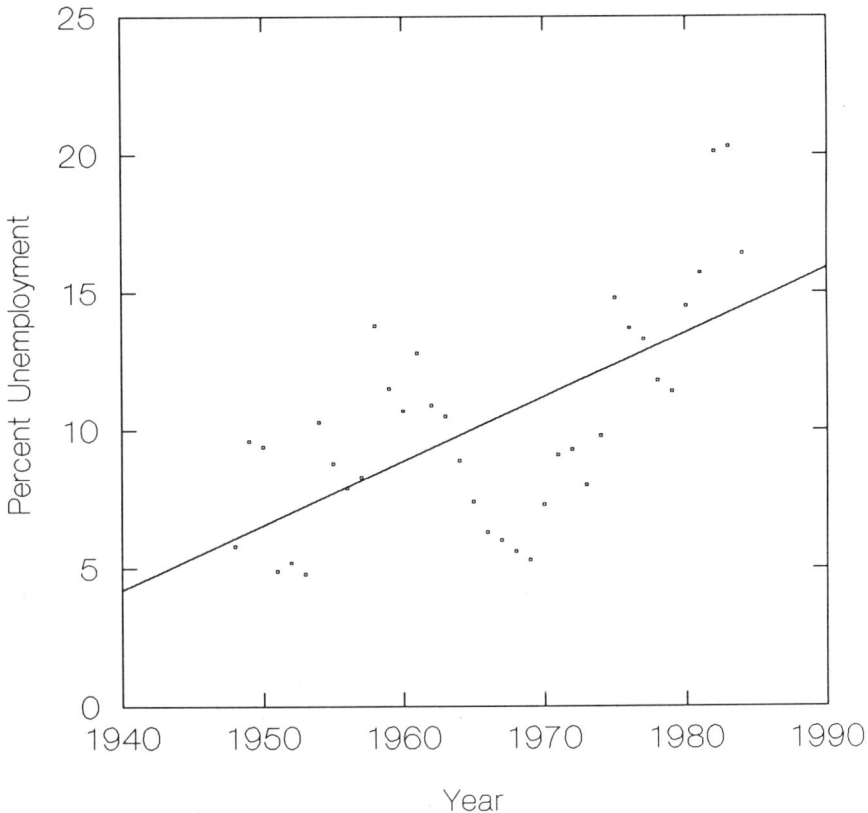

FIGURE 9.2. Yearly black male unemployment rates with trend line imposed, U.S. data.

up are those associated with short-term and long-term patterns. There are two technical problems working at cross purposes. In order to assess long-run trends, it is necessary to suppress short-run trends (short-run noise). Conversely, if the data are smoothed to make the long-run trends visible, then the possibly relevant information contained in the short-run behavior is lost. These differing patterns can be modeled simultaneously, but the process is involved (see Box & Jenkins, 1976; McCleary & Hay, 1980), and we will mention these strategies below. However, the elementary techniques for enhancing the perception of long-run trend or sharpening the picture of short-run variation are easily grasped. Engineers, thinking in terms of waves and periodic motion, refer to high pass filters (let the short-run motion through to be seen) and low pass filters (let the long-run motion through to be seen). What are these elementary techniques?

To allow an enhanced view of long-run patterns, smooth the time series

TABLE 9.1. Slopes for black male unemployment on time estimated by least squares. Selected time periods 1948–1984, U.S. data.

Time period	Slopes
1948–1984	+0.23
1964–1974	+0.22
1965–1975	+0.62
1964–1974	+0.22
1963–1973	−0.04
1962–1972	−0.21
1961–1971	−0.51
1960–1970	−0.68

Source: Statistical Abstract, 1986.

by taking a series of short-run averages. The simplest of these averages is an equally weighted moving average, say for five data points. Figure 9.3 shows the black male unemployment data smoothed with a moving average of width five, and the result is dramatic—the long-term behavior or (business) cycle jumps out forcefully.

In contrast, to see the short-run noise clearly, it is useful to take out the long-term trend. An inspection of Figure 9.3 suggests that a fairly complicated model might be required. But there is a simpler approach. An elementary strategy that is very often sufficient is to model the long-run trend in first approximation by taking first differences of the original unsmoothed time series, i.e., by a measurement manipulation. The procedure is straightforward. To obtain first differences, subtract observation n from observation $n - 1$. Thus the value of a variable in a given year is subtracted from that of the previous year. This is repeated throughout the time series. Clearly, the first observation becomes a missing value. To form second differences, repeat the same the procedure, but now operate on the just-transformed first differenced series. It should be evident to the reader that for the second differenced series, an additional observation must take a missing value. Hence, if the original series had no missing values, the first differenced series will miss the first observation, and the second differenced series will miss both the first and second observations. When first differences are taken, the results may be depicted as in Figures 9.4 and 9.5. Figure 9.4 shows that the time trend through the differenced data is nearly flat (first differencing indeed captures most of the long-term trend), and Figure 9.5 displays a reasonably convincing portrait of short-run noise. The noisy short-run pattern is usually the occasion for rejoicing, since it suggests a complex trending model is not necessary for many purposes.

An alternative verbal description of the success of taking first differences, i.e., the new trend line is essentially flat, is to say that the series tracks. It follows a simple autoregressive form of order one. Still another

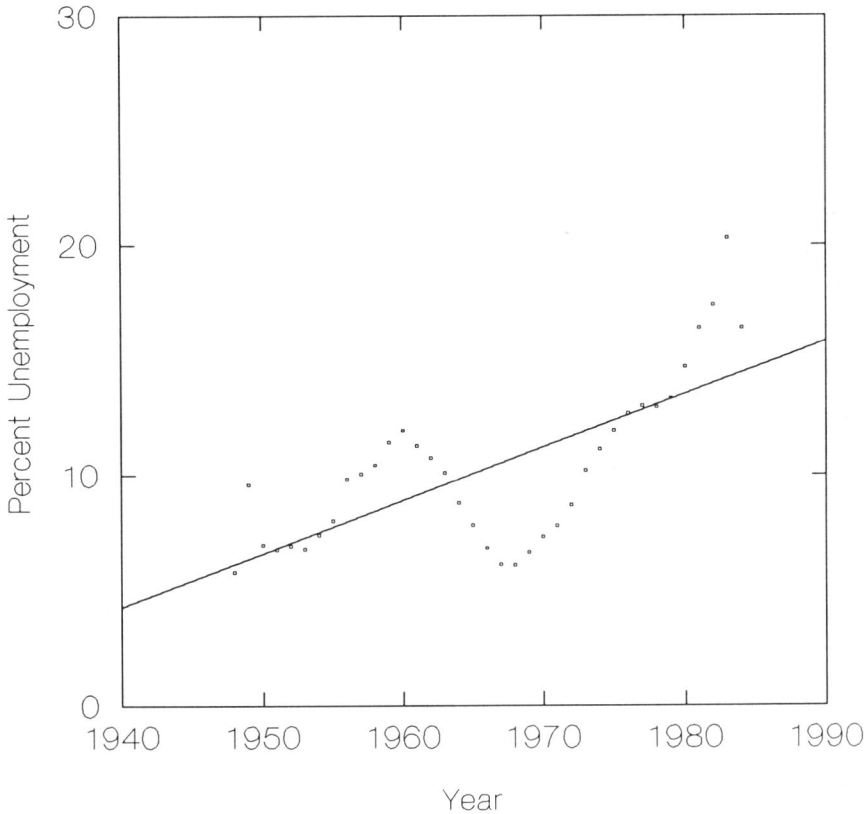

FIGURE 9.3. Yearly black male unemployment rates smoothed with a moving average of width five, U.S. data.

phrase used to describe this outcome is to say the series is linear in first differences.

Knowing whether or not a series tracks in simple fashion is a useful bit of information in developing an appropriate representation of the data. Visual inspection of the original plot warns us that the overall behavior is more complicated. This insight is reinforced by the plot of the smoothed data around the trend line in Figure 9.3. Even so, it is beneficial to outline a frequently useful technique for detecting tracking by counting the sign changes in the direction of movement of the series. This is easily done from a plot like that in Figure 9.1. There are 37 data points plotted in that figure and, thus, 36 possible changes of direction once the first direction is established (start from either end). A count reveals 15 changes of direction, which compares with the predicted value from a fair coin model of 18 changes. This is presumptive evidence of no tracking; but our visual inspection led us to the conclusion there is some tracking, and it may have a

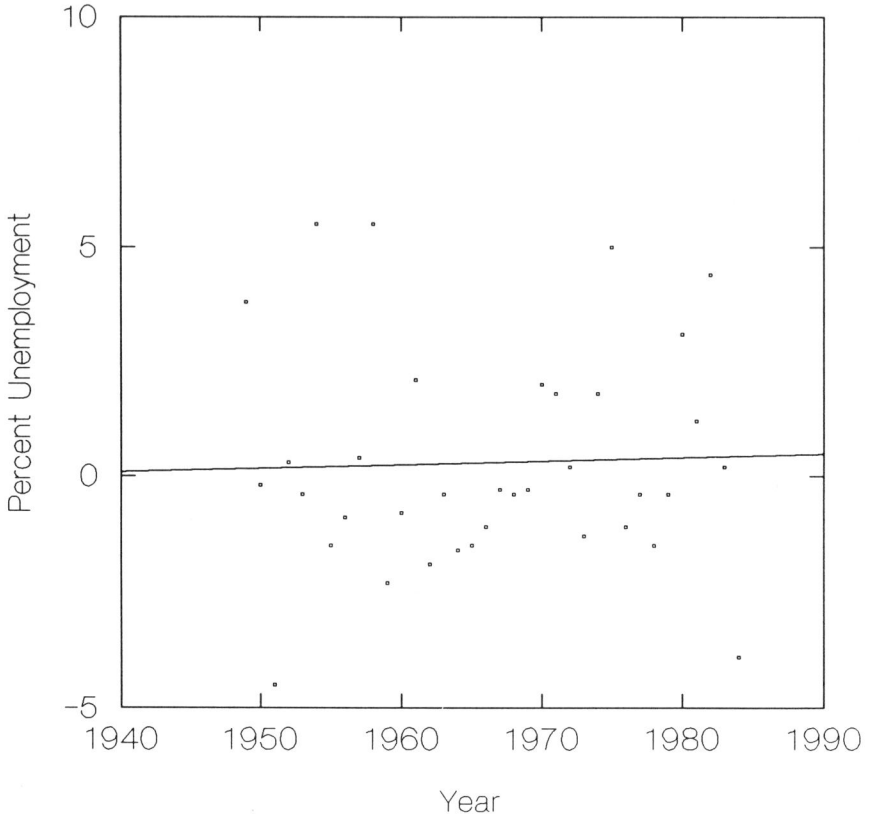

FIGURE 9.4. First differences of yearly black male unemployment rates with trend line imposed, U.S. data.

longer period. The moral is that there is not substitute for plotting the data and having a look. If a similar count is made for first differences and then second differences (losing an additional degree of freedom each time), there are 21 observed changes in each of these two further differenced series—slightly above the 14 expected by chance and systematically above the mean in both cases. Combining this simple counting exercise with our visual inspections suggests that a technically more satisfactory representation of the trend in the data might require a model that takes account of a possibly more complicated structure of internal dependencies between past and present for these data.

A number of strategies are available. One of these strategies is to follow the entire Box-Jenkins program. This has been set out elsewhere (McCleary & Hay, 1980) and is beyond the scope of this chapter. A second

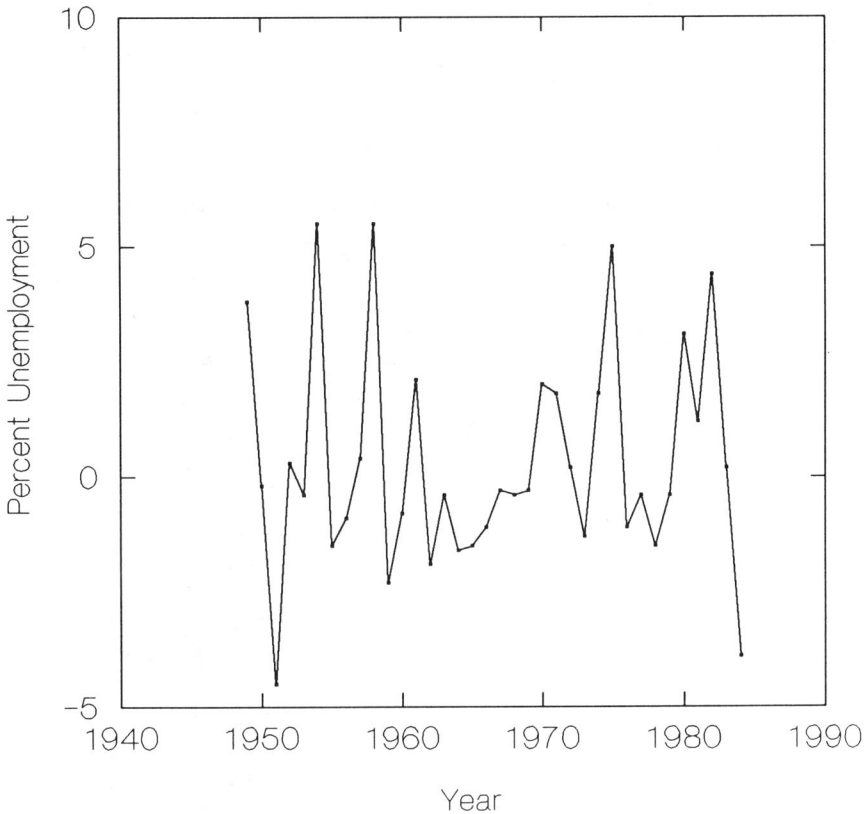

FIGURE 9.5. Line plot of first differences of yearly black male unemployment rates, U.S. data.

strategy is to imagine what components are required to represent the series in Figure 9.1. It is clear that a representation of trend is required and also that some sort of representation for cyclical motion is required. One could, for example, fit a trend on time, save the residuals, and fit a trigonometric function (a periodic function) to the residuals. Thus, one would obtain a model in two steps.

A step upward in mathematical complexity provides a somewhat more straightforward approach. A discrete time difference equation of a sufficiently high order could be estimated capturing in one statistical procedure both the trend and the oscillations about the trend. The simplest structure that will suffice is a third order difference equation—an autoregression of the observed series on its previous three lags. Such a structure has the analytic capability of representing long-term growth in a richer variety of forms than a simple straight line on time and of allowing the data to determine whether or not the oscillations are approximately sinusoidal (Goldberg, 1958; Huckfeldt, Kohfeld, & Likens, 1982). A good introduction to simple statistical strategies for analyzing time series is Chatfield (1975), which also provides an intermediate introduction to the theoretical probability considerations underlying the statistically much more complex autoregressive integrated moving average (ARIMA) modeling.

Three useful suggestions emerge from our discussion. First, always plot the data and examine the scatter carefully. Second, to see the long-run trend, smooth the data and plot the smoothed observations. Third, to see the short-run behavior, subtract out the long-run trend and plot the residuals. Simple moving averages and empirical first differencing are frequently very useful techniques in practice as long as one remembers to always plot and examine the results.

Before and After

In the analysis of the impact of public policies, the basic question is always the same: Did the policy have the desired effect? A prior question, more fundamental indeed, is this: Did the policy have any effect at all? Before/after time-series designs are calculated to answer such questions. Some measure of the behavior of interest is assembled for a time period prior to the adoption of an enforcement policy or the change of law. A current example of great interest to criminology is the recently upheld federal law designed to ensure similar sentences for equivalent offenses. However, in criminology *the* classic example is the Connecticut crackdown on speeding (Campbell & Ross, 1968). The success of this design depends on a large number of assumptions that assure that the design is in fact equivalent to a controlled experiment. As the literature on such designs illustrates, it may be quite difficult to assure that these assumptions are satisfied and statistical analysis has been associated overwhelmingly with the work of Campbell and his associates (Campbell & Ross, 1968; Campbell & Stanley, 1966; Cook & Campbell, 1979).

Depending on the length of the time periods that are available, the richness of the behavioral record, and the inherent metric of the events that have been recorded, different measurement strategies become available. On the low end are simple frequency counts, while on the high end are slope estimates embedded in complex statistical time-series models. Since before/after designs are basically attempts to estimate trends even if the trend is a step function, all the cautionary remarks with respect to time trends apply. Particularly troublesome for such designs is the influence of end point choices (beginning and ending observations) on estimates of averages or slopes. We do not develop these themes further here, and the interested reader should start with the classics already mentioned.

Panels

Panel designs, present several useful alternatives for analyses. They are particularly well suited to situations where development over time is a significant concern. Such designs identify a group of subjects or outcome measures and then track them over a period of time, making observations or measurements of the variables of interest on a periodic basis. This design is suitable for measuring change for individuals as well as in policy effects. There are at least two important advantages presented by the panel approach. First, subjects of interest can sometimes be matched on a set of relevant characteristics from some similar population. Both groups can then be followed over time, allowing for some experimental control. Second, individuals in a panel provide their own control in a sense. Past measures of behavior (either by individuals or policy units such as states, cities, or criminal justice agencies like the police) can be compared with measures of subsequent behavior. The latter measures can be compared with prior measures, allowing for corrections or adjustments in light of historical events or changes.

Perhaps the best known panel study is that of juvenile offenders by Wolfgang et al. (1972) and Wolfgang, Thornberry, and Figlio (1987). This study used a cohort of males born in Philadelphia in 1945. This study tracked a large number of identified youths until they reached the age of majority in 1963 and, ultimately, into adulthood. The clear advantage of being able to control for periodicity is evident in this design. An additional study of delinquency that uses the cohort design has been done by Shannon (1988) for youths in Racine, Wisconsin. Another excellent example of the use of longitudinal design to measure and explain delinquent behavior was done by Elliott et al. (1982). This design used multiple birth cohorts as part of the National Youth Survey to focus specifically on drug use and delinquency in the context of testing a theoretical model of delinquent behavior. Recent debate over criminal career research has highlighted several of the important issues underlying the use of longitudinal studies. The ongoing debate between Gottfredson and Hirschi (1988) and Blumstein, Cohen, and Farrington (1988a, 1988b) highlights the importance of the design for investigations of criminal or delinquent behavior.

While the focus on behavior in panel studies has been most prominent, they are also useful in attempting of assess the impact of policy or legislative changes. The analysis presented in the latter half of this chapter is an example of such an application. Others abound in the literature, perhaps the most famous of which is the application of a time-series design to crackdowns on speeding in Connecticut by Campbell and Ross (1968). The work of Sherman and Berk (1984) serves to illustrate the different results that may be obtained when one uses a cross-sectional design and a panel design. Their examination of the deterrent effect of arrests for domestic assaults showed significantly different results for each approach. In dynamic processes such as deterrence, the use of a method that captures the changing nature of variables is clearly advisable. Other relevant applications in the policy area include McCleary et al. (1982) and Greenberg and Kessler (1982).

Such designs are not a methodological panacea, however. There are several drawbacks to such designs, some practical, some more analytic in nature. First, they tend to take a long time to collect data for and, thus, tend also to be quite costly. The resources in both time and money to invest in such projects is seldom available. Another practical problem is obtaining access to the breadth of records—many officially kept, many confidential—needed to make such designs function well. A major threat to the validity of such an approach can be found in the inability to control on history. Historical events, which may affect subjects differentially, are unpredictable and quite uncontrollable. Additionally, researchers are often unable to select subjects in a random fashion, further limiting generalizations one may make from the data. The problem of attrition is also quite significant. It is almost a certain fact that attrition affects the pool of subjects in a nonrandom fashion. This reduces the validity of explanations that may be based on data analyzed in this fashion. Extended discussions of these and other methodological issues can be found in Mason, Winsborough, Mason, and Poole (1973), as well as in the two-volume work Handbook of Longitudinal Research by Mednick, Harway, and Finello (1984). The latter is an excellent reference providing methodological explanations as well as specific applications of the technique in a variety of contexts.

As with any approach, there are limitations and attractive features. The most important consideration is that the approach be well suited to both the question at hand and the data to be used for analysis.

Non-causal Time-Series Analysis

It is possible to approach the analysis of time-series data from a radically different perspective. Rather than seek the causes of change, it is possible to attempt to model the time series as parsimoniously as possible, i.e., to obtain the best fitting model with the smallest number of parameters for the series based only on properties of that series. Intuitively, the future behavior of the series is predicted at each point in time from a limited number of prior values of the series. Such techniques have proved to be very powerful tools in a wide range of applications (Box & Jenkins, 1976; McCleary & Hay, 1980; Norpoth, 1986). The acronym for such analyses, mentioned previously is ARIMA modeling.

The approach to the analysis of time series by means of ARIMA modeling is based on a battery of statistical models. The most important requirement in applications is first to render the series stationary in order to apply the modeling techniques. A frequent first step is to take differences of the series under investigation, just as was done above under the discussion of trends. Intuitively, a stationary series is one that may bounce around in the short run but does not have any long-run-trend component.

An interesting variant of some of these ideas, which has been developed in both the ARIMA context and in a somewhat more straightforward manner in a regression context, is known as Granger causality. Granger had a powerful insight into the relationship between causation and a set of measurements ordered in time. Essentially, he argued that if some series is caused at time t by a set of causal variables, it is also likely caused at time $t - 1$ by the same set of causal variables, and at time $t - 2$, and at time $t - 3$, and so on. A fair implication is that, except for perhaps some attenuation caused by time lags, all the causes that determine a process at time t are already contained in the values measured for the process at previous time periods. Hence, previous values of a measured process can serve as surrogates for all the independent causes that have not been measured directly. A good example of this is found in Fox (1978), where the best predictor of crime is crime at $t - 1$. Granger develops these ideas to provide strategies for determining direction of causation between interdependent series and for evaluating the contribution of variables contending for causal roles. The interested reader should consult the original sources (Granger, 1963, 1969; Granger & Hatanaka, 1964).

Causality

The driving force for time-series research in criminology is to determine the causes of change in some process of interest. What are the causes of this process? What is the relative significance of a cause under conditions where multiple causes are thought operative? Frequently, such investigations focus on aspects of public policy and the impact of decisions of law enforcement officials (including judges).

Such investigations typically focus on one or more time series of interest made up of events to be explained or accounted for and other events presumed to be causal on theoretical grounds. For example, if executions (for murder) deter surviving individuals from committing murder, then a pair of time series for both murders and executions in a specified jurisdiction should bear certain specifiable relationships to each other. But not even the most ardent proponent of capital punishment believes that swift justice or its lack is the only causal force affecting the frequency of murder. Hence, other time series measuring other potential causes of murder come into play. Very soon the picture becomes complex, and several variables must have their role assessed along with the role of capital punishment.

In such circumstances, a number of considerations dealing with interdependence of the series influence the statistical treatment. The most important notion from the perspective of causality, however, is easily illustrated with executions and murder. Simple-minded approaches will not work. For example, the correlation between murders and executions may be positive simply because, in the presence of a death-penalty law, if murder frequencies go up the probability of executions likely will also go up. Thus, the two series are likely to be positively correlated, leading to the perhaps erroneous conclusion that executions cause murders. The most powerful causal ordering principle that can be invoked in such situations is precedence in time. Thus the time order of the variables attains greater significance. In this case, it can be studied by assessing whether executions last year determine murders this year. We can be relatively confident that data organized in this fashion do not reflect more executions simply because there are more murders and, hence, that they present a cleaner evaluation of the question of interest: Does capital punishment deter murder?

In criminology, deterrence studies have been plagued by the problem of simultaneous causation. The unsatisfactory state of such investigations led to a full-scale review by a committee of the National Academy of Sciences (Blumstein et. al., 1978). Again, it is easy to illustrate the problem but much more difficult to suggest an approach to fix it. Consider police arresting criminals and criminals committing crimes. Nothing can be more elementary than the observation that as crime increases, if police are doing their job, then so will the number of arrests increase. Conversely, if crime is infrequent, then so will be arrests. This means that police deterrence efforts (arrests) and criminal behavior (say, burglaries) will be positively associated. This can be interpreted in silly-minded fashion as showing that arrests increase crime. Clearly, the sensible interpretation is that crimes cause arrests. However, the question of interest is whether or not those arrests deter *other* crimes. And this has proved to be a refractory problem motivating many investigations as well as the National Academy report. Establishing a time precedence for the relevant series has turned out to be difficult in many deterrence studies. In the case of murder and executions, the case treated in the next section, the time precedence principle is somewhat easier to apply and has a relatively unambiguous interpretation on a priori theoretical grounds.

We now turn to an extended example of a time-series investigation. The basic issue is an evaluation of the policy significance of capital punishment in influencing murder rates in eight midwestern states. Several technical problems in time-series analysis are illustrated in the development, and the principle of time precedence is used in formulating the basic model. This example serves to illustrate many of the methodological issues raised in this section.

Murder in the Midwest

Capital punishment has generated a good deal of debate wherever it has been practiced. In addition, it is an issue that has prompted analysis from scholars in a variety of disciplines. Most disciplines have contributed to the debate over the existence, effect, and imposition of the death penalty. This work has been accelerated, no doubt, by the certification of the death penalty by the U.S. Supreme Court in *Gregg v. Georgia* (1976) and the subsequent executions.

Three topics of debate have received the most attention in this context. First, the legal merits of capital punishment have been debated in the courts and state legislatures and by the public. These debates have been most concerned with procedural issues and, in particular, have concentrated on Eighth Amendment concerns regarding "cruel and unusual punishment." Most of this debate has centered around the way in which the penalty has been imposed. In this context, the discriminatory or unpatterned imposition of the death penalty has been the principal concern of these studies. Thus, questions about the nature of the victim, characteristics of the offender, and contribution of aggravating circumstances to the sentencing decision have been the hallmarks of this approach. As a second concern, many have debated the moral or ethical merits of the death penalty. This tradition is perhaps the oldest and most consistent theme in the analysis of the death penalty. Opponents have emphasized that executions represent legalized killing performed in the name of the state. As such, they argue, these practices are without moral justification and merely serve to substitute one killing in place of another (Amsterdam, 1977; Conrad, 1983; Schwarzschild, 1982). Proponents of the death penalty have argued that when the death penalty is not imposed, a serious moral wrong is committed. These arguments have stated that it is a moral injustice not to impose the death penalty, and they stem from the traditional retributionist contention that those who commit an offense have earned a penalty. From this perspective, when such persons go unpunished an injustice has been committed (Hook, 1961; Van den Haag, 1982).

None of the other debates, though, has received the attention that the deterrent effect of capital punishment on homicides has received. The studies in this area have increased significantly in frequency and in methodological and statistical rigor in the last decade. Research in this area has evolved from early studies that employed contiguous states as the basis for analysis. In these analyses, states with roughly similar social and demographic characteristics would be compared to determine if their homicide rates differed. Differences in this criterion variable were presumed to be primarily the result of the primary existence of the death penalty. Such analyses (Bailey, 1974; Lempert, 1983; Sellin, 1958; Sutherland, 1925) have consistently found that there is no significant difference in homicide rates between similar states that vary only as to the existence of the death penalty. A methodological advance came in the evolution of such analyses with the advent of correlational studies. The works of Schuessler (1952) and Bailey (1977) are the best known examples of this trend. They, too, attempted to determine whether a relationship between executions and the death penalty and other exogenous variables could be demonstrated. They, also, failed to demonstrate a deterrent effect for executions. The current vogue in deterrence studies is the use of multivariate statistics. In addition to multiple predictors, these analyses have incorporated the use of lagged variables, as well as a variety of techniques to minimize autocorrelation effects. Such techniques lend themselves particularly well to the use of time-series designs, a practice that represents an advance in data as well as method. Including a large number of points in time, deterrence studies can now more accurately document the effect of executions. These studies can also be categorized by the type of data used. Typical of most deterrence studies in the 1970s was the use of cross-sectional data. Aggregates of jurisdictions, typically states, would be grouped together for analysis. Recently, single jurisdictions have been employed more frequently in time-series analyses. This strategy preserves the advantages of longitudinal designs but eliminates some of the potential difficulties inherent in cross-sectional studies, especially where consequences for public policy are likely applications of the results.

The analyses presented here are consistent with these recent trends in deterrence research, and a time-series design for the analysis of the deterrence question in eight midwestern states is developed. A 50-year time series is employed to assess the effect of executions on homicides in eight midwestern states that differ in death penalty. Four of those states, Ohio, Indiana, Illinois, and Missouri, have had executions during this time period and currently have capital punishment statutes. Three states have not had executions during this time period, Wisconsin, Minnesota, and Michigan, and a fourth, Iowa, has had very few executions (14), but all four currently do not have capital punishment legislation and, thus, are included as controls in this study. This design provides the joint advantage of using data from states from a particular region as the units of observation and analysis while also allowing the pooling of data from related jurisdictions.

Data Sources

The data on executions for this study were provided by the U.S. Bureau of Prisons. Specifically, the authors have received an enumeration of the yearly number of executions by state for the time period 1931 to 1980. These data made possible the time-series nature of the analysis, as well as the approach that uses single jurisdictions (states) as the unit of analysis. The dependent variable, i.e., the annual rate of murder and nonnegligent manslaughters, was drawn from the Uniform Crime Reports. Other exogenous variables were drawn from the *Statistical Abstracts*. These variables were selected based on an analysis of the death-penalty and homicide literature. A dual criterion was applied in the selection decision: whether or not the variable was identified in the literature as having both empirical and theoretical relevance to variations in homicide rates. The final group of controls included in the analyses are the proportion of the state population that was white males ages 15 to 29, the proportion that was nonwhite males ages 15 to 29, the proportion that was living in urban areas, and a dummy variable that measures whether or not executions took place in a given year.

These eight states were chosen for a variety of reasons. First, they represent perhaps the most homogeneous area of the country—they share a common agricultural, ethnic, and urban history. They were settled by immigrants from Ireland, Poland, Italy, Germany, and the Scandinavian countries, primarily in the early 1900s. In addition, they all experienced a great influx of minorities in the early 1950s. Each of the states (with the exception of Iowa) has a major urban center, and all have a dependence on agriculture for state livelihood. What makes these states even more attractive as candidates for analysis in this study is the fact that exactly half of the states (four) have executed people consistently throughout the period and currently have death-penalty legislation on the books. In addition, three of the states have never imposed the death penalty (Michigan, Minnesota, and Wisconsin), and one of them (Iowa) has imposed it very seldom (14 times) in the 50-year period included in this study. None of this last group of states currently has valid death-penalty legislation. Thus, what is presented by these states is the opportunity to examine a naturally occurring experiment. The fact that these states are in the same region, that they share many similar characteristics save their executions policies, and that they are demographically similar are design advantages in assessing our central question.

There are a number of reasons why this analysis focuses on these eight states. First, these states represent a similar region of the country and, as such, are likely to include the effect of the communication of information about executions in one state to another state. A second reason is more closely related to the nature of the analysis to be performed here. Because executions are typically not a frequent practice, a state with a relatively low number of executions presents special difficulties, i.e., when the independent variable occurs infrequently, it is more difficult to draw inferences from results. Therefore, from a strictly methodological viewpoint, these eight states are desirable units of analysis because of the natural experiment presented by the similarity of the states and because of their differing capital punishment policies.

Literature Review

The evidence on the existence of a deterrent effect from the death penalty is nearly unequivocal. Beginning with the work of Sellin (1958), must studies have shown there to be no deterrent effect. The Sellin study compared the homicide rate of similar contiguous states, one that had the death penalty, some that did not. The differences between the states' homicide rates in each case were negligible. This led Sellin to conclude that there was no deterrent effect for the death penalty. This conclusion has been called into question on a number of grounds by Ehrlich (1975). However, this comparative approach has been recently resurrected by Lempert (1983). He addressed the Ehrlich criticisms by comparing states based on the number of executions they have had, not on the mere existence of the death penalty. Lempert used Ehrlich's (1975) well-known finding that each execution saves approximately eight lives as the basis for his hypothesis that states with more executions should enjoy lower homicide rates when the contiguous comparisons are made. Lempert found results almost identical to those reported by Sellin 25 years earlier; there is no evidence that the death penalty or the use of executions serves as a deterrent to homicides.

A number of studies have purported to demonstrate the deterrent effect argued for by its advocates, while others have failed to uncover such an effect. Typical of those works that have demonstrated a deterrent effect are the studies of Ehrlich (1975, 1977) and Yunker (1976). Each employed national data in his analysis. Ehrlich's well-publicized study (1975) (cited by the majority in the *Gregg* decision that lifted the Supreme Court prohibition on executions) demonstrated a strong deterrent effect, indicating that approximately eight lives were saved for every execution that occurred between 1933 and 1969. His study was called into question on a number of grounds by Bowers and Pierce (1975), Barnett (1981), Klein, Forst, and Filatov (1978), and McGahey (1980). Among the primary criticisms offered of the Ehrlich (1975) work were the identification restrictions and the lack of homogeneity of structural relations over time (Klein et al., 1978). Additional criticisms included: (1) the use of data aggregated to the national level, (2) the exogenous variables in the equation, and (3) the years included in the time series.

A significant criticism of the applications of Ehrlich's (1975) work to policy questions has been the focus on his use of the states aggregated as a single unit. This procedure has the unfortunate effect of comingling the effect of the independent variables, most of which show considerable variation from one jurisdiction to another. This produces the inferential dilemma noted earlier. Some have contended that his model was misspecified. Other criticisms of this work have argued that Ehrlich (1975) failed to use enough independent variables or that he failed to include the correct ones. While one may quibble ad infinitum about variable selection, this criticism seems merited.

Ehrlich's (1975) time series ends in 1969, just after the suspension of use of executions by most states and before the abolition of the death penalty by the Supreme Court in 1972. Thus, he included a period of high homicide rates with no executions at the tail end of his time series. One suspects that this is the segment of his time series that produces his high negative correlations. Indeed, Kleck (1979), using a time series that extended into the seventies, reported no evidence for the deterrent effect found by Ehrlich (1975).

While Ehrlich's (1975) work represents the most statistically sophisticated of those that have shown a deterrent effect, it has been so widely
criticized (see, also, Barnett, 1981; Forst, 1977; Friedman, 1979; Passell,
1975) as to render its conclusions highly suspect. (Indeed, Bowers's, 1984,
replication of Ehrlich's (1975) analysis, using the same data and analytic
technique, failed to find the same results.) Yunker (1976) demonstrated an
even stronger deterrent effect than did Ehrlich (1975). However, his data,
method, and results were severely criticized by Fox (1977), who noted severe misspecification problems in the analysis. Thus, it appears that those
studies that have demonstrated a negative relationship between executions
and homicides are fraught with methodological problems.

Studies that have focused on a single state as the unit of analysis have
failed to find a deterrent effect. Bailey's studies of Noth Carolina (1978a),
Utah (1978b), Oregon (1979a), California (1979b), and Ohio (1979c) and
Decker and Kohfeld's (1984) study of Illinois have all demonstrated a consistent finding; executions exert no deterrent effect on homicide rates.
However, Bailey's work is not without its own problems. His time series
spanned 1910 to 1962; however, it does not have 53 time points as one
would with annual data. Rather, he used sociodemographic data from the
census years as proxies for the real values of the 2 years preceding and
following the decennial census years. Thus he included only 25 data points,
less than half of the total number of years in his time series. His last data
point was 1962, over 20 years ago, and is therefore somewhat dated, given
the change in homicide rates from 1962 to 1980. In addition, he performed
no test for autocorrelation and failed to include a consideration of the
possible effect of a time trend upon the analysis. Clearly, these methodological problems suggest that a replication of these analyses that deal with
these problems at the state level would prove useful.

What is apparent from this literature review is that the overwhelming
majority of results show no deterrent effect. This finding is even more convincing in terms of the policy debate regarding the death penalty. The burden of proof must rest with the proponents of the death penalty. That is,
those who contend that a deterrent effect exists should be pressed to
demonstrate conclusively the results of their work. This is consistent with
both the basic assumption of the scientific method—that he burden of
proof rests on rejecting the null hypothesis—and the significance of the
penalty. The studies reported on here point strongly to a single conclusion:
Executions have little impact on the homicide rate. This conclusion holds
over a variety of studies and methodologies. Over 20 studies examining the
deterrence issue were examined, and only 3 of them found a deterrent
effect. Each of these studies has been severely criticized in the literature.
The studies that failed to support the deterrence notion were varied in level
of aggregation, data, technique, control variables, and site. Given the
nature of social science analysis, it would be inappropriate to depend on
a single study as the basis for guiding policy for such an important issue,
as was the case in the *Gregg* decision. The variations in method and data

among the studies that fail to find a deterrent effect support the claims of those who claim that no deterrent effect exists.

The Current Analysis

In light of these findings, we have performed several different analyses. The time-series nature of these data makes it possible to address the deterrence issue from a variety of perspectives. The nature of the data allows us to illustrate a number of methodological issues important to time-series analysis.

First, graphs of the patterns of homicides for each of the states over time are presented. This analysis allows us to examine the different patterns of variation in the two different kinds of states. That is, the homicide rate for the four death-penalty states and the four non-death-penalty states as aggregates are compared. Following this, the mean homicide rates of the two groups of states are compared, in order to minimize the effect of outliers and extreme variations in the time series. The next segment of the analysis presents a generalized least squares approach. Several controls that have been demonstrated to have both theoretical and empirical relevance to homicide rates are included in the models. Among the models that are included here is a regression analysis of the eight states pooled. This was done in order to determine the effect of executions while controlling for demographic variables. Next, the four execution states are analyzed in separate regressions. This analysis was complemented by a look at the four non- (or low) execution states and hence provides a comparison of the coefficients for each of the variables across the two kinds of states.

Findings

Figure 9.6 presents a plot of the mean homicide rates for the eight states. The states with the death penalty are represented with a plus (+), and those without the death penalty are represented with a box ([ ]). The first and most striking result to be observed is the fact that the states with the death penalty have a considerably higher mean homicide rate for every year in the time series. Equally striking is the similarity of the patterns. The three peak eras of homicide rates (early 1930s, years around 1950, and the general escalation throughout the 1970s) are the same for both groups of states. The same is true of the dips in the pattern, as well as the overall trend. This indicates that the major difference between the two kinds of states is a difference of level and that the pattern is relatively constant across the eight states. This finding provides support for the contention noted earlier, that states from a similar region are good candidates for such

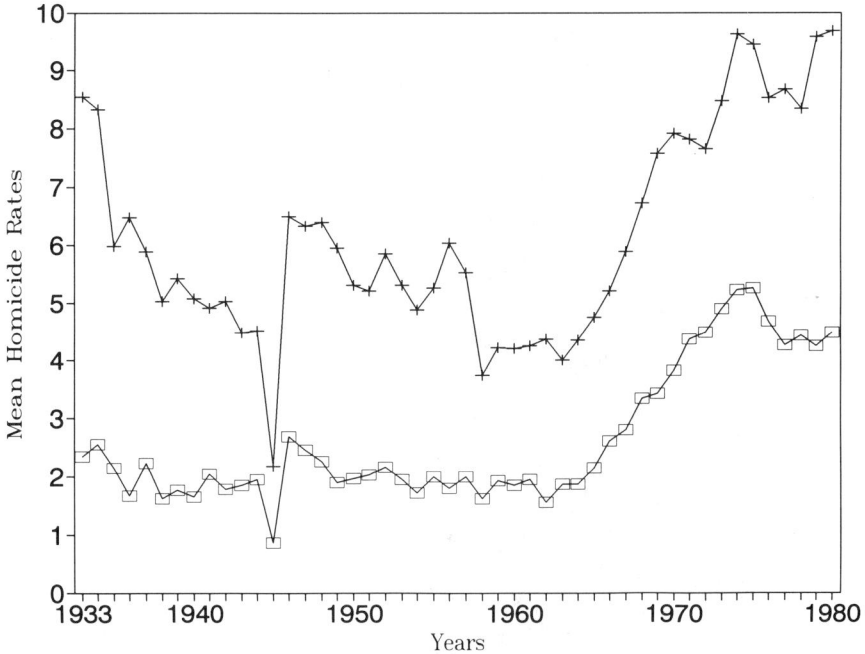

FIGURE 9.6. Mean homicide rate for the four death-penalty states + (Illinois, Indiana, Missouri, and Ohio) compared with the mean homicide rate for four non-death-penalty states □ (Minnesota, Michigan, Wisconsin, and Iowa).

an analysis because of the existence of many of the same factors that may be influencing crime, in general, and homicide rates, in particular. While no firm conclusions about the effect of the existence of the death penalty can be drawn from this graphical presentation, one thing is clear—those states with the death penalty and executions in this time period have consistently and considerably higher homicide rates.

The results shown in Figure 9.7 confirm the results shown in Figure 9.6. In this graph, Michigan is eliminated from the group of states without the death penalty. This serves to reduce and flatten out the plot of homicide rates for this group of states. Michigan is a state with a higher homicide rate than the remainder of the non-death-penalty states and also exhibits other important demographic differences when compared with the remainder. With this outlier removed from the analysis, it becomes clear that the differences in homicide rates are generally even greater than evidenced by the display in Figure 9.6.

Figure 9.8 provides a more detailed analysis of the homicide rates for the four death-penalty states: Indiana, Illinois, Missouri, and Ohio. Indiana is the state with the consistently lowest homicide rate in this group, while

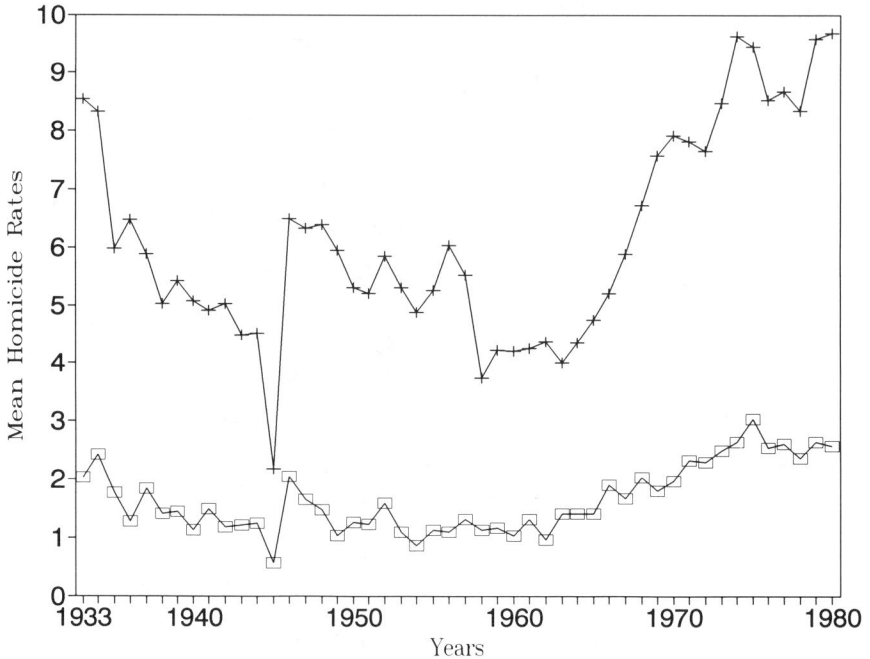

FIGURE 9.7. Mean homicide rate for the four death-penalty states + (Illinois, Indiana, Missouri, and Ohio) compared with the mean homicide rate for three non-death-penalty states □ (Minnesota, Wisconsin, and Iowa).

Missouri and Illinois tend to define the upper limits for these states. The variation across these four states is not particularly large though, with the exception of the first 2 years in the time series for Missouri. Figure 9.9 is the counterpart to Figure 9.8 for the non-death-penalty states. The results of this eighth graph show rather clearly the reasons for removing Michigan from the seventh graph. Michigan is clearly an outlier that has homicide rates closer in scale to the non-death-penalty, nonexecution states.

   We must now ask what conclusions are to be drawn from these last four graphs. The results were rather striking in their consistency and clarity. States with executions and the death penalty have consistently higher homicide rates. This appears to provide support for the brutalization hypothesis expressed throughout the literature. States that have executions tend to have higher homicide rates. Some contend that this is linked to the greater tolerance for violence in states where the government condones and engages in taking life. An alternative explanation would be that those states that have high homicide rates tend to respond to this phenomenon by executing offenders. The case of Michigan, with a relatively high homicide rate and no death penalty, seems to contradict this though and to offer at least preliminary support for the brutalization hypothesis. These graphs,

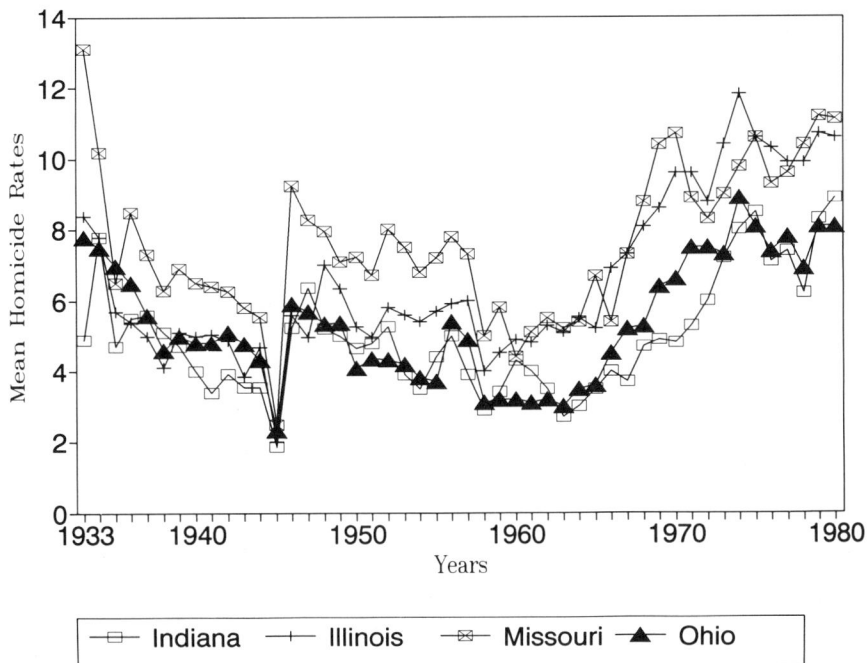

FIGURE 9.8. Homicide rates for the four-death-penalty states (Indiana, Illinois, Missouri, and Ohio): 1933–1980.

however, do not provide us with the ability to control for other variables that may be affecting the relationship. Thus, we turn to the results of the regressions.

In order to assure that executions occur before the further crimes they are presumedly deterring, executions are measured with a time lag of 1 year. Thus, for example, the murder rate for 1940 is associated in the regressions with the execution measure for 1939. It may well be that in the case of executions as a variable, they measure a generalized atmosphere and public attitude with respect to the death penalty in a state. It turns out that one obtains nearly identical statistical results independent of the lag structure on the measure of executions. Nevertheless, we adhere to the theoretically appropriate principal of time precedence in order to provide an unambiguous order to the direction of causality between executions and murders.

In Table 9.2, a regression is presented for the eight states pooled. Overall, 84% of the variation in homicide rates is explained by the five independent variables. This is a relatively high r-squared, though not uncommon in time-series analyses. All of the predictor variables are significant, but it is most interesting to focus on the last two, i.e., the number of executions and

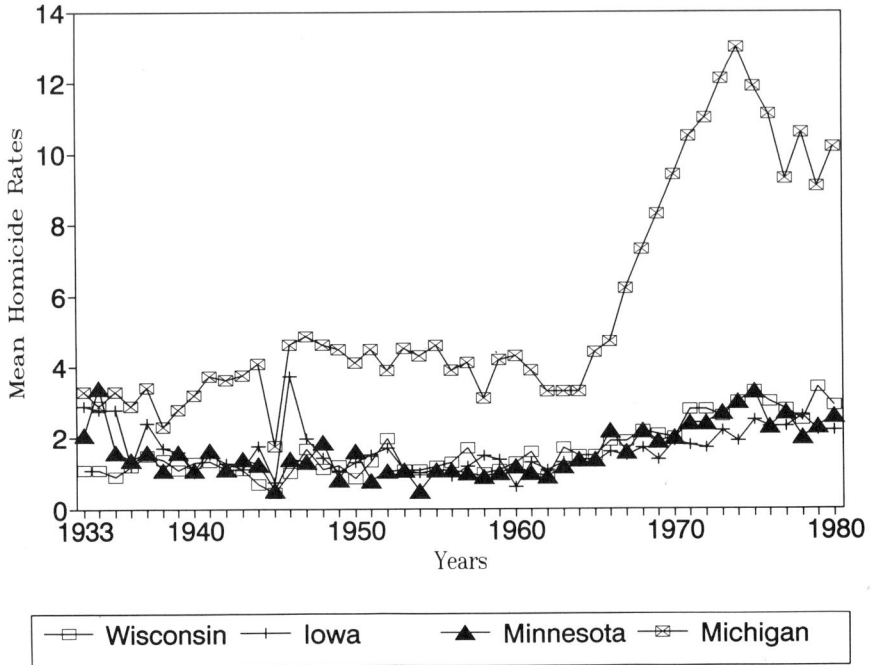

FIGURE 9.9. Homicide rates for the four non-death-penalty states (Michigan, Minnesota, Iowa, and Wisconsin): 1933–1980.

the dummy variable, whether or not a state has the death penalty. Both of these variables are positive, contradicting what deterrence theory would predict. If deterrence theory is correct about the effect of executions, both should be inversely related to the number of homicides in a state. However, this is clearly not the case. These results, therefore, provide additional support for the explanations provided earlier for the graphs, that executions and homicides are positively related. The two most important variables in explaining homicide rates are the percentage of nonwhite males 15 to 29 years old and the percentage of the state's population living in an urbanized area. Thus, these results are consistent with the preceding results in noting the overwhelming role played by demographic factors in explaining variation in homicide rates over time.

In Table 9.3, regressions for each of the death-penalty states are analyzed individually. While less variation is accounted for in each of these states than the eight taken as a whole, a considerable amount is explained by these models. Since these are all execution states, the dummy variable was dropped from the analysis, and only the number of executions (lagged 1 year) was used to represent the contention of deterrence theory that executions deter homicides. Here this variable is significant for only two

TABLE 9.2. Regression results for the model using pooled data for the eight midwestern states of Illinois, Indiana, Ohio, Missouri, Michigan, Wisconsin, Minnesota, and Iowa: 1933–1980. The dependent variable is homicide rate per 100,000 population in each state per year ($N = 384$).

Variables	Regression results
R^2	.84
Intercept	2.62[a]
	(.86)[b]
	3.01**[c]
Percent white males	.21
(15–29 years old)	(.048)
	4.49***
Percent nonwhite males	6.46
(15–29 years old)	(.22)
	29.00***
Percent urbanized	−8.16
	(.98)
	−8.29***
Number executions	.137
	(.033)
	4.15***
Death penalty state	.848
(1 = DP, 0 = No DP)	(.16)
	5.24***

a Unstandardized regression coefficients
b Standard error of the coefficient
c Scores: $*p < .05, **p < .01, ***p < .001$

states, Illinois and Indiana, and positive for all four states. Urbanization and the percentage of nonwhite males 15 to 29 years old are again the two critical variables in explaining the changes in homicide rates over time for these four states. This is particularly true for Missouri, the state that has the consistently highest homicide rates. Thus, whether aggregated as a group of eight states or analyzed separately, there is not support for the deterrence effect of executions. In fact, the analyses support the contrary notion.

Table 9.4 presents the results of regressions for each of the non-death-penalty states. In these four states, roughly equivalent percentages of the variation are explained as in death-penalty states. While Iowa and Illinois are on the low end, both Michigan and Wisconsin have extremely high r-squared figures, .85. Again, the percentage of nonwhite males 15 to 29 years old is the key variable. In Iowa, which has had a very small number of executions, the variable representing the number of people executed

226   Carol W. Kohfeld and Scott H. Decker

TABLE 9.3. Regression results for the model in the four states that use the death penalty or have had it on the books for the entire time period: Ohio, Indiana, Illinois, Missouri, 1933–1980. The dependent variable is homicide rate per 100,000 population.

Variables	Ohio	Indiana	Illinois	Missouri
R²	.63	.57	.76	.49
Intercept	−11.3	22.8	−10.5	56.3[a]
	(22.3)	(10.9)	(30.1)	(21.7)[b]
	−.51	2.08*	−.35	2.60**[c]
Percent white males	.73	−.20	.56	−2.54
(15–29 years old)	(.31)	(.44)	(1.11)	(1.09)
	2.07*	−.66	1.26	−2.29*
Percent nonwhite males	4.04	13.5	4.35	19.7
(15–29 years old)	(3.78)	(3.77)	(2.10)	(5.55)
	1.04	3.58***	2.07*	3.55***
Percent urbanized	7.35	−40.8	7.99	−66.9
	(30.7)	(17.3)	(35.6)	(25.1)
	.24	−2.35*	.22	−2.66**
Number executions	.090	.28	0.93	.16
	(.062)	(.13)	(.12)	(.19)
	1.48	2.10*	.80	.84

a Unstandardized regression coefficients
b Standard error of the coefficient
c Scores: $p < .05$, ** $p < .01$, *** $p < .001$

(lagged 1 year) is not significant, and its regression coefficient is extremely small although it is negative.

Next Steps

The data for the preceding analyses are included in the Appendix. A number of manipulations of these data are instructive. Students interested in studying trend analysis can easily select a state and apply smoothing by moving averages and the removal of trends by repeated differencing plotting their results after each manipulation. A good exercise is to estimate the trend lines for each state on time by ordinary least squares, draw the lines on separate graphs, and plot the observed data. Repeating this exercise for smoothed data may be revealing. It is particularly instructive to plot smoothed data for a simple moving average filter with differing widths, or windows of, say, three observations, then five observations, then seven observations. Comparing the plots for a given state for these differing smoothers will vividly portray the way in which smoothing progressively

TABLE 9.4. Regression results for the model in the four states that never used the death penalty (or used it rarely, Iowa) for the entire time period: Minnesota, Wisconsin, Michigan, Iowa, 1933–1980. The dependent variable is homicide rate per 100,000 population.

Variables	Minn.	Wisc.	Mich.	Iowa
R^2	.52	.85	.85	.38
Intercept	−7.22	29.5	−4.01	8.74[a]
	(2.61)	(9.95)	(23.4)	(4.12)[b]
	−2.76**	2.96**	−.17	2.12*[c]
Percent white males	.34	−.49	.38	−.10
(15–29 years old)	(.08)	(.20)	(.41)	(.15)
	4.25***	−2.40*	.92	−.69
Percent nonwhite males	−4.65	16.3	7.29	24.4
(15–29 years old)	(5.34)	(4.07)	(1.12)	(9.29)
	−.87	4.01***	6.54**	2.63**
Percent urbanized	9.62	−44.3	−2.47	−18.1
	(4.46)	(14.5)	(28.5)	(7.45)
	2.16	−3.05**	−.09	−2.43*
Number executions				−.08
				(.10)
				.86

a Unstandardized regression coefficients
b Standard error of the coefficient
c Scores: $p < .05$, **$p < .01$, ***$p < .001$

suppresses short-run variation in the time series. Taking the opposite tack, i.e., removing long-run trends, can also be carried out. Once more, first differences, second differences, and third differences of the same series within one state should be compared. Computing a trend line for such differenced data will allow an assessment of how adequate first or second or third differencing has been in removing trend from the data. These same techniques can be invoked to evaluate the statistical soundness of replications of the regressions reported in Tables 9.2, 9.3, and 9.4. For example, statistical inferences concerning the coefficients in the regressions are justified if the remaining error, the residual error, does not exhibit a time trend. This question can be directly examined by a plot and the computation of the correlation between the residual and its lag. It can also be examined visually. If the residual exhibits pronounced autocorrelation, the usual direction of first attempts at statistical repair is taken by, you guessed it, forming first differences of the variables believed to still contain or to be causing the trend effects. For example, one might wish to repeat the regressions using first differences of the murder rates as the dependent variable and, among the independent variables, including the first difference of executions rather than its level. After this is done, the residuals may be recovered and once more examined for the presence of systematic trend rather than independent short-run noise. The truly adventurous reader might wish to evaluate whether or not pooling of the data is justified. The essential issue here is whether the time-series regressions for individual states are statistically indistinguishable from the regression for the data for all states combined. A succinct summary of the major issues in pooling can be found in Maddala (1977, pp. 320–333). Many other possibilities for using these data exist.

Good estimating!

References

Amsterdam, A.G. (1977). In opposition to death penalty legislation. In H. Bedau (Ed.), The death penalty in America (pp. 42–47). New York: Oxford University Press.

Bailey, W.C. (1974). Murder and the death penalty. Journal of Criminal Law and Criminology, 65(3), 416–423.

Bailey, W.C. (1977). Imprisonment v. the death penalty as a deterrent to murder. Law and Human Behavior, 1(3), 239–260.

Bailey, W.C. (1978a). An analysis of the deterrent effect of the death penalty in North Carolina. North Carolina Central Law Journal, 10, 29–52.

Bailey, W.C. (1978b). Deterrence and the death penalty for murders in Utah: A time series analysis. Journal of Contemporary Law, 5(1), 1–20.

Bailey, W.C. (1979a). Deterrence and the death penalty for murder in Oregon. Willamette Law Review, 16(1), 67–85.

Bailey, W.C. (1979b). The deterrent effect of the death penalty for murder in California. Southern California Law Review, 52(3), 743–764.

Bailey, W.C. (1979c). The deterrent effect of the death penalty for murder in Ohio: A time series analysis. Cleveland State Law Review, 28(1), 51–81.

Barnett, A. (1981). The deterrent effect of capital punishment: A test of some recent studies. Operations Research, 29(2), 346–370.

Blumstein, A., Cohen, J., & Farrington, D.A. (1988a). Criminal career research: Its value for criminology. Criminology, 26(1), 1–36.

Blumstein, A., Cohen, J., & Farrington, D.P. (1988b). Longitudinal and criminal career research: Further clarifications. Criminology, 26(1), 57–74.

Blumstein, A., Cohen, J., & Nagin, D. eds. (1978). Deterrence and incapacitation: Estimating the effects of criminal sanctions on crime rates. Washington, D.C. National Academy Press.

Bowers, W. (1984). Legal homicide: Death as punishment in America, 1864–1982. Boston: Northeastern University Press.

Bowers, W., & Pierce, G. (1975). The illusion of deterrence in Issac Ehrlich's research on capital punishment. The Yale Law Journal, 85(2), 187–208.

Box, G.E.P., & Jenkins, G.M. (1976). Time series analysis: Forecasting and control (rev. ed.). San Francisco: Holden-Day.

Campbell, D.T., & Ross, H.L. (1968). The Connecticut crackdown on speeding: Time series data in quasi-experimental analysis. Law and Society Review, 3, 33–53.

Campbell, D.T., & Stanley, J.C. (1966). Experimental and quasi-experimental designs for research. Chicago: Rand McNally.

Chatfield, C. (1975). The analysis of time series: Theory and practice. New York: Wiley.

Conrad, J.P. (1983). The state as killer. American Bar Foundation Research Journal, 2, 451–464.

Cook, T.D., & Campbell, D.T. (Eds.). (1979). Quasi-experimentation: Design & analysis issues for field settings. Chicago: Rand McNally.

Decker, S., & Kohfeld, C. (1984). A deterrence study of the death penalty in Illinois: 1933–1980. Journal of Criminal Justice, 12(4), 367–379.

Ehrlich, I. (1975). The deterrent effect of capital punishment: A question of life and death. American Economic Review, 65, 397–416.

Ehrlich, I. (1977). Capital punishment and deterrence: Some further thoughts and additional evidence. Journal of Political Economy, 85(4), 741–788.

Elliott, D., Huizinga, D., & Ageton, S.S. (1982). Explaining delinquency and drug use. The National Youth Survey. (Behavioral Research Institute: Project Report No. 21). Boulder, CO.

Forst, B.E. (1977). The deterrent effect of capital punishment: A cross state analysis of the 1960's. Minnesota Law Review, 61, 743–767.

Fox, J.A. (1977). The identification and estimation of deterrence: An evaluation of Yunker's model. Journal of Behavioral Economics, 2(2), 225–242.

Fox, J.A. (1978). Forecasting crime. Lexington, MA: Lexington Press.

Friedman, L.S. (1979). The use of multiple regression analysis to test for a deterrent effect of capital punishment: Prospects and problems. In E. Bittner & S. Messinger (Eds.), Criminology Review Yearbook (pp. 61–87). Beverly Hills, CA: Sage.

Goldberg, S. (1958). Difference equations. New York: Wiley.

Gottfredson, M., & Hirschi, T. (1988). Science, public policy, and the career. Criminology, 26(1), 37–56.

Granger, C.W.J. (1963). Economic processes involving feedback. Information and Control, 6, 28–48.

Granger, C.W.J. (1969). Investigating causal relations by econometric models and cross-spectral methods. Econometrics, 37, 424–438.

Granger, C.W.J., & Hatanaka, M. (1964). Spectral analysis of economic time series. Princeton: Princeton University Press.

Greenberg, D.F., & Kessler, R.C. (1982). The effect of arrests on crime: A multivariate panel analysis. Social Forces, 60(3), 771–790.

Gregg v. Georgia, 428 U.S. 153, 96 Sup. Ct. 2909 (1976).

Hook, S. (1961). The death sentence. The New Leader, 44, 18–20.

Huckfeldt, R.R., Kohfeld, C.W., & Likens, T. (1982). Dynamic modeling: An introduction. (Sage University Paper series on Quantitative Applications in the Social Sciences, series no. 07-027). Beverly Hills, CA: Sage.

Jenks, C. (1987). Genes and crime. New York Review of Books, 34(2), 33–41.

Kleck, G. (1979). Capital punishment, gun ownership and homicide. American Journal of Sociology, 84(4), 882–910.

Klein, L., Forst, B., & Filatov, V. (1978). The deterrent effect of capital punishment: An assessment of the estimates. In A. Blumstein, J. Cohen, & D. Nagin (Eds.), Deterrence and incapacitation: Estimating the effects of criminal sanctions on crime rates (pp. 336–360). Washington, DC: National Academy Press.

Kohfeld, C.W., & Sprague, J. (1988). Urban unemployment drives urban crime. Urban Affairs Quarterly, *24*(2), 215–241.

Lempert, R. (1983). The effect of executions on homicides. Crime and Delinquency, *29*(1), 88–115.

Long, S.K., & Witte, A.D. (1981). Current economic trends: Implications for crime and criminal justice. In K.N. Wright (Ed.), Crime and criminal justice in a declining economy (pp. 69–143). Cambridge, MA: Oelgeschlager, Gunn & Hain.

Maddala, G.S. (1977). Econometrics. New York: McGraw-Hill.

Mason, K., Winsborough, H.H., Mason, W.M., & Poole, K.W. (1973). Some methodological issues in cohort analysis of arrival data. American Sociological Review, *38*, 242–258.

McCleary, R., & Hay, R.A., Jr. (1980). Applied time series analysis for the social science. Beverly Hills, CA: Sage.

McCleary, R., Nienstedt, B.C., & Erven, J.M. (1982). Uniform crime reports as organizational outcomes: Three time series experiments. Social Problems, *29*(4), 361–372.

McGahey, R. (1980). Dr. Ehrlich's magic bullet: Econometric theory, econometrics, and the death penalty. Crime and Delinquency, *26*(4), 485–502.

Mednick, S., Harway, M., & Finello, K. (Eds.). (1984). Handbook of longitudinal research (2 vols.) New York: Praeger.

Norpoth, H. (1986). Transfer function analysis. In W.D. Berry & M.S. Lewis-Beck (Eds.), In new tools for social scientists (pp. 241–274). Beverly Hills, CA: Sage.

Passell, P. (1975). The deterrent effect of the death penalty: A statistical test. Stanford Law Review, *28*, 61–80.

Schuessler, A. (1952). The deterrent effect of the death penalty. Annals, *54*, 284–297.

Schwarzschild, H. (1982). In opposition to death penalty legislation. In H. Bedau (Ed.), The death penalty in America (pp. 364–370). New York: Oxford University Press.

Sellin, T. (1958). The death penalty. In the Model penal code. tentative draft no. 8.

Shannon, Lyle. (1988). Criminal career continuity: Its social context. New York: Human Sciences.

Sherman, L.W., & Berk, R.A. (1984). The specific deterrent effects of arrest for domestic assault. American Sociological Review, *49*(April), 261–271.

Sprague, J. (1980, April 7–11). *Two variants of aggregation processes and problems in elementary dynamic and contextual causal formulations*. Paper delivered at the Shambaugh Fund sponsored lectures, Department of Political Science, University of Iowa, Iowa City.

Steffens, L. (1931). The autobiography of Lincoln Steffens. New York: Harcourt, Brace.

Sutherland, E. (1925). Murder and the death penalty. Journal of Criminal Law and Criminology, *15*, 522–536.

Van den Haag, E. (1982). In defense of the death penalty: A practical and moral analysis. In H. Bedau (Ed.), The death penalty in America (pp. 323–332). New York: Oxford University Press.

Wolfgang, M., Figlio, R.M., & Sellin, T. (1972). Delinquency in a birth cohort. Chicago: University of Chicago Press.

Wolfgang, M., Thornberry, T.P., & Figlio, R.M. (1987). From boy to man, from delinquency to crime: The follow-up study to delinquency in a birth cohort. Chicago: University of Chicago Press.

Yunker, J.A. (1976). Is the death penalty a deterrent to homicide? Some time series evidence. Journal of Behavioral Economics, *1*(2), 45–81.

Appendix to Chapter 9
Data

State Code	Year	Number executions	Homicide rate/100,000	Per capita income	Percent unemployed	Percent urban	Population in 1,000	Percent nonwhite males 15–29	Percent white males 15–29
10	30	8	–	–	–	67.8	–	–	–
10	31	10	–	–	–	67.7	6694	0.633	11.76
10	32	7	–	–	–	67.6	6717	0.629	11.82
10	33	11	7.80	–	–	67.5	6740	0.625	11.87
10	34	7	7.50	–	–	67.4	6763	0.621	11.92
10	35	10	7.00	–	–	67.3	6787	0.617	11.98
10	36	6	6.50	–	–	67.2	6798	0.614	12.05
10	37	1	5.60	–	–	67.1	6809	0.611	12.12
10	38	12	4.60	–	–	67.0	6837	0.606	12.17
10	39	10	5.00	–	–	66.9	6886	0.600	12.17
10	40	2	4.80	–	–	66.8	6920	0.595	12.21
10	41	4	4.81	815	–	67.1	6926	0.624	12.11
10	42	2	5.11	988	–	67.5	6950	0.652	11.99
10	43	5	4.79	1204	–	67.8	6888	0.688	12.02
10	44	2	4.33	1298	–	68.2	6834	0.724	12.04
10	45	7	2.34	1326	–	68.5	6880	0.750	11.87
10	46	2	5.91	1314	–	68.8	7484	0.717	10.84
10	47	5	5.69	1441	–	69.2	7754	0.719	10.39
10	48	7	5.35	1534	–	69.5	7949	0.727	10.07
10	49	15	5.37	1436	–	69.9	7995	0.749	09.94
10	50	4	4.08	1612	–	70.2	7978	0.777	09.89
10	51	4	4.34	1806	–	70.5	8038	0.785	09.84
10	52	4	4.32	1926	–	70.8	8524	0.754	09.31
10	53	4	4.20	2050	–	71.2	8463	0.773	09.40
10	54	4	3.80	1983	–	71.5	8720	0.763	09.14
10	55	0	3.70	2070	–	71.8	8966	0.755	08.91
10	56	4	5.40	2184	–	72.1	9118	0.755	08.79
10	57	1	4.90	2255	3.8	72.4	9281	0.754	08.65
10	58	6	3.10	2184	7.8	72.8	9491	0.749	08.48
10	59	1	3.20	2328	4.7	73.1	9612	0.751	08.40
10	60	2	3.20	2331	5.3	73.4	9739	0.753	08.31
10	61	1	3.10	2330	7.4	73.6	9876	0.785	08.50
10	62	2	3.20	2392	5.7	73.8	10038	0.813	08.66
10	63	2	3.00	2516	5.1	74.0	10173	0.843	08.85
10	64	0	3.50	2641	4.3	74.2	10080	0.891	09.23
10	65	0	3.60	2845	3.6	74.3	10201	0.921	09.42
10	66	0	4.50	3056	2.9	74.5	10330	0.950	09.60
10	67	0	5.20	3204	3.2	74.7	10414	0.982	09.81
10	68	0	5.30	3501	2.9	74.9	10516	1.011	10.01
10	69	0	6.40	3801	2.8	75.1	10563	1.046	10.25
10	70	0	6.60	3977	4.2	75.3	10664	1.074	10.44
10	71	0	7.50	4175	5.2	75.4	10724	1.100	10.54
10	72	0	7.50	4512	4.3	75.5	10722	1.131	10.70
10	73	0	7.30	5070	3.5	75.6	10743	1.160	10.83
10	74	0	8.90	5549	4.8	75.7	10737	1.192	11.00
10	75	0	8.10	5778	9.1	75.8	10735	1.224	11.16
10	76	0	7.40	6432	7.8	75.9	10690	1.260	11.36
10	77	0	7.80	7084	6.5	76.0	10696	1.291	11.52
10	78	0	6.90	7812	5.4	76.1	10749	1.316	11.62
10	79	0	8.10	8775	5.9	76.2	10731	1.349	11.80
10	80	0	8.10	9462	7.6	76.3	10798	1.372	11.88

State Code	Year	Number executions	Homicide rate/100,000	Per capita income	Percent unemployed	Percent urban	Population in 1,000	Percent nonwhite males 15–29	Percent white males 15–29
11	30	1	–	–	–	55.5	–	–	–
11	31	1	–	–	–	55.5	3257	0.451	11.79
11	32	2	–	–	–	55.4	3280	0.448	11.84
11	33	3	4.90	–	–	55.4	3304	0.445	11.89
11	34	4	7.80	–	–	55.3	3318	0.443	11.96
11	35	2	4.70	–	–	55.3	3332	0.441	12.04
11	36	2	5.50	–	–	55.3	3353	0.438	12.09
11	37	5	5.60	–	–	55.2	3374	0.436	12.14
11	38	8	5.10	–	–	55.2	3386	0.434	12.23
11	39	3	4.70	–	–	55.1	3403	0.432	12.29
11	40	0	4.00	–	–	55.1	3435	0.428	12.30
11	41	0	3.38	705	–	55.2	3458	0.442	12.20
11	42	1	3.91	879	–	55.3	3488	0.455	12.08
11	43	0	3.53	1092	–	55.4	3399	0.485	12.38
11	44	0	3.53	1144	–	55.5	3434	0.497	12.23
11	45	1	1.86	1199	–	55.5	3432	0.514	12.22
11	46	1	5.23	1168	–	55.6	3657	0.499	11.45
11	47	0	6.36	1287	–	55.7	3729	0.505	11.21
11	48	0	5.20	1389	–	55.8	3820	0.508	10.93
11	49	3	4.99	1290	–	55.9	3896	0.513	10.70
11	50	1	4.65	1520	–	56.0	3946	0.522	10.55
11	51	1	4.78	1651	–	56.6	4095	0.514	10.18
11	52	0	5.26	2081	–	57.3	4149	0.518	10.06
11	53	0	3.90	2168	–	57.9	4175	0.526	10.01
11	54	0	3.50	2155	–	58.6	4235	0.529	09.88
11	55	0	4.40	1903	–	59.2	4330	0.528	09.68
11	56	0	5.00	1977	–	59.8	4463	0.522	09.40
11	57	0	3.90	2010	4.6	60.5	4540	0.523	09.25
11	58	0	2.90	1990	8.2	61.1	4595	0.527	09.15
11	59	0	3.40	2102	5.1	61.8	4616	0.534	09.12
11	60	0	4.30	2181	5.2	62.4	4677	0.537	09.02
11	61	1	4.00	2213	6.8	62.6	4711	0.575	09.28
11	62	0	3.50	2350	4.9	62.9	4663	0.625	09.70
11	63	0	2.70	2478	4.4	63.1	4694	0.663	09.96
11	64	0	3.00	2588	4.0	63.4	4856	0.682	09.95
11	65	0	3.50	2867	3.1	63.6	4922	0.714	10.12
11	66	0	4.00	3076	2.6	63.9	4999	0.743	10.27
11	67	0	3.70	3188	3.2	64.1	5053	0.775	10.47
11	68	0	4.70	3410	3.2	64.4	5093	0.809	10.68
11	69	0	4.90	3669	2.7	64.6	5143	0.840	10.88
11	70	0	4.80	3787	4.8	64.9	5202	0.869	11.05
11	71	0	5.30	4027	5.6	65.1	5242	0.890	11.17
11	72	0	6.00	4391	4.9	65.4	5286	0.909	11.28
11	73	0	7.20	4998	3.7	65.6	5304	0.933	11.44
11	74	0	8.00	5263	5.2	65.9	5330	0.956	11.58
11	75	0	8.50	5609	8.6	66.1	5313	0.986	11.82
11	76	0	7.10	6257	6.1	66.3	5313	1.013	12.02
11	77	0	7.40	6921	5.7	66.6	5350	1.033	12.14
11	78	0	6.20	7696	5.7	66.8	5374	1.055	12.28
11	79	0	8.30	8686	6.4	67.1	5400	1.076	12.42
11	80	0	8.90	8936	7.8	67.3	5490	1.085	12.41

Illinois Code 12

State Code	Year	Number executions	Homicide rate/100,000	Per capita income	Percent unemployed	Percent urban	Population in 1,000	Percent nonwhite males 15–29	Percent white males 15–29
12	30	6	–	–	–	73.9	–	–	–
12	31	10	–	–	–	73.9	7687	0.594	12.21
12	32	5	–	–	–	73.8	7727	0.589	12.18
12	33	5	8.40	–	–	73.8	7768	0.583	12.14
12	34	8	7.80	–	–	73.8	7782	0.580	12.15
12	35	10	5.70	–	–	73.7	7797	0.576	12.15
12	36	2	5.40	–	–	73.7	7827	0.572	12.14
12	37	7	5.00	–	–	73.7	7857	0.567	12.12
12	38	4	4.10	–	–	73.7	7866	0.564	12.13
12	39	4	5.10	–	–	73.6	7890	0.560	12.12
12	40	4	5.00	–	–	73.6	7905	0.556	12.13
12	41	2	5.05	865	–	74.0	7963	0.597	11.90
12	42	4	4.86	1010	–	74.4	8015	0.638	11.69
12	43	1	3.85	1226	–	74.8	7695	0.710	12.04
12	44	2	4.68	1309	–	75.2	7711	0.755	11.87
12	45	1	2.01	1416	–	75.6	7650	0.808	11.83
12	46	0	5.58	1501	–	76.0	8147	0.802	10.97
12	47	2	4.97	1624	–	76.4	8286	0.831	10.66
12	48	0	7.02	1722	–	76.8	8488	0.853	10.28
12	49	2	6.33	1618	–	77.2	8626	0.881	09.99
12	50	3	5.26	1826	–	77.6	8753	0.909	09.72
12	51	0	4.98	1929	–	77.9	8825	0.925	09.60
12	52	4	5.79	1768	–	78.2	8913	0.940	09.46
12	53	1	5.60	1936	–	78.5	9039	0.950	09.29
12	54	0	5.40	1834	–	78.8	9193	0.957	09.09
12	55	0	5.70	2251	–	79.1	9361	0.963	08.89
12	56	0	5.90	2385	–	79.5	9363	0.985	08.84
12	57	0	6.00	2447	3.7	79.8	9559	0.987	08.62
12	58	1	4.00	2435	6.3	80.1	9832	0.981	08.34
12	59	0	4.50	2610	4.8	80.4	9974	0.988	08.19
12	60	0	4.90	2624	4.2	80.7	10113	0.995	08.04
12	61	0	4.80	2672	5.8	80.9	10258	1.053	08.20
12	62	2	5.30	2844	4.7	81.2	10098	1.144	08.61
12	63	0	5.10	2915	4.4	81.4	10182	1.207	08.81
12	64	0	5.50	3042	3.8	81.6	10580	1.232	08.74
12	65	0	5.20	3302	3.4	81.8	10693	1.288	08.91
12	66	0	6.90	3532	2.7	82.1	10836	1.339	09.05
12	67	0	7.30	3752	3.0	82.3	10947	1.394	09.22
12	68	0	8.10	3993	3.0	82.5	10995	1.455	09.43
12	69	0	8.60	4288	3.0	82.8	11039	1.516	09.65
12	70	0	9.60	4486	4.1	83.0	11128	1.571	09.82
12	71	0	9.60	4775	4.8	82.9	11191	1.615	09.90
12	72	0	8.80	5126	4.5	82.9	11244	1.661	09.99
12	73	0	10.40	5801	3.7	82.8	11176	1.725	10.18
12	74	0	11.80	6337	4.2	82.8	11131	1.785	10.35
12	75	0	10.60	6735	7.1	82.7	11197	1.828	10.43
12	76	0	10.30	7432	6.5	82.6	11193	1.882	10.56
12	77	0	9.90	7768	6.2	82.6	11228	1.930	10.66
12	78	0	9.90	8745	6.1	82.5	11243	1.981	10.78
12	79	0	10.70	9823	5.5	82.5	11229	2.036	10.93
12	80	0	10.60	1052	6.8	82.4	11427	2.053	10.87

State Code	Year	Number executions	Homicide rate/100,000	Per capita income	Percent unemployed	Percent urban	Population in 1,000	Percent nonwhite males 15–29	Percent white males 15–29
13	30	0	–	–	–	68.2	–	–	–
13	31	0	–	–	–	67.9	4798	0.543	12.76
13	32	0	–	–	–	67.7	4789	0.544	12.90
13	33	0	3.30	–	–	67.4	4780	0.546	13.03
13	34	0	2.90	–	–	67.2	4809	0.544	13.06
13	35	0	3.30	–	–	66.9	4838	0.541	13.09
13	36	0	2.90	–	–	66.7	4903	0.534	13.02
13	37	0	3.40	–	–	66.4	4968	0.528	12.95
13	38	0	2.30	–	–	66.2	5056	0.520	12.83
13	39	0	2.80	–	–	65.9	5156	0.510	12.68
13	40	0	3.20	–	–	65.7	5275	0.499	12.50
13	41	0	3.73	790	–	66.2	5404	0.543	12.20
13	42	0	3.62	970	–	66.7	5531	0.586	11.91
13	43	0	3.76	1230	–	67.2	5423	0.654	12.15
13	44	0	4.08	1307	–	67.7	5465	0.704	12.05
13	45	0	1.77	1260	–	68.2	5483	0.757	12.01
13	46	0	4.63	1266	–	68.7	5867	0.759	11.22
13	47	0	4.85	1424	–	69.2	6064	0.785	10.86
13	48	0	4.63	1493	–	69.7	6175	0.820	10.66
13	49	0	4.49	1443	–	70.2	6270	0.856	10.50
13	50	0	4.11	1682	–	70.7	6420	0.883	10.25
13	51	0	4.47	1753	–	71.0	6502	0.883	10.11
13	52	0	3.88	1941	–	71.2	6635	0.877	09.90
13	53	0	4.50	2124	–	71.5	6825	0.863	09.61
13	54	0	4.30	2017	–	71.8	7028	0.848	09.33
13	55	0	4.60	2145	–	72.0	7236	0.834	09.05
13	56	0	3.90	2158	–	72.3	7441	0.821	08.79
13	57	0	4.10	2141	6.6	72.6	7537	0.820	08.67
13	58	0	3.10	2099	13.8	72.9	7646	0.817	08.54
13	59	0	4.20	2253	8.5	73.1	7753	0.816	08.41
13	60	0	4.30	2313	6.7	73.4	7848	0.815	08.30
13	61	0	3.90	2270	10.2	73.4	7954	0.886	08.54
13	62	0	3.30	2416	6.9	73.5	8029	0.958	08.81
13	63	0	3.30	2581	5.5	73.5	8116	1.028	09.05
13	64	0	3.30	2764	4.8	73.6	8187	1.099	09.31
13	65	0	4.40	3060	3.9	73.6	8357	1.154	09.46
13	66	0	4.70	3269	3.5	73.6	8512	1.209	09.61
13	67	0	6.20	3387	4.6	73.7	8630	1.268	09.80
13	68	0	7.30	3703	4.3	73.7	8696	1.333	10.05
13	69	0	8.30	3987	4.0	73.8	8781	1.394	10.27
13	70	0	9.40	4133	7.0	73.8	8890	1.450	10.45
13	71	0	10.50	4430	8.2	73.5	8961	1.479	10.56
13	72	0	11.00	4817	8.3	73.2	9013	1.511	10.69
13	73	0	12.10	5540	6.9	72.9	9061	1.544	10.82
13	74	0	13.00	5928	7.4	72.6	9098	1.578	10.96
13	75	0	11.90	5991	12.5	72.3	9111	1.616	11.13
13	76	0	11.10	6994	9.4	72.0	9113	1.655	11.31
13	77	0	9.30	7619	8.2	71.7	9148	1.689	11.45
13	78	0	10.60	8442	6.9	71.4	9189	1.721	11.58
13	79	0	9.10	9269	7.8	71.1	9207	1.758	11.74
13	80	0	10.20	9951	10.6	70.8	9262	1.787	11.86

State Code	Year	Number executions	Homicide rate/100,000	Per capita income	Percent unemployed	Percent urban	Population in 1,000	Percent nonwhite males 15–29	Percent white males 15–29
14	30	0	–	–	–	52.9	–	–	–
14	31	0	–	–	–	53.0	2990	0.058	12.52
14	32	0	–	–	–	53.0	3015	0.062	12.50
14	33	0	1.10	–	–	53.1	3040	0.067	12.48
14	34	0	1.10	–	–	53.1	3055	0.071	12.50
14	35	0	0.90	–	–	53.2	3070	0.076	12.52
14	36	0	1.20	–	–	53.3	3079	0.081	12.57
14	37	0	1.50	–	–	53.3	3088	0.085	12.61
14	38	0	1.40	–	–	53.4	3098	0.090	12.65
14	39	0	1.10	–	–	53.4	3121	0.094	12.64
14	40	0	1.30	–	–	53.5	3144	0.098	12.62
14	41	0	1.32	649	–	53.9	3143	0.107	12.51
14	42	0	1.11	808	–	54.4	3121	0.116	12.48
14	43	0	1.10	1003	–	54.8	3011	0.129	12.81
14	44	0	0.69	1084	–	55.3	2978	0.140	12.83
14	45	0	0.44	1184	–	55.7	2946	0.150	12.85
14	46	0	1.00	1208	–	56.1	3137	0.150	11.95
14	47	0	1.67	1337	–	56.6	3219	0.154	11.53
14	48	0	1.11	1400	–	57.0	3261	0.160	11.27
14	49	0	1.23	1329	–	57.5	3326	0.165	10.93
14	50	0	0.84	1467	–	57.9	3449	0.167	10.44
14	51	0	1.33	1624	–	58.5	3416	0.181	10.51
14	52	0	1.99	1726	–	59.1	3483	0.189	10.28
14	53	0	1.10	1762	–	59.7	3516	0.199	10.15
14	54	0	1.10	1706	–	60.3	3628	0.204	09.81
14	55	0	1.20	1786	–	60.8	3694	0.212	09.60
14	56	0	1.30	1872	–	61.4	3740	0.220	09.46
14	57	0	1.70	1920	3.0	62.0	3802	0.228	09.28
14	58	0	1.00	1936	5.1	62.6	3863	0.235	09.10
14	59	0	1.10	2116	3.2	63.2	3915	0.242	08.95
14	60	0	1.30	2156	3.9	63.8	3964	0.249	08.82
14	61	0	1.60	2194	5.0	64.0	4022	0.273	09.04
14	62	0	0.90	2283	4.1	64.2	4019	0.300	09.40
14	63	0	1.70	2364	4.1	64.4	4061	0.323	09.65
14	64	0	1.50	2507	3.9	64.6	4165	0.341	09.75
14	65	0	1.50	2740	3.4	64.8	4232	0.361	09.92
14	66	0	1.90	2973	3.2	65.1	4274	0.383	10.16
14	67	0	1.90	3152	3.6	65.3	4303	0.405	10.42
14	68	0	2.20	3371	3.4	65.5	4345	0.426	10.64
14	69	0	2.10	3512	3.3	65.7	4378	0.447	10.88
14	70	0	2.00	3712	4.6	65.9	4429	0.467	11.07
14	71	0	2.80	3912	5.2	66.0	4471	0.478	11.26
14	72	0	2.80	4207	5.0	66.1	4526	0.488	11.41
14	73	0	2.60	4781	4.5	66.2	4539	0.502	11.67
14	74	0	3.00	5210	4.5	66.3	4566	0.514	11.88
14	75	0	3.30	5616	6.9	66.3	4589	0.527	12.10
14	76	0	3.00	6293	5.6	66.4	4610	0.540	12.33
14	77	0	2.80	6890	4.9	66.5	4644	0.551	12.52
14	78	0	2.50	7597	5.1	66.6	4679	0.562	12.70
14	79	0	3.40	8419	4.5	66.7	4720	0.572	12.87
14	80	0	2.90	9348	5.8	66.8	4706	0.589	13.18

State Code	Year	Number executions	Homicide rate/100,000	Per capita income	Percent unemployed	Percent urban	Population in 1,000	Percent nonwhite males 15–29	Percent white males 15–29
15	30	0	–	–	–	49.0	–	–	–
15	31	0	–	–	–	49.1	2614	0.044	12.45
15	32	0	–	–	–	49.2	2643	0.052	12.46
15	33	0	2.10	–	–	49.2	2673	0.059	12.47
15	34	0	3.40	–	–	49.3	2695	0.066	12.52
15	35	0	1.60	–	–	49.4	2717	0.073	12.56
15	36	0	1.40	–	–	49.5	2731	0.080	12.64
15	37	0	1.60	–	–	49.6	2746	0.087	12.72
15	38	0	1.10	–	–	49.6	2753	0.094	12.83
15	39	0	1.60	–	–	49.7	2771	0.100	12.90
15	40	0	1.10	–	–	49.8	2797	0.107	12.92
15	41	0	1.65	589	–	50.3	2758	0.110	12.92
15	42	0	1.12	751	–	50.7	2664	0.116	13.20
15	43	0	1.41	916	–	51.2	2578	0.123	13.45
15	44	0	1.26	955	–	51.7	2521	0.128	13.56
15	45	0	0.53	1066	–	52.1	2534	0.129	13.29
15	46	0	1.41	1102	–	52.6	2713	0.123	12.24
15	47	0	1.32	1195	–	53.1	2789	0.122	11.73
15	48	0	1.88	1340	–	53.6	2850	0.121	11.30
15	49	0	0.82	1227	–	54.0	2916	0.120	10.88
15	50	0	1.64	1397	–	54.5	2996	0.119	10.43
15	51	0	0.80	1478	–	55.3	3012	0.121	10.34
15	52	0	1.06	1558	–	56.0	3043	0.123	10.21
15	53	0	1.10	1624	–	56.8	3073	0.125	10.09
15	54	0	0.50	1644	–	57.6	3132	0.125	09.87
15	55	0	1.10	1710	–	58.3	3174	0.126	09.72
15	56	0	1.10	1767	–	59.1	3260	0.126	09.44
15	57	0	1.00	1850	4.5	59.9	3314	0.126	09.26
15	58	0	0.90	1916	7.0	60.7	3334	0.128	09.18
15	59	0	1.00	1962	5.3	61.4	3378	0.129	09.04
15	60	0	1.20	2066	4.6	62.2	3426	0.130	08.89
15	61	0	1.00	2149	5.7	62.6	3470	0.142	09.15
15	62	0	0.90	2236	4.9	63.0	3461	0.156	09.55
15	63	0	1.20	2370	4.8	63.5	3500	0.167	09.81
15	64	0	1.40	2432	4.0	63.9	3558	0.178	10.01
15	65	0	1.40	2666	4.0	64.3	3592	0.189	10.28
15	66	0	2.20	2904	3.0	64.7	3617	0.200	10.56
15	67	0	1.60	3079	3.0	65.1	3659	0.211	10.79
15	68	0	2.20	3326	3.2	65.6	3703	0.221	11.01
15	69	0	1.90	3579	2.9	66.0	3758	0.230	11.20
15	70	0	2.00	3855	4.4	66.4	3815	0.239	11.37
15	71	0	2.40	4032	5.9	66.5	3854	0.236	11.57
15	72	0	2.40	4332	5.6	66.6	3877	0.234	11.82
15	73	0	2.70	5144	4.7	66.7	3890	0.233	12.10
15	74	0	3.00	5450	4.3	66.8	3917	0.231	12.33
15	75	0	3.30	5779	5.9	66.8	3921	0.230	12.63
15	76	0	2.30	6153	5.9	66.9	3954	0.227	12.83
15	77	0	2.70	7129	5.1	67.0	3980	0.225	13.06
15	78	0	2.00	7847	3.8	67.1	4008	0.223	13.28
15	79	0	2.30	8760	4.2	67.2	4060	0.220	13.41
15	80	0	2.60	9724	4.3	67.3	4076	0.218	13.66

Iowa Code 16

State Code	Year	Number executions	Homicide rate/100,000	Per capita income	Percent unemployed	Percent urban	Population in 1,000	Percent nonwhite males 15–29	Percent white males 15–29
16	30	0	–	–	–	39.6	–	–	–
16	31	1	–	–	–	39.9	2482	0.082	12.13
16	32	0	–	–	–	40.2	2488	0.082	12.16
16	33	0	2.90	–	–	40.5	2495	0.082	12.20
16	34	0	2.80	–	–	40.8	2509	0.082	12.20
16	35	3	2.80	–	–	41.1	2524	0.081	12.20
16	36	0	1.20	–	–	41.5	2511	0.082	12.33
16	37	0	2.40	–	–	41.8	2498	0.083	12.46
16	38	4	1.70	–	–	42.1	2494	0.083	12.55
16	39	0	1.60	–	–	42.4	2520	0.082	12.49
16	40	1	1.00	–	–	42.7	2540	0.082	12.46
16	41	1	1.52	609	–	43.2	2505	0.086	12.48
16	42	0	1.28	812	–	43.7	2427	0.091	12.73
16	43	0	1.11	983	–	44.2	2319	0.098	13.16
16	44	1	1.76	966	–	44.7	2246	0.105	13.41
16	45	1	0.73	1105	–	45.2	2225	0.019	13.37
16	46	2	3.73	1150	–	45.7	2384	0.104	12.32
16	47	0	1.99	1144	–	46.2	2429	0.105	11.94
16	48	0	1.44	1507	–	46.7	2487	0.105	11.51
16	49	1	1.05	1292	–	47.2	2551	0.105	11.07
16	50	0	1.30	1449	–	47.7	2627	0.105	10.61
16	51	0	1.53	1522	–	48.2	2619	0.106	10.51
16	52	1	1.70	1593	–	48.8	2645	0.105	10.29
16	53	0	1.10	1539	–	49.3	2663	0.105	10.09
16	54	0	1.00	1667	–	49.8	2665	0.105	09.96
16	55	0	1.10	1571	–	50.3	2692	0.105	09.74
16	56	0	0.90	1641	–	50.9	2718	0.104	09.53
16	57	0	1.20	1806	2.8	51.4	2742	0.104	09.32
16	58	0	1.50	1863	3.2	51.9	2731	0.105	09.24
16	59	0	1.40	1953	2.6	52.5	2745	0.104	09.08
16	60	0	0.60	2017	3.0	53.0	2761	0.104	08.90
16	61	0	1.30	2124	3.8	53.4	2779	0.113	09.08
16	62	2	1.10	2189	3.2	53.8	2774	0.123	09.33
16	63	0	1.30	2304	2.9	54.3	2780	0.133	09.54
16	64	0	1.30	2356	2.6	54.7	2746	0.144	09.89
16	65	0	1.30	2727	2.3	55.1	2742	0.154	10.14
16	66	0	1.60	2992	2.0	55.5	2762	0.163	10.30
16	67	0	1.50	3087	2.4	55.9	2793	0.171	10.42
16	68	0	1.70	3264	2.4	56.4	2803	0.180	10.61
16	69	0	1.40	3519	2.7	56.8	2805	0.189	10.83
16	70	0	1.90	3750	3.5	57.2	2832	0.197	10.96
16	71	0	1.80	3877	4.0	57.7	2859	0.200	11.12
16	72	0	1.70	4318	3.5	58.2	2884	0.203	11.29
16	73	0	2.20	5347	2.9	58.8	2863	0.210	11.63
16	74	0	1.90	5302	2.2	59.3	2855	0.216	11.93
16	75	0	2.50	5894	4.3	59.8	2861	0.221	12.17
16	76	0	2.30	6439	4.0	60.3	2874	0.225	12.38
16	77	0	2.30	6878	4.0	60.8	2888	0.229	12.59
16	78	0	2.60	7873	4.0	61.4	2896	0.233	12.81
16	79	0	2.20	8589	4.1	61.9	2902	0.238	13.05
16	80	0	2.20	9358	4.6	62.4	2914	0.242	13.26

State Code	Year	Number executions	Homicide rate/100,000	Per capita income	Percent unemployed	Percent urban	Population in 1,000	Percent nonwhite males 15–29	Percent white males 15–29
17	30	5	–	–	–	51.2	–	–	–
17	31	0	–	–	–	51.3	3711	0.760	11.43
17	32	3	–	–	–	51.3	3742	0.752	11.37
17	33	6	13.10	–	–	51.4	3773	0.745	11.30
17	34	2	10.20	–	–	51.4	3785	0.741	11.29
17	35	5	6.50	–	–	51.5	3798	0.737	11.27
17	36	1	8.50	–	–	51.6	3796	0.735	11.30
17	37	4	7.30	–	–	51.6	3794	0.734	11.34
17	38	8	6.30	–	–	51.7	3781	0.735	11.40
17	39	2	6.90	–	–	51.7	3783	0.733	11.42
17	40	2	6.50	–	–	51.8	3788	0.731	11.43
17	41	1	6.39	621	–	52.8	3805	0.736	11.24
17	42	1	6.25	758	–	53.7	3800	0.745	11.11
17	43	0	5.79	896	–	54.7	3750	0.763	11.12
17	44	2	5.52	991	–	55.7	3535	0.818	11.65
17	45	2	2.49	1101	–	56.6	3481	0.839	11.68
17	46	2	9.26	1134	–	57.6	3713	0.795	10.80
17	47	3	8.28	1197	–	58.6	3807	0.783	10.40
17	48	0	7.96	1339	–	59.6	3832	0.786	10.19
17	49	2	7.09	1286	–	60.5	3907	0.779	09.86
17	50	1	7.23	1446	–	61.5	3956	0.777	09.60
17	51	1	6.71	1519	–	62.0	4047	0.770	09.35
17	52	1	8.01	1671	–	62.5	3994	0.791	09.43
17	53	2	7.50	1732	–	63.0	4063	0.788	09.23
17	54	0	6.80	1747	–	63.5	4076	0.796	09.16
17	55	1	7.20	1805	–	64.0	4128	0.797	09.01
17	56	0	7.80	1905	–	64.6	4244	0.785	08.72
17	57	1	7.30	1940	4.1	65.1	4259	0.792	08.65
17	58	0	5.00	2037	5.6	65.6	4240	0.806	08.65
17	59	0	5.80	2145	4.2	66.1	4286	0.807	08.52
17	60	0	4.40	2196	4.6	66.6	4331	0.809	08.40
17	61	0	5.10	2254	6.0	66.9	4378	0.851	08.56
17	62	0	5.50	2384	5.3	67.3	4316	0.915	08.94
17	63	1	5.20	2354	4.8	67.6	4328	0.964	09.17
17	64	2	5.40	2446	4.2	68.0	4442	0.990	09.18
17	65	1	6.70	2667	3.7	68.3	4467	1.034	09.38
17	66	0	5.40	2817	3.3	68.7	4523	1.071	09.51
17	67	0	7.30	3003	3.4	69.0	4539	1.116	09.72
17	68	0	8.80	3268	3.4	69.4	4568	1.158	09.90
17	69	0	10.40	3467	3.2	69.7	4640	1.188	09.98
17	70	0	10.70	3713	4.6	70.1	4688	1.223	10.12
17	71	0	8.90	3940	5.3	69.8	4734	1.246	10.21
17	72	0	8.30	4206	4.9	69.5	4747	1.277	10.38
17	73	0	9.00	4831	4.1	69.2	4768	1.305	10.53
17	74	0	9.80	5056	4.6	68.9	4777	1.336	10.71
17	75	0	10.60	5476	6.9	68.6	4767	1.373	10.93
17	76	0	9.30	6005	6.2	68.4	4787	1.401	11.07
17	77	0	9.60	6654	5.9	68.1	4822	1.425	11.19
17	78	0	10.40	7342	5.0	67.8	4860	1.447	11.29
17	79	0	11.20	8132	4.5	67.5	4867	1.478	11.47
17	80	0	11.10	8982	6.0	67.2	4917	1.496	11.54

10
Assessing the Potential of Secondary Data Analysis: A New Look at the Gluecks' *Unraveling Juvenile Delinquency* Data[1]

JOHN H. LAUB, ROBERT J. SAMPSON, and KENNA KIGER

Introduction

Until recently, one of the most neglected areas in research methodology was the secondary analysis of existing data. Attention to the potential strengths and weaknesses of secondary data analysis is especially important at this time in light of recent calls in the field of criminology for conducting more longitudinal research (see Farrington, Ohlin, & Wilson, 1986). For example, the Program on Human Development and Criminal Behavior (1989) is currently designing a series of prospective longitudinal studies. In addition to these primary data collection efforts, the Program encourages the secondary analysis of existing longitudinal data sets. Secondary analysis of existing data sets may well provide a potential gold mine as a method of research.

This chapter examines various issues surrounding the secondary analysis of existing data. First, we briefly outline some of the strengths and weaknesses of secondary data analysis as a research method. Then, to illustrate this research strategy in action, we discuss our current work, which involves coding, recoding, computerizing, and reanalyzing a classic study on the causes of crime and juvenile delinquency. The data we refer to were collected by Sheldon and Eleanor Glueck during the period 1940 to 1965 (see Glueck & Glueck, 1950, 1968). Specifically, we examine several issues regarding the validity of the Glueck data. We believe that our research represents a creative use of archival data and suggests the large potential of this method for future criminological research.

Secondary Data Analysis

Once a data source has been selected for secondary analysis, the quality of the data must be evaluated. Researchers may have access to the actual raw data that were collected (secondary data) and/or the previously published summaries of these data (secondary sources) (Stewart, 1984). If one is fortunate enough to gain access to both sources of information, these can be jointly used in a cross validation of both the raw data and published figures.

The advantages and disadvantages of secondary data analysis have been systematically examined by only a few researchers (see Hyman, 1972; Kiecolt & Nathan, 1985; Stewart, 1984). One advantage of using secondary data is that the time and costs of obtaining, preparing, and analyzing archival data are usually less compared with the cost and time involved in the initiation of a new data collection effort. Although acquiring and analyzing an existing data set (raw data or machine-readable data) will take time, patience, and effort, the overall time/resource commitment will undoubtedly be less than the original data collection and analysis. This is especially true in the secondary analysis of existing longitudinal data sets (see Colby & Phelps, 1990).

Secondary data analysis can also be used for comparative purposes with newly collected data or combined with other primary data for an assessment of various trends (Kiecolt & Nathan, 1985; Stewart, 1984). For instance, data from earlier studies of crime may provide a useful benchmark of comparison in two ways. First, secondary data analysis may identify findings that are consistent over time and, as a result, may increase overall confidence in the findings. Second, secondary analysis of data may provide crucial information on findings that are different from contemporary studies and help to identify findings that seem to be specific to a particular cohort and/or period.

Of course, secondary analysis of existing data sets is not problem free. A major disadvantage is that the original data collection may not be suitable to address the important theoretical, research, or policy questions facing the field. For instance, the existing data may not focus on the appropriate unit of analysis (Stewart, 1984). If the data collected are in an aggregate form, while the present research question concerns individual-level occurrences, then clearly, secondary data analysis may not be suited to the research question at hand. As noted by Stewart (1984, p. 24) "the degree of precision, the types of categories used, and the method by which the data are collected are often dictated by the intent of the study." The original intent of the researchers then may confound interpretations derived from a secondary data analysis. The choice of the data source must be dictated by the research question. One must avoid what Kiecolt and Nathan (1985, p. 14) refer to as the "data set in search of analysis" approach. Researchers using secondary analysis must be even more sensitive to this concern given their lack of control over the original data collection process.

In addition to this major disadvantage, there are several key concerns regarding the validity of the secondary data. One of the most fundamental concerns in criminological research is the validity of the phenomenon we seek to explain. Specifically, are our measures actually capturing the theoretical construct of interest? The validity of a particular set of data may be suspect due to errors in the original data collection and compilation that may have occurred during the interviewing, coding, and/or keypunching processes. More important, validity may also be "of concern to the extent that survey items [used] are imprecise measures of the concepts a secondary analyst has in mind, or that variables [selected] have been poorly operationalized" (Kiecolt & Nathan, 1985, p. 14). Again, to the extent that one has access to secondary data rather than secondary sources, some of these potential stumbling blocks can be addressed through rigorous analysis of the raw data.

Overall, there are a number of different data sets available for secondary data analysis. Stewart (1984) provides a list of both governmental (e.g., Census data, the National Crime Survey) and nongovernmental (e.g., the Gallup polls) sources. In addition, Boruch and Pearson (1988) present a description of a series of national longitudinal surveys in the United States that are available for secondary analysis (e.g., the High School and Beyond Survey). There also exist numerous data archives in the United States; some, like the Inter-University Consortium for Political and Social Research at the University of Michigan, provide machine-readable social science data, and others, like the Henry A. Murray Research Center of Radcliffe College, collect and catalogue raw data files for reanalysis (Colby & Phelps, 1990; see, also, Kiecolt & Nathan, 1985, which contains a complete listing of data archives in the United States and abroad). Also, the National Institute of Justice provides a listing of data sets from the various projects funded by the Institute as a way of encouraging secondary data analysis and fostering continued use of collected data beyond the life of the original project (see Wiersema, Loftin, & Huang, 1988).

The Glueck Data

As indicated above, a key question in assessing the usefulness of secondary data is the extent to which these existing sources can address the current research questions facing the field. A recent report by a National Academy of Sciences (NAS) panel on criminal careers strongly recommended that prospective longitudinal studies be implemented that would examine: (a) the developmental experiences engendering compliant behavior, (b) behavioral precursors of subsequent criminality, (c) influence on subsequent behavior of interactions with the juvenile and criminal justice systems, and (d) factors associated with career termination (Blumstein, Cohen, Roth, & Visher, 1986, p. 200). In our project (Laub & Sampson, 1987), we proposed a research strategy that would address the concerns of the NAS report but with existing data. Our research entails a reanalysis of a major prospective data base that contains nearly all of the data elements and design characteristics noted by the NAS panel as ideal (Blumstein et al., 1986). The data we are currently reanalyzing are drawn from the classic study of juvenile delinquency by Sheldon and Eleanor Glueck—*Unraveling Juvenile*

Delinquency (*UJD*). Published in 1950, *UJD* was a cross-sectional study of 500 official delinquents matched with 500 nondelinquents on the basis of low-income residence, age, race/ethnicity, and IQ (see Glueck & Glueck, 1950). After publication of this work, for over a 15-year period, the Gluecks conducted an extensive follow-up of all delinquents and nondelinquents in the original *UJD* study, resulting in a longitudinal data set covering the life events of all the boys in the sample up to age 32 (see Glueck & Glueck, 1968). These data offer a potentially rich source of information on the causes and correlates of crime and delinquency over the life course.

Overall, Sheldon and Eleanor Glueck adopted an eclectic approach to the study of the causal processes involved in human motivation and behavior. Not only did they engage in a multidisciplinary approach but they also believed that a meaningful integration of various disciplines such as sociology, economics, psychology, and biology would be best achieved through the integration of data from several levels and sources of inquiry (Glueck & Glueck, 1950).

The Gluecks' research team collected data on the 500 delinquent and 500 nondelinquent male subjects over a 25-year period. The delinquent sample contained persistent delinquents recently committed to two correctional schools—the Lyman School for Boys, located in Westboro, Massachusetts, and the Industrial School for Boys in Shirley, Massachusetts (Glueck & Glueck, 1950, p. 27). The nondelinquent sample was drawn from the public schools in the city of Boston. Their sampling procedure was designed to maximize differences in delinquency—an objective that by all accounts succeeded (Glueck & Glueck, 1950, pp. 27–29).

In addition to the features discussed above, one unique aspect of the study was that the Gluecks utilized a matched sample research design. Specifically, all of the delinquent boys were matched on a case by case basis with the nondelinquent boys on four characteristics: age, general intelligence, race/ethnicity, and residence in low-socioeconomic-status neighborhoods—all classic criminological variables thought to influence both delinquency and official reaction (see Sampson, 1986). Both the delinquents and nondelinquents were white males who grew up in lower class neighborhoods of central Boston. These neighborhoods were regions of poverty, economic dependency, and physical deterioration and were usually adjacent to areas of industry and commerce—what Shaw and McKay (1942) would have termed socially disorganized neighborhoods (Glueck & Glueck, 1950, p. 29). Hence, all boys grew up in similar high-risk environments with respect to poverty and exposure to delinquency and antisocial conduct (Laub & Sampson, 1987).

The average age of the delinquent boys at the time this study began was 14 years 8 months, and the average age for the nondelinquents was 14 years 6 months. The age range for all of the boys at the initiation of the study was 9 to 17 years. As for ethnicity, 25% of both groups were of English background; another 25% were Italian; 20% were Irish; less than 10% were old American, Slavic, or French; and the remaining were Near Eastern, Spanish, Scandinavian, German, or Jewish. Finally, as measured by the Wechsler-Bellevue test, the delinquents had an average IQ of 92 and the nondelinquents, 94.

Data for each subject were collected in three waves: data at first interview (average age 14), at the subject's 25th birthday, and at the subject's 32nd birthday. A wealth of information on social, psychological, biological, developmental, family, SES/employment, school performance, and life events were collected on the delinquents and controls in the period 1939 to 1948. For example, some of the key items regarding family life include parental criminality and alcohol use, parental education and intelligence, family mobility, economic status, family structure (e.g., divorce/ separation), and patterns of discipline and supervision by parents. Theoretically relevant items for school/employment include onset and nature of school misconduct, educational attainment, employment history, work habits, and educational/occupational ambitions. Among others, there are also numerous indicators of recreational and leisure-time activities, peer relationships and influence, church attendance, and personality profiles gleaned from psychiatric interviews (Laub & Sampson, 1987). These data were collected by examining a variety of official sources including criminal justice agencies (e.g., police, court, and correction), as well as school records and social welfare and mental health records.

The authors are currently restoring, coding, computerizing, and reanalyzing the Glueck longitudinal data files. One unexpected discovery was the existence of boxes of computer cards that contained data from the Glueck study. Although the cards were quite old and in a multiple punch format (most modern card readers cannot read cards containing multiple punch codes), we were able to read them and re-create the basic data as derived from the Gluecks' coding scheme. A considerable amount of time was spent validating these coded data. Our validation scheme contained a number of steps. First, frequencies were checked (whenever possible) for the coded variables with the published secondary sources of data. Also, the logic and substance of each variable were examined. In addition, we selected a 10% random sample of cases from the raw data files and for each case checked the values generated by the computer card to the values for those variables found in the raw data files. Overall, we found an extremely high level of agreement between the raw data and the coded data (generally 98% or higher).

In addition, and unknown to most criminologists, the Gluecks collected data regarding delinquent acts and other forms of misbehavior from parents, teachers, and the subjects themselves. This serves as an example of the serendipity that can result when an investigator has access to raw records from the original study. Moreover, we believe the combination of self-, parental, and teacher reports plus official records provides an excellent opportunity to develop valid measures of delinquent and antisocial conduct for our substantive analysis, as well as assisting us in validating the Glueck data overall. Thus, in addition to the previously mentioned technical validation strategy, we examine the construct and predictive validity of the Glueck data by comparing the self-, parent-, teacher-, and officially reported indicators of the misbehaviors of the boys. As noted by Kiecolt and Nathan (1985), when data can be presented by multiple independent sources, confidence in the validity of the data is increased if these sources arrive at similar conclusions.

Self-Reported Data

During Wave 1 of the Gluecks' data collection, psychiatric interviews were conducted with each of the boys in the study. These interviews dealt with personality and behavioral characteristics and were intended to supplement information that had been derived from the extensive social investigation of the home environment as well as other investigations (e.g., Rorschach tests). In addition to asking questions concerning the boy's various activities, such as club memberships, play places, academic/vocational ambitions, and church attendance, the psychiatrist also questioned the boys with respect to their misbehaviors.[2] As noted by the Gluecks (1950), the initial hesitancy on the part of the boys in discussing their misbehaviors (particularly those that had not yet come to the attention of the police) seemed to dissipate as the boys realized the confidential nature of the study (p. 61).

The interviews of the boys regarding their own misbehavior were initiated in 1939. It is interesting to note that virtually all existing literature reviews of the early self-report studies cite Short and Nye (1957, 1958) as the first definitive self-report study and Porterfield (1946) and Wallerstein and Wyle (1947) as the earliest but crude version of this method (see Hindelang, Hirschi, & Weis, 1981; O'Brien, 1985; Weis, 1986). As with many of the Gluecks' contributions to criminology, their early use of the self-report method as well as the breadth of their use of this method has been overshadowed by the concern for their lack of a singularly sociological focus as well as by perceived methodological inadequacies in their research (Laub & Sampson, 1988).

Parent-Reported Data

The Gluecks' research team conducted interviews with parents (usually mothers) in the home of each boy in the study in order to obtain information about the home atmosphere, family finances, and family background and geneology, as well as the boy's developmental health history and his leisure-time habits. Within the context of this interview, there were also questions asked about the boy's misbehaviors. These home interviews were also supplemented by information from the records of various social agencies (Glueck & Glueck, 1950, p. 160).

Teacher-Reported Data

In addition to obtaining the written school records for each boy in the study, which contained information on their grades and truancies and other possible misbehaviors, the Gluecks' investigator also interviewed the boy's most recent teacher. The focus of the interview was to "determine how the delinquents and nondelinquents behaved in school during their most recent full year" (Glueck & Glueck, 1950, p. 149). Inquiries were made with respect to the boy's adjustment to his schoolmates and participation in curricular and extracurricular activities as well as his misbehavior in school (Glueck & Glueck 1950, p. 51). Teachers were provided with a list of behavioral characteristics relating to conduct at school and were asked to record which characteristics described the subject (Glueck & Glueck, 1950, p. 149).

Official Data

Criminal history data for each boy were gathered from extensive record checks of police, court, and correctional files and cover the period from first arrest to age 32. Some of the information available includes: the number of arrests, the number of convictions, correctional experiences over time, the type of dispositions, offense-specific arrest sequences, and the length of time of all correctional experiences as well as the number of probation/parole revocations (see Glueck & Glueck, 1950; 1968).

In sum, the Gluecks collected information from a variety of different sources on a wide range of delinquent and other antisocial behaviors. Moreover, the Glueck data come very close to the suggestion by Farrington et al. (1986, pp. 18–19) that "data about crime should include arrest reports, self-reports, and (to the extent possible) the reports of peers, parents and teachers. Moreover, these reports should focus not only on crime and delinquency, but other measures of misconduct like truancy, drug and alcohol use, problems at school, etc." (see, also, Weis, 1986). The range of data collection by the Gluecks is truly impressive, and the restored Glueck data provide a potentially rich secondary data source for reanalysis. At the same time, the multiple sources of information on crime and other misbehaviors allow for extensive analysis of the validity of the basic Glueck data. More precisely, both the construct and predictive validity of the Glueck data can be examined through a comparison of the multiple sources of unofficial and official data collected across the similar domains of behavior.

Validity

Cook and Campbell (1979, p. 38) state that construct validity is established when an empirical variable is a valid measure of the underlying theoretical notions under discussion. The ideal situation in establishing construct validity is to find "convergence across different measures" and "divergence between measures . . . of related but conceptually distinct 'things'" (Cook & Campbell, 1979, p. 61). In the field of criminology, this test of validity typically entails a comparison of an official data source with an unofficial data source like self-report data. Because the data collection by the Gluecks focused on a variety of different reporters (e.g., official, semi-official, and self-report), we can initially assess the extent of construct validity at a number of different levels.

Construct validity in our case would be established to the extent that our multiple measures of delinquent and antisocial behavior are consistently interrelated. Boruch and Pearson (1988) outlined the criteria for assessing the usefulness and quality of existing longitudinal and cross-sectional surveys and suggested that analysis should be done concerning the extent to which different measures of the same concept yield similar results. Although most unofficial delinquency such as self-reports are validated by a comparison to official records, external validation criteria can also include criteria other than official records, such as teacher and parental reports of delinquent and/or deviant behavior. With the Glueck data then, we can potentially establish construct validity not only *across* settings such as official record versus self-report but also *within* unofficial sources, through a comparison of parental and teacher reports of juvenile misconduct. Farrington (1988) has noted that an analysis of multiple measures of behavior reduces the likelihood that relationships that are found among constructs are due to measurement bias.

On the other hand, predictive validity concerns a future criterion and assesses whether or not it is correlated with our relevant measures. This form of validation measures our ability to predict future events. With the Glueck data, we can use the data collected at Time 1 to predict events at Time 2 and Time 3. For instance, do self-reports collected at Time 1 predict official criminality at Time 2? At Time 3?

Construct Validity

Table 10.1 displays the complete list of delinquent conduct and other antisocial behavior reported by the three types of respondents. As is evident, the offenses range from the less serious, although important, items (e.g., smoking, drinking) to the more serious items (e.g., stealing, arson). In addition to covering many types of misconduct across varying levels of seriousness, the domain of behavior studied is in many cases similar for each reporter.

We created various scales containing items that were collected across all three groups of reporters. This allowed us to examine the degree of overlap among the reporters and address the issue of construct validity. Table 10.2 presents the correlations among parent, teacher, and self-reported indicators across several types of crime. Overall, the degree of overlap is substan-

TABLE 10.1. Self-reported, parent-reported, and teacher-reported items in *Unraveling Juvenile Delinquency** coded data.

Self-reported	Parent reported	Teacher reported
Smoking	Smoking	Smoking
Drinking	Drinking	Untruthfulness
Running away	Running away	Stubbornness
Bunking out	Bunking out	Profanity
Gambling	Gambling	Quarrelsomeness
Late hours	Late hours	Cheating
Truancy	Truancy	Truancy
Stealing rides	Stealing rides	Disobedience
Sneaking admissions	Sneaking admissions	Impudence
Begging	Begging	Disorderliness
Destructive mischief	Destructive mischief	Destroys school
Auto stealing	Auto-stealing	materials
Impulsive stealing(m)	Impulsive stealing(m)	Stealing
Impulsive stealing(s)	Impulsive stealing(s)	Cruelty, bullying
Planful stealing(t)	Planful stealing(t)	Tantrums
Planful stealing(fbg)	Planful stealing(fbg)	Defiance
Arson	Arson	
	Lying	
	Stubbornness	
	Vile language	
	Pugnacity	
	Tantrums	

Note. (m) = minor
   (s) = serious
   (t) = trivial
   (fbg) = for big gain
* S. and E. Glueck (1950). New York: Commonwealth Fund.

TABLE 10.2. Relationships among self-, parent-, and teacher-reported indicators of delinquency, by type of crime/misconduct ($N = 1,000$)[a].

A. Smoking/drinking		Parent	Teacher
	Self	.75*	.51*
	Parent	—	.40*
B. Truancy		Parent	Teacher
	Self	.93*	.95*
	Parent	—	.91*
C. Vandalism		Parent	Teacher
	Self	.33*	.49*
	Parent	—	.23
D. Theft		Parent	Teacher
	Self	.72*	.40*
	Parent	—	.68*

[a] Cell entries are gamma coefficients.
* $p < .01$

tial and in the expected direction. For instance, the cross-setting validity of misbehaviors that inherently involve both parties (such as truancy) shows the strongest relationships. At the same time, there appears to be some divergence between items that represent different concepts, like teacher reports of behavior at school and parental reports of behavior at home or in the neighborhood. In all cases (except the correlation between parent- and teacher-reported vandalism), these coefficients are significant at the .01 level.

We also created a total unofficial measure of delinquency, which is a composite of all self-, parent, and teacher reports, as well as a summary measure of the unofficial reports for each particular offense (e.g., truancy as reported by parents, teachers, and self). Scales were also constructed that reflected the total amount of delinquency (all types) within a setting and are designated as "self-report total," "parent-report total," and "teacher-report total." The measure "official delinquency" is operationalized as the presence of an official (police) record for the juvenile.

In establishing the validity of our measures across settings, we can compare both unofficial and official reports for the same individuals. Again, due to the rich nature of the Glueck data, we can compare these two sources not only in general but also by specific crime types. In Table 10.3A, we display the correlations between the specific types of unofficial delinquency summary measures with a total composite measure of unofficial and official delinquency. All of the correlations between our crime-specific unofficial summary measures and our totals of unofficial and official delinquency are significant, thus illustrating a high degree of concurrent validity among the Glueck measures. Truancy has the highest correlation with both official and unofficial total delinquency, while the summary variable reflecting auto-theft has the lowest concurrent validity for both official and unofficial delinquency.[3] These results are not surprising, as we would expect the cross-setting agreement to be greater for those offenses inherently involving both parties. It is less likely that auto-theft would come to the attention of school officials compared with an offense like truancy or theft.

Table 10.3B displays the cross-setting convergence of the total reports of delinquency for each unofficial source. The reports of the boys themselves and their parents were more likely to agree than those between the boys and their school officials or the school officials and the parents. Overall, our total self, parent, and teacher measures correlate well with one another.

Predictive Validity

Much of the previous assessment of the validity of measures across settings, i.e., cross-situational consistency, has been a psychological assessment of the extent to which individuals maintain certain characteristics across various conditions, sources, or time. As with the delinquency litera-

TABLE 10.3. Pearson correlation coefficients among official and unofficial summary delinquency measures ($N = 1,000$).

A. Unofficial summary measures	Total unofficial delinquency	Official delinquency
Truancy (S + P + T)[a]	.86*	.80*
Runaway (S + P)	.83*	.72*
Theft (S + P + T)	.84*	.79*
Smoke/drink (S + P + T)	.74*	.60*
Vandalism (S + P + T)	.59*	.47*
Car-hop (S + P)	.81*	.66*
Auto-theft (S + P)	.44*	.41*
Incorrigible (P + T)	.56*	.41*
Self-report total	.92*	.82*
Parent-report total	.88*	.76*
Teacher-report total	.67*	.54*

B.	Self	Parent	Teacher
Self-report total	—	.72*	.45*
Parent-report total	—	—	.44*
Teacher-report total	—	—	—

[a] S = self-report
P = parent report
T = teacher report
*$p < .01$

ture, the study of the longitudinal nature of cross-setting consistency has been limited, the focus being the cross-sectional nature of the consistency of various personality dimensions (Loeber & Dishion, 1984; Olweus, 1979; Tremblay, LeBlanc, & Schartzman, 1988). A review of longitudinal data sets of aggressive behavior and reaction patterns as reported by individuals other than the subjects themselves found a greater degree of cross-setting consistency across time than had been previously suggested (Olweus, 1979). Teacher assessments of various antisocial behaviors and personality traits in their students have been shown to be good predictors of future social adjustment (Loeber & Dishion, 1984). Tremblay et al. (1988) recently tested the predictive utility of teacher and peer ratings and found that unofficial indicators of conduct could be used to predict self-reported aggression and antisocial behavior. Farrington (1985) assessed the extent to which later official records could be predicted by earlier data gathered from parents, teachers, and peers, as well as from the subjects. This study found that the best single predictor of adult official criminality was self-reported juvenile delinquency.

As previously noted, the Glueck research design was longitudinal in nature and therefore provides criminal history data for the boys from first

TABLE 10.4. Predictive-validity correlation coefficients within the original delinquent group ($N = 438$)[a].

Later official delinquency	Total reported delinquency (at mean age of 14)
Misdemeanors age 17–25	.24*
Felonies age 17–25	.19*
Lambda age 17–25	.22*
Misdemeanors age 25–32	.20*
Felonies age 25–32	.10
Lambda age 25–32	.20*

[a] Date are available at all three interview waves for 438 of the original 500 delinquents.
*$p < .01$

TABLE 10.5. Predictive relationship between total reported delinquency (mean age of 14) and later official delinquency within the original nondelinquent group ($N = 500$).

	Total unofficial delinquency		
	Low	Medium	High
Proportion officially delinquent by age 17	3.5	6.3	13.4
	($N = 7$)	($N = 9$)	($N = 21$)

Note. Gamma = .47 ($p < .01$)

arrest until age 32. Although official records were collected across all time periods, the amount of self-reported behavior at Time 2 (age 25) and Time 3 (age 32) is limited. A few questions were asked concerning participation in illicit occupations and bad habits, which included various illegal activities, but overall the later self-report data are, relatively speaking, lacking in detail. Thus, it is not possible to test the predictive capacities of self-report data with reference to delinquent and criminal behavior across all three time periods. However, it is possible for us to test the predictive strength of our self-report measures at Time 1 with official criminality at Times 2 and 3.

Tables 10.4 and 10.5 display the results of our analysis. First, within the original delinquent group, we correlated our measure of total reported delinquency and misconduct at Time 1 with later arrests for misdemeanors, felonies, and a crude measure of lambda (the number of crimes per month free), respectively, both at Time 2 (age 17 to 25) and Time 3 (age 25 to 32). The Glueck data in Table 10.4 illustrate not only that official delinquency can be predicted by the self-reports of the boys at age 14 but also that our predictive capacity holds with respect to specific types of crimes at 25 and 32. Only the coefficient for felonies at age 25 to 32 was not significant at the .01 level. In addition, the frequency of offending during both of the later time periods was significantly correlated with the early self-report measures.

Although by design there was a control group of 500 boys who were designated as nondelinquent according to their lack of an official record and self-reported delinquency, some of these boys did self-report delinquent acts during the interview at Wave 1. Similarly, parents and teachers reported misbehaviors for these boys. Based on the level of unofficial reported delinquencies, we can assess the degree to which the original nondelinquent boys were likely to gain an official record by age 17. Table 10.5 indicates that those boys whose total reported level of delinquency was low at Time 1 were the least likely to have a future official record (3.5%). Conversely, as would be expected if our measure of delinquency is stable across time, those boys whose total reported delinquency was at the highest level at Time 1 were the most likely to have a later official record (13.4%). The gamma coefficient between total reported unofficial delinquency at mean age 14 and official delinquency at age 17 is .47 and significant at the .01 level.

Overall, then, the Gluecks' self-, parent-, and teacher-reported data display good predictive validity up to age 32 within the original delinquent group. Moreover, these same data display predictive validity for the original nondelinquent group up to the age 17. Unfortunately, at this time, data on the criminal activity of the control group up to age 32 is not yet available for analysis. As noted by Farrington (1973), the usefulness of our predictive abilities at this level has theoretical rather than practical implications. It is not likely that we would have valid self-reports from respondents if respondents knew that their self-reports of criminal behavior were to be used by the criminal justice system in the identification of candidates for selective incapacitation or some other criminal justice system intervention.

Limitations

Prior discussions of validity in criminological research have centered on the measurement of both official records and self-reports. The general limitations of both sources of data are well-known and need not be repeated here (see Hindelang et al., 1981, and O'Brien, 1985, for reviews). However, there are some specific limitations in the Glueck data set (and, as a result, our subsequent analysis) that should be noted.

Overall, the Gluecks were not particularly concerned about measurement error in their use of the self-report technique. This measurement error could result from respondent bias, interviewer effects, and/or poor question construction in the Glueck interview schedule. This insensitivity to methodological concerns by the Gluecks has potential implications for our study. For instance, it is not possible to trace patterns of communication between parents and teachers regarding each boy's behavior. If such communication occurred, it could have influenced reporting practices, and our interpretation of the parental and teacher reports as independent measures of delinquency and other misconduct would be inaccurate.

There also could be variation among teachers, parents, and the boys themselves in the interpretation of the behavioral characteristics asked about in the study. Similarly, we have no way of assessing the extent of differential validity among the various respondents. The Gluecks themselves have stated, "The delinquents' parents certainly knew far less, or were perhaps unwilling to admit what they actually knew, than the parents of the non-delinquents in regard to the bad habits of the boys" (1950, p. 130)

Moreover, given the design of the study, most of the delinquents had not been in the classroom and under the observation of teachers for some months (i.e., since their commitment to a correctional facility). At the same time, the nondelinquents were currently know to their teachers (Glueck & Glueck, 1950, p. 149). This raises the possibility of retrospective bias and a possible "halo" effect. Kerlinger (1973, p. 549) has defined a halo effect as "a tendency for the rating of one characteristic to influence the ratings of other characteristics." To the extent that teachers knew the subject under discussion was incarcerated, how did this knowledge affect their reporting of behavioral characteristics concerning school conduct for that subject while he was in school? Conversely, if it was known that the Gluecks were inquiring about nondelinquents in the school setting, did this knowledge affect reporting practices among teachers? Unfortunately, we have no way of systematically addressing these methodological concerns.

Concluding Remarks

This chapter presents a variety of themes for consideration by the reader. Three points bear repeating. First and foremost, our research reanalyzing the basic Glueck data illustrates the unlimited potential of secondary data analysis in the field of criminology. With careful attention to the important theoretical and methodological questions, secondary research can be a cost-effective alternative to original data collection and, in a timely manner, be used to address some of the key issues facing the field of criminology. Such secondary data analysis will be enhanced to the extent that investigators have access not only to machine-readable data but also to the raw data as well. As noted by Colby and Phelps (1990, p. 253), one obstacle to secondary data analysis is the "perception that reanalyses involve simple recombinations of existing information and . . . are atheoretical and uncreative." Colby and Phelps (1990, p. 253) also point out that many graduate programs discourage secondary data analyses for doctoral dissertations; thus, a golden opportunity for experience in conducting secondary data analysis is lost.

Second, our analysis of the self-, parent, and teacher reports of delinquency and other antisocial behavior among the subjects in the Glueck study shows that the basic Glueck data are indeed valid and can be used in a substantive analysis. Specifically, both the construct and the predictive validity of the Glueck data were established in our analysis above. Moreover, our results are consistent with other research using the self-report technique as well as parental and teacher reports (e.g., Farrington, 1989; Farrington & West, 1981; Hindelang et al., 1981). Therefore, various types of reporters can provide valid information with regard to the underlying construct of juvenile delinquency and other juvenile misconduct.

Third, our analysis of predictive validity suggests a linkage between antisocial and delinquent behavior in early adolescence (14 years of age) and criminality in late adolescence and young adulthood. This finding held true for those originally assigned to the delinquent group and those originally defined as nondelinquent controls. Recall, though, that at this time, follow-up data on the official criminal histories of the control group are available only up to age 17. Of course, our finding is not unique to the Glueck data (see e.g., Farrington, 1989; Farrington & West, 1981; Loeber, 1982; Olweus, 1979; West & Farrington, 1977).

In sum, the Glueck data drawn from parental, teacher, and self-reports can be used as independent measures of behavior or as general assessments of the juvenile's overall conduct. Such information is quite helpful to an investigator from both a theoretical and a methodological standpoint. At the same time, the longitudinal data collected by the Gluecks allow us to explore the predictive validity of their data over time. Such an analysis is crucial both for the sake of data preparation for further secondary data analysis and for the theoretical import such findings have for the study of crime generally.

Endnotes

1. This is a revised version of a paper presented at the annual meeting of the American Society of Criminology in Chicago, Illinois, November 12, 1988. The data utilized in this study are part of the Sheldon and Eleanor Glueck study materials of the Harvard Law School Library and are on long-term loan to the Henry A. Murray Research Center of Radcliffe College. This project was supported in part by a grant from the National Institute of Justice (87-IJ-CX-0022). The support of the Henry A. Murray Research Center and Erin Phelps is also gratefully acknowledged.

2. These self-report data sometimes resulted in transferring a previously designated nondelinquent to the delinquent group or eliminating the boy from the study altogether. In fact, 36 cases originally selected as nondelinquents were eliminated

from the study. This is not to say that boys in the nondelinquent group did not report any misbehavior whatsoever. In fact, during the interview, about 25% reported some misbehavior (Glueck & Glueck, 1950, p. 29).
3. Auto-theft and incorrigibilty have equally low correlation coefficients (.41) with official delinquency.

References

Blumstein, A., Cohen, J., Roth, J., & Visher, C. (Eds.). (1986). *Criminal careers and "career criminals."* Washington, DC: National Academy Press.

Boruch, R., & Pearson, R. (1988). Assessing the quality of longitudinal surveys. *Evaluation Review*, *12*(1), 3–55.

Colby, A., & Phelps, E. (1990). Archiving longitudinal data. In D. Magnusson (Ed.), *Methodological issues in longitudinal research* (pp. 249–262). Cambridge, England: Cambridge University Press.

Cook, T.D., & Campbell, D.T. (1979). *Quasi-experimentation: Design and analysis issues for field settings*. Chicago: Rand McNally.

Farrington, D. (1973). Self-reports of deviant behavior: Predictive and stable? *Journal of Criminal Law and Criminology*, *64*, 99–110.

Farrington, D. (1985). Predicting self-reported and official delinquency. In D. Farrington & R. Tarling (Eds.), *Prediction in criminology* (pp. 150–173). Albany, NY: SUNY Press.

Farrington, D. (1988). Studying changes within individuals: The causes of offending. In M. Rutter (Ed.), *Studies of psychosocial risk: The power of longitudinal data*, (pp. 158–183). Cambridge, England: Cambridge University Press.

Farrington, D. (1989). Self-reported and official offending from adolescence to adulthood. In M. Klein (Ed.), *Cross-National research in self-reported crime and delinquency* (pp. 399–423). Norwell, MA: Kluwer Academic Publishers.

Farrington, D., & West, D. (1981). The Cambridge study in delinquent development. In S.A. Mednick & A.E. Baert (Eds.), *Prospective longitudinal research: An empirical basis for the primary prevention of psycho-social disorders* (pp. 137–145). Oxford: Oxford University Press.

Farrington, D., Ohlin, L., & Wilson, J.Q. (1986). *Understanding and controlling crime: Toward a new research strategy*. New York: Springer-Verlag.

Glueck, S., & Glueck, E. (1950). *Unraveling juvenile delinquency*. New York: Commonwealth Fund.

Glueck, S., & Glueck, E. (1968). *Delinquents and nondelinquents in perspective*. Cambridge, MA: Harvard University Press.

Hindelang, M., Hirschi, T., & Weis, J. (1981). *Measuring delinquency*. Beverly Hills, CA: Sage.

Hyman, H. (1972). *Secondary analysis of sample surveys*. New York: Wiley.

Kerlinger, F. (1973). *Foundations of behavioral research* (2nd ed.). New York: Holt, Reinhart and Winston.

Kiecolt, K.J., & Nathan, L. (1985). *Secondary analysis of survey data*. Beverly Hills, CA: Sage.

Laub, J., & Sampson, R. (1987). *Criminal careers and crime control. A matched sample longitudinal research design* (an unpublished proposal to the National Institute of Justice Crime Control Theory and Policy Program).

Laub, J., & Sampson, R. (1988). Unraveling families and delinquency: A reanalysis of the Gluecks' data. *Criminology, 26*(3), 355–380.

Loeber, R. (1982). The stability of anti-social child behavior: A review. *Child Development, 53*, 1431–1446.

Loeber, R., & Dishion, T. (1984). Boys who fight at home and school: Family conditions influencing cross-setting consistency. *Journal of Consulting and Clinical Psychology, 52*, 759–768.

O'Brien, R. (1985). *Crime and victimization data*. Beverly Hills, CA: Sage.

Olweus, D. (1979). Stability of aggressive reaction patterns in males: A review. *Psychological Bulletin, 86*(4), 852–875.

Porterfield, A. (1946). *Youth in trouble*. Fort Worth, TX: Leo Potisham Foundation.

Program on Human Development and Criminal Behavior. (1989). Phase II Final Report to the John D. & Catherine T. MacArthur Foundation & the National Institute of Justice. Unpublished document.

Sampson, R. (1986). Effects of socioeconomic context on official reaction to juvenile delinquency. *American Sociological Review, 51*, 876–885.

Shaw, C., & McKay, H. (1942). *Juvenile delinquency and urban areas*. Chicago: University of Chicago Press.

Short, J., and Nye, I. (1957). Reported behavior as a criterion of deviant behavior. *Social Problems, 5*, 207–213.

Short, J., & Nye, I. (1958). Extent of unrecorded juvenile delinquency: Tentative conclusions. *Journal of Criminal Law and Criminology, 49*, 296–302.

Stewart, D. (1984). *Secondary research*. Beverly Hills, CA: Sage.

Tremblay, R., LeBlanc, M., & Schartzman, A. (1988). The Predictive power of first-grade peer and teacher ratings of behavior: Sex differences in antisocial behavior and personality at adolescence. *Journal of Abnormal Child Psychology, 16*(5), 571–583.

Wallerstein, J., Wyle, C.J. (1947). Our law-abiding law-breakers. *Probation, 25*, 107–112.

Weis, J. (1986). Issues in the measurement of criminal careers. In A. Blumstein, J. Cohen, J. Roth, & C. Visher (Eds.), *Criminal Careers and "Career Criminals"* (pp. 1–51). Washington, DC: National Academy Press.

West, D., & Farrington, D. (1977). *Who becomes delinquent?* London: Heinemann.

Wiersema, B., Loftin, C., & Huang, W.S.W. (1988). *Data resources of the National Institute of Justice* (3rd ed.). Washington, DC: U.S. Department of Justice.

Biographies

Trevor Bennett is the Senior Research Associate at the Institute of Criminology, Cambridge University, England. He received his Ph.D. from the University of Kent in 1977. He is the author of several books and many articles dealing with crime and deviance. Currently, he is carrying out a project funded by the Home Office on community policing in Britain.

Thomas J. Bernard is Associate Professor of Administration of Justice at the Pennsylvania State University. He has written in the area of criminology and sociology theory, including *The Consensus-Conflict Debate* (Columbia University Press) and *Theoretical Criminology* (Oxford University Press). He is currently writing a book on the history, philosophy, and law of juvenile justice.

Scott H. Decker received the Ph.D. in Criminology from Florida State University. He is currently Professor and Chair of Administration of Justice at the University of Missouri-St. Louis. He holds an appointment as a Fellow in the Center for Metropolitan Studies. His research has focused on a variety of policy issues including the impact of diversion programs, deterrence issues, racial justice, and evaluations of police policies. He is currently engaged in anethnographic study of residential burglars. He serves as Project Director for the St. Louis Drug Use Forecasting Project.

Elizabeth Piper Deschenes is a consultant with the RAND Corporation in Santa Monica, California and a Research Sociologist with the UCLA Drug Abuse Research Group in the Neuropsychiatric Institute at the University of California Los Angeles. She has published articles on the violent juvenile offender in the 1958 Philadelphia Birth Cohort and is co-author of several articles with Jeffrey Fagan on the Violent Juvenile Offender Project. Her most recent writings are on the effectiveness of legal supervision in controlling narcotic addiction and criminal behavior, including "Modeling the Longitudinal Impact of Legal Sanctions on Narcotics Use and Property Crime, in the *Journal of Quantitative Criminology*. Research interests include evaluation of intensive aftercare for chronic juvenile offenders, substance use, delinquency and crime, and criminal careers of drug-addicted offenders.

Jeffrey Fagan is Associate Professor in the School of Criminal Justice at Rutgers University. His research interests and recent publications include drug-crime relationships, youth gangs, violence in families, and the jurisprudence of crimes by adolescents. He is author, together with Joseph Weis, of *Drug Use and Delinquency Among Inner City Youths* (Springer-Verlag, forthcoming), and is editor of the *Journal of Research in Crime and Delinquency*.

Julie Horney is Associate Professor of Criminal Justice at the University of Nebraska at Omaha. She earned her Ph.D. in experimental psychology at the University of California, San Diego and then spent a post-doctoral year studying the law and field research methods. She has recently completed a multi-jurisdiction study on the impact of rape reform legislation (with Cassia Spohn), and is currently working on a new approach to measuring crime commission rates of individual offenders through self-reports.

Patrick Jackson is Associate Professor of Criminal Justice at Sonoma State University, California. He is the author of *The Paradox of Control* (New York: Praeger) and numerous articles on methods, deviance, jails, arson, pretrial preventive detention, youth gangs, the effects of counsel on court dispositions and others. His current work deals with the reasons for charge reduction among felony defendants and the long-term effects of parole supervision.

Kenna Kiger is a Ph.D. candidate in the Department of Sociology at the University of Illinois at Urbana-Champaign. Her doctoral studies focus on patterns of offending throughout the criminal career. She teaches undergraduate courses as well as serves as the research assistant to the project currently reanalyzing the three wave longitudinal data derived from the Gluecks' *Unraveling Juvenile Delinquency* study.

Carol W. Kohfeld is Associate Professor of Political Science and Fellow in the Center for Metropolitan Studies at the University of Missouri-St. Louis. Her current research interests include urban crime, race and politics, and the impact of the death penalty. Her work has appeared in *Criminology, Journal of Research in Crime and Delinquency, Law and Society Review, Political Methodology, and Urban Affairs Quarterly*. Her most recent book, co-authored with Robert Huckfeldt, is *Race and the Decline of Class in American Politics* (University of Illinois Press, 1989).

John H. Laub is Associate Professor at the College of Criminal Justice at Northeastern University, Boston, Massachusetts. His current research interests include juvenile offending, juvenile victimization, and the history of the criminological discipline. He also is conducting a reanalysis of the three wave longitudinal data derived from the Gluecks' *Unraveling Juvenile Delinquency* study.

R. Richard Ritti received the Ph.D. in Organizational Behavior from Cornell University. He is Professor of Administration of Justice and Sociology at the Pennsylvania State University. He has held research positions with Western Electric and the IBM Corporation, as well as a previous academic position with Columbia University Graduate School of Business. Dr. Ritti served as an Associate Editor of Social Problems and on the Executive Council of The American Association for Public Opinion Research. In 1989 he was honored as Distinguished Scholar at the 25th Anniversary meeting of the Midwest Business Association. He is author of three books, including *The Ropes To Skip and the Ropes to Know* (Wiley). Current research interests are in the relationship between the cultural environment of public organizations, organizational structures, and perceive effectiveness.

Robert J. Sampson is Associate Professor in the Department of Sociology and the Institute of Government and Public Affairs at the University of Illinois at Urbana-Champaign. His current research focuses on community structure and crime, deterrence theory, and contextual models of victimization. He also is conducting a reanalysis of the three wave longitudinal data derived from the Gluecks' *Unraveling Juvenile Delinquency* study.

Cassia Spohn is Professor in the Department of Criminal Justice at the University of Nebraska at Omaha. Her current research interests include racial and gender disparities in the processing of criminal defendants and decision making by black and female judges. She and Julie Horney recently completed a multi-jurisdiction study of the impact of rape law reform.

Paul E. Tracy, Jr. is Associate Professor of Criminal Justice, and formerly Director of the Graduate School of Criminal Justice, at Northeastern University. Dr. Tracy's research interests generally concern the measurement and analysis of juvenile delinquency careers; legal issues in juvenile justice; trends and patterns in juvenile homicide; and prediction models of criminal careers. For the past ten years Dr. Tracy has been working on the collection and analysis of data for the 1958 Philadelphia Birth Cohort. Recently, he also completed a cohort study in Puerto Rico, and has begun another birth cohort study in Wuhan Province, People's Republic of China. He is the author of three books and numerous articles in the sociology and criminology literature.

Sandra Wexler received the Ph.D. from the University of California, Berkeley, School of Social Welfare. Her research interests have centered on issues relating to children and families, and in particular have focused on behaviors that tend to be stigmatized or characterized as deviant. During the past ten years, she has been involved in studies of wife battering, child physical and sexual abuse, and runaway, homeless and prostituting youth. Dr. Wexler is presently conducting a study of AIDS risk behaviors among out-of-school adolescents. Her publications include articles on various aspects of family violence and its relationship to delinquency.

Richard Wright is Associate Professor of Addministration of Justice and a Fellow in the Center for Metropolitan Studies at the University of Missouri-St. Louis. He received his Ph.D. in Criminology from Cambridge University in 1980. He is co-author of *Burglars on Burglary: Prevention and the Offender*. He also has written many articles dealing with matters such as sexual assault, the decriminalization of homosexuality, heroin use, and property crime. Lately, his research has focused on the offender's perspective and the emerging field of cognitive criminology. At present, he is conducting an ethnographic study of active residential burglars funded by the National Institute of Justice.

Author Index

A

Adams, J. 147
Ageton, S.S. 153, 198, 211
Akers, R.L. 9
Amsterdam, A.G. 215
Anderson, B.F. 113, 115, 129
Anderson, J.E. 180
Anglin, M.D. 120–121
Atkinson, P. 146–148
Ayres, R. 195

B

Babbie, E.R. 79–80, 85, 90, 95
Bachman, G.G. 39
Bailey, W.C. 215, 219
Bakel, D.A. 95
Banks, W.C. 84
Barnett, A. 218–219
Becker, G. 95
Becker, H.S. 79, 91
Ben-Yehuda, N. 121
Benn, G.J. 120
Bennett, L.A. 86, 91, 93
Bennett, T. 139, 141–144, 148, 149
Benney, M. 148
Berk, R. 108–110, 147, 211
Bernard, T. 1, 3, 4, 9, 10, 13, 14
Beyleveld, D. 139
Biderman, A.D.
Binder, A. 85
Black, D. 32
Blumberg, H.H. 95
Blumstein, A. 22, 160–164, 211, 214, 243

Boland, B. 44–46
Boret, L. 138
Boruch, R.F. 108–109, 112, 243, 248
Boucher, R.J. 123
Bowers, W. 218
Box, G.E.P. 205, 208, 212
Bradburn, N.M. 95, 100
Braiker, H.B. 158
Brereton, D. 195
Briar, S. 32
Brodsky, S.L. 92
Brown, B.S. 120
Brown, C.E. 110
Brown, E.D. 111, 128
Bulmer, M. 148
Burgess, R.L. 9

C

Campbell, D.T. 100, 108–109, 116–117, 125–126, 129–132, 154, 191–194, 210–211, 247–248
Canter, R.J. 153, 198, 211
Cantor, D. 42
Carey, S. 139
Carpenter, C. 139–145, 148
Carroll, J. 141
Casal, J. 85–86, 93
Casper, J.D. 195
Cernkovich, S.A. 14
Chambliss, W. 108–109, 139, 140, 145
Chappell, N.L. 87
Clark, J. 32
Clarke, R.V. 111–112, 114–115, 139
Cocozza, J. 123–124

Cohen, J. 22, 42, 160–164, 211, 214, 243
Conley, C.H. 44–46
Conrad, J.P. 215
Cook, T.D. 109, 116–117, 126, 129, 191, 210, 247, 248
Cornish, D.B. 9, 111
Cox, M. 95
Cox, S.J. 45, 219
Cressey, D. 4, 140
Crouch, B.M. 171–173, 186

D
Decker, S. 219
DeFleur, M.L. 5
Deikman, D. 110
Dickson, W.F. 111
Dill, F. 43–46, 136, 142
Dishion, T. 251
Dodge, R.W. 38
Dole, P. 120
Dye, T.R. 167

E
Ehrlich, I. 218–219
Elliott, D.S. 39–41, 114, 139, 153, 198, 211
Empey, L.T. 110
Ennis, B.J. 123, 125
Epperlein, T. 168, 186, 193
Erickson, M.L. 110
Erikson, K. 85
Erven, J.M. 198, 212

F
Fagan, J. 111, 118, 126, 128
Farrington, D. 109–110, 148, 154, 157–164, 211, 214, 241, 247, 251
Feeney, F.F. 43–46, 136, 142
Feinberg, S.B. 110
Ferguson, L.R. 88–89
Ferracutti, F. 6
Figlio, R.M. 6, 154, 157, 158, 211
Filaton, V. 203
Finello, K. 212
Finkelhor, D. 84–85, 90
Fiske, D.W. 100, 108

Foley, J.P. 181, 184, 189, 195
Forst, B. 45, 203, 219
Fox, J.A. 219
Frankel, M.R. 88, 96, 99, 101
Frasier, C. 147
Freeman, H.E. 113
Freidman, C.S. 219
Fuller, C. 95

G
Garafalo, M.J. 4
Garner, J.A. 109
Gebhard, D. 79
Geerken, M. 23, 32, 35
Geis, G. 85
Gelles, R.J. 79, 84, 86, 91, 93
Giallombardo, R. 146
Gilchrist, I. 81
Gillespie, D. 80, 82–83, 92–93
Giordano, P.G. 14
Glass, G.V. 193
Glassner, B. 139–145, 148
Glueck, E.J. 138, 157–159, 241–243
Glueck, S. 138, 157–159, 241–243
Gold, M. 39
Goldberg, S. 210
Goldkamp, J. 117
Goodman, S. 142
Gordon, A.C. 129
Gordon, R. 6
Gottfredson, M. 3, 4, 9, 27, 139, 160–162, 211
Gove, W.R. 23, 32, 35
Granger, C.W.J. 201, 213
Green, S. 39
Greenberg, D.F. 160
Greenwood, P. 158
Guggenheim, M. 118, 126

H
Hagan, J. 163
Hammersley, M. 146–148
Hammes, R.R. 97–98
Haney, C. 84
Hare, A.P. 95
Hartstone, E.C. 111, 128
Harway, M. 212

Hatanaka, M. 213
Hauck, M. 95
Hay, R.A. 199, 205, 208, 212
Henshel, R. 139
Hess, D. 195
Hilbert, R.A. 85
Hindelang, M.J. 42, 246, 253, 255
Hirschi, T. 3, 9, 14, 39, 160–162, 246, 253, 255
Hook, S. 215
Hopkins, R.H. 97–98
Horney, J. 167, 186
Horowitz, I. 81
Huang, W.S.W. 243
Huckfeldt, R.R. 210
Huemann, M. 175–176, 184–186, 193
Hughes, E. 148
Hughes, M. 23, 32
Huizinga, D. 39–41, 153, 198, 211
Humphrey, L. 81
Hunt, R.C. 124
Hyman, H. 242

I
Ianni, F. 148
Irwin, J. 122, 141, 144, 146

J
Jackson, P.G. 26, 33, 42
Jacoby, J.E. 123
Jenks, C. 203
Johnson, L.D. 39
Jones, H.H. 81
Judd, C.M. 79, 80, 85, 95

K
Kearney, K.A. 97–98
Kelling, G.L. 110
Kemeny, U.G. 12
Keveles, G. 124
Kidder, L.H. 79, 80, 85, 95
Kiecolt, K.J. 242, 246
Kimmel, A.J. 80–81
Kinard, E.M. 84–85, 88–89, 92–93
King, F.W. 95
Kinsey, A. 79

Kleck, G. 218
Klein, L. 218
Klockars, C.B. 91, 110, 143
Knight, B.J. 159
Knowles, B.A. 153, 198, 211
Kobrin, S. 149
Kohfeld, C. 203, 210, 219
Kozal, H.L. 123

L
LaRossa, R. 86, 91, 93
Lasch, C. 79
Laub, J. 245
Lavin, M. 158
LeBlanc, M. 251
Lehnen, R.G. 34
Lempert, R. 186, 191, 215, 218
Lempert, R.O. 109
Lentzner, H.R. 38
Likens, T. 210
Lipton, D. 108
Litwack, T.R. 123–125
Loeber, R. 162, 251
Lofland, J. 147
Loftin, C. 175–176, 184–186, 193, 243
Logan, C.H. 108
Lucianoric, J. 45, 219
Lueptow, L. 97–98
Lundman, R. 32

M
Macklin 84
Maltz, M.D. 25, 35, 129
Marquart, J.W. 171–173, 186
Martin, C. 79
Martin, W. 44–46
Martinson, R. 108
Mason, K. 212
Mason, W.M. 212
Master, L. 97–98
Mauss, A.L. 97–98
Mayhew, P. 114, 115, 139
McCall, G. 139, 141–146
McCleary, R. 129, 168, 186, 193, 198, 199, 205, 208, 212
McCord, J. 157, 159

McDowall, D. 129, 175–176, 184–186, 193
McGahey, R. 218
McGlothlin, W. 120, 121
McPheters, L.R. 10
Mednick, S. 212
Megargee, E.J. 123
Merry, S. 140, 143
Merton, R.K. 10, 13–14, 80
Milgram, L. 81, 85
Miller, E. 146
Mills, M. 81
Moll, K.D. 34
Monahan, J. 123, 125
Morris, N. 81
Mueller, S.A. 97–98
Murphy, S. 122

N
Nagin, P. 3
Nathan, L. 242, 246
Neal, D. 195
Nerporth, H. 212
Nettler, G. 6
Newman, R.G. 120
Nienstedt, B.C. 198, 212
Nye, F.I. 14
Nyswander, M.E. 120

O
O'Brien, R. 253
Ohlin, L.E. 109–110, 154, 241, 247, 251
O'Malley, P.M. 39
Osgood, D.W. 39

P
Palloni, A. 163
Passell, P. 219
Pate, T. 110
Pearson, R. 248
Pelto, G. 148
Petersilia, J. 158
Peterson, M. 158
Phelps, E. 242, 254
Pierce, G. 218
Piliavin, I. 32

Polish, S.M. 158
Polsky, N. 140, 143–147
Pomeroy, W. 79
Poole, K.W. 212
Porterfield, A. 39
Pugh, M.D. 14

Q
Quinney, R. 5

R
Reamer, F.G. 100–101
Reimer, D.J. 39
Reiss, A.J., Jr. 22, 32, 38
Rengert, G. 139, 142, 144
Rezmoric, E.L. 109, 113–114, 126, 128
Ritti, R. 1
Robeson, J. 108
Robison, J.D. 123
Roethlisberger, F.J. 111
Rosenbaum, M. 122
Ross, H.L. 154, 168, 181, 184, 186, 189, 192–195, 211
Rossi, P.H. 108–109, 113
Roth, J.A. 22, 243
Russell, D.E.F. 84

S
Sampson, R. 244–245
Savitz, L.D. 23, 26, 32
Schantz, M. 195
Schartzman, A. 251
Schlesinger, L.B. 123, 124
Schuessler, A. 215
Schwartz, C. 148
Schwartz, I. 26
Schwartz, M. 148
Schwarzschild, H. 215
Sechrest, L. 111, 128
Sellin, T. 6, 154, 157, 198, 215–218
Shannon, L. 117, 154, 163, 211
Sherman, L.W. 80, 110, 211
Shover, N. 146
Sinclair, I. 112
Singer, B. 110
Singer, F. 95–96, 98–99, 101, 111

Skogan, W. 32, 34, 38
Smith, E.W. 123
Smith, G. 108
Snyder, H.N. 161, 162
Sobal, J. 95–97, 99, 111
Sones, R. 44–46
Spohn, C. 167, 186
Sprague, J. 200, 203
Stanley, J.C. 116, 125, 129–132, 191–
    194, 210
Stapleton, W.V.L.E. 111
Steadman, H.J. 123–124
Steffens, L. 202
Steinmetz, S.K. 79, 84
Stewart, D. 241
Strain, L.A. 87
Straus, M.A. 7, 9, 84
Stronge, W.B. 10
Sudman, S. 95, 100
Sutherland, E.H. 4, 9, 140, 215
Sykes, R. 32

T
Teitelbaum, L.E. 111
Tenur, J.M. 110
Thompson, T.L. 97–98
Thornberry, T. 123, 211
Toch, H. 139, 149
Torgerson, W.S. 13
Tracy, P. 57, 159
Tremblay, R. 251
Trend, N.G. 91

V
Van den Haag, E. 215
Visher, C.A. 22, 109, 243
Vold, G.B. 3, 4, 9, 14
Von Hirsch, A. 120

W
Wald, M. 195
Walerstein, J. 246
Walker, N. 138, 140
Warner, L. 44–46
Wasilchick, J. 139, 142, 144
Wax, M.L. 85, 89, 90, 93
Weaver, F. 141
Weir, A. 43–46, 136, 142
Weis, J.G. 246, 253, 255
Weisheit, R.A. 97–98
Weiss, C.H. 178, 181–182, 247
Wenk, E.A. 123
West, D.J. 25, 146, 148, 157–159
White, S.O. 111, 128
Whitebread, C., II. 195
Whyte, W.F. 85
Wiersema, B. 243
Wiley, E.D. 124
Wilks, J. 108
Wilson, J.Q. 109–110, 154, 241, 247,
    251
Winsborough, H.H. 212
Wirtanen, I. 39
Witte, A. 108–109
Wolfgang, M.E. 6, 80, 154, 157, 158,
    211
Wright, R. 139, 141–144, 148–149
Wyle, C.J. 246

Y
Yelaja, S.A. 78, 80, 86–87, 90–92
Yunker, J.A. 218, 219

Z
Zeisel, H. 112
Zimbardo, P. 84, 94

Subject Index

A

Accuracy 22, 23, 117–120, 123, 202
Age effect 163
Aggregate 41, 90, 16, 120, 199, 216, 218, 219
Analysis 198–202, 216, 219
Anonymity 83, 90
Antecedent measures 125
Anti-Arson Act 26
Archival data sources 186, 187, 242
Arithmetic mean 62, 75, 220
Artifactual settings 111
Associations 6, 57, 71, 75, 96–97, 156, 223
At risk 70
Attribute 75
Attrition 43, 110, 163, 212
Autocorrelation 219, 227
Autoregressive integrated moving average modeling (ARIMA) 210, 212
Averages 52

B

Bail Reform Act 179–180
Bar graph 64, (chart) 76
Barefoot v. Estelle 123
Base-rate 123, 131
Before/after time series designs 210
Belmont Report 82
Bivariate association (relationship) 52, 55, 57
Bounding 35
Bureau of Justice Statistics (BJS) 35, 42

C

Cambridge Somerville Study 157
Career criminals 160
Case approach 45, 46
Causal factor 4, 109, 213–214
Causality 15, 117, 156, 213, 223
Census data 243
Central tendency 62–63
Chain of referrals 145
Cleared 27
Code of Federal Regulations (CFR) 82, 83, 87
Coding 241
Coefficients 227, 250
Cohort 118, 121, 124, 131, 153, 242
Cohort effect 163
Communality 80
Composite measure 250
Computerized case-selection procedures 194
Computerized data base 190
Concept 4, 23, 51, 75, 250
Conceptionalized 128
Concurrent validity 250
Conditioning variables 15, 56, 57
Confidentiality 83, 90, 96, 99–101, 188, 212, 246
Confounding 114–115
Consent
  informed 95
  voluntary 81, 84
Constant error 129
Construct validity 12, 246–248
Context bound 123
Contiguous states 215, 218

Contingency table 55
Contingent association 52, 56, 57
Continuum 94
Control group 118, 126, 157, 253, 255
Control theory 14
Control variables 3, 56–57, 100, 111,
    191, 192, 198, 219
Controlled experiment 210
Convergence 250
Correlates 55, 250
Correlation 7, 130, 248, 250, 253, 255
Counts 53, 58
Court-based statistics 22, 186
Covariates 126, 127
Crime classification 32, 33
Crime prevention 32, 33, 109, 139
Crimes known to the police 26
Criterion variables 52, 59, 215
Cross-checks 39, (see also Overlap 248)
Cross-sectional 152–153, 200, 211, 216,
    251
Cross-setting validity 250
Cumulative percentage 72
Cutting point 116
Cyclical 209

D
Dangerousness 117–119, 123
Data collection 2, 23, 132, 154–155,
    187–188, 194, 196, 202, 219, 242,
    254
Decision making 109, 120, 126, 138, 141
Deductive 7
Degree of freedom 208
Denominator 36
Department of Juvenile Justice 118
Dependent variable 15, 16, 52, 59, 109,
    128–129, 138, 156, 216, 227
Descriptive statistical measures 52
Deterrent effect 182, 193, 211, 217–218
Deviant scores 130
Dichotomized 53, 75, 94, 128
Direct experiments 112
Directly related 52
Disaggregated 97, 127
Disaggregation 127
Disinterestedness 80
Distribution 51, 160

District of Columbia Court Reform Act
    117
Drug Use Forecasting (DUF) 153
Dummy variable 217, 244

E
Elaboration 8, 52, 57, 59
Empirical 122, 199, 202
Epidemiological 22
Etiological 22
Event history analysis 163
Evidence 183, 207
Exogenous variables 216, 218
Experimental design 15, 100, 109–110,
    191–192
  controlled 210
  direct 112
  indirect 112
  natural 113–133, 186, 217
  quasi-experimental designs 113, 115,
    191, 201
  true experiment 15, 17, 112–133
Explaining variation 224
Extraneous 57

F
Face to face interviews 100
Factor analysis 53
Failure rate 119
False positives 119, 123, 124
Federal Bail Reform Act of 1966 117
Federal Bureau of Investigation's
    Uniform Crime Report (UCR) 63,
    168, 186, 189
Federal Property and Administrative
    Services Act of 1949 91
Field settings 17, 109, 139
First order data 147
Folk theory 3
Follow-up data 255
Freedom of Information Act 91
Frequency 52–54, 58, 245, 253

G
Gallup polls 39
Gamma 253

Generalizability 39, 126, 128, 130–132, 157, 159
Generalization 7, 129
Generalized least squares 220
Granger causality 201, 213
Grounded theory 127
Group A offenses 42

H
Halo effect 254
Hawthorne effect 111
Hierarchy rule 33–34, 38, 42, 43
High School and Beyond Survey 243
Histogram 57–58; 66, 76
Historical data 46
History effect 116, 129, 132, 155, 163, 191–193, 212
Homogeneity 218
Horizontal bar chart 69
Household crimes 35–36
Hypothesis 2, 6, 109, 127, 149, 152, 155, 200, 218, 222
Hypothetical cases 186

I
Incidence 2, 40–42, 51, 59, 153–154, 157
Incident Based Reporting (IBR) 42, 87, 89
Independent variable 16, 52, 109, 111–114, 125–127, 129–132, 139, 156, 218, 223, 227
Index crimes 26–27
Indirect experiments 112
Induction 7.
Inferential statistics 52, 109, 218, 227
Informed consent 40, 84
Institutionalist 22
Instrumentation effects 129, 156, 163, 194
Interaction effects 15, 126
Intergroup contamination 109
Internal dependencies 208, 213
Internal validity 116, 125, 128, 130–132, 194
Interrupted time-series design 177, 191–194
Inter-University Consortium for

Political and Social Research 46, 243
Interval 128
Intervening variable 138
Intervention 194
Interviewer bias 38
Interviewers 39, 168, 247, 253
Invariant 160–161
Inversely related 10, 224

K
Kansas City Preventive Patrol 110

L
Lag structure 198, 216, 223, 227
Lambda 161–162
Latent goals 178, 181
Legal impact research 167–168, 178, 181–196
Level of analysis 42
Life-course perspective 163
Line chart 72, 76
Linear 207
Linear regressions 117
LISREL 16
London cohort studies 158, 159
Long run patterns 205, 210, 213, 227
Long term goals 182
Longitudinal 52, 121, 152, 241, 251

M
Main effects 15
Manhattan Bail Project 112
Manifest goals 179, 181
Marginal gain 119, 126
Matched sample 126, 157, 211, 244
Matching techniques 116
Maturation effect 129, 132, 155, 163
Mean 62, 75, 220
Measurement bias 248
Measurement by fiat 13
Measurement error 130, 253
Measurement level 11
Median 119
Michigan Felony Firearm Statute 175, 181

Miranda v. Arizona 195
Misspecified 218
Mode 71
Monitoring the Future survey 39
Mortality effects 129
Mortality tables 43
Moving averages 226
Multicohort design 39
Multidisciplinary approach 244
Multiple birth cohorts 211
Multiple interrupted time-series designs 116, 191
Multiple time-series design 154, 192–193
Multiway cross-tabulation 55

N
National Academy of Sciences (NAS) 109, 214, 243
National Commission for the Protection of Human Subjects of Biomedical and Behavioral Research 82
National Crime Survey (NCS) 22, 23, 35, 37, 40, 202, 243
National Institute of Justice 109, 153, 159, 243
National Research Service Award Act 82, 83
National Youth Survey (NYS) 22, 39, 153, 211
Natural experiment 113–133, 186, 217
Necessary condition 18, 41
Negatively related 75
Newton's Law 11
New York Family Court Act 118, 119
Nominal 128
Non-equivalent groups 191
Null hypothesis 2, 8, 219
Nuremberg Code 80, 81

O
Offender-based data systems 22
Offender-based Transaction Statistics (OBTS) 24, 43
Offender's perspective 138
Office of Juvenile Justice and Delinquency Prevention 159

Open-ended semistructured interviews 142, 148
Operational definition 12, 119, 243
Operationalization (operationalism) 12, 13, 95, 178, 183, 250
Ordinal 128
Ordinary least squares 226
Organized skepticism 80
Outcome measures 183, 186, 198

P
Panel 153, 211
Parameters 70, 143, 162, 212
Parsimoniously 212
Participant observation 2, 139, 143, 149, 172, 183
Path analysis 15–16
Percentage change 27, 52, 54, 76
Period effects 119, 130–132, 163
Periodicity 202, 211
Philadelphia Birth Cohort 52, 154, 157–159
Plot 199, 204, 208–209, 210
Policy research 16, 211
Pooled data 216, 223
Population 17, 132, 143–144, 157
Positive relation 10–11, 214, 224
Positivism 139, 214
Positivistic 22
Post-test only control group design 125
Precision 130
Prediction instruments 123
Predictive accuracy (efficacy) 119, 123, 126
Predictive utility 251–252
Predictive validity 132, 246–248, 253, 255
Preintervention baseline 195
Pre-reform 194
President's Commission of Law Enforcement and Administration of Justice 34
Pre-test/post-test control group design 125
Pretesting 127, 130
Prevalence 41, 42, 51, 53, 153–154, 157–158, 161

Primary data (original) 23, 42, 155, 241–242
Probability 96, 109, 159, 214
Professional codes 82
Program of Human Development and Criminal Behavior 241
Project Camelot 81
Proportion 54
Prosecutor Management Information Systems (PROMIS) 43
Prospective 126, 155, 163, 241, 243
Proximate goals 178, 181, 182
Proxy variables 32
Public opinion data 23
Public records 187–188

Q

Qualitative 16, 46, 51, 75, 86, 121, 199
Quantitative 15, 42, 46, 51, 75, 121, 201
Quasi-experimental designs 113, 115, 191, 201
Questionnaires 39

R

RAND: inmate surveys 158
Random assignment (randomization) 112, 114, 126, 128, 130
Random sampling (selection) 33, 35, 46, 100, 109–111, 119, 123–127, 144, 155, 245
    see also Probability sample 96
    naturally random 112
    random distribution 131
Range of variation 39
Rate, defined 62
Rational choice 9
Raw data 241, 243, 245
Raw frequency 74
Recall 155
Recidivism 127, 159, 162
Records 196
Refractory problem 214
Regression artifacts 129–130
Regression-discontinuity designs 116
Regression equation 16, 202, 220, 223
Rehabilitation 108

Reliability 16, 21, 22, 39, 42, 123, 148–149, 184, 226
Replication 110, 131–132, 207, 219
Representative 21, 39, 40, 98, 143–144, 153, 155, 163, 209
Research design 15, 121, 125–126, 130, 160–164
Residual error 227
Respondent bias 253
Respondent mortality 40
Response pattern 156
Response rate 96, 98, 100
Response set 39
Retrospective 140, 154–155, 159, 163
Retrospective bias 255
Rigor 112
Risk/benefit assessment 80, 83, 92

S

Sample 14, 17, 111, 126, 132, 144, 153, 167, 244
Sampling 125
Sampling error 130, 155
Scatterplot 199, 210
Schall v. Martin 117–119, 125–126, 132
Secondary data 154–155, 241–255
Selection artifact 123
Selection bias 130
Selection maturation interactions 116
Selective incapacitation 160, 253
Self-reported data 14, 23, 39, 40, 246
Series incidents 38
Short-run seasonal variations 200, 227
Short-run trend 202, 205, 206, 210
Short-term effects 182
Significant 6, 119, 176–177, 215
Simple trend estimation 203
Simultaneous causation 214
Skewed 57
Slope 201
Snowball sampling 144–145
Social control theory 173
Social structure strain theory 13
Solomon four-group designs 125
Specifiable relationship 213
Specification 179, 180, 183
Speedy trial laws 179
Spurious 52–57, 117, 198

Standardized 54, 60, 74, 76, 127, 149, 189
Stationary series 213
Statistical abstract 216
Statistical regression 130
Statistical significance 52, 96–99, 100, 169, 177, 189, 193, 210, 250
Stepwise regression 15–16
Strain theory 13–14
Subject reactivity 114
Substantive significance 98
Sufficient conditions 18, 82
Surrogate observer 142
Symbolic objectives 181
Systematic 42, 127, 133, 149, 202, 242, 254
Systematic biases 202, 242, 254
Systematic errors 42

T
Tarasoff decision 92
Target selection 141
Telescoping 155
Temporal order 156 (*see also* Causal Factor, Causality)
Testing effect 132, 156
Theoretical construct 242
Theoretical goals 120
Theory 18, 199
Time frame 194
Time lags 163, 213
Time period 203
Time points 219
Time-series 153, 167, 200
Time-series design analysis 154, 168, 198, 199, 201, 223
Tracking 43–44, 207, 211
Treatments 17, 11, 191, 192
Trends 71–76, 153, 199–203, 226, 242
Triangulation 100
True experiment 15, 17, 112–133
Truncated response 39
Tuskegee syphilis study 81

U
Ultimate goals 178, 181
Unfalsifiable 110–112, 114, 118

Unidimensional 128
Uniform Crime Reporting programe (UCR) 22, 189, 216
Unit of count 46
Universalism 80
Unraveling Juvenile Delinquency (UJD) 244
U.S. Bureau of Prisons 216
U.S. Census Bureau 35
U.S. Department of Health and Human Services (DHHS) 82, 83, 86, 87, 90, 102
U.S. Department of Justice 35
U.S. Public Health Service 81
U.S. Supreme Court 120, 124, 186, 195, 215, 218

V
Validity 8, 21–23, 33, 39, 42, 55, 109– 110, 116, 118, 123, 125–126, 148, 184, 189–191, 212, 217, 242, 245
concurrent 250
construct 12, 246–248
cross-setting 250
external 125, 128
internal 116, 125, 128, 130–132, 194
predictive 132, 246–248, 253, 255
Variable, defined 11
conditioning 15, 56, 57
control 3, 56–57, 100, 111, 191, 192, 198, 219
criterion or dependent 15, 16, 52, 59, 109, 128–129, 138, 156, 215–216, 227
dummy 217, 244
exogenous 216, 218
independent 16, 52, 109, 111–114, 125–127, 129–132, 139, 156, 218, 223, 227
intervening 138
proxy 32
Variable selection 218
Variation, explained 224
range of 39, 203
short-run seasonal 200, 227
Vectors 128
Verifiability 9
Vertical bar chart 57, 66

Victim surveys 23, 34
Voluntary consent 81, 84

W
Watergate 81, 102
Wave 121, 245

Wechsler-Bellevue test 245
Wickersham Commission 25, 43
Weighted 33

Y
Youth in Transition studies 39